A PLUME BOOK

WHAT EVERY AMERICAN SHOULD KNOW ABOUT WHO'S REALLY RUNNING THE WORLD

MELISSA ROSSI is the author of *What Every American Should Know About the Rest of the World* (Plume, 2003) and *The Armchair Diplomat on Europe* (Penguin UK, 2005). She also has written for *Newsweek, National Geographic Traveler,* and MSNBC.

ALSO BY MELISSA ROSSI

*What Every American Should Know
About the Rest of the World*

WHAT EVERY AMERICAN
SHOULD KNOW ABOUT
WHO'S REALLY
RUNNING THE WORLD

The People, Corporations, and Organizations That Control Our Future

Melissa Rossi

A PLUME BOOK

PLUME
Published by Penguin Group
Penguin Group (USA) Inc., 375 Hudson Street, New York, New York 10014, U.S.A.
Penguin Group (Canada), 90 Eglinton Avenue East, Suite 700,
Toronto, Ontario, Canada M4P 2Y3 (a division of Pearson Penguin Canada Inc.)
Penguin Books Ltd., 80 Strand, London WC2R 0RL, England
Penguin Ireland, 25 St. Stephen's Green, Dublin 2, Ireland (a division of Penguin Books Ltd.)
Penguin Group (Australia), 250 Camberwell Road, Camberwell, Victoria 3124, Australia
(a division of Pearson Australia Group Pty. Ltd.)
Penguin Books India Pvt. Ltd., 11 Community Centre, Panchsheel Park,
New Delhi – 110 017, India
Penguin Books (NZ), cnr Airborne and Rosedale Roads, Albany, Auckland 1310, New Zealand
(a division of Pearson New Zealand Ltd.)
Penguin Books (South Africa) (Pty.) Ltd., 24 Sturdee Avenue, Rosebank,
Johannesburg 2196, South Africa

Penguin Books Ltd., Registered Offices: 80 Strand, London WC2R 0RL, England

First published by Plume, a member of Penguin Group (USA) Inc.

First Printing, December 2005
10 9 8 7 6 5 4 3

Credits: Page 20 courtesy of Brandy Lorenz. Page 53 courtesy of Matt Dellinger and *The New Yorker*. Pages 89 and 91 courtesy of the FDA History Office. Page 126 copyright © 2004 David I. Gross. Page 180 courtesy of Darrell Gooding. Page 201 courtesy of AP Photo/Scott Stewart. Page 224 copyright © 2005 Charles Lewis. Page 244 courtesy of the Center for Defense Information. Page 270 courtesy of AP Photo/Michael Euler. Page 304 courtesy of the Saudi Information Office, Washington, D.C. Page 334 courtesy of R. Darrow Bernick.

Ⓟ REGISTERED TRADEMARK—MARCA REGISTRADA

LIBRARY OF CONGRESS CATALOGING-IN-PUBLICATION DATA

Rossi, M. L. (Melissa L.), 1965–
  What every American should know about who's really running the world : the people,
corporations, and organizations that control our future / Melissa Rossi.
    p. cm.
  Includes bibliographical references and index.
  ISBN 0-452-28615-8
  1. Power (Social sciences) 2. Power (Social sciences)—United States. 3. Elite
(Social sciences)—United States. 4. Conservatism—United States. 5. Pressure groups.
6. Corporations—Political activity. 7. United States—Politics and government—2001– I. Title.
  HN49.P6R67 2005
  320.52'086'210973—dc22   2005020886

Printed in the United States of America
Set in Helvetica and RotisSerif

*To Melik Boudemagh,
a stellar cook and a brilliant researcher*

Contents

Acknowledgments

This book would be nothing more than a mountain of papers with a writer buried under it had I not been fortunate enough to work with some truly dedicated people who brought this project to fruition. My editor at Plume, Emily Haynes, spent many long hours with this monster, slaving over it on vacations and weekends, stitching together the assorted pieces and adding her astute insights along the way. Visionary Trena Keating, the head of Plume, gave this book the green light, and Norina Frabotta tended to the thousands of details, giving 200 percent to line up all the parts. Matt Giarratano marshaled the book through the different phases, and Gary Brozek started the ball rolling and offered undying support. Thanks to copy editor Sheila Moody, who pulled together all the finer points and provided numerous helpful comments. Book designer Eve Kirch came up with a novel way to present the information, and Melissa Jacoby designed the cover. To everyone at Plume who pulled out the stops to make this happen, I am deeply grateful. Other benevolent forces were also at work. I met research king Melik Boudemagh in a café when he asked why I was lugging around a library wing's worth of books—with names like *True Lies, Welcome to the Machine,* and *Confessions of an Economic Hit Man.* Melik immediately burrowed into the tomes, and his lust for information was so compelling that I asked him to sign on. Melik, who'd previously worked in investment firms for substantially better pay, spent days and nights digging up reports and articles, uncovering new pieces of the vast puzzle. Some of the people and issues I was writing about in this book deeply depressed me, and I was starting to get bitter and cranky, when I began encountering the projects of other people who made me happy that they were alive and communicating their thoughts. I highlight some of them as "Agents of Change." I am also thankful to the people who offered their insights, including David Wright of the Union of Concerned Scientists, Paul Kerr of the Arms Control Association, and Michael O'Hanlon of the Brookings Institution. The FDA's History Office (which runs a fabulous Web site) dug up photos, as did the Saudi embassy in DC. My whirlwind of an agent, Bill Gladstone, continually cheered me on and my friends and family tolerated me when I called up hissing and sputtering over whatever I had discovered that day. It would require another book to list everyone who helped, but to all of them I am deeply indebted.

Introduction

These are unusual times. In fact, they are bizarre. In the course of little more than four years, reason, caution, and international diplomacy in the country that has long been a global leader lauded for such traits have been shoved out of the window by fear, paranoia, and aggression: "Out of our way," seems to be the U.S. government's motto of the day. Like the mirrors in the fun house, little is as it appears. The government routinely deceives us and runs propaganda campaigns. Those who try to tell us what is happening are frequently rejected as "Bush bashers" and "American haters" or are pressured into retractions, while those who regurgitate slimy half-truths, nationalistic nonsense, and utter lies are hailed as patriots. In the name of spreading democracy and liberty around the world, we are losing ours, as groups who have kidnapped and twisted the founding principles of this country—and have nabbed even the images of the founding fathers themselves, whom they claim to hold dear—steamroll their agendas across the land and the planet. Surveillance needs to be turned on the citizenry, we are told, to prevent future terrorist attacks; centuries-old rights, such as the right to be free unless we are charged with a crime, don't hold anymore; conventions against torture have been tossed aside as quaint; the international community that questions us is dismissed as irrelevant; those who attack us are said to do so simply because they are evil. Often it seems that this era is a chapter out of George Orwell's *1984*: The propaganda machine is churning out misinformation, an all-seeing eye is beginning to trail us, and even the Ministry of Truth's slogans—"War Is Peace, Freedom Is Slavery, Ignorance Is Strength"—seem to match the motives of the current administration. These are also unusual times in that there appears to be little reason to trust that the executive branch of the government and many corporations are working in the ways they have promised to. It is crucial that citizens know the changes that are occurring at rapid-fire pace and react accordingly, but the information we need is hidden and blurred; it's difficult to grasp the real issues at hand. Rarely do we see news articles about the United States' moves to dominate outer space, the superpricey national missile defense system that is being erected around us, the robots that are showing up on the battlefield, or how extremely powerful religious radicals tied to the U.S. government are trying to push us into a theocracy. The majority of Americans don't know that the food we are eating is genetically modified—and never before tested on humans—or that leading advisors to the Bush administration are suspected of being Israeli spies or that our cell phones are now tracking devices.

That's why I wrote this book: to try to unravel what is going on and who is behind it. The book you're looking at, however, is not the one I initially intended to write. When I started this, I imagined it would simply identify the big wheels that make our world spin, that it would point out the good and the bad, highlight important issues, and voilà, the end. I aimed to be as balanced and objective as possible and to give the parties who are examined equal say in presenting their views. While some criticism seemed inevitable, I truly did not plan to condemn so many of the powers that be. In the course of researching this, however, the initial plan changed as the dangers of what is happening became impossible to ignore, and I opted not to give all parties equal time in explaining their views, as frequently they appear to be happy to whitewash and fabricate their answers. My goal became not to cover as wide a swatch as I had originally planned, but to point out the groups who pose the gravest threats to Americans, the residents of the world's most powerful country and a group that is being hoodwinked.

As I illustrate in this book, a small group of extremists—many of whom have worked together before—are redesigning the mechanics of this country. They are trying to redraw the world, and they are shrinking our rights in the process. The media has stopped holding the powers that be accountable for their actions, and the legislature, where many extremists now hold powerful seats, is an arena where some are trying to upset the balance of power—including attempts to disempower the courts. And meanwhile, lying is so common it's nearly acceptable, and those who point out the lies are drowned out by official denials. We're losing the truth, we're losing perspective, we're losing the original ideals of this country and our birthrights are vanishing with them.

However, some people are loudly fighting these changes. They're standing up as individuals and saying "No, I won't take this!" and exposing the deceit that's been shoved down our throats and blocking the dangerous moves under way. They're blowing whistles within the government and pointing out the fibs of the powers that be. They're forming organizations that document the truth. They're writing books and they're putting classified documents and lost information on their Web sites. And they're waiting for more people to stand up and join them. I've highlighted some of these catalysts throughout this book as "Agents of Change"—and there are many more.

*   *   *

We tend to forget our own power in this age, but individuals—many of whom started out without any advantages—put what is happening today into motion. They had a vision, they pursued it, and even if I don't respect the end result of some of these players, I do respect them for having a plan and for getting up to bat. Meanwhile, a third of Americans are pretty much tuned out: They don't vote, they don't pay attention to news, they apparently don't care. And even those who care often feel helpless—"There's nothing I can do," they've told me numerous times, unknowing perhaps that that is exactly the complacent attitude that allows those with questionable agendas to push them through.

There are things we can do:

1. *Search out information.* As noted in the Resources section in the back, there are numerous new fonts of knowledge that can supply us with reports and facts missing from the everyday news. The alternative media is in full bloom, and international news sources supply a wider variety of perspectives.

2. *Discuss the issues of the day with your friends and colleagues.* Don't let issues die. Already people speak of 9/11—all the facts of which have not yet been revealed—in the same way they speak of the JFK assassination. "We'll never know," they say with a shrug. Well, the reason we don't know what happened with JFK's death is because the people let the issue fade. They did not demand the truth. And many are not demanding more inquiries on recent occurrences, be it September 11 or the torture at U.S.-run prisons abroad. Demand that the truth be told.

3. *Speak out—to congresspeople, in op-eds, in letters to companies.* For an idea of how to organize, check out the Christian Right/social conservative site Focus on the Family (www.family.org). Follow this group's lead, but you can call, fax, and write the same congresspeople and organizations and say just the opposite if you wish.

4. *Join groups—or start your own.* (See "Resources," page 407.)

5. *Applaud the groups and actions you like, and loudly protest those you don't.* Make noise.

6. *Turn out for public hearings on local matters.*

7. *Run for office.*

Whatever you do, please don't take what you are about to read sitting down. What is happening in the United States—and the world—is truly alarming. We are at a historical crossroads. The ideals of democracy are being shredded, as are our rights, and what happens in the future is up to us.

Melissa Rossi
June 13, 2005

PART I

THE RIGHT

1. BRIEFING:

The Mighty Right

The United States is the world's lone superpower, with military muscle unmatched by any other country and a tendency to impose its will in all corners of the planet—we're even trying to dominate outer space. So it bears asking: Who is really running the United States? On the surface, at least, it's hard not to come up with a simple answer. The Right.

An identifying marker of the Right is a tendency to divide most everything into blacks and whites, but the Right itself does not so neatly fit into such stark divisions. The Right is not synonymous with Republicans, nor is it one group of people who all share the same values or push the same program. A rich mix of conservatives of all types—from the Christian Right to neocons—are orchestrating profound changes currently shaking up the United States. Elements of the American Right include:

- **Social conservatives:** Opposed to abortion, euthanasia, gay marriage, and the cheapening of American culture through pornography and trashy TV, music, and movies; often exhibit fervent nationalism.
- **The Christian Right:** Often linked to social conservatives, they are antiabortion, anti-euthanasia, and anti-homosexuality. Hoping to embed Christian values in American culture, many believe in literal interpretations of the Bible and that we are living in the "End Times"—the end of the world as prophesied in the New Testament's book of Revelation. They frequently blur divisions between church and state, and want to limit the courts' powers to enforce any split between the two. Ultraright Christians want to establish a militant biblical theocracy, punishing with death those who break the Ten Commandments.
- **Neoconservatives:** Neocons, of whom quite a few are Jewish, are hawkish, nationalistic, and idealistic. They believe the United States should militarily intervene in world affairs to overthrow dictatorships and implant democracy.

- **Economic Right:** Adherents believe business should not be burdened with government regulations and laws, and that the free market should dictate the economy.
- **One-issue conservatives:** Guaranteeing rights to gun ownership, overturning legal abortion, and lowering taxes are all issues that have galvanized their own right-wing factions.
- **Libertarians:** Getting government off our backs is the goal of libertarians, who typically are pro-gun, anti-taxes, and anti-regulations for industry; some also support legalizing drugs and prostitution.
- **Radical right-wingers:** Whether they blow up abortion clinics, run secret militias and survivalist camps, or attack foreigners, these factions of the Right are often entirely antigovernment.

When one peers beyond headline news at what is happening in the United States, it looks like an agenda that fell out of a conspiracy theory book. Alas, it isn't, as a slew of new books, reports, and academics are warning. The various factions of the Right have overcome their differences and work as a unified bloc, albeit one often led by extremists. Among the dramatic changes currently taking place in the United States:

- Attacks on the constitutionally designed system of checks and balances, including attempts to strip the courts of power to interpret the Constitution
- A movement to install a militant Christian theocracy: This group already has taken over factions of the Republican Party
- The transformation of the federal government into little more than a tax-collecting military machine
- The weakening of U.S. federal regulatory agencies, increasingly run by the industries they are supposed to regulate
- Propaganda and disinformation from government being presented by the media as the product of independent reporting
- Infringement of our rights—from our privacy to our ability to initiate legislation

Predictably, some key players initiating these changes hold power seats in the Bush administration: Donald Rumsfeld is bringing Big Brother to the battlefield and weaponizing outer space, and Dick Cheney, a font of disinformation, has welcomed militant neocons onto the team. Others catalysts sit in the Republican-dominated Congress: Representative Tom DeLay (R-Texas) wants to Christianize the American government and disempower the courts, and Senate Majority Leader Bill Frist (R-Tennessee), who may be buttering up Christians for his predicted 2008 presidential bid, endorsed the Christian Right's charge that Democrats were attacking people of faith—because Democrats threatened to filibuster over Senate approval of Supreme Court judges. Many of the powermongers, however, work their magic in arenas outside of government. Famous in conservative circles, these leaders are largely unknown and unwatched by the public. A few of the behind-the-sceners that deserve close scrutiny:

- **Paul Weyrich** (head of the Free Congress Foundation): He cobbled together the right-wing machine.
- **Richard Perle** and **Michael Ledeen** (Bush administration advisors): These neocons whisper in the ears of Secretary of Defense Rumsfeld and Vice President Cheney, pushing what's good for Israel as what's good for the United States.
- **Tim LaHaye** (political strategist; author of the *Left Behind* series): Bringing biblical prophecy into government decisions, he recruits out of fear via his best-selling books.
- **James Dobson** (Focus on the Family; Family Research Council): Antigay, antiabortion, and Christian-valued child psychologist Dr. Dobson is a dangerously powerful guru; 200 million worldwide tune in to his radio and TV broadcasts each day. Through his charity, Focus on the Family, and lobby group, Family Research Council, he mobilizes millions of supporters to call politicians or corporations and recite his views. The Family Research Council, for example, convinced the Bush administration to cut off U.S. funding for United Nations programs distributing condoms in AIDS-plagued countries.
- **Howard Phillips:** To hack the U.S. Constitution to a more palatable size and bring the Bible to the government, the well-connected Phillips started the Constitution Party.
- **Richard Viguerie** (Free USA): Fund-raiser and direct-mail whiz Viguerie, who invigorated numerous conservative causes, now takes out full-page ads attacking the AARP in his Free USA campaign to push privatized Social Security.
- **Grover Norquist** (Americans for Tax Reform): Anti-taxman Norquist wants "to cut government in half . . . to get it down to the size where we can drown it in the bathtub."[1] Holds popular Wednesday breakfasts in DC, where archconservatives strategize over lattes.

Paul Weyrich

A few of the organizations that Weyrich founded or cofounded:

▶ Moral Majority (he coined the term)
▶ Heritage Foundation (conservative think tank)
▶ Free Congress Foundation (lobbying arm)
▶ American Legislative Exchange Council (law-writing machine)
▶ Council for National Policy (the spine of the Republican Party)

Banish the idea that one person can't make a difference. College dropout and former radio broadcaster Paul Weyrich drew the map for social conservatives and the Christian Right to become the stewards of the Republican Party, and ultimately the country. Accidentally invited to a Democratic Party strategizing event in 1969, Weyrich was dumbfounded: He says at the meeting reporters promised to get editorial board endorsements from the *Washington Post*, and the Brookings Institution said it would support Democratic positions with its think tank reports. It seemed to the young Republican that the Democrats of that era were running a virtual political machine. Weyrich set out to design just such a machine for conservatives, and to "coach" the religious Right on how to become political activists.[2] His first task: create a Christian right-wing think tank that would bombard the White House and congressmen with reports on what stands to take on policies and how to vote. In 1973, with funding from Joseph Coors and Richard Scaife, he founded the Heritage Foundation, the keystone of the modern conservative movement. (See "The Heritage Foundation," page 189.) Initially laughed off as a think tank minus brains, the Heritage Foundation soon evolved into one of the country's most forceful institutions. Now many Republicans in Congress heed Heritage voting recommendations as their bible.

Also in 1973, Weyrich launched an important vehicle to connect the demands of the right-wing and Big Business directly with lawmakers: the American Legislative Exchange Council. Composed of corporate representatives, social conservatives, and legislators, this group writes the laws it wants to be governed by—and puts them directly in the hands of congressmen, many of whom are members. Hundreds of laws written up by ALEC are adopted in state legislatures every year.

To engage the Christian Right as foot soldiers of social change, Weyrich convinced televangelist Jerry Falwell to form the Moral Majority in 1979. With its stated mission "to defend the free enterprise system, the family and Bible morality" the Moral Majority illustrated the growing power of the organized Christian

Right in the 1980s, with millions of activists writing letters protesting anything from condom advertisements to racy TV programs. In 1981, Weyrich helped fill the roster of Tim LaHaye's ultraconservative strategizing forum—the Council for National Policy—bringing billionaires, political conservatives, and religious extremists to the five-hundred-strong gang that would before long be the controlling faction of the Republican Party.

> *Weyrich helped spread the Christian cause by investing in satellite broadcasting systems to beam the good word to tens of millions of households nationwide.*

Although the organizations he created have deeply altered the American political environment, Weyrich—like many conservatives—isn't satisfied with the progress that's been made. American culture—with its Jerry Springers, sleazy music videos, reality shows, and porno channels—had been "captured by the other side," he lamented in 1999.[3] Conservatives had but one option, he opined: cleave themselves culturally—with their own media, entertainment, schools, and universities, creating "a complete, separate, parallel structure."[4] And slowly, but surely, between home schooling, new Christian colleges, and an expanding network of TV stations, magazines, Internet sources, and books, that idea too, like every other Weyrich idea, is blossoming.

If the American people do not fully comprehend the nature of what is unfolding in their country, it's understandable. The power moves are often hidden behind emotional issues that blur what is actually at stake. A few examples of these "veiled issues":

- The controversy over the Ten Commandments in federal buildings encompasses more than publicly stating what most Americans would happily endorse as ideals for human behavior—that it is bad to lie and kill, and good to honor your parents. The current Ten Commandment furor is an engineered move to link the Bible with the Constitution, and to open the door to an Old Testament–based theocracy.
- The Constitution Party is actually trying to limit the Constitution and is working to "restore our government . . . and our law to its Biblical foundation."[5]
- The dispute over forty-one-year-old Terri Schiavo, who had been in a coma since 1990 and whose husband wanted to detach her feeding tube, concerned more than the right to live and the right to die. Politicians, particularly those of the Christian Right, used the Schiavo case to further their

agenda to deflate the muscle of the courts. When a federal court ruled in March 2005 that Schiavo's husband had the right to take her off her lifeline, congressmen—mostly Christian Republicans—rushed back to Congress during the recess to save Terry. The bill they hastily passed to block the court's decision, however, wasn't about Terry at all. In a larger context, it was a move to strip the courts of their might—and to throw off the system of checks and balances. Why do many conservative Christians want to lessen the power of the courts? Because the courts legalized abortion, took mandatory prayer out of schools, and recently ruled that sodomy in Texas is legal—all decisions that make many conservative Christians' blood boil.

- Attempts to shut down the tort system that allows class action suits against manufacturers in state courts (which tend to grant larger awards) aren't just about protecting businesses from crushing lawsuits. The 2005 bill that President Bush signed is also an attempt to slash the power of individual states and, most importantly, to strangle the Association of Trial Lawyers, which is the biggest contributor to the Democratic Party.

Just as confusing as trying to discern the true objective in political power plays is trying to figure out who is most heavily influencing the government in dictating what agendas the White House should endorse and what laws Congress should adopt. Think tanks are powerful in planting these ideas—and most are now churning out ideas and reports endorsed by the Christian Right and their corporate donors. Lobbyists also are skilled in persuading, as is cold cash contributed to politicians' campaigns. While some policy-shaping groups are well known—the National Rifle Association; Big Pharma's lobbyist group, PhRMA; and the American Conservative Union among them—the hand that is most stealthily and dramatically shaping our country is the Council for National Policy, a shadowy organization of ultraconservatives, radical Christians, and the megamoneyed. Without the blessing of this group, it's said, a Republican presidential candidate won't get far.

 Council for National Policy

Description: An education forum for radical right-wingers that is believed to direct the Republican Party
Founded: 1981 by Tim LaHaye

High-Profile Members, Past and Present:
   Billionaires: Herbert and Nelson Hunt, Joseph Coors, Amway founder
      Richard DeVos, Howard Ahmanson
   Christian Right: James Dobson, theocracy pusher Rousas Rushdoony, Jerry
      Falwell, Pat Robertson
   Political types: Tom DeLay, John Ashcroft, Tommy Thompson, Ed Meese,
      Howard Phillips, former U.S. energy secretary/current Focus on the
      Family president Donald Hodel
   Other notables: Oliver North, NRA head Wayne LaPierre, Phyllis Schlafly,
      representatives of Rev. Sun Myung Moon (reportedly a major contributor)

"One day, before the end of this century, the Council will be so influential that no president, regardless of party or philosophy, will be able to ignore us or our concerns or shut us out of the highest levels of government."

—COUNCIL FOR NATIONAL POLICY'S FIRST EXECUTIVE DIRECTOR WOODY JENKINS,
A LOUISIANA STATE CONGRESSMAN, TO *NEWSWEEK* IN 1981

A potpourri of the extremely religious, extremely conservative, extremely wealthy, and extremely powerful, the Council for National Policy is, unsurprisingly, an extremist group. Headquartered in Virginia, the group couples Christian über-right-wingers with tax-reform conservatives (a faction that includes billionaires), and commands such clout that such bigwigs as Donald Rumsfeld, Dick Cheney, John Bolton, Clarence Thomas, and Alberto Gonzales are delighted to speak before its five hundred members, all of whom pay thousands a year in membership fees if tapped to join. Credited with shoving the government to the right, CNP is believed to have installed ultraconservatives in state and national government, and its meetings provide the network for financial backing of assorted conservative causes; most importantly, this group is said to green-light or impede the progress of presidential hopefuls—George W. Bush got the seal of approval when he was grilled by the group privately in 1999, and Senator Bill Frist, who received CNP's Jefferson Award in 2004, may be next.

The Council for National Policy is believed to be the group Hillary Clinton was referring to when she talked about a Far Right conspiracy against her and her husband; along with billionaire Richard Mellon Scaife, CNP spearheaded the Clinton impeachment.

Peppered with members who want a Bible-based theocracy, this potent group is extremely secretive. It doesn't have a Web site, send out brochures, or announce award ceremonies to the press, and it shirks the media spotlight. Although CNP's nonprofit educational status mandates that it have transparency and produce materials for the public, this locked-doors, invitation-only group shuts out the public and the press. In 1992, the IRS yanked its nonprofit status, but CNP ultimately yanked it back.[6] Three times a year, members meet for clandestine conventions that last several days, during which they hammer out strategies for installing more ultraright-wingers and furthering Far Right Christian causes. Although precise details aren't known about what they are stirring up next, the group packs a wallop: Donald Rumsfeld reportedly called them "the heart of a great conservative movement," and Indiana Congressman Mike Pence has praised them as "the most influential gathering of conservatives in America."[7] More frightening is the assessment of Barry Lynn, who heads Americans United for Separation of Church and State. "[T]hese are the genuine leaders of the Republican Party," he told *Church and State* magazine. "If the CNP gets its way, the First Amendment, along with the rest of the U.S. Constitution, will be replaced with fundamentalist dogma."[8]

▶▶ ◀◀

Over the past three decades, the Right, in all its varieties, has vastly reshaped the U.S. government—from our regulatory agencies such as the FDA and EPA, which are now so laughably lax there seems no point in having them (and abolishing them is exactly what many right-wingers want), to our beefed-up military and relaxed laws on gun control. But the most impressive quality of the Right is how it has been able to unite many factions to accomplish conservative goals. Granted, part of the process involved dragging along those who weren't aware of what was happening—including moderate Republicans who didn't notice their party was being hijacked by Christian extremists. As the Far Right shows where it is actually heading, the conservatives' power may recede. And lately, the Right is starting to fragment: Master strategist Paul Weyrich's Free Congress is hooking up with liberal groups and griping about the Patriot Act's intrusion into our private lives, centrist Republicans such as John McCain are teaming up with centrist Democrats to decry Congress's attempt to weaken the judiciary, and Bush's approval rating even from Republicans is on the decline. How long the Right will continue trying to dictate the national agenda is anyone's guess, but the institutions they've erected—and the changes already in the works—may be hard to stop. At best, the Right's actions will leave deep scars, at worst, thou may be killed if thou utters a profanity.

2. THE CHRISTIAN RIGHT:

Introducing the Handmaiden's Tale?

Notable Numbers

- 59 percent: Proportion of Americans who believe the "End Times" are here or coming soon[1]
- 42 percent: Proportion of Americans who attend church at least once a week[2]
- 25–36 percent: Proportion of Americans estimated to be born-again Christians[3]
- 37 percent: Proportion of Americans who endorse religious leaders influencing government decisions[4]
- 1 million: Number of children being home-schooled[5]

Snapshot

"America is the most religious country in the rich world, with churches full, evangelicals on the march and the Almighty popping up all over public policy."

—JOHN MICKLETHWAIT AND ADRIAN WOOLDRIDGE, *CONSERVATIVE POWER IN AMERICA*

Maybe the stampede to church is a reaction to heart-pounding fear, utter confusion, and down-in-the-gutter decadence. Maybe the pull of heaven is growing stronger or maybe the new megachurches, with their daycare centers, gyms, cafés, and counseling groups, offer a comfort and community not found anywhere else. Perhaps the new wave of evangelicalism is the result of a well-orchestrated Jesus marketing blitz that has brought the Lord into households via satellite, radio, Internet, and cable—and is scaring the bejeezus out of the masses with best-selling fables, such as the *Left Behind* series, which spells out the hell on earth that awaits those who don't sign on as born-again Christians.

THE END TIMES

Left Behind, a wildly successful twelve-part fictional series cowritten by preacher Tim LaHaye, graphically details the "End Times" that some believe are predicted in the last book of the New Testament, Revelation. LaHaye's series opens with "the Rapture"—cars across the planet careen into poles, passengers disappear from planes, pregnant women find their wombs are suddenly empty as the Lord yanks children and born-again Christians to the heavens, while their dentures and prosthetics are left behind along with all the nonbelievers. The world government is run by the Antichrist and hellacious plagues haunt those who aren't plucked up by God, until finally Jesus returns to wage the battle of Armageddon and rule the earth for a thousand years. Religious scholars criticized LaHaye's lurid interpretations, saying the chapter isn't meant to be taken literally, and literary reviewers trashed the religious horror story. LaHaye, the brains behind the books' story line (coauthor Jerry Jenkins actually wrote it), got the last laugh. After September 11, the books' popularity skyrocketed—with totals now well over the 60 million mark, ringing in close to $1 billion in sales. Some credit the series with boosting the number of evangelical Christians and note that its success was in part due to Wal-Mart displaying it prominently in its stores.[6]

Whatever its basis, obsession with the End Times is having odd geopolitical implications.

- Some hardcore Christians are opposed to allowing Palestinians to have their own state. According to End Times prophecy, Jesus won't return until the Jews fully occupy all of the Holy Land.
- The Christian ultraright are also trying to Christianize government, believing that this too is a requirement for Jesus to reenter the earthly plane.

Those anxious about when the big day will arrive can consult www.rapture ready.com, which features an Armageddon clock, currently poised at three minutes to midnight. Even handier: Site visitors can print out a prewritten, undated letter, for the day when the Rapture occurs. Once they realize they are being yanked up by God, the chosen just have to date the note and stick it on the fridge to explain, to those who didn't make the final cut, why they won't be home for dinner.

The Profiteering Prophet
Tim LaHaye

Don't mistake *Left Behind* author Tim LaHaye merely for a writer who struck the mother lode with his blend of religious propaganda and Hollywood horror. The self-proclaimed expert in biblical prophecy—he had previously written over three dozen nonfiction books about the final days, none of them terribly successful—is an ultraconservative Christian strategist, and his novels are tools to empower his cause. At seventy-seven, the wiry Baptist has the plasticky look of someone who's been cosmetically remolded a few too many times. Critics say LaHaye likewise has molded and reshaped the ideas of the Bible's "Revelation" to fit in with his political plan. The *Left Behind* series that weaves in LaHaye's prejudices—he cast the head of the United Nations as the Satanic Antichrist—is only the latest of his evangelical campaigns to win souls and recruit Christians to the Republican cause. Nobody—not even televangelist Pat Robertson, who mobilized millions with his Christian Coalition—has been more crucial in the political rise of the Christian Right. LaHaye helped rev up the right-wing machine that Paul Weyrich built (see "Paul Weyrich," page 6) and cofounded the Moral Majority with Jerry Falwell in 1979. He helped wife Beverly found Concerned Women for America, whose half a million members rally against abortion, gay rights, and the Equal Rights Amendment. (The duo went on to cowrite a book about Christian marriage.)

LaHaye, as well as some older "Reconstructionists," are linked to the rabidly anticommunist John Birch Society formed in the 1950s. Deeply paranoid and seeing "red" everywhere, this group was so extreme they accused President Dwight D. Eisenhower of being a Commie. They also loathe the United Nations, seeing it as a tool to instate world government.

LaHaye, who has sat on boards of organizations created by Rev. Sun Myung Moon (whose money helped fund LaHaye's American Coalition for Traditional Values),[7] has also started up Southern Baptist churches, Christian schools, family values groups, and even his own think tank to promote creationism. But LaHaye's most inspired move came in 1981, when he created the Council for National Policy, whose roster includes many who want to trade democracy for theocracy.

Though currently at the height of popularity, not long ago LaHaye was banished to social pariahdom. Religious consultant for Jack Kemp's 1987 Republican primary campaign, LaHaye resigned within days after his foes revealed that he had previously damned Roman Catholicism as "a false religion." One of LaHaye's churches ran a program to convert Catholics, complete with brochures calling the Pope "the Antichrist." His campaign to save America's soul finally paid off. Now the multimillionaire lives in a gated community of Palm Springs, alongside a golf course, in a mansion gleaming with worldly riches. Nevertheless, his life isn't always heavenly: He recently lashed out at Cloud Ten Pictures, the production company that produced the movie *Left Behind*, which he thought was such a cheesy celluloid version of his masterpiece that he sued. Must have been more proof for LaHaye that the devil rules the judiciary when the court sided with the production company. Not to worry: Mr. Holy Moneybags formed a production company of his own, perhaps funded with the cool $42 million or so he landed for a new book series about an archeologist traipsing through the Holy Land.[8]

The United States has certainly been bit by the Bible bug: While 77 percent of Americans consider themselves Christians at least in name, up to a third (possibly more) of Americans now identify themselves as evangelical—born-again—Christians.[9] Over half of Americans believe the horrific "End Times" of the apocalypse are coming down the pike.

> *End Times fever has crept into TV: NBC aired a spooky miniseries,* Revelations, *in spring 2005 and even Homer Simpson recently developed Rapture-itis—ultimately persuading the Holy Father to postpone his Christian "pull-up."*

As they pile into churches—some of them megachurches with congregations of ten thousand or more, complete with huge video-screen projections of the preaching, and theatrics like rain storms, thunder, and even tanks rolling down the aisles—the fervent are finding more than pleas for their souls and their dollars: The Republican Party is calling out for their votes, filling their ears with promises of reinstilling traditional family values, and putting millions of voter pamphlets in their hands.

More than any other group, the Christian Right, once linked to Democrats, are now faithful to the GOP, which seriously courted them, marketed to them, and brought their values into the party. It paid off.[10]

- 64 percent of those who attend church more than once a week voted for Bush
- 58 percent of those who attend church weekly voted for Bush

"I pledge allegiance to the Christian flag, and to the Savior for whose kingdom it stands. One Savior, crucified, risen and coming again, with life and liberty for all who believe."

—OATH RECITED AT RECENT RECLAIMING AMERICA FOR CHRIST CONFERENCE IN FLORIDA[11]

THE UNITED STATES OF THE LORD?

The Christian Right includes many who recognize the founding fathers' calls for a separation between church and state. However, some of the movement's ultraright leaders—including LaHaye, economist Gary North of the Institute for Christian Economics, Gary DeMar of American Vision and the California-based Chalcedon Foundation—want the country to be a Christian nation, with God as the acknowledged supreme power, the Bible as the rule book, and the entire government an organ of Christendom, holding down the fort till Jesus returns. Those pushing for a true theocracy often sound like a Christian Taliban.

Southern Baptist preacher Dr. Bruce Prescott is one of a growing number of Christians and scholars who take the threat of the Christian Reconstructionists quite seriously.[12] Prescott says the Reconstructionists are trying to:

- "Make the Ten Commandments the law of the land"
- "Reduce the role of government to the defense of property rights"
- "Require 'tithes' to [Christian] agencies to provide welfare services"
- "Close prisons [and] reintroduce slavery"
- Put to death those not practicing Christianity or guilty of the crimes of cursing, Sabbath breaking, sodomy, witchcraft, incorrigibility in children, as well as murder and rape
- "Close public schools"
- Strip women of their rights and install strong-male-dominated families

Two of the many recent moves that indicate the theocracy pushers are serious:

- In 2004, over three dozen U.S. representatives and senators cosponsored the Constitutional Restoration Act. The bill called for God to be named as sovereign leader of the country and for judges who recognized the distinction between church and state to be impeached and possibly imprisoned. Even if it doesn't pass, given the warm response it received from the Christian Right, this bill will surely rise again.
- Numerous bills in Congress are attempting to strip the power of the courts, including preventing the courts from having a say in matters about religion.

Those watching the growing power of the radical Christian Right see the Ten Commandments as the issue that could lead to a religious takeover. What the Reconstructionists are trying to do, they caution, is use the Ten Commandments to force recognition that the Bible is the basis for the U.S. Constitution, and therefore the basis for U.S. law.[13]

Some surveys have shown that up to 25 percent of Americans would support a Bible-based government.[14]

THE TEN COMMANDMENTS

Cecil B. DeMille couldn't have known the hell that would result from his 1951 movie *The Ten Commandments* (starring Charlton Heston). To promote the film, DeMille encouraged the Fraternal Order of the Eagle—a military group—to donate carvings of the Ten Commandments to public squares and government buildings across the land. Five decades later, those monuments are the source of loud controversy: Progressives are bellowing that the commandments are marrying religion to government while the Christian Right is screaming that their beliefs are being attacked. Ultraright Christians, in a publicity stunt of their own, are installing more monuments of the Ten Commandments in government buildings. The biggest fireworks exploded in Montgomery when Alabama Chief Justice Roy Moore—a Republican who wants to use the Bible as law—ordered a 2.6-ton granite monument of the commandments to be placed in the lobby of Alabama's state judiciary. Several groups, including the Southern Poverty Law Center, seeing it as a challenge to the concept of separation between church and state, sued Moore. A federal judge ruled that the monument had to be removed, and Moore's colleagues on the state Supreme Court upheld the judgment. Moore still wouldn't call in the movers, and in November 2003 both Moore and the monument were forcibly pried from the state building. Moore became an instant martyr, and the Christian Right rallied around his cause. (Ever since being ousted from the Alabama judiciary building, Roy's rock has been on the road: The most famous copy of the commandments since the original is on tour, appearing in two dozen states by spring 2005.)

Currently the U.S. Supreme Court heard several cases on the Ten Commandments in 2005. In one case, it ruled the display of the Ten Commandments (alongside other historical monuments) was legal on federal property. In a second case, concerning the commandments hanging inside Kentucky courthouses, the Supreme Court ruled it was unconstitutional. The issue is sure to launch more battles as the Christian ultraright seeks to replace words first written on parchment paper with words carved in stone.

Close-up

These days the Christian Right has plenty of reason to cry out "Hallelujah." They have a born-again Christian in the White House preaching about saving America "soul by soul" and waging a "crusade" against "evildoers" such as the non-Jesus-loving countries on the "Axis of Evil." The American people—typically secular at least in their politics—are buying it, often not even noticing that biblical phrases and images—"a day of fire" and "the maker of heaven and earth" are woven into presidential speeches.

"America . . . proclaims liberty throughout all the world and to all the inhabitants thereof."

—PRESIDENT GEORGE W. BUSH, SECOND INAUGURAL ADDRESS[15]

"And ye shall . . . proclaim liberty throughout all the land unto all the inhabitants thereof."

—LEVITICUS 25:10

Upon entering the White House in 2001, President George W. Bush's first move was to introduce his controversial program for "faith-based initiatives"—which uses religious groups to carry out social programs from food aid delivery to drug counseling. The program did not garner Senate approval, but no matter: Bush signed it into law by executive order in December 2002. The federal government is shoveling billions of dollars into religion-based programs—including those of Pat Robertson and Rev. Sun Myung Moon's Unification Church.[16]

Over $2 million of the faith-based initiative funding went to a program started by a man who saw the light while in prison—and now counsels former inmates on how to stay out of jail. Former presidential advisor Charles Colson once advised President Nixon to firebomb a DC think tank, the Brookings Institution, which he warned was too liberal.[17] What got him tossed behind bars, however, was his involvement in Watergate. While there, he wrote Born Again, *and Colson, reportedly a Reconstructionist,[18] started up the Prison Fellowship Ministries to help keep convicted criminals from a repeat "vacation" in prison.*

A galvanizing cause for the Christian Right is reversing the landmark *Roe v. Wade* decision that legalized abortion in 1973; they even have "Roe"—the woman whose case went to the Supreme Court—in their league, saying she is now antiabortion and working to strike down the law. Internationally, antiabortion Christian groups such as the Family Research Council have helped to slash funding for birth control and abortion, possibly contributing to the spread of AIDS worldwide. Because of their loud unsubstantiated claims that U.S. funding to the United Nations Population Fund resulted in coerced abortions in China—even though over 160 other groups sent to verify that claim refuted it—the $34 million of U.S. federal funding typically given to that agency was cut off. Now many family planning clinics in Africa, which also counsel on AIDS, don't have money and don't have condoms.

In March 2005, Ellen Sauerbrey, the U.S. delegate to the United Nations, was heckled and booed at a UN conference for women when she lectured about abstinence and demanded that an antiabortion clause be inserted into a UN document about women's rights. Outside of the Vatican, Nicaragua, Panama, and Costa Rica, no other country supported the amendment.[19]

Drawn together through groups such as Focus on the Family—which has over 2 million members—the Christian Right has serious muscle and frequently flexes it. Whether through floods of letters and calls or threats of boycotts, they have recently launched campaigns to:

- Pressure Kraft to drop its support of the Gay Olympics[20]
- Force Proctor & Gamble to withdraw support for a local law that called for ending discrimination against gays[21]
- Convince Tyson Foods to stop buying advertising spots on TV shows they believed were provocative[22]

Hardcore Christians are also rewriting science to eliminate, or at least refute, Darwin's theory of evolution. Across the United States, more and more states stamp notices on their textbooks saying evolution is only a theory while others mention "intelligent design," the idea that animals, including humans, are so complex that they must have been created by a being, somewhere, that is intelligent.

Kansas kicked up the evolution controversy: In 1999 it erased Darwin's theory from most textbooks. Three years later, textbooks in Georgia were required to bear a sticker stating that evolution was only an unproven theory. In October 2004 the school board in Dover, Pennsylvania, required that alternatives to evolution also be taught. The next month, the school board in Grantsburg, Wisconsin, voted to allow creationism to be taught. But the movement to teach that God created man may be devolving. Darwin's theory is now being rewritten back into Kansas textbooks, and in Georgia stickers are being pulled off.

Sometimes it's hard to discern a definite path that the Christian Right—and their much more extreme brethren, the Christian ultraright—are following as they ascend in power. But there's a plan in place, say those who are watching and those whom they've tried to recruit. Stripping courts' power, handing social services over to religion, and bringing the Lord's word into the government and the schools are all part of a program to marry religion and politics—now mostly a clandestine affair. But there's one problem: Not all Christians want to follow the herd.

"There are many non-'right' Christians who oppose the [theocracy] movements, but they are kinder, gentler folk, and they don't fight in the mud, nor do they get much media attention. Among 'evangelical' churches the 'proper' and expected way to think is to strongly support these theocratic movements—after all, we 'have to' support God and the Bible. I hear it all the time."

—PASTOR LARRY HARVEY, JUNE 2005[23]

Behind the Scenes

The Bush administration has brought many of the Christian Right into its fold. Among the religious Right he shepherded in:

- Former attorney general John Ashcroft, active in the Pentecostal Assemblies of God and a member of the Council for National Policy
- Kay Coles James, formerly of the Family Research Council, now director of the U.S. Council of Personnel; some fear she will preferentially hire born-again Christians
- W. David Hager, Bush's appointee to the FDA's Reproductive Drugs Advisory Committee and a Christian gynecologist who wrote a book recommending the use of prayer to relieve menstrual cramps
- J. Robert Brame, a Bush appointee to the National Labor Relations Board; was unable to take the position after activists loudly protested that Brame had been a member of the Reconstructionist group American Vision

The U.S. Supreme Court may soon be headed by hardcore Christians Antonin Scalia (reportedly a member of Catholic extremist group Opus Dei) or Clarence Thomas (also rumored to be Opus Dei), both Bush favorites.

Agent of Change
Dr. Bruce Prescott

"Christians need to look at themselves through the eyes of Jews—particularly, through the eyes of those who were herded into boxcars and slaughtered like cattle in the Holocaust," says Dr. Bruce Prescott. "Jews need to look at themselves through the eyes of Muslims—particularly, through the eyes of those who were displaced from their homes in Palestine. Muslims need to look at themselves through the eyes of Baha'is. We all need to look at ourselves through the eyes of the hungry and the homeless, the impoverished and the imprisoned. If we have the courage to honestly look at ourselves through the eyes of others who are strange and foreign to us or who have been injured and ignored by us, then I believe our hearts will open and the whispering of God's still, small voice will begin to ring loud and clear in our ears."[24]

Southern Baptist Dr. Bruce Prescott. "Religious liberty for everyone—not just Christians— is our first freedom."

Dr. Bruce Prescott is a Southern Baptist with a blog, an evangelical who wants to keep religion out of government. "True believers in the Christian Reconstructionist movement are serious and determined, and the movement provides intellectual, spiritual and financial support for a network of activists who are a rising political force," he says. "Someplace there is a tipping point and it will be too late to turn back from the trajectory these theocrats are steering us. I think we are approaching the danger zone."

Besides in his sermons and at interfaith conferences, Prescott lambasts the ongoing merging between church and state in his blog (mainstreambaptist.blogspot.com)—pointing out political shenanigans, such as Ohio's recently unveiled "Restoration Project," promoted by Ohio's secretary of state, which calls upon two thousand Christian leaders to become "patriot pastors"—filling their churches with voter guides and handing over the addresses of their flocks to the Republican Party. Prescott has written about how he witnessed Texan Reconstructionists (including high-powered judges and lawyers) overtaking the Republican Party in Houston, and he has called attention to a brochure by a Houston theocracy-pusher that urges Christians to vote in elections—twice. "The number of people who actually admit to being Christian Reconstructionists is small," says Prescott. "But the number of people who have been influenced by them—picking and choosing aspects of their agenda—is very large. Few who have been influenced by Reconstructionism are aware of the entire agenda."

3. THE BUSHES:

Texan Blue Bloods

George H. W. Bush (b. 1924)   CIA director: 1976–77
                                   U.S. vice president: 1980–88
                                   U.S. president: 1989–92
George W. Bush (b. 1946)   Texas governor: 1994–2000
                                   U.S. president: 2001–present
John Ellis "Jeb" Bush (b. 1953)   Florida governor: 1998–present

Notable Numbers

- $7.6 million to $19 million: George W. Bush's worth[1]
- $1.5 million: Jeb Bush's worth[2]

Snapshot

If a submarine periscope hadn't poked up in the Pacific on September 2, 1944, this page would be blank. There would never have been a presidential election swindle in 2000, there may not have been a savings and loan crisis in 1988, and Terry Schiavo would have passed away without all the hoopla. Religion would not be entwined so deeply into the White House, the U.S. government might not have deceived its citizens quite so many times, and the country probably would never have invaded Iraq—the first time or the second. We would never have heard the term "Axis of Evil" and September 11 might have passed by as just a lovely autumn day. But when that sub, the *Finback*, pushed out of inky water long enough to grab the lone occupant of a lifeboat, it set into motion a number of actions that would profoundly shape the United States for many decades ahead.

On the plastic raft was a shivering twenty-year-old pilot whose fighter plane had been shot down hours earlier in the skies over Chichi Jima, southwest of Japan. His name was George H. W. Bush. His first thought when he saw the periscope extend out of the water: "Jeez, I hope it's one of ours."[3] It was.

Except perhaps when it comes to Japanese food—he vomited all over the Japanese prime minister during a 1992 state visit to Tokyo—George H. W. Bush is extraordinarily lucky: The close brush with death during World War II ended happily for him (not so for his gunner, whose parachute wouldn't open), and he escaped unscathed from a 1993 assassination attempt in Kuwait. He and his wife, Barbara, were not on that private plane in December 2004 that crashed (killing all occupants) en route to picking them up for a speaking engagement. And the forty-first president also emerged from numerous close brushes with scandal with barely a scratch on his armor.

Reagan was said to be the Teflon president, but his veep was fairly stick-free himself. The dirt that didn't cling to George Bush Sr. includes:

- Not named as a major player in the Iran-Contra affair by Congress (thanks to Congressman Dick Cheney, who kept Bush's name clean)
- Little fallout for pardoning all convicted in Iran-Contra scandal (thanks to nonattentive American public)
- Never publicly chastised for his extramarital affairs (thanks to forgiving media)
- Never officially faulted for green-lighting the arming of mujahideen in Afghanistan (thanks to nobody understanding the implications)
- Never officially blasted for what may have been an unnecessary invasion of Iraq, or for deceiving the public about the reasons for doing so
- Rarely mentioned as being a top paid speaker for Rev. Sun Myung Moon (thanks to sleeping reporters)

It shouldn't come as a big surprise that the former president slips out of tight situations with Houdini-like skills: The senior Bush was very tapped into the CIA—as well as Big Money, Big Power, and Big Oil, and if one colleague couldn't fix a problem, another one could. That certainly came in handy for his sons, to whom he passed his connections like a dominant gene. With the help of Pappy's Rolodex, the Bush boys have snagged millions of dollars, erased legal woes, and even snatched elections. Senior's lucky streak and his influential pals, however, still haven't been enough to fully ward off the boys' HSP—or High Screwup Potential. Whether you are talking about George W., Jeb, Neil, or Marvin, they all seem to suffer from a unique gift: the Opposite Midas Touch. Once the boys pick up any golden opportunity placed before them, it turns to dust, ultimately.

> *Officially listed as CIA director in 1976 under President Ford, the elder Bush may have been part of the intelligence agency long before his résumé notes it. Atop a 1963 FBI document concerning the death of John F. Kennedy, J. Edgar Hoover reportedly had written: "George Bush of the CIA," and rumors swirl that Senior was part of the anti-Castro CIA activity throughout the 1960s.*

Close-up

When George Herbert Walker Bush, son of wealthy financier and liberal congressman Prescott Bush, said his solemn "I dos" alongside Barbara Pierce in 1945, he would not merely be keeping the family name alive. He and his wife would produce a line of Texan princes that would try to do what only the Kennedys before them had succeeded at, and then only briefly: become reigning American royalty.

With four handsome and charming sons (and a shoved-to-the-sidelines daughter, Dorothy), a high-profile, accomplished father, and a road that some say was prepaved by friendly powers in the U.S. military and intelligence communities,[4] from Bush Sr.'s perspective a family power grab appeared to be in the stars. Except, that is, for one thing: His sons, the young, heavy-boozing, skirt-chasing Bush boys—who had notoriously bad taste in friends—initially didn't have the slightest interest in politics, wanting little more than to lay their paws on mountains of money.

> *The boys may be charismatic, but Harvard professors they ain't. Perhaps it goes back to their upbringing: According to one visitor to their childhood home, Marjorie Perloff, the house was notably lacking in books. Perloff says young Dorothy Bush admitted that the Bushes didn't even own an encyclopedia.[5]*

While their father's career was soaring, the boys' floundered, and their attempts at finding their callings were consistently pathetic. George Junior—a rip-roaring alcoholic—headed several oil ventures that came up dry. Jeb had a talent for getting sucked into Florida real-estate deals with dicey partners and for falling into assorted fly-by-night schemes such as selling water pumps in Nigeria. Neil also embarked on oil and gas ventures that went bust. Marvin, who had a life-threatening colon disease, was an investment banker with a knack for picking losing horses. Despite the fact that they all wallowed in their so-called careers for many years, the boys typically blew through millions, thanks to Dad's buddies who invested in the kids' financial black holes—and fished them out whenever they messed up, which was often.

A SAMPLER OF THE BUSH BOYS' IFFY MOVES

- In June 1990, George W. cashed in his stock in Harken—an oil company that had absorbed his other dying oil ventures and suddenly looked healthy, thanks to a contract for exploration in Bahrain. The sale of the stock brought George over $848,000, but he didn't report it to the SEC for another seven months. The situation was curious: Within a few weeks of Bush selling off his shares, Harken's stock was almost worthless—due to the impending war in Iraq. The question arose that perhaps George, whose father was president and planning the war in Iraq, may have been tipped off to the upcoming military showdown and ditched the stock before it plummeted in value. An SEC investigation soon followed, but the president's son was officially cleared of accessing insider information.

- In Florida, Jeb and his business partner bought an office building in 1985, using a third party—who defaulted on the $4.56 million loan, a factor in the crumbling of the Broward Bank in Sunrise. Curiously, federal investigators opted to devalue the property—and Jeb and partner kept the building after forking over a mere $500,000. The remainder of the tab was eaten by taxpayers.[6]

- Jeb may have also played a role in the Iran-Contra affair. In 1985 he served as middleman, running a request for medical aid from the Nicaraguan contras to his father, then vice president.[7]

- Jeb, who was a real estate agent for the country's largest HMO, International Medical Centers, also lobbied the Department of Health and Human Services to waive any cap on the amount of Medicare funding that IMC could receive. The Miami-based HMO took in over $1 billion in federal Medicare funding, and Jeb claimed that he had been duped when the thuggish CEO Miguel Recarey (who carried a fancy gun under his suit jacket) was later charged with fraud and ripping off Medicare for many millions.[8] Before the fraud was uncovered, the HMO, reportedly linked to both the mafia and the CIA, was believed to have been treating Nicaraguan contras.

- Neil helped finance his business stinkers by snagging a director's seat at Denver's Silverado Banking, Savings and Loan, which tossed $200 million of loans at Neil's financiers. They defaulted, a key factor in the 1988 crash of the institution, which rattled savings and loans institutions nationwide. Taxpayers got hit with the bank's $1 billion tab.

But where some might see abject failure, Senior (who, granted, was tossing back strong meds that might have colored his view) saw hope and a political
future—especially after his 1988 presidential campaign, when his offspring
seemed to blossom and show their hidden talents. In fact, Senior may have owed
his presidency to none other than until-then-couldn't-do-nothin'-right George:
Recently off the hooch, George had "found the Lord" while attending a men's
prayer group in Midland, Texas. And that discovery, it turned out, was indeed a
godsend, smoothing the way for his father to secure the very much needed votes
of the Christian Right.

GEORGE AND GEORGE, TAKE ONE

George W. may never have seen the light, or the light of the Oval Office, had
he not showed up at the family's Maine vacation compound one weekend in
1986 and proceeded to get trashed during a Bush bash, so much so that he
greatly offended one of his mother's closest friends, slurring into her ear, "So
what's sex like after fifty, anyway?"[9] Before you could say "going to hell in a
handbasket," Senior had Rev. Billy Graham on the line, who swooped into the
sorry sod's life and as George W. would later say, planted "a mustard seed of
faith." Shortly thereafter, George shoved aside his beloved bourbon and was
"born again"—this time as an evangelical Methodist. Showing the extremist ten-
dencies of a "dry drunk," George W. so fervently embraced his new life with the
Lord that his religion sparked a few family showdowns, including heated de-
bates about whether you had to be Christian—and a born-again at that—to enter the pearly gates of heaven. (George W. insisted yes, but Billy Graham, called
in for counsel on the matter, sided with Barbara and said no.) But George's new
passion was ultimately a boon. In the 1988 Republican primaries, Senior was
slapped with a nasty surprise: Televangelist Pat Robertson was leaving Bush behind in the dust as he snatched up the votes like dollars out of the donation basket, state after state. Suddenly, W was an asset, and was hauled in as advisor:
The newborn Christian met with the country's religious leaders, informing them
of his "conversion" and assuring them with carefully chosen words that his pa
would be responsive to their demands. The church leaders were duly impressed
with Junior—and Senior subsequently kicked Pat Robertson to the sidelines,
winning both the 1988 primaries and the election. And W saw firsthand that this
faction of Christian Right voters was a veritable vein of power—and one that he
could easily tap.

"I'm going to tell them the five turning points in my life. Accepting Christ. Marrying my wife. Having children. Running for governor. And listening to my mother."

—GEORGE W. BUSH RUNNING HIS PLAN TO WOO CHRISTIANS BY DOUGLAS WEAD, HIS RELIGIOUS ADVISOR.[10] UNKNOWN TO BUSH, WEAD WAS TAPING MANY OF THEIR INTIMATE CONVERSATIONS AND WOULD LATER BETRAY BUSH'S CONFIDENCE BY MAKING THE TAPES PUBLIC.

After the Bush 1988 presidential campaign, a new plan was hatched to take advantage of the boys' newfound skills in politics. George W. would aim to become governor of Texas, Jeb would shoot for Florida, and Neil would make a run for Colorado. Although there were a few false starts, by the 1990s the Bush boys were indeed well on their way.

- With Karl Rove as his strategist, George knocked popular Texas governor Ann Richards out of her seat, becoming the main man in Texas in 1994; he was reelected in 1998.
- Jeb stepped in as Florida's governor in 1998, reelected in 2002.
- Neil, embroiled in an ugly divorce, and tainted by the Silverado Savings and Loan debacle, hasn't yet manifested his part of the political plan. However, his business deals in Asia have brought other perks. Asian businessmen often sent lovely women to Neil's hotel room for a little hanky-panky, a fact that came out during Neil's 2003 divorce.[11]

Texas and Florida, never known as squeaky clean, above-the-board states, both pack a punch. Texas has a whopping 34 electoral votes (second only to California's 55) and Florida has 27 of the country's total 538. Texas holds most of the country's oil refineries and the last drops of the mainland's oil; Florida is home to NASA's Kennedy Space Center and CENTCOM, the key command post from which U.S. military operations in the Middle East are directed. In Texas, the Bushes are friendly with the oil billionaires and have welcomed in the Saudis; in Florida, Jeb is close to wealthy Cuban hardliners said to control the Cuban community's votes.[12] And in both states, the ultraconservative religious Right runs megachurches and lubes the political machine, all the while beaming lovingly at the born-again Bush boys.

Texas writer J. H. Hatfield asserted that George W. was busted for cocaine in 1972, but that the record was expunged. Shortly after writing his controversial book, Fortunate Son*, Hatfield, too, was permanently expunged. In July 2001, Hatfield died in a motel room under mysterious circumstances that were alleged to be suicide.*

As politicians, George W. and Jeb, the clan's third generation to hold office, showed themselves to be far more conservative than their father or granddad.

- As Texas governor, George W. distinguished himself as being the American who had fried the most people—152. (By comparison, Illinois has executed twelve since 1977.)
- Although George W. is widely believed to have been a cocaine user himself,[13] as governor he toughened up laws on cocaine, mandating a minimum five-year prison term for first-time offenders caught possessing less than a gram—about a sugar packet's worth of the powder. Some estimate that nearly 10 percent of Texas's prison population is now there for cocaine offenses.
- George W. ushered religion into the state social program, budgeting state funds for church-based counseling programs.
- Contrary to his actions regarding Terri Schiavo in 2005, George W. signed a law in 1999 giving Texas physicians the right to pull the plug on patients requiring life support—even if the family objected.
- Jeb, who, after failing to grab the Florida governorship in 1994, became a born-again Christian and is pro-life, intervened in 2002 to prevent the abortion planned for a mentally retarded ward of the state who had been raped while in state care.
- Jeb slashed funding for drug rehab programs and stiffened penalties for drug users, but they didn't apply to his daughter Noelle, who was popped for illegal drugs several times—including being busted for possession of crack at her drug treatment center.
- In 2003, Jeb signed "Terri's Law" preventing the state-court-approved removal of the feeding tube to Terri Schiavo, who had been in a coma since 1990. In 2005, he again tried to block the state-court-approved removal of the feeding tube. This time he turned it into a federal effort, working with the U.S. Congress and his brother the president to bring Republicans back to Congress during a recess to pass a law allowing Congress to direct the matter to the federal courts. The bill, signed by President Bush, was rejected by a Florida federal court.
- Since his bro became pres, Jeb has successfully pushed for a number of presidential pardons for convicted Cuban criminals, including known terrorist Orlando Bosch, who tried to sink a Polish ship off of Miami and is be-

lieved to have been behind the 1976 attack of a Cubana flight that killed seventy-three. Another head-scratcher: his nomination of Cuban lawyer Raoul Cantero to the state Supreme Court, despite Cantero's glaring lack of judicial experience.[14]

- As governor, Jeb initiated a number of controversial programs regarding data mining, including pioneering a program with MATRIX, a system that critics say gives too much info to the state.

- But what Jeb is best known for is helping his big brother win the 2000 presidential election, which was among America's stinkiest. Among the many strange occurrences in the Florida presidential election: Tens of thousands of Democrats who should have been eligible to vote were prevented from doing so in a mix-up, hanging chads weren't correctly counted, and suitcases full of uncounted votes were discovered in hotel rooms days after the election.

With George W. in the White House—the first time a son had followed his father there since the Adamses two centuries before—the Bush Machine was primed to roll. But a small headache emerged, for Senior at least. Junior wasn't necessary listening to what Pops had to say. In fact, he'd apparently handed over most of the workings of the White House to his inner cadre—Cheney, Rumsfeld, and Wolfowitz—while he jetted off to his ranch.

GEORGE AND GEORGE, TAKE TWO

Although some have speculated that Dad's words guide the actions of his eldest son, George Senior reportedly had little to do with George Junior's plan to invade Iraq in 2003; in fact, he opposed it. Being of the conservative realist school, Senior valued the UN and bristled at the new administration's cocky go-it-alone attitude and willingness to flip off the Security Council and mock "Old Europe." A former CIA director, the elder Bush was also alarmed at the Bush team's belligerent bullying of the intelligence community to cough up the information that they needed to support the lies that had already slithered out of their mouths. Senior, who had invaded Iraq with a true coalition of the world's power-mongers (not just Britain and a few minor league suck-ups), warned of alienating allies and the hazards of unilateralist moves. Former national security advisor Brent Scowcroft, former secretary of state James Baker, and former secretary of state Lawrence Eagleburger also tried to talk some sense into the young'un and his dangerous neocon friends, even if they had to write op-eds to do it. The younger Bush asserted his independence and demonstrated his screwup potential again in his refusal to heed their advice.

Father Knows Best?

"We would have been forced to occupy Baghdad and, in effect rule Iraq. . . . Going in and thus unilaterally exceeding the United Nations mandate would have destroyed the precedent of international response to aggression we hoped to establish. . . . Had we gone the invasion route, the United States could conceivably still be an occupying power in a bitterly hostile land. It would have been a dramatically different—and perhaps barren—outcome."

—GEORGE H. W. BUSH AND BRENT SCOWCROFT EXPLAINING WHY THE U.S. MILITARY PULLED BACK FROM IRAQ IN THE 1991 GULF WAR[15]

TRICKLE-DOWN POLITICS

Senior passed on a legacy that skipped over the Clinton years, and very literally blew up in Junior's face—on September 11, 2001. Two keys events related to the 9/11 attacks:

- As VP in the 1980s, Senior gave the thumbs-up to help fund and train Arab Muslim mujahideen fighting the Soviets in Afghanistan—the same warriors who would later form al-Qaeda.
- As president, Senior launched the Persian Gulf War in 1991—under questionable circumstances then as well—and helped trigger the ire of Osama bin Laden, who'd begged the Saudi ruling family to let his mujahideen warriors take out Saddam.

Behind the Scenes

Rich, powerful fathers pass on more than their millions and their business connections to their sons. They also pass on a crushing weight—as George Bush Sr. knew well. Upon becoming president, he requested a study of presidential offspring. Written by advisor Douglas Wead, the report, "All the Presidents' Children," looked at the progeny of presidents from John Adams to Ronald Reagan and showed a high propensity among them for scandals, accidental deaths, and raging alcohol abuse.

George H. W. Bush, who sat on the board of drug maker Eli Lilly, bought United Fruit in 1969, the banana importer notorious for its role in the U.S.-engineered overthrow of Guatemala's democratically elected president in 1954.

It must make some statement in the nurture v. nature debate that George W.—given the same opportunities as his father—turned out so differently. Both Georges attended prep school at Andover, both attended Yale, both were members of Skull and Bones (the secret society in which members are said to masturbate in a coffin as part of the initiation), and both were aided by their fathers in setting the initial direction of their careers. But George H. W.'s pa helped him only once—in snagging a job at Texas oil company Dresser Industries, where George H. W. made his first millions. Senior soon became powerful within his own right. With rare exception throughout his career, George W. has used his father like an invisible cane.

POP'S UNSEEN HANDS

A few occasions when Senior and friends have smoothed out George's uneven career:

- With funding from Senior's friends, Harken bailed out W's ailing Spectrum 7 oil company in 1986.
- At W's behest, Senior's pals pooled together the money to buy the Texas Rangers baseball franchise in 1989.
- The Carlyle Group (where Senior and Baker worked as consultants) gave W a job as director of Caterair in 1990–94; at board meetings, he did little but tell dirty jokes.[16]
- Pops brought in Karl Rove as W's strategist in the 1990s.
- George Shultz put together W's education team in the late 1990s, to prepare him for the 2000 presidential campaign.
- James Baker was hauled out to make sure the Florida judgment went W's way in the 2000 election.
- James Baker was sent to the Middle East in 2004 as an official U.S. envoy to try to obtain forgiveness of some of Iraq's outstanding debts.

In violation of the Presidential Records Act, George W. Bush recently signed an executive order preventing release of over sixty thousand Reagan-era documents, which may have brought to light his father's involvement in Iran-Contra and other scandals of the day.

Whereas George H. W. Bush slipped out of office without any permanent dirt on his hands, George W. seems to be tattooing himself with india ink. But not to worry: With luck, Jeb will come along and help him wash off any lingering stains.

Jeb's rising national and international profile seems to portend that he'll make a run at the White House as well. (Pundits are predicting that Jeb will either run as veep on a ticket with Dick Cheney in 2008 or as the presidential candidate with Condoleezza Rice as his VP.) And Jeb may be the slickest, most conservative, and scariest Bush of all.

4. BUSH INSIDERS:

The Vulcans

The Vulcans

Dick Cheney, vice president
Donald Rumsfeld, secretary of defense
Condoleezza Rice, secretary of state
Paul Wolfowitz, president of the World Bank
Stephen Hadley, national security advisor
Karl Rove, political strategist

Notable Numbers

- $30 million to $110 million: Dick Cheney's estimated worth
- $60 million to $130 million: Donald Rumsfeld's estimated worth

Snapshot

Brainy, polished, and telegenic, the hawks that circle George W. Bush are a cunning cabal. Already big shots who shined as power players in previous administrations, as millionaire CEOs in the private sector, or as heady thinkers in lofty academia, they've inadvertently formed the "Most Powerful Club" and their names are now as well known as the president's. Whether you're talking about Dick Cheney ("the most powerful vice president"), Donald Rumsfeld ("the most powerful defense secretary"), Karl Rove ("the most powerful political strategist"), or Condoleezza Rice ("the most powerful woman in the world"[1]), the supporting cast President Bush assembled when he slipped into the Oval Office in 2001 is the hardest-hitting, most ruthless bunch to ever pull up chairs in the White House's Situation Room. *Hawks* wasn't a strong enough term for these warmongers: They jokingly dubbed themselves the Vulcans, apparently in reference to *Star Trek*'s coldly calculating egghead, Mr. Spock.

THE BUSH LEGACY (THUS FAR)

Since 2001, the Bush administration has:

- Blasted military spending ($455.5 billion in 2004;[2] $288 billion in 2000[3])
- Sucked the budget dry ($412 billion deficit in 2004)[4]
- Introduced a preemptive defense strategy
- Okayed first-strike use of nuclear weapons by the United States
- Launched the "War on Terror," authorizing the United States to attack suspected terrorists anywhere in the world (and lured other countries to sign on by dangling arms deals)
- Gave the U.S. government new rights to snoop, arrest, and detain civilians
- Wove religion into the White House and federal government
- Issued ground-breaking executive orders, including one authorizing extreme methods of interrogation, such as unleashing attack dogs on prisoners in their cells, and another that exempts all personal presidential papers from the public record
- Appointed John Bolton to the UN without Senate approval
- Made the United States look like a global jerk

The Vulcans knew what they wanted from their very first days in power: to take out Saddam, and to put in a $200+ billion[5] National Missile Defense system to intercept enemy missiles,[6] both items that looked like tough sells back before the United States became an irrational heap of rattled nerves post-9/11.

Recent books by Bush's former treasury secretary Paul O'Neill and former counterterrorism expert Richard Clarke attest to the administration's obsession with regime change in Iraq from the earliest staff meetings. The British press reported in 2001 that by Bush's second week in office, he was meeting with British Prime Minister Tony Blair to plot how to take down Saddam.

BUSH'S BRAINS

When political planner Karl Rove and the Republican machine in Texas began making serious noises about Gov. George W. Bush making a run for the 2000 presidency, at least two people recognized that the governor, not a MENSA member candidate on his brightest of days, was a true imbecile in the international department. Karl Rove could spell out the magic phrases to memorize and spit out during speeches, but what if the press asked Bush about, heaven forbid, a foreign country? Bush's knowledge of life outside the United States included little except for a few trips to Mexico, where he learned such key phrases as *"Hola, amigo. ¿Qué tal?"*

George Shultz, former secretary of state under Bush Sr., and Dick Cheney, Senior's secretary of defense, stepped in to help the young'un learn World 101. They lassoed a team of cerebral types out of deep thought and assembled their impromptu school in Texas.[7] Dr. Condoleezza Rice was provost at Stanford (where she also "thought" for the Hoover Institute, a conservative think tank), Dr. Paul Wolfowitz was dean of the School of Public Policy at Johns Hopkins, and lawyer Stephen Hadley worked on weapons issues for think tanks, recommending that the United States take a more easygoing approach about using nuclear weapons in conventional warfare.

For more than a year before Junior hit the campaign trail in 2000, the trio gave him a nonstop crash course in global geopolitics. Despite his high-caliber teachers, the future president was not a quick study and still often seemed overwhelmed when the talk turned to matters overseas: He's been known to confuse Sweden and Switzerland, Slovenia and Slovakia, but perhaps can now identify Iraq on a map. The sages' efforts paid off in other ways, however. When the Supreme Court ruled that Bush had won the 2000 election, Wolfowitz snagged the title of deputy secretary of defense, Rice became national security advisor, and Hadley became Rice's assistant NSA.

While Bush gives a nod to many of the recommendations his high-IQ supporting cast makes, the two who appear to have a direct line to George W.'s gray matter are his vice president, whom many believe is directing the administration with help from the neocons, and Bush's longtime buddy Karl Rove, a college dropout who may be the slyest of the bunch.

The Vulcans were poised to ensure that the Bush II presidency would be a no-nonsense, battle-happy era of wars, resource grabs, and defensive strategies that would haunt us for years to come. But before operations were fully under way—before they had time to unveil their war plans—they were hit with the most terrifying occurrence of American history: the 9/11 attack. While it is impossible to have a rational reaction to such a mouth-droppingly brutal act, the Vulcans, as is their wont, reacted to an extreme, both militarily and domestically. The administration imposed a quasi–police state, complete with censorship, propaganda, and Big Brother's watchful eyes.

There is a school of thought that the global "discipline program" that Bush and his Vulcans put into place post-9/11 wasn't really a reaction at all. Some believe the Bush administration purposefully disregarded warnings and "let it happen"[8]— to create an opportunity to launch its military plans. Even if the Bush administration wasn't complicit in the attacks, some believe that it seized the opportunity to push through an agenda that was already in the works.

> "[B]e very cautious not to seek political advantage by making incendiary suggestions, as were made by some today, that the White House had advance information that would have prevented the tragic attacks of 9/11."
>
> —VICE PRESIDENT DICK CHENEY, WARNING DEMOCRATS IN CONGRESS NOT TO BE "IRRESPONSIBLE" BY POINTING OUT THAT THE WHITE HOUSE HAD BEEN WARNED ABOUT THE HIGH LIKELIHOOD OF ATTACKS.[9] IT LATER CAME OUT THAT AN AUGUST 6, 2001, PRESIDENTIAL BRIEFING POINTED OUT THE INCREASING PROBABILITY OF AL-QAEDA STRIKING THE COUNTRY; THE BRIEFING CARRIED THE HEADLINE "BIN LADEN DETERMINED TO STRIKE IN U.S."

STRANGE COINCIDENCES

Appointed by President Bush in May 2001 "to oversee the development of a coordinated national effort" for emergency preparedness, Vice President Cheney reportedly had ordered a "drill" for the National Reconnaissance Office in Chantilly, Virginia. In the fake attack, the intelligence agency—which runs the country's spy satellites—would respond as if a small plane had rammed into one of the agency's four towers. Eerily, the drill, which Cheney had scheduled months before, was to launch at 9 A.M.—on Tuesday, September 11, 2001.[10] FEMA—the Federal Emergency Management Agency—was also setting up to run emergency drills in Manhattan the same day.[11] The press entirely missed the National Reconnaissance story until August 2002, and the rumors about FEMA had been brushed off as conspiracy theories, until New York's Mayor Giuliani testified before the 9/11 Commission in 2004. Both raise more questions about September 11, the truth of which has yet to emerge, being blocked by the powers that be.

As this elitist group manipulated and exploited the reaction to September 11, alarming the masses with their new color-coded terror levels and warnings of other unforeseen attacks and their inability to prevent them, they changed life in America, rewriting defense policies and rescripting American values from previous tolerance to stark either/or terms. The Bush administration launched the United States on a new paranoid and xenophobic voyage as significant as any in history. They worked the attack into a means to sell their favorite war toys, including National Missile Defense. America needed more money for military operations, they told Congress, which handed them a check for over $400 billion—some $120 billion more than the Clinton defense budget. America needed to more closely watch its people, they told Congress, which hurriedly passed the privacy-shredding Patriot Act. America needed to launch a War on Terror, and start by attacking Afghanistan, they informed legislators and the American people, both of whom gave the moves a loud "aye."

Calming Words à la the Vulcans

"The prospects of another attack against the United States are almost certain . . . not a matter of if, but when."

—VICE PRESIDENT DICK CHENEY

"It's only a matter of time [when terrorists will strike again]."

—SECRETARY OF DEFENSE DONALD RUMSFELD

"There will be another terrorist attack. We will not be able to stop it."

—FBI DIRECTOR ROBERT MUELLER

The most impressive achievement of the Bush team was to spin September 11 into a reason to attack Iraq, which had been their goal all along. With little regard to fact, these manipulators stirred emotions, made links where they didn't exist, and successfully created the blurry image of a fictional monster apparently called Ossaddama bin Hussein. Still today many Americans will say the United States went into Iraq over September 11—even when there is not a thin thread of evidence tying the two.

BALD-FACED INTELLIGENCE FAILURES?

Those who wish to be generous can excuse the administration for making conclusions based on faulty information. However, before the words "weapons of mass destruction" tumbled out of the Vulcans' mouths, intelligence agents were warning that they could not substantiate many of the claims the Vulcans wanted to make. A confidential Defense Intelligence Agency report given to the White House in September 2002 notes that "[We have] no reliable information on whether Iraq is producing or stockpiling chemical weapons"; intelligence also tried to delete the line about Iraq buying uranium from the presidential speech. But to no avail: The Bushies were winding up for the home run.

- *"Simply stated, there is no doubt that Saddam Hussein now has weapons of mass destruction."*—Dick Cheney, addressing Veterans of Foreign Wars 103rd National Convention, Aug. 2002
- *"We do know that he [Saddam Hussein] is actively pursuing a nuclear weapon."*—Condoleezza Rice on CNN's *Late Edition*, Sept. 8, 2002
- *"The Iraqi regime could launch a biological or chemical attack in as little as forty-five minutes."*—George Bush in radio address to the nation, Sept. 26, 2002
- *"Facing clear evidence of peril, we cannot wait for the final proof, the smoking gun, that could come in the form of a mushroom cloud."*—George W. Bush in a speech in Cincinnati, Oct. 7, 2002
- *"The British government has learned that Saddam Hussein recently sought significant quantities of uranium from Africa."*—George W. Bush, State of the Union address, Jan. 28, 2003
- *"My fellow citizens, at this hour, American and coalition forces are in the early stages of military operations to disarm Iraq, to free its people, and to defend the world from grave danger."*—George W. Bush, Mar. 19, 2003
- *"We found the weapons of mass destruction . . . [F]or those who say we haven't found the banned manufacturing devices or banned weapons, they're wrong, we found them."*—George W. Bush, May 29, 2003, in a White House interview with Polish TV.[12] Bush's incorrect statements stunned the media and flew in the face of reality.

The actions of Bush's paid coterie have not only rankled the world, they've rankled at least some of those within government, who have been known to refer to the Vulcans as "the crazies" and "the nuts."[13] Bush's brains have certainly exhibited a zeal for achieving their goals, and anyone who has resisted them or questioned what they are doing has been steamrolled.

Dissenters

Just file away that idea of healthy debate, the right to one's own opinion, or even the need for correct information. Bush's support staff has attacked, smeared, and belittled all who have dared question them—including those within the administration. A few of the victims:

▶ *Colin Powell:* Never mind that he was secretary of state. When Powell questioned the intelligence about Iraq's WMDs, the supposed links between Hussein and al-Qaeda, and the sort of invasion planned, he was sidelined by the Cheney-Rumsfeld-Wolfowitz troika and ultimately pushed out of office for the second term.

▶ *Richard Clarke:* "Who cares about a little terrorist in Afghanistan?" Wolfowitz reportedly asked the "tsar of counterterrorism" in April 2001;[14] after 9/11, when Clarke reported that there was no evidence that Saddam was behind the attack, he says he fell victim to a Vulcan smear campaign. After he left the post in January 2003, Clarke testified before the 9/11 Commission that the administration totally botched preparation for the attack, and he wrote a tell-all book.

▶ *Paul O'Neill:* The former secretary of the treasury disagreed with the administration about everything from Iraq to "SEC overreach." Forced to resign in December 2002.

▶ *Ambassador Joseph Wilson:* Sent to Niger, he could not confirm that Iraq bought uranium there—and blasted the administration's claims to the contrary. The White House subsequently attempted to discredit him, and oops, someone slipped it out to the press that his wife was a CIA agent.

▶ *Hans Blix:* The UN's chief weapons inspector couldn't find WMDs in Iraq. Became victim of attempts to discredit him.

▶ *Scott Ritter:* The UN weapons inspector stated that there were no WMDs left in Iraq. Was subsequently exposed as an alleged child abuser.

▶ *Germany:* After Chancellor Schröder questioned the wisdom of attack in Iraq, Rumsfeld sniped that Germany (and France) were "Old Europe." White House response: to begin moving U.S. troops out of German bases, killing the local cconomies.

▶ *France:* After President Chirac said France would veto a UN approval of Iraq attack—prompting Republican Congressman Walter Jones to rename French fries "freedom fries"—the United States attacked France economically, even banning imports of foie gras, mumbling something about facilities being unclean.

▶ *Mary Robinson:* As head of the UN High Commission on Human Rights, the former president of Ireland criticized Bush government actions in Afghanistan. White House response: to very actively push her out of her UN post. (That did indirectly save her life, however. The next human rights commissioner, Brazilian Sergio Vieiera de Mello, died when a UN building in Iraq was bombed.)

▶ *Cynthia McKinney:* The U.S. representative from Georgia criticized war plans, pointed out links between the Bush administration and arms dealer Carlyle, and said she thought the whole 9/11 ordeal was highly suspicious. Became focus of a smear campaign and lost her 2002 reelection bid.

▶ *Paul Wellstone:* An outspoken critic of the Bush administration and opposed to the war in Iraq, the senator died in a 2002 plane crash.

When President Bush was forced to admit in late 2004 that, gosh, there really wasn't any link between al-Qaeda and Saddam after all, and geez, no weapons of mass destruction uncovered in Iraq either, the United States looked like a bumbling idiot internationally. But even when torture of prisoners in Iraq was shamefully exposed, at least half the country stood waving their flags madly behind the president, while the other half stood openmouthed, especially when George W. Bush was voted in for a second term in 2004.

Ever since the Bush team took over the control panel in 2001, life in America has been rife with ironies.

- In the name of making our world safer, this administration has destabilized the whole planet, making a mockery of international institutions and negating traditional bonds with Europe while overthrowing governments and unleashing violence in Afghanistan and the Middle East.
- In the process of inflicting democracy worldwide, our own democracy has eroded and such long-cherished ideals as freedom of speech and the right to privacy have vanished.
- In the name of toppling repressive dictators, the American people have been propagandized and slammed with lies.
- And, despite the billions this bunch has spent to wage the "War on Terror" and strong-arm the rest of the world into shaping up, the number of terrorists attacks worldwide is soaring. In 2003, there were 175 terrorist attacks. In 2004, there were 651.[15]

Then again, perhaps we really can't blame simple Bush, whom some view as a backseat president who has handed the keys to his advisors while he takes an eight-year nap. As for who has taken the United States to these new lows, look at the Vulcans who have been driving the car. Lord knows where they will be taking us next.

Close-up

Well, they sure aren't wallflowers. Aligned or alone, the Vulcans get noticed, standing out for ambition, conviction, and ability to accomplish their dreams, even if it might entail shoving aside competitors along the way.

- Master manipulator Karl Rove, who once ran a direct-mail outfit out of Austin, is credited with bringing Republicans to power in Texas.
- As CEO and president of drug company G. D. Searle, Rumsfeld earned awards as "Outstanding Chief Executive Officer" from *Wall Street Transcript* and *Financial World*.
- Cheney, who served four presidents in positions ranging from White House chief of staff to secretary of defense, became a six-term congressperson in 1978, and later turned Halliburton into a company worth billions.
- Condoleezza Rice, who graduated from college cum laude at age nineteen and earned her master's and doctorate by age twenty-five, became the first female provost of the Political Science Department at Stanford before her fortieth birthday.

If they often appear to work as a well-oiled power machine, it's because this bunch has worked together before. Almost all their political pasts are interwoven, with most working closely during at least one administration. But no two of the Vulcans have worked more tightly than VP Dick Cheney and Secretary of Defense Don Rumsfeld, both of whom previously wracked up extensive political experience as secretaries of defense and White House chiefs of staff during the Nixon and Ford administrations—with Dick sticking around through the Reagan and Bush Senior years as well. Don had originally opened the door for Dick, when he hired the congressional aide to work at the Office of Economic Development in 1969—and Don had pulled Dick with him as he soared up the ranks to White House chief of staff. Dick seemed to shadow Don in his career moves: Dick too became chief of staff, when Don became defense secretary, a position that Dick would also hold. The duo made a dynamic team, even after they left government: They were both part of emergency drills in the 1980s, and both were star members of the neoconservative Project for a New American Century, the war-happy advocacy group that demanded that Clinton oust Saddam from Iraq (in a letter that both Dick and Don signed). Having conquered the private sector, where both served as CEOs (Dick of Halliburton, Don of Searle), the old guys—by then Don was in his seventies and Dick in his sixties—were filthy rich by the time they creaked back into the capital in 2001, revved up to make one last run in the power seats. They do have their differences: Dick is the quiet, behind-the-scenes controller; Don is the brusque, bossy sort. Their business styles were different too: Don was cutthroat but usually aboveboard; as head of Halliburton, Dick pulled numerous shady moves, including financial hanky-panky that now has the SEC examining Halliburton's books. But both are able to spout false information like a nonstop fountain and both brush off calls for accountability like lint from their fine suits.

A decade or two younger than Cheney and Rumsfeld, the other Vulcans paid their political dues during the 1980s. Paul Wolfowitz, Rumsfeld's sidekick as deputy secretary of defense during Bush's first term, worked under Cheney during the Bush Sr. administration, when one of his tasks was weakening arms control treaties. The defense policy that Wolfowitz authored for Bush Sr. gave the United States preemptive strike powers, but back then it was highly controversial and hastily watered down.

> *The Bush administration's current defense policy that Wolfowitz helped to author is nearly an exact replica of his original plan, then seen as too aggressive, now seen as what's right.*

Condoleezza Rice was quite familiar with the White House as well. The Stanford political science professor had served as special advisor on Soviet affairs to Bush Sr., specializing in the energy-producing regions of central Asia. Condoleezza's former assistant, Stephen Hadley—now filling Rice's seat as national security advisor—also goes back to the Bush Sr. days, when he worked as a Defense Department analyst. Even Karl Rove got his connection through Bush the Elder: The ex-president was so impressed with the sleazy campaigns Rove was running in Texas that he introduced him to his son.

We should use nuclear weapons. That was the opinion of Stephen Hadley, Linton Brooks, and Stephen Cambone in the January 2001 report they coauthored for the National Institute for Public Policy. Nuclear weapons, they said, could counter threats of "weapons of mass destruction used by regional powers." And the nukes should be used as insurance as well: "To ensure that enemy facilities or forces are knocked out and cannot be reconstituted," they wrote, "attacks with nuclear weapons may be necessary." The Bush administration applauded their opinion and rewarded them with plum jobs, including Hadley's appointment as national security advisor, Brooks's as head of the National Nuclear Security Administration, and Cambone's as undersecretary of defense for intelligence.[16]

> *The "low-yield" nuclear weapons that Hadley, Brooks, and Cambone support— which the National Academy of Sciences recently reported could kill 1 million per weapon—are in development.*

Control Freak
Karl Rove

Publicly, President Bush calls Karl Rove "the Architect," crediting him with Bush's political victories; privately, the president calls his bespectacled, fleshy-faced friend "Turd Blossom"—a nickname whose origins may best be left to future historians to unravel. Formerly a senior advisor to Bush and since 2005 the White House deputy chief of staff in what some consider a conflict of interest, Rove indeed combines the attributes of both of the names. He skillfully draws master plans on how to shape public opinion and win elections—and he pulls slimy tricks to do it, perhaps learned from his mentor Donald Segretti, who went to prison for Watergate. Skilled at screwing his opponents throughout his rise as a College Republican, one of Rove's first tactical coups in Texas was targeting tort law that allowed class action lawsuits: Despite claims of fighting greed, it is more likely Republican Rove was taking a whack at the Trial Lawyers of America, who are the financial lifeline for the Democratic Party. Obsessed with drawing out the millions of Christian Republicans who had stayed home for the 2000 elections—preventing Bush from winning the popular vote in that presidential election—Rove wanted them at the polls in 2004 and pushed for campaign volunteers to unethically supply telephone directories of their churches' members for last-minute campaign calls. Rove also helped orchestrate the linking of the presidential election with the vote on gay marriage (which Bush loudly opposed during the campaign), with Rove vowing to evangelicals that constitutionally banning same-sex unions would top the priority list in 2005.

The gravest concerns for voters in the 2004 presidential election, as noted from exit polls—where many had just voted no on gay marriage—were the country's "moral issues"; one guesses they were not talking about unjust wars or the torture at Abu Ghraib.

Rove was accused by Ambassador Joseph Wilson (who in 2003 disputed the Bush claim that Saddam Hussein bought uranium in Niger) as the blabbermouth who outted CIA agent Valerie Plame (Wilson's wife) by leaking info to neoconservative writer Robert Novak; the FBI is conducting an investigation into the federal offense of exposing an agent. Some, including U.S. Rep. Maurice Hinchey, suspect Rove may have had a hand in the forged Killian documents slipped into *60 Minutes*'s paws.[17] Future reporters now may steer clear of examining

Bush's past after that fiasco, which blasted Dan Rather and four others out the door at CBS for erroneously reporting on the president's conduct as a member of the National Guard. As hired strategist for over two decades (his direct-mail company came in handy for campaigning) Rove strategized numerous victories for the Republican machine in Texas and Republicans onto the Supreme Court in heavily Democratic Alabama (the state where the Ten Commandment controversy now runs deepest), and he's persuaded fellow Republicans to run or not to run with a phone call. He is rumored to have been behind numerous of the era's nastiest smears, among them reportedly engineering an attack on Senator John McCain (Bush's opponent in the 2000 primaries) through fake "push polls" in South Carolina: Voters were asked if they would vote for McCain if they knew he'd fathered an illegitimate black child (which McCain hadn't). Rove's power in the White House is immense—detractors call him "Bush's brain" and "the copresident"—and few get to Bush without going through him. Some say that those going against Bush are smacked with subsequent Rove rumormongering and slips to the press, and bloggers at least speculate that the man who loves to play the homophobia card is secretly gay; over the blogs, rumors abound that Rove was quite fond of male escort/faux White House reporter Jeffrey Gannon.

> *Who says you need a college education to make it? Active in politics since his teens (he admits that as a college Republican, he stole a Democratic senator's letterhead and printed flyers—which he handed out at soup kitchens—promising loose women and free booze to those who attended a political rally), Rove apparently was too busy politicking to make it to classes: He never earned a college degree.*

Bush's Heavy Lifters
Dick Cheney

There are two ways to look at Richard B. Cheney. If you close your eyes and toss back a few shots of tequila, you might view him as a kindly grandfatherly sort who is entirely a self-made man. A former football captain and honor student, he married the pyrotechnic baton-twirling Homecoming Queen; at her majorette show's end, his job was to dutifully extinguish her flaming wand in a can of water.[18] As a 1978 U.S. congressional candidate in Wyoming, he wrote a letter to every Montanan asking for their vote, despite his recent heart attack (he's since had three more). Cheney is a man who dutifully worked his way up from the bottom: At points in his career he was in charge of White House table settings, and now he's in charge of setting the White House agenda.

But there's a more sinister take to Dick Cheney, one perhaps betrayed by his snaking half-smile. The man who flunked out of Yale is suspected by some to have been a campus narc reporting on demonstrations in the 1960s; others sniff that he's a brownnoser who rose to the top by never appearing too ambitious, too threatening, or too bright. His most questionable deeds may have taken place in the 1990s, when he was Bush Sr.'s secretary of defense. Given the difficult task in 1990 of persuading Saudi Arabia's monarch to allow the U.S. military to "crash" in his country for a few months to prepare what would be "Desert Storm," Cheney may have deceived Saudi King Fahd. The king wasn't keen on the idea of hosting the U.S. military—his religious people so hate infidels roaming through the kingdom, and besides, Saddam had promised he wouldn't attack Saudi Arabia. But when Cheney showed up at his door bearing a damning satellite photo, Fahd changed his mind and invited the foreigners in. The photo showed that Saddam's forces were amassing right at the Saudi border. Problem is, some journalists contend that the photo was fake.[19] Another problem: Cheney promised that U.S. troops would pack up as soon as the war was over, but in fact thousands stayed. Fourteen years later, we're only now finalizing a pullout from Saudi Arabia, having overstayed the visit a bit.

While defense secretary, Cheney also initiated a significant change in military power that would behoove him financially: He began outsourcing military duties to private companies, setting up engineering firm Halliburton to become a prime recipient of contracts. From 1995 to 2000, Cheney took the helm as CEO of Halliburton, which now is the top recipient of Iraq reconstruction contracts. Cheney parted with millions of dollars' worth of Halliburton stock in 2000, just weeks before the stock value plunged, leading some to wonder if he had an insider tip-off.

As vice president, Cheney's behavior has been entirely opaque in an era that demands transparency. In 2002, he would not hand over notes about his secret meetings with Enron head Kenneth Lay and others in the National Energy Policy Development Group; when the Government Accountability Office launched an investigation, he supplied them with complete jibberish and lists of random numbers—and a pizza receipt. Sierra Club and the GAO filed a lawsuit to finally gain access, although many pages are still missing, including those that might have detailed any Cheney involvement in pressuring India to sign a big Enron contract weeks before the company went bust. To top it off, his energy plan simply increased American reliance on oil and recommended ripping up the Arctic National Wilderness Reserve to squeeze out a few drops. At least Cheney does have a soft side: He supports homosexual rights—one of his two daughters is gay.

The most frightening thing about Cheney may his ultraconservative wife, the former baton twirler Lynne. A director for Lockheed (he sat on the board of Boeing) until 2001, and a fellow at neocon bastion the American Enterprise Institute, the second lady has founded right-wing organizations such as the American Council of Trustees and Alumni. ACTA is best known for blacklisting university professors or others who speak out in ways ACTA considers unpatriotic. The organization published scathing reviews of the blacklisted professors in *Defending Civilization: How Our Universities Are Failing America and What Should Be Done About It.* But Lynne's writings also spills into fiction. Her novel *Sisters*, which came out shortly after Cheney's second cardiac arrest, features a philandering senator who dies of a heart attack while rolling in the hay with his girlfriend; in the novel, his wife takes over his post. In fact, some assert that Lynne Cheney was originally on Bush's list of potential running mates;[20] her husband erased her name when he volunteered himself for the job. He also pulled Rumsfeld in as secretary of defense.

 ## Donald Rumsfeld

Donald Rumsfeld may be the single most influential person in the United States. His hands, perhaps more than any others, have helped to sculpt twenty-first-century America. Whether we're talking about the possibly hazardous fake sugar[21] we stir into our coffee or the United States' chillier relations with our number one trade partner, Canada; whether the topic is the international ire over the United States' moves to dominate space or the inflated amount of our taxes going to ill-conceived wars; behind it all one finds the fingerprints of Donald H. Rumsfeld. A go-getter even as a child—neighborhood mothers chided their sons for not being as driven as little Donny—Rumsfeld is a cutthroat überachiever who has made the world a much more lethal place. As the most radical secretary of defense in U.S. history, Rumsfeld is dramatically modernizing American defense capabilities (ushering in an era of expensive "smart" weaponry)—and supporting the use of nuclear weapons in conventional war. Rumsfeld launched us into a quagmire in Iraq—price tag $150 million a day[22]—with no coherent exit strategy in sight. Under Rumsfeld's watch, torture has become commonplace in Iraq, Afghanistan, and Guantánamo Bay, while the CIA flies some detainees to other countries where prison authorities specialize in electrifying means to get them to talk.

Rumsfeld's Pentagon now spends more than $1.2 billion a day.

Rumsfeld's effect is divisive. Disliked by the military, whose pre-Iraq advice he sneered at and whose power he minimized at the Pentagon,[23] he sharply elbowed the more moderate secretary of state, Colin Powell, out of the way during the lead-up to the Iraq War and wrestled away the State Department plans for that country's reconstruction.

WHAT DON'S BEEN DREAMING UP AT DEFENSE

Tired of relying on the CIA, which did not link Saddam Hussein to al-Qaeda or document the presence of nuclear weapons in Iraq, in late 2001 Rumsfeld demanded a new intelligence organization—one that would answer to him. This intel group would do more than just gather info—it would have the authority to kill terrorists and a freer rein to do whatever was considered necessary to maximize results from interrogations. They could hire notorious underworld figures, the sort that the DoD would disavow having on its payroll. The Strategic Support Branch (code name: Icon) was working secretly for the Department of Defense since 2002 until its cover was blown in 2004 by the *Washington Post*.[24] Given the task of squeezing information out of detainees at Guantánamo Bay—their techniques were later used at Abu Ghraib[25]—the unit is now on clandestine missions from Somalia to Bosnia.

The man who not so secretly aspired to be president started his power trip long before 2001, when President George W. Bush tapped him for defense secretary. Polished Rumsfeld was a four-term U.S. representative in the 1960s, and held high-ranking positions in the Nixon and Ford administrations, but he remained a political heavyweight even while shining in the private sector. In the last decade he has headed several congressional commissions that dictated U.S. policy. Among them: "the Rumsfeld Missile Defense Commission" and "the Rumsfeld Space Commission." Hawks such as then speaker of the house Newt Gingrich were joyous at the assorted Rumsfeld commissions' findings, including:

▶ that we desperately needed a National Missile Defense program (to counter threats from rogue North Korea, until then not considered a missile threat), and
▶ that we desperately needed space weapons (an extension of National Missile Defense) and a military force to protect our satellites.

"The U.S. is an attractive candidate for a 'Space Pearl Harbor.'"

—2001 REPORT FROM "THE RUMSFELD SPACE COMMISSION," AKA THE COMMISSION TO ASSESS UNITED STATES NATIONAL SECURITY SPACE MANAGEMENT AND ORGANIZATION[26]

Handily, as secretary of defense, Rumsfeld is in the ideal position to ram through both National Missile Defense and the weaponization of space. The youngest secretary of defense under President Gerald Ford when he was forty-three, Rumsfeld, now seventy-three, is currently the oldest defense secretary. "Once in a while," he told the *New York Times,* "I'm standing here, doing something. And I think, 'What in the world am I doing here?'" Sometimes we wonder the same.

A FEW MORE RUMMY VICTORIES

Rumsfeld also has profoundly shaped the United States by:

- Bringing the private sector into war. Under Rumsfeld, DoD has handed out numerous contracts to private military contractors including Halliburton, Blackwell, CACI, and DynCorp.
- Weakening international bonds. He slammed Germany and France, calling them "Old Europe," while also sidelining the United Nations.
- Appointing neoconservatives to high-level Pentagon positions.
- Changing the reasons for warring. As outlined in the Pentagon's "National Security Strategy" and "Nuclear Posture Review" of 2002, U.S. policy now allows for preemptive first strikes against perceived enemies and green-lights nuclear war if certain allies are attacked.
- Increasing power of the Defense Policy Board. He boosted its size from nineteen to thirty members, named Richard Perle as its director, and heeds the board's advice.
- Allowing "aggressive interrogation techniques" to become standard drill.
- Introducing a whole new form of noncommunication: Rummyspeak.

"As we know, there are known knowns
There are things we know we know.
We also know there are known unknowns.
That is to say we know there are some things we do not know.

But there are also unknown unknowns,
The ones we don't know we don't know."

—D. H. Rumsfeld, Feb. 12, 2002, Department of Defense briefing;
the secretary's unintentional poetic gifts were first lauded by online
magazine *Slate,* which presented his comments in verse form[27]

The man who knows how to get results (except for his failed plans of running for president) is now under fire for botching operations in Iraq and permitting the use of torture by U.S. military personnel. His newest trick, when asked about reports investigating the abuse at American-run prisons, is to feign ignorance and insist he hasn't seen them.

> "As you know, you go to war with the army you have. They're not the army you might want or wish to have at a later time."
>
> —RUMSFELD'S 2004 RESPONSE TO A SOLDIER IN KUWAIT WHO COMPLAINED
> THAT TROOPS IN IRAQ DID NOT HAVE PROPERLY ARMED VEHICLES; IT
> CAUSED AN UPROAR AND MORE CALLS FOR RUMSFELD TO RESIGN

Whether Donald Rumsfeld is prescient or paranoid with his calls (and orders) for trillions of dollars' worth of armaments, the man has altered the military and the country for decades to come. Although Rumsfeld never set up in the Oval Office, he has exerted more power than many presidents and his mark won't be easily erased when he leaves government—that is, if they can ever pry him out of his chair.

MEET THE SUPPORT STAFF

Condoleezza Rice, Secretary of State (2005–present)

Sometimes you have to wonder if Condi is really a white Texan oilman disguised as a black preacher's daughter. The Bush administration's personal goddess of war—tending more toward scary Indian deity Shiva than the Greeks' graceful bow-wielding Athena—knows so much about petroleum (particularly in the former Soviet Union) that, until recently, she sat on the board of Chevron. (The oil boys liked her so much they named a Chevron supertanker after her.) Then again, she has far more skills than an American oilman: She speaks Russian and French, plays the piano and flute, and is a dream on ice skates. Most of the press sickeningly fawns over the articulate professor, as if applauding the fact that she is smart, female, and black—a combination some of us don't think is so rare, albeit hard to find in the aptly named White House. In the months following September 11, Condi was more or less the weekend president, making appearances on big-time shows while Bush was apparently too frayed to show up.

> *"As I was telling my husb— As I was telling President Bush . . ."*
> —*Condi's slip-up at a dinner party in 2004*

Condi held up well, despite the many fingers wagging at her for the 9/11 screwup, when as national security advisor, she was accused of blundering badly by not making al-Qaeda a priority. In fact, even though intelligence agents were screaming that al-Qaeda was up to something, Condi ignored them; her lack of attention to the matter was illustrated on September 11, 2001, when she was scheduled to make a presentation on the pressing need for National Missile Defense, which would have done nothing to counter the terrorists. She initially blew off calls to testify before the 9/11 Commission—and blocked the investigation by refusing to declassify information. (Under pressure, she put in an appearance and declassified a fraction of one report.) Now secretary of state, the so-called Warrior Princess and maestro at the ivories certainly is type A in her life, but she isn't much of a leader in the Bush house, where she typically seems to blindly follow the leads of Cheney and Rumsfeld. On the world arena, perhaps she will fare better than at her desk in DC, where the administration wheels her out for her trademark polished appearances before the TV cameras, but doesn't hand her much power. Maybe she can turn on that charm and thaw relations with North Korea, but one doubts it. Despite her occasional warm smiles, and the heated anger she sometimes emanates—as when, during Rice's Senate confirmation hearing, Barbara Boxer nailed Condi for the many lies spewed about Iraq—the secretary of state appears icy in her negotiations, and has already flip-flopped on policy more times than a Mexican jumping bean. Nevertheless, if she can bring peace in the now turbulent Middle East, or calm down North Korea, perhaps her failure as an effective national security advisor will melt away, just like the memory that she once worked as foreign policy advisor for not just a Democrat—which Condi herself used to be—but a liberal Democrat, Gary Hart.

"In 1984 and 1988, Condi worked on Hart's presidential campaigns. Today's story that she has always been a Republican is simply a myth."

—Professor Alan Gilbert, who taught Rice
at the University of Denver[28]

Stephen Hadley, National Security Advisor (2005–present)

A lawyer in a previous incarnation, nerdy Hadley took the blame for the administration's false claim that Iraq bought "yellowcake" uranium in Niger, and was handsomely rewarded: He now sits in Condi's vacated seat. Duck and cover: He advocates nuclear warfare, being a proponent—along with Rumsfeld—of "mininukes."

Paul Wolfowitz, President of World Bank (2005–present), Deputy Secretary of Defense (2001–05)

Wolfowitz is a very influential player—see "Powermonger" on page 64.

Behind the Scenes

"Americans need to watch what they say, watch what they do."

—WHITE HOUSE SPOKESMAN ARI FLEISHER, PRESS BRIEFING, SEPT. 26, 2001

They've frightened us. They've made Americans hated around the world. They've stifled us. They've tried to beat us into submission while they've exaggerated, fibbed, and fancily embroidered the truth. They've lied to us and continue to hide the truth. They've subjected us to propaganda. They've manipulated the press. They've endangered us. They've bungled international affairs, creating needlessly dangerous situations. They've miscalculated military endeavors. They've misspent our money. They're weaponizing space. They've ripped away our constitutional rights. They've violated human rights. They've damaged international relations and pulled us out of important treaties. They've blurred the distinction between church and state. And did we mention they lied? And they are starting to get called on it. Their thick veil of secrecy is being pierced, their shams are being exposed, their standing—with their fellow countrymen and with the rest of the residents of the planet—is crashing.

Even Republican Congressman Walter "freedom fries" Jones now says there was "no justification" for the American attack in Iraq. Apparently it's okay to call the taters "French fries" again.

What country is the biggest threat to the world?

- In a BBC World News poll conducted in late January 2005, of twenty-two thousand people living in eighteen countries, 58 percent said they thought President Bush would have a negative effect on the world.
- In a 2003 poll conducted by *Time* via the Internet, 87 percent considered the United States a bigger danger to world peace than North Korea (7 percent) or Iraq (6 percent).
- A March 2005 survey in Australia found that the United States was not even among the top ten most liked countries, falling behind even China and France.
- A survey of residents in twenty-three countries conducted by GlobeScan and the University of Maryland released in April 2005 showed that the United States was negatively perceived in fifteen of those countries.

> "Our survey shows that Europe's star has risen as America's has declined under the Bush administration."
>
> —DOUG MILLER OF GLOBESCAN[29]

"I don't think anybody could have predicted that they would try to use an airplane as a missile . . . Had this president known a plane would be used as a missile, he would have acted on it."

—CONDOLEEZZA RICE TELLING WHAT APPEARS TO BE YET ANOTHER WHOPPER.[30] THEN AGAIN, PERHAPS IT'S THE TRUTH—PERHAPS BUSH DIDN'T NOTICE THAT AT THE G-8 CONFERENCE HE'D ATTENDED JUST MONTHS BEFORE, THE USE OF AIRCRAFT AS MISSILES WAS AN EMPHASIZED SECURITY CONCERN.

"[That's] an outrageous lie. And documents can prove it."

—FBI ANALYST SIBEL EDMONDS, WHO HAD TRANSLATED DOCUMENTS THAT COUNTERED THE OFFICIAL WHITE HOUSE LINE ABOUT NO PREVIOUS WARNINGS ABOUT THE ATTACKS. CITING STATE SECURITY PRIVILEGE, THE DEPARTMENT OF JUSTICE GAGGED HER FROM SPEAKING OUT, BUT EDMONDS WAS ASKED TO TESTIFY BEFORE THE 9/11 COMMISSION, PREDICTABLY IN PRIVATE. HOWEVER, HER TESTIMONY SO RATTLED THE WHITE HOUSE THAT CONDOLEEZZA RICE, WHO'D REFUSED TO TESTIFY BEFORE THE COMMISSION PREVIOUSLY, SUDDENLY VOLUNTEERED TO APPEAR.[31]

Several campaigns have been launched to impeach President Bush, including one by former U.S. attorney general Ramsey Clark.

Agent of Change
Seymour Hersh

Hanging somewhere in the White House, there may be a dartboard with Seymour Hersh's picture on it. Since about the minute the son of a dry cleaner first started banging out his articles, back then on a manual typewriter, presidents and secretaries of defense have been yelping in response. In the late 1960s, Hersh sold a story to an obscure newswire about the torture and death of nearly five hundred Vietnamese by American troops gone haywire: Initially rejected by all the major news services, his article about the My Lai massacre and the courtmartial of commanding officer Lt. William Calley earned him a Pulitzer Prize and a job

at the *New York Times.* Hersh took aim at
Henry Kissinger, reporting on his clandestine orders to bomb Cambodia, and he wrote
a book on Israel's secret nuclear program
and Mossad's capture of Mordechai Vanunu,
the Israeli who blew their cover. He suffered
a drop in popularity when he targeted JFK
in a book that portrayed Kennedy as a sex
addict who brought prostitutes around to the
White House. But many of the most important works of Hersh, now sixty-eight, have
rolled off his printer in the years when most
people would have already retired, an act
which the DoD no doubts wishes he would
perform.

*Seymour Hersh, rebel reporter who
makes the White House cringe*

"When you looked at the war reporting on
Iraq, it was unbelievable. All the great journalists and major outlets developed
laryngitis, with the notable exception of Seymour Hersh."

—Charles Lewis, Center for Public Integrity

Hot-tempered, "roll up the sleeves and figure out what is really going on" investigator Hersh has horrified the Bush administration as he digs up its nasty secrets and holds them up for the whole world to see in the pages of the highbrow
New Yorker. He was the first print reporter to tell the story of the torture at Abu
Ghraib, where he reported interrogators were using many procedures okayed by the
DoD, and he tattled on Secretary of Defense Rumsfeld when Rumsfeld created an
answer-to-nobody-but-Rumsfeld secret intelligence agency—which Hersh reports
was also involved in prisoner abuse. He blew Richard Perle's sideline business when
he reported that the then-chairman of the Defense Policy Board, which urged the
DoD to rev up the war machine (at one point considering Saudi Arabia as a target),
hit up Saudis to invests hundreds of millions of dollars in his security investment
program, a move that struck many as unsavory. Hersh has reported that the CIA is
being sidelined and that Iran is next in the administration's crosshairs. And each
piece he writes is typically greeted with howls and hisses from the Bush administration and particularly the Pentagon, which dashes out sputtering press releases
denying Hersh's allegations and pointing out that most of his high-level sources
aren't named (although their identities are known to *New Yorker* editor David
Remnick). However, time and time again, Hersh has been proven correct. We don't
know what motivates Hersh—a ground-breaking individualist who dislikes giving interviews—but we know that without Seymour Hersh's unflinching reporting,
we'd all be even more in the dark about what the powers that be are really up to.

RED FLAG
Iran-Contra: The Shadow Continues

When a small plane flew over Nicaragua on the fifth of October 1986, swooping so low that the Nicaraguan army shot it down, we got our first clue that a shadow government was operating within the White House. When the plane's lone survivor—Eugene Hasenfus, a construction worker hired as a freelance undercover operative—parachuted to safety, he told Nicaraguan authorities that he worked for the CIA. And the arms on the plane, it turned out, were being sent by the United States to Nicaraguan rebels, an act expressly forbidden by Congress. It was the first thread that came loose in the complex ball of yarn that became known as the Iran-Contra affair, a scandal that involved trading missiles for hostages and funneling money to a CIA-formed Nicaraguan rebel force—an event that showed that Ronald Reagan wasn't in charge of the White House.

> *Some believe that a secret cabal running the White House, and delving into covert activities such as Iran-Contra, was in fact directed by Vice President George H. W. Bush, previously director of the CIA.*

As the story further unraveled, the American public was shown a few of the key players—Lt. Col. Oliver North and National Security Advisor John Poindexter among them—but the tale was never fully unwound. The CIA's involvement with delivery of drugs that many believe was part of a fund-raising effort for the contras never fully came to light, nor did the identities of those at the tip of the conspiratorial pyramid. CIA head William Casey, who helped dream up the plot, conveniently died of a brain tumor before he could testify about Iran-Contra. And Vice President George H. W. Bush, whom subsequent investigations showed had full awareness of what was going on with Iran-Contra, was shielded: His participation was shushed up in large part by a congressman from Wyoming, who sat on the House committee investigating Iran-Contra—Dick Cheney.

> *The contras, who numbered about seven thousand, often worked out of Honduras, where current Director of National Intelligence John Negroponte was then U.S. ambassador.*

THE BASICS OF IRAN-CONTRA

In the same way that money launderers clean their money in elaborate schemes, the illegal activities that wove together to create what would be called the Iran-Contra affair were hard to unwind. One background issue was that Congress was controlled by Democrats, who were quick to block many Reagan administration moves. Thus several objectives of the administration went underground and became entwined:

- The Reagan administration wanted to free American hostages, many of them CIA employees, who had been kidnapped in the early 1980s and were being held in Lebanon by Iranian radicals.
- To aid in their release, the administration opted to sell arms to Iran, despite that act being forbidden by the Democratic-majority U.S. Congress.
- The Reagan administration also wished to overthrow the Communist Sandinistas in Nicaragua: The Cuban-backed government had been fairly elected in 1979, after the ruling family of dictators, the U.S.-friendly Somozas, were shoved out.
- To knock out the Sandinistas, the CIA put together a guerrilla force called the contras, which had at its core the National Guard from the Somoza era, but also contained mercenaries from other countries, including Honduras, where many of the contras were trained by the CIA.

Several problems emerged in pursuing these objectives.

First off, there was the illegality issue: Both arming Iran and aiding the contras were prohibited by Congress. This problem was solved by simply ignoring Congress—and later lying to Congress—by forming a tight cabal of insiders from the National Security Council and the CIA.

The other problem was how to fund the contras. The two agendas became linked. Iran got its arms, but was overcharged for them—and the surplus money went to fund the faux rebels.

Another problem emerged: that money wasn't enough. Millions more were donated—and illegally funneled through a tax-exempt foundation, National Endowment for the Preservation of Liberty. (The Saudi Arabian royal family, Rev. Sun Myung Moon, Pat Robertson, and the Heritage Foundation were among the big supporters and donors.)

Still, that money wasn't enough. One missing part of the funding formula, which the CIA admits was happening, though it denies it was involved, was cocaine smuggling.[32,33] Small planes shuttled off to the United States loaded up with white stuff and came back with arms destined for assorted parts of Latin America, including those hiding the contras.

A few weeks after the plane was shot down in Nicaragua, exposing the covert U.S. aid to the contras, another bit of information came out: A Lebanese paper, *Al Shiraa*, reported that the United States had been selling arms to Iran in exchange for hostage release, and the Iranian government confirmed it. Oliver North, who was in charge of the operation, was fired. So was National Security Advisor John Poindexter—who was replaced by Frank Carlucci. A number of investigations were launched, but even those who were convicted were let off through appeals and presidential pardons.

The truth about this scandal—which parties were involved and how far it went—has never been fully revealed. And it may never be. Over sixty thousand documents of the Reagan era that were about to be declassified were instead hidden from the public. In 2001, President George W. Bush, whose father's role may have been ascertained through those papers, ordered them sealed.

THE PLAYERS, IRAN-CONTRA, THEN AND NOW

Elliott Abrams

Then: As assistant secretary of state for human rights and humanitarian affairs under Reagan, neocon Abrams covered up the massacres of thousands of civilians in El Salvador; in the 1986 investigation he lied to Congress about his knowledge of Iran-Contra and his role soliciting $10 million from the Sultan of Brunei for contra funding. In 1991, pleaded guilty to two misdemeanor counts of lying to Congress. Pardoned by Bush Sr. in 1992.

Now: Previously George W. Bush's advisor on Middle Eastern affairs, Abrams was promoted in 2005 to deputy national security advisor for global democracy strategy. Also has been a paid speaker for Rev. Sun Myung Moon.

John Poindexter

Then: As Reagan's national security advisor, Poindexter orchestrated the selling of arms to Iran for the funding of Nicaraguan rebels. In 1990, convicted on five felony counts, including conspiracy, defrauding the government, lying to Congress, and destroying evidence relating to Iran-Contra. Convictions overturned.

Now: Works on research projects funded by federal defense agency DARPA; until recently, headed the government's Total Information Awareness program pulling together a vast record on us all.

John Negroponte

Then: Ambassador to Honduras from 1981 to 1985, Negroponte looked the other way while death squads ran amok, and was accused of running contra activities out of Honduras.

Now: Under George W. Bush, he served as UN ambassador (2001–04) and U.S. ambassador to Iraq (2004–05). Since spring 2005, he's been director of National Intelligence.

John Bolton

Then: Blocked information from getting into congressional mitts during Iran-Contra investigation.

Now: Although blocked by Senate from taking seat as U.S. ambassador to the United Nations, appointed as temporary UN respective by Bush.

Otto Reich

Then: Headed Office of Public Diplomacy, rapped by Congress for "covert propaganda activities." According to Fairness and Accuracy in Reporting, "In a campaign to tarnish the Sandinistas and gild the Contras, Otto Reich's Office of Public Diplomacy pressured U.S. media and planted ghostwritten articles and editorials."

Now: Assistant secretary of state for Western Hemisphere affairs; Cuban American Reich loathes Fidel Castro and, like his colleague John Bolton, has accused Cuba of making biological weapons.

Oliver North

Then: Marine lieutenant colonel and counterterrorism coordinator for Reagan's National Security Council, coordinated the on-the-ground operations and became the face of Iran-Contra during the 1987 televised congressional hearing. In 1989, he was found guilty of three felonies—destroying evidence, lying to Congress, and accepting a bribe—but the verdict was thrown out in 1990.

Now: Correspondent for Fox News, ultraconservative columnist, author, and talk-radio celebrity. Also reported to be a member of Council on National Policy.

Edwin Meese

Then: Attorney general who was forced to resign in the wake of Iran-Contra.
Now: Scholar at the Heritage Foundation.

Eugene Hasenfus

Then: The CIA supply plane "cargo pusher" whose confession first cracked the seal on the Iran-Contra case, Hasenfus was held in Nicaraguan prison for ten weeks in 1986. He later demanded that the U.S. government pay for damages in the amount of $805,000. The government, which never recognized him as an official employee, declined to pay.

Now: Last seen exposing himself in the parking lot of a Wisconsin Wal-Mart.[34]

Ultimately the hostage release idea had a dud payoff. Perhaps angry that the arms bore inflated prices, the Iranians released only three hostages from Lebanon. And then they kidnapped three more—holding thirty hostages, the survivors of whom were released in 1992, long after most Americans had forgotten they were even there. Also relegated to the dustbins of history: the fifteen thousand or so Nicaraguans killed by the contras, fighting a bogus, Reagan-sponsored war.

5. THE NEOCONS:

Professional Alarmists

Neocon VIPs

Paul Wolfowitz, World Bank president and former deputy secretary of
   defense
John Bolton, UN ambassador and former undersecretary for arms control
   and international security at State Department
Richard Perle, former chairman of Defense Policy Board
Michael Ledeen, freelance advisor to Bush administration

Organs

Project for the New American Century
Center for National Security
American Enterprise Institute
The Weekly Standard

Headquarters

Washington, DC

Notable Number

- $70 billion to $100 billion: Amount neocons think annual defense budget
  should be further increased

Snapshot

Ever wonder exactly who sat down and came up with George W. Bush's polarizing 2001 ultimatum "Either you are with us or you are with the terrorists"? Or who drew the jagged line connecting Iraq, Iran, and North Korea on the melodramatic-sounding "Axis of Evil"? What about who immediately seized the September 11 attack as a (bogus) reason to invade Iraq? Answer: the neoconservatives—aka the neocons—with Paul Wolfowitz (new head of the World Bank), John Bolton (new U.S. ambassador to the United Nations), and Richard Perle (vastly influential outside advisor) leading their pack.

GENESIS STORY

Many neocons started out as Democrats. They ideologically and politically cleaved from their colleagues in the 1960s and 1970s, when the left-leaning Dems opposed Vietnam, criticized the country's direction, and advocated arms reductions. Appalled—this brainy bunch loathes arms control and claimed that the Soviets would soon attack—they pulled a 180, most becoming Republicans and all supporting massive military buildup. (Several leading neocons, including Richard Perle and former CIA director James Woolsey remain Democrats.) Back in the Reagan years, when the United States was dueling the "Evil Empire," the neocons emerged as the political force that defied détente with the Soviets. In fact, their attempts to derail moves to end the arms race with the Russians was one of the key ideas behind this group who describe themselves as "liberals who were mugged by reality."

The hardcore Christian Right is currently trying to spell out the U.S. domestic agenda, but neocons—many of whom are Jewish—are dictating the United States' lines and actions in the world theater, most of which are beneficial to Israel. Regimes now featured prominently on the neocons' "Get Rid of Next" list just happen to be the same regimes that Israel wouldn't mind not bumping into at the next UN shindig. And at least a few neocons, including Richard Perle, have been suspected of being Israeli informants.

WHO'S NEXT

Government advisor Michael Ledeen and other weighty neocons have a new wish list. A few neocon picks for who to take out next:

- Iran's Islamic government (want their oil, possible nuke program, threat to Israel)
- Syria's al-Assad dictatorship (geographically blocks a direct pipeline from Iraq, Hezbollah hangout, threat to Israel)
- Saudi Arabia's monarchy (want their oil, al-Qaeda is running amok there, threat to Israel)
- Egypt's Mubarak dictatorship (strategic location, threat to Israel)
- North Korea's Kim dictatorship (annoying, possesses nukes, threat to all)

In fact, some pundits say that the neocons, once behind-the-scenes players who have now grabbed center stage, have so successfully intertwined American foreign policy with their own agenda that they've essentially hijacked the White House. And this isn't the first time they've done it.

"The CIA denied it. They tried to convince people that we were really crazy. I mean, they never believed that the Soviet Union was a driving force in the international terror network."

—MICHAEL LEDEEN, ADVISOR TO THE U.S. SECRETARY OF STATE, 1981–82.[1]
IN FACT, THE SOVIET UNION NEVER WAS FOUND TO BE A DRIVING FORCE IN THE INTERNATIONAL TERROR NETWORK, ALTHOUGH LEDEEN SNIFFED THE RUSSIANS BEHIND EVERY RADICAL GROUP FROM THE IRA TO THE PLO.

This is the very same bunch that, in the 1970s and 1980s, whipped the U.S. arms-buying establishment into a frenzy over fears that the United States would be attacked by Soviets. Much like their alarms over Saddam Hussein's WMDs, their hysterical information about the Soviet threat also turned out to be false. In both cases, however, the result was the same: Defense budgets soared. No wonder these powerful "Chicken Littles" have so many friends in the arms industry.

NEOCON IDEALS

Well-educated, articulate, and driven, the hardcore neocons may number but a few thousand, if that, but these political idealogues have carved an impressive niche in modern politics: Neocons are high-ranking government officials (including Pentagon number three Douglas Feith), editors of such publications as the *Wall Street Journal* (Max Boot), columnists for right-wing papers (Robert Kagan), thinkers at right-wing think tanks (Michael Ledeen), and other VIPs (James Woolsey) who have the full attention of Donald Rumsfeld, Dick

Cheney, and George W. Bush, all of whom mirror neocon views on matters of military and world domination.

Simply put, the neocon idealogy is to:

- Remodel the United States as a fighter against evil—a "benevolent hegemon"—and take control of the world, unleashing democracy wherever the country drops its bombs and sinks its flag
- To achieve this, arm the United States to the hilt (with pricey high-tech weaponry) and dominate not only earth but space and cyberspace
- Take aggressive military action against anyone perceived as an enemy— first-strike attacks and nuclear weapons are viable military options
- Ignore international bodies, including the UN, unless they agree with the United States
- Militarily protect Israel as well as South Korea and Taiwan, including threatening to use nuclear weapons if those countries are attacked

---

Ignoble Untruths

Neocons were deeply influenced by gloomy political philosopher Leo Strauss. A man who believed the world was as black and white as 1950s TV (he adored Gunsmoke *and* Perry Mason*),[2] he stressed the necessity of filling commoners' heads with "noble truths"—which is to say, propagandistic lies—in order for an elitist group to pursue its own agenda of what was best for society.*

Although their errors are legendary, the neocons' boo-boos grow bigger with time. One of their most stunning bloopers was wheeling Iraqi dissident Ahmed Chalabi into the "Does Saddam Have WMDs?" debate. Pentagon advisor Richard Perle had befriended the banker from Jordan, pitching Chalabi as the man who had the dirt on Saddam Hussein's formidable arsenal. And that noble truth had far-reaching consequences: It legitimized the 2003 war in Iraq, for starters.

NEOCON WHOPPER: AHMED CHALABI

Secretary of State Colin Powell, for one, didn't buy it. When the neocons began parading Richard Perle's makeshift Iraqi Ahmed Chalabi—who hadn't stepped foot in Iraq since the 1960s—Powell smelled a rat. "I can't substantiate his [Chalabi's] claims. He makes new ones every year," Powell told *USA Today* in

2003. Chalabi, the neocons insisted, was the real deal: Not only did he have insider information on the horrors committed by Saddam, insisted Richard Perle and Paul Wolfowitz, so did Chalabi's friends. Thanks to the neocon push and the enthusiasm of Secretary of Defense Rumsfeld and Vice President Cheney, the government spent millions to keep Chalabi in fine style—and to import his friends. In fact, with help from the government's favorite propagandist, John Rendon, Chalabi put together a political group of dissidents: the Iraqi National Congress. This would be the ruling party of the new Iraq, crowed the neocons. They were so sure that Chalabi would be elected president by the soon-to-be-democratic Iraqis, that neocons dubbed him "the George Washington of Iraq" as they carted Chalabi and pals before the press. And that notion was as flimsy as the one that Iraq would soon be a tranquil democracy.

Judith Miller at the New York Times *apparently swallowed Chalabi's highly dubious assertions. Her reporting pounded home the notion that there were undoubtedly weapons of mass destruction in Iraq.*

Now it appears that Chalabi and his pals (like the Bush administration itself) were shooting empty bullets. Once the United States had invaded Iraq, Chalabi—seen as the fake that he was—was promptly rejected by his fellow Iraqis. And the kingdom of Jordan was soon on his trail, pursuing criminal charges: The Jordanian government convicted Chalabi of bank embezzlement and sentenced him to twenty-five years. Chalabi fled to Switzerland to avoid serving the sentence. Worse, it appears that Chalabi may have been an Iranian spy, paid by Tehran to load up the U.S. government and media with horse puckey. After all, Iran too wanted its old foe, Saddam Hussein, out.

"It's hard to conceive that it would take more forces to provide stability in post-Saddam Iraq than it would take to conduct the war itself and secure the surrender of Saddam's security forces and his army. Hard to imagine."

—PAUL WOLFOWITZ IN A CONGRESSIONAL TESTIMONY, FEBRUARY 2003, WHEN HE WAS YET AGAIN MISCALCULATING

Powermonger
Paul Wolfowitz

Accomplishment: Dreamed up the Bush Doctrine.

Friendly and affable, Wolfowitz is a hawk in dove's clothing. The former college dean at Johns Hopkins has rearranged U.S. military policy: He's chucked out such old-fashioned ideas as peaceful negotiation and containment, endorsing instead bare-fanged aggression and preemptive strikes, including kicking open the door to nuclear war.

> *Star neocon Paul Wolfowitz believes, as do most neocons, that near-constant military action for the rest of time will be needed to keep the United States in the saddle.*

But maybe he's wrong—he certainly has been before. His last four years as deputy secretary of defense were just as costly as they were riddled with error. Apparently mistaking the people of the world for simpletons who view life only in stark black and white, he concocted Bush's "with us or with the terrorists" ultimatum that struck even countries friendly with the United States as highhanded; Wolfowitz also drew harsh criticism as the architect of the war in Iraq, the cost of which, in lives, money, and effects, was vastly underestimated. Wolfowitz, who wanted to invade Iraq days after September 11, was wrong about Saddam's WMDs (and Iraq's link to al-Qaeda), and he was wrong about Iraqi dissident Ahmed Chalabi. Lacking military experience himself, Wolfowitz was also wrong about how many troops it would require to take Iraq: He initially estimated that Iraq could be taken with 40,000 troops—although many experts now feel that even the 100,000+ Rumsfeld sent in weren't enough. Wolfowitz really showed his cluelessness with his unflinching conviction that the American troops would be welcomed as liberators in Iraq, even though Middle East experts were bellowing that an invasion would soon trigger mayhem and resentment against the United States, as indeed it has. While that notion of planting democracy may have looked good on the blackboard, Wolfowitz overlooked factoring nonstop insurgency into his dreamy prewar formula.

> *"There is a lot of money to pay for this. It doesn't have to be U.S. taxpayer money," Wolfowitz assured Congress days before the United States invaded*

> *Iraq in 2003. "We are talking about a country that can finance its own recon-*
> *struction—and relatively soon." Cost of invading Iraq: over $200 billion U.S.*
> *taxpayer dollars as of mid-2005.*

That Bush rewarded Wolfowitz for his expensive miscalculations with an appointment to become president of the World Bank doesn't quite add up; Europeans, who could have vetoed the appointment, initially regarded him warily. However, easygoing Wolfowitz charmed the EU bunch when he visited Old Europe in March 2005. Wolfie admitted with a chuckle that he knew he was a controversial figure, but assured the across-the-ocean gang that the more they knew him, the more they would like him; critics might call that yet another noble truth, having found exactly the opposite to be the case.

As high-ranking government officials and as powerful outside consultants, the neocons have demanded that the United States stomp heavily, speak loudly, think selfishly, and carry a big weapon (and brandish it in the face of the world).

In the neocons' book, notions such as arms control and multilateral agreements that aim to benefit the whole world are for wussies. During the Bush administration, they've ripped the United States loose of numerous treaties, including:

- the Anti-Ballistic Missile Treaty with Russia
- the Chemical Weapons Convention
- the Comprehensive Test Ban Treaty (prohibiting nuclear testing underground)
- the International Criminal Court on war crimes
- the Kyoto Protocol designed to cut emissions linked to global warming

> *"It was the happiest day of my government service,"* John Bolton *chirped to the* Wall Street Journal *upon sending notice that the United States would pull out of previous commitments to support the International Criminal Court.*

Never mind that most members of this group wriggled out of military service, and just overlook the fact that their ideas about planting the freeze-dried concept of democracy in countries the United States leaves scarred and smoking haven't taken root. Neocons look down from their lofty posts and see all sorts of situations where they want to direct U.S. soldiers to correct the problem, believing that the United States has the right and the need to kick up war wherever it pleases, for whatever reason, and to hell with what the rest of the globe thinks. There is a whole world of evil to slay and even if it requires nuclear war to eradicate ne'er-do-wells—and show the planet who is boss—well, say the neocons with a shrug, so be it.

The Neocons sayeth, and the Bush administration doeth, seems to be the rule lately. Neocon recommendations recently heeded include:

- Waging war on Iraq
- Launching National Missile Defense
- Opening the Arctic National Wildlife Refuge to oil exploration
- Developing more usable nuclear weapons and pushing the right to use nuclear warfare, even if the target countries do not have nuclear arms
- Attempting to control outer space by advocating that the United States send weapons up there

---

Another major neocon influence is Albert Wohlstetter, a nuclear strategist and RAND Corporation thinker who is rumored to have been the basis for Stanley Kubrick's wacked-out Dr. Strangelove.

 ZOOM

The Roaring Lion
John Bolton

Accomplishments: Through numerous administrations, in assorted State Department roles, he has magnificently succeeded in offending coworkers, foreign countries, and international agencies.

Does he suffer from migraines? Do his hemorrhoids rage? Is he actually bald and wearing a wig? Why is bespectacled and mustachioed John Bolton—an articulate, wealthy, Yale-educated lawyer who isn't all that bad-looking—not only the administration's most aggressive and belligerent official, but downright nasty, the kind of guy who wouldn't just stomp out of a party if his gal glanced at another guy but would shoot the beer keg on his way out? Whatever the reason, the foul-tempered, ultraconservative superunilaterist is alarming in his rude contempt for nearly any other person or country's right to pipe up and he's infamous for unnecessarily stomping on toes:

▶ After the anthrax scare in 2002, he couldn't simply state that the United States (which shudders at the thought of foreigners inspecting its bioweapons facilities) didn't wish to sign a UN agreement banning biological weapons: He had to sabotage the entire UN meeting to make his point.[3]

▶ When intelligence agents couldn't confirm his allegations that Cuba was developing biological weapons of mass destruction, he threatened to have the agents fired, according to a former senior intelligence officer, Alan Foley.

▶ Sent to meet with North Korea's Kim Jong Il in 2003—a delicate situation that had taken months of negotiations and China's insistence to arrange— Bolton proved that he was more of a loose cannon than the dictator: He so ferociously slammed Kim in a speech given in South Korea just before the scheduled meeting—one spiced up with frequent use of the words "tyrant," "tyranny," and "dictatorship"—that Kim slammed the figurative door in Bolton's face, refusing to see him.[4] It's been iceville with Pyongyang ever since.

"He's a kiss-up, kick-down sort of guy."

—CARL FORD, FORMER CHIEF OF THE BUREAU OF INTELLIGENCE AND RESEARCH AT THE
STATE DEPARTMENT IN APRIL 2005 BEFORE THE SENATE COMMITTEE HOLDING
BOLTON'S CONFIRMATION HEARINGS. FORD TESTIFIED THAT BOLTON TRIED TO
CAN AN AGENT WHOSE INVESTIGATION DID NOT SUPPORT BOLTON'S CLAIMS.

An even more compelling question than what's eating Mr. Bolton, however, is why on earth President Bush would appoint this affirmed anti-diplomat to the institution that has been an ongoing target for Bolton's criticisms and mean-spirited digs. Many took the Bush nomination of Bolton as meaning that Bush hopes to demolish the United Nations from within. They may be right.

"There is no such thing as the United Nations," Bolton sniped in 1994, adding that if the New York headquarters "lost ten stories, it wouldn't make a bit of difference."

The March 2005 news of the nomination (which requires Congressional approval) unleashed a wave of fury, including from five dozen ambassadors and former ambassadors who signed a letter demanding that the Senate veto Bolton's confirmation. What sort of nuanced diplomacy can we expect from a man who told National Public Radio in 2000 that if he were in charge of the UN Security Council it would "have one permanent member [the United States] because that's the real reflection of the distribution of power in the world." In August 2005, when the Senate still had not approved Bolton, Bush sidestepped the prob, appointing him as a temporary UN ambassador until 2007.

Bolton is on the record for blustery finger pointing: In 2002, at a speech before the Heritage Foundation dramatically entitled "Beyond the Axis of Evil," he announced that the United States had undeniable proof that Cuba was manufacturing biological weapons; his proclamation was quickly followed by a loud announcement from U.S. intelligence denying that claim. In summer 2003, when he was scheduled to assert before Congress that Syria possessed weapons of mass destruction, a panicked CIA blocked his testimony, apparently not wanting to be forced yet again to find evidence to support another neocon noble truth.

Where Bolton could kick up the biggest dust storm, in the UN, is in the touchy area of Taiwan, an island that operates almost autonomously of China, but which Beijing still claims is part of "One China." Bolton delights in loudly demanding that Taiwan be recognized as independent—having been paid tens of thousands of dollars by Taiwan to lobby for its cause. Even though he theoretically is no longer on Taiwan's payroll, Bolton still makes a stink about it, infuriating sensitive Beijing in the process. And that may be just what the man who opposed free trade with China is trying to do. If China gets flustered and makes a move on Taiwan, the United States (or so neocons have promised) will swoop in to defend the island. And according to Bush administration U.S. Nuclear Posture Reviews, the United States would use nuclear arms in that fight.[5] And that's just another reason why we shudder: not only that Bolton has an iota of power, but that this anti-diplomat is now the United States' representative to the world.

Close-up

Frankly, when they see neocons coming their way, those in power should have one rapid response: run. After all, neocons are usually, if not always, wrong. Their ability to defy statistical probability goes back to 1976, when they formed Team B, a vehicle put into place under CIA director George H. W. Bush. It was the first large-scale neocon show of the dangers of their hype: They simultaneously were given the means to defy reality, manipulate public opinion, and foreshadow how expensive and dangerous their erroneous, wacked-out ideas could be.

TEAM B.S.[6]

It was founded on an absurd premise—that the Soviet wizards had created such frighteningly advanced weapons that U.S. intelligence couldn't detect them, and whose existence, therefore, was impossible to prove. Thus was born Team B, a trademark neocon lesson in ridiculousness. The background was this: In the 1970s, Secretary of State Kissinger had negotiated a détente with the Soviet Union. Certain hawks, including the defense secretary under President Ford—Donald Rumsfeld—didn't like that move at all. Certain neocon academics postulated that we would be blown away in a sneak attack by the Soviets, and accused the CIA of underestimating the Soviets' capability.[7] Even though there was no evidence to support his assertion, Rumsfeld announced to Americans in 1976 that the Soviets had been "very busy" building up secret weapons that were going to be unleashed on the United States and take it down. Rumsfeld pushed CIA director George H. W. Bush to form a committee to speculate what the Soviets might be up to. This committee—called "Team B"—worked on war game strategies for the CIA in the 1970s, but they were guided not by facts or real information; they relied only on their paranoid fantasies. Armed with their imaginations, Team B—which included Paul Wolfowitz—concocted a hostile world of noble truths. Regarding Soviet satellites, they imagined they were laser ray weapons; they constructed scenarios involving a sophisticated antiballistic missile system; and they envisioned wildly advanced intercontinental missiles hurtling our way. The simple fact that Team B couldn't prove that the mad Soviet scientists were inventing these hypothetical weapons was just one measure, said Team B, of how incredibly scary the arms were. The CIA didn't buy Team B's nightmare scenarios, and initially neither did Congress. Frustrated that their plan to rearm America was failing, the neocons from Team B revived the Committee on the Present Danger—a disbanded group that, back in 1950, had been yelling that the Soviets would invade any second. Bellowing that the Russians were coming—and with weapons we couldn't even see—the alarmist Committee on the Present Danger attracted conservative politicians including presidential candidate Ronald Reagan. And when Reagan stepped into the White House in 1980, so did the neoconservatives from Team B and their unfounded neuroses. Paul Wolfowitz headed the State Department's policy office, Richard Perle was assistant secretary of defense, and neocon thinker Michael Ledeen was called in as a presidential advisor to Reagan. With the paranoiacs whispering in his ear, Reagan launched the biggest military buildup the United States had yet seen. And for absolutely no good reason.

Team B's fantasy scenarios triggered $1 trillion of arms buying.[8]

"In retrospect, Team B's conclusions were wildly off the mark."

—FAREED ZAKARIA, *NEWSWEEK*

Both arms purchases and the neocons' power ballooned through the 1980s until 1992, when the neocons' rise abruptly stalled: Bill Clinton won the presidential election, and his administration gave the alarmists the boot. They kept busy, however—and not just writing *The Weekly Standard* and the *Wall Street Journal* or banging out warnings from their desks at the American Enterprise Institute or sitting on the board of Frank Gaffney's Center for Security Policy. Their main vehicle for publicity—and one that gained them a hearty nod from more traditional conservatives—was the Project for the New American Century, the platform they used to bark orders at Clinton.

 ## Project for the New American Century (PNAC)

The Clinton years may have been good for the economy—arms sales to foreign countries was a mainstay of his foreign policy—but the neocons, along with their out-of-office buddies Donald Rumsfeld and Dick Cheney, fretted. Now that the Cold War was over, the United States would never arm itself so lavishly again, and arms sales could plummet permanently. They devised the perfect solution for alerting the government, the media, and the general public about the need to keep buying. In 1997, they founded a report-issuing think tank, which also served as a lobby crying out that the American hold on twenty-first-century dominance was slipping away. The Project for the New American Century gives its premise away in its name: The century would belong to the United States, at least if we followed PNAC's stellar advice.

Lining up not only Rumsfeld and Cheney, but former defense secretary Frank Carlucci and the man soon to be Florida's governor—Jeb Bush—they cranked out orders to President Clinton, attaching their John Hancocks to the letters: The Democrat had to bolster the military at once, they reprimanded in 1997; the next year they lectured Clinton, again in a well-publicized letter, to invade Iraq. But in 2000, they released their pièce de résistance. The report that PNAC released that year, "Rebuilding America's Defenses," spelled out the plan to keep the United States at the top of the heap far into the future.[9]

Among the demands dictated in the 2000 PNAC report were that the United States must:

▶ "[C]ontrol space and cyberspace"
▶ Create "a new military service—U.S. Space Forces—with the mission of space control"

▶ "[D]evelop and deploy global missile defenses to defend the American homeland and American allies, and to provide a secure basis for U.S. power projection around the world"

▶ "[E]xploit the [high-tech] revolution in military affairs to insure the long-term superiority of U.S. conventional forces" (e.g., unmanned spy drones)

▶ "[I]ncrease defense spending . . . adding $15 billion to $20 billion to total defense spending annually"

In other words, the United States should hand over trillions of dollars because these guys were getting paranoid again.

Other influential neocon "organs" include:

- *American Enterprise Institute, a think tank that churns out reports calling for increased military spending*
- *Center for Security Policy: Headed by weapons nut Frank Gaffney, CSP boasts top-shelf advisors Richard Perle, Douglas Feith, and Jeane Kirkpatrick*
- *Jewish Institute for National Security Affairs: JINSA commands that the United States keep arming itself, and also coordinates trips for U.S. military brass to travel to Israel*

Extremely helpful in shoving George W. Bush into office (the neocons saw in the Texan the opportunity for an expanded military), neocons are reaping the rewards. The Bush administration adores them, their militaristic and confrontational recommendations are quickly transformed into U.S. policy, and their heavy hitters soar to power positions and become the United States' talking heads to the world. An added bonus: Nearly all of the "directives" from the Project for the New American Century were written into Bush policy.

THE GANG

Besides working for the government, neocons—many of them think-tank scholars—are asked to sit on government-appointed expert panels such as the Defense Policy Board, which makes recommendations for the Pentagon. A few neocon notables working both within and outside the government:

- **Richard Perle:** Chairman of weighty Defense Policy Board, 2001–03. (See "Perle's Wisdom?," page 73.)

- **Douglas Feith:** The Pentagon's third most powerful; put together the Defense Policy Board and organized a separate intelligence team on Iraq that contradicted the CIA, assuring the White House of links between al-Qaeda and Iraq.
- **Michael Ledeen:** White House advisor, columnist for the conservative *National Review*, and author of *The War Against the Terror Masters*, scholar Ledeen is worshipped by the Bush administration as a guru, despite (or perhaps because of) his inability to utter a sentence without using the phrase "terror masters." When he was employed as an advisor to President Reagan he spiced up his banter with a different buzz phrase—"terror network." Ledeen contended that all international terrorists—from the PLO to the IRA— were part of a Soviet plot. He's now gunning for Iran and Syria, and recommending the United States strike there next.
- **Elliot Abrams:** See "Iran-Contra," page 54.
- **James Woolsey:** Former CIA director; now sits on Defense Policy Board.
- **"Scooter" Libby:** Former chief of staff to Vice President Dick Cheney.
- **William Kristol:** Editor of neocon bible *The Weekly Standard* and founder of the Project for the New American Century.
- **Irving Kristol:** The godfather of the neocons, and Bill's proud pa.
- **Robert Kagan:** Senior associate at Carnegie Endowment for International Peace who believes Americans and Europeans occupy different planets.
- **Robert Novak:** Newspaper columnist who outted CIA agent Valerie Plame.
- **Max Boot:** Fellow at Council on Foreign Relations; influential author and former *Wall Street Journal* editor.
- **Frank Gaffney:** Briefly employed by Defense Department during Reagan administration, he was so goofy even then that Defense Secretary Frank Carlucci showed him the door. Later founded influential Center for Security Policy.

Although they held powerful posts in the Bush administration, neocons didn't have quite so much clout until the September 11 attacks. Within days, the Pentagon's number two and number three men—Paul Wolfowitz and Douglas Feith respectively—as well as Defense Advisory Board chairman Richard Perle—began squawking incorrectly about Saddam Hussein's connection to September 11 (none established) and hammering home the idea that he possessed weapons of mass destruction of all types (none found). Now claiming that we actually went into Iraq to unlock the Iraqis' shackles, these absolutists, waving the democracy-for-all flag, are currently pushing the United States toward war with a half dozen other oppressive regimes—in countries that just happen to hold resources that we want, and are located in strategic regions that would allow the United States to move closer to the neocons' stated goal of world hegemony.

Behind the Scenes

Given their war-loving stance, it's no surprise that many neocons are also professionally and financially linked to the arms industry, often working as consultants for the arms makers and sometimes hawking weaponry and security investments themselves, while serving as advisors to the government—situations that some might call conflicts of interest.

 ## Perle's Wisdom?

Richard Perle, a pal of Defense Secretary Rumsfeld and widely respected by men who love arms, is one of the loudest voices in developing Bush's defense strategies. His influence reaches back decades. In the Defense Department and on the National Security Council during the Reagan administration, he was tapped to accompany the president to Iceland for a meeting with Gorbachev about arms control—which, predictably, Perle opposed. (Reagan, for once, didn't listen.) Amusing, bright, a fabulous chef, and the author of numerous books, Perle has strong ideas—he hates the UN, advocates taking out Saudi Arabia and Libya as well as Iran and Syria, and is all tied up with Israel. For a think tank linked to Likud, the party of Israeli Prime Minister Ariel Sharon (with whom he is chums), Perle cowrote a 1995 defense strategy report advocating that Israel further beef up its military and refuse to negotiate with the Palestinians. Until recently, Perle was a director of the *Jerusalem Post* and a director of its owner, the Hollinger Group. Hollinger recently accused him not only of raiding the corporate piggy bank, but of using the media chain, which also owns the *Telegraph* in London and the *Chicago Sun-Times*, to push his political agenda.[10] He also produces TV segments about political matters for PBS, and has the unusual practice of demanding that he be paid for interviews with the media. Perle also has a history of attracting scandals. In 1970, while an aide to Sen. Henry Jackson, for example, an FBI wiretap reportedly caught him leaking classified info to Israel,[11] and in 1983 he was investigated for recommending that the United States buy arms from an Israeli agent who had paid him $50,000. While hard-selling the "invade Iraq" idea as Defense Advisory Board chairman in 2001, a *New Yorker* article by Seymour Hersh revealed, Perle also was part of a security-related investment firm, Trireme, that stood to benefit if there was war. Perle met with several Saudis, soliciting them to invest $100 million in Trireme, according to the article.[12] During that time, he was also paid $750,000 by Global Crossing to lobby for a satellite program the company wanted to sell to China, which had been blocked by the Pentagon.[13] Although a Defense Department investigation cleared him of any ethical breach, it sure didn't look wholesome that Perle was financially tied to Loral Space & Communications, which profited greatly when the Pentagon rented satellite space during the 2003 Iraq invasion.[14]

> That Perle had the nerve to hit up Saudis for money for his security investment firm was ironic. Not long before, Perle had invited a RAND thinker to speak in front of the Defense Advisory Board, an event that caused a huge flap, since the speaker suggested that the United States invade Saudi Arabia and take over its oil fields.

While on the Defense Policy Board, Perle also wrote a piece for the *Wall Street Journal* lauding a Boeing scheme to convince the U.S. Air Force to lease one hundred aerial refueling planes at a price that would have cost billions of dollars more than simply buying the aircraft. Perhaps Perle was just bad with his math, or perhaps the $20 million that Boeing reportedly had just invested in his company Trireme had something to do with his endorsement. He reportedly also blabbed confidential info about investment opportunities in Iraq to board members of Goldman Sachs.

Perle resigned the chairmanship post in 2003, but kept a seat on the Defense Board until 2004. As usual, despite all the hoo-hah, Perle somehow emerged a still-respected voice in the political advice department. But he's not so revered in Congress, where Perle had appeared in fall 2002, pressing the urgent case to go to war with Iraq. Congress called him back in spring 2005 to inquire why his information had been so wrong. Perle blamed the intelligence community's "appalling incompetence," and then launched a real conspiratorial doozy. "There is reason to believe," he said, "that we were sucked into an ill-conceived initial attack aimed at Saddam himself by double agents planted by the regime."[15] Speaking of working double-time, Perle is again being investigated by the FBI for leaking classified information about Iran.[16]

In their drive to keep the United States permanently poised at the top, the neocons have positioned the country as an overarmed, cocksure monster that is increasingly disliked by the rest of the world. Wealthy and elitist, the neocons lie to the common man and don't shirk at using the country's young men and women as cannon fodder. They've introduced their neuroses into policy—including regarding any political compromise as the equivalent of appeasing Hitler during

World War II—and they've made their ideological priorities, including protection of Israel, South Korea, and Taiwan, reasons to launch a nuclear war, which could lead to worldwide destruction. We can point fingers at the neocons for being so deranged, but perhaps we should point them instead at the powers that be who time and time again actually heed the neocons' psychotic advice.

PART II

FOOD AND DRUG

6. BRIEFING:

How Big Pharma Works

Frequently cast as greedy villains whose CEOs make millions a year, drug makers such as Pfizer, Johnson & Johnson, GlaxoSmithKline, and Merck often appear more motivated by the almighty buck than by a shred of altruism as they kick prices for their healing elixirs into a realm that many Americans and most of the world can't afford. Popular drugs, such as anticholesterol drug Lipitor, anti-ulcer drug Nexium, and antidepressant drug Zoloft, ring in at $2 to $4 per day, while cancer drugs such as Procrit can cost $1,000 a shot and Genentech's Avastin costs nearly $45,000 for the full treatment.

LEADING PHARMACEUTICAL COMPANIES WORLDWIDE, 2004

(Sales in $ Billion)[1]	
Pfizer	50.9
GlaxoSmithKline	32.7
Sanofi-Aventis	27.1
Johnson & Johnson	24.6
Merck & Co. Inc.	23.9
Novartis AG	22.7
AstraZeneca Plc.	21.6
Hoffman-La Roche	17.7
Bristol-Myers Squibb Co.	15.5
Wyeth	14.2

Whenever questioned about the reasons for their painfully high drug prices, company spokesmen wheel out the same feeble excuse with a sigh: Research and development are costly, they say, so exorbitant that it costs them over $800 million per drug to bring the average medicine to your corner drugstore.

> *Critics say the industry's much batted around $800 million figure is terribly inflated. Marcia Angell, former editor in chief of the* New England Journal of Medicine, *estimates the amount it costs to bring a drug to market is closer to $100 million per drug, if that.*[2] *Consumer group Public Citizen concurs with Angell's figure.*

> *PhRMA claims that the industry spends over $30 billion a year in research and development. Critics dispute that figure, too.*

TRIALS AND TRIBULATIONS

Like a fine wine, every pharmaceutical pill or capsule you pop in your mouth is the product of years of work and fine-tuning. Of every one thousand molecules and potential drugs explored, claims PhRMA, the powerful mouthpiece of the industry, only one makes it to clinical trials. From trials, only one in five makes it onto the FDA's desks for approval, where about 80 percent make the grade. But before they are approved, drugs go through costly clinical studies, which are farmed out to entities called contract research organizations, which conduct thousands of trials all over the world—increasingly in developing countries where they don't pay the human guinea pigs much.

Big Pharma claims that if Americans—who pay far more for their pills than anyone else—don't pay full price, then the budget for medical research will shrivel up and we'll never find the antidote for heart disease, Alzheimer's disease, and cancer. Experts, including former editor in chief of the *New England Journal of Medicine* Marcia Angell, say that claim is bunk, and point out that most drug companies are not introducing novel drugs, but copycats of popular medicines already on the market; she says that their main concern is squeezing every penny out of their blockbusters while they hold the patent, and marketing similar drugs to replace their blockbusters when the patent expires.[3] Drug patents last twenty years, and the clock starts ticking the minute a drug starts clinical trials.

WHY DRUGS HURT TO BUY

Discovering, testing, and manufacturing drugs are not the only costs that are passed on to consumers. Other critical factors in pricing drugs include:

- There are no price controls on pharmaceutical drugs in the United States.
- In 2004, pharmaceutical companies spent $3.7 billion in direct-to-consumer advertising in print media and on TV, a jump of 27 percent over the previous year's DTC budget, according to *Medical Marketing and Media.*[4]
- The pharmaceutical industry spent $759 million on lobbying from 1998 to 2004.[5]
- The industry coughed up over $87 million for political campaigns from 1998 to 2004.[6]
- Drug companies spend a fortune buying favors with doctors. For example, they offer physicians huge consulting fees to sit on evaluation teams for a few hours; pay for doctors' required continuing education; fund doctors' ongoing research; and sometimes just send doctors a multizeroed unsolicited check; all to lure them into prescribing that company's latest drug—even when another older, generic drug will work just as well or better.

According to the Center for Public Integrity, the pharmaceutical industry spends more on lobbying than any other industry. For every one U.S. congressperson, there are 4.5 drug industry lobbyists swarming around.

Corporate druglords successfully manipulate politicians to enact other measures that ensure they can keep commanding top dollar. In 2004, when the Medicare Act was up for debate, some congressmen pushed to have the government regulate drug prices, as governments do almost everywhere else. Panicked, Big Pharma sent out the lobbyists to make sure that didn't happen—and, predictably, Big Pharma succeeded in this effort. Just as frightening to them was another bill on the table that year: The Drug Reimportation Act would have allowed companies to reimport American drugs at Canadian prices, which are 30 to 80 percent less. Drug company lobbyists helped stomp out that idea as well.

SAVING MONEY THE CANADIAN WAY

Lately, U.S. residents have been spending some $760 million a year buying drugs in Canada. The drug industry is lobbying Congress to seal up that financial drain, and companies are threatening to cut off drugs to Canada if that country keeps selling to U.S. citizens. "If you take the supply intended for 25 million people in Canada," Pfizer CEO Hank McKinnell warned on PBS's *Newshour*, "and make it available to 250 million people here in the United States, there's going to be shortages in Canada."[7] Even if the federal government wouldn't approve of bringing in drugs at Canadian prices, nearly half of the state legislatures in the United States are making moves to allow it; some state legislators have even launched state-sponsored programs to buy drugs from abroad.

Billy Tauzin, former head of the House Energy and Commerce Committee that oversees the drug industry, was a main author of the 2004 Medicare Prescription Drug Bill that guarantees billions in sales for pharmaceutical companies and prohibits the government from tampering with drug prices. Shortly thereafter, he took up a lucrative offer to sign on as president and CEO of the powerful Pharmaceutical Research and Manufacturers Association (PhRMA), the heavy-lobbying trade association for the industry.

Despite their many legislative victories, drug companies are feeling the heat. The furor over Vioxx—which caused a minimum of twenty-seven thousand heart attacks—caused calls for new industry standards, including an independent board that tracks drug safety once the pharmaceuticals hit the shelves. The media, particularly the *Los Angeles Times* and the *Wall Street Journal*, are all over these guys with stellar reporting, and meanwhile consumers are getting miffed. As things currently stand, many Americans simply can't afford to take drugs.

2004: BIG PHARMA'S ANNUS HORRIBILIS

It had looked so hopeful: For much of the year, drug sales were soaring—reflecting huge jumps in prescriptions written for children as well as yet more Americans joining the ranks of the antidepressed. Drug companies had convinced Congress to adopt the Medicare legislation they wanted and to ban imported drugs from Canada. The FDA was still madly stamping approvals and ignoring reports about the dangers of assorted drugs already on the market. But problems sprang up:

- Even though the FDA had closed its eyes to them, studies from the British medical community kept circulating that showed that antidepressants increased the likelihood of suicide among children. The reports were so damning that the British government had banned most antidepressants for minors in 2003.

- Riled up by the British findings, the U.S. medical community in turn demanded that the FDA call for "black boxes"—the most severe warnings—to be added to the labels of all antidepressants.
- The New York district attorney's office chomped into GlaxoSmithKline for fraud concerning its antidepressant Paxil, which caused severe withdrawal reactions, including fainting and "electric zaps" in the brain, in up to 85 percent of those who took it.
- Supplies of flu shots in the United States dried up when the UK shut down the labs of main manufacturer Chiron.
- Merck yanked Vioxx from the market due to its increased risk of heart attacks.
- The FDA's David Graham testified before the Senate Finance Committee that Vioxx was responsible for the deaths of tens of thousands, and that at least five more drugs should be yanked from the shelves, including Pfizer's Bextra.
- The media—and state prosecutors—went after Big Pharma's practice of kickbacks to physicians, and Congress called for a new drug approval board; even the *Journal of the American Medical Association* wrote an editorial calling for a new monitoring agency.

Together, they spelled the worst year in the drug industry's history, and they pointed to the need for vast change—a need that Big Pharma will probably ignore.

Big Pharma has other headaches, to boot: Patents for many blockbusters are expiring, and many companies, including Merck, don't have much in the pipeline. Despite the money they've had to play with and their alliances with biotech companies, most pharmaceutical companies simply aren't that inventive these days. They mostly rely on "me-too's"—drugs that are similar to ones already on the market—and they are routinely criticized for not making much progress on conquering disease. A day of reckoning may be drawing near for the companies that until recently were the world's most profitable, and in the meantime, the best thing about being a pharmaceutical company is that an endless store of antidepressants and painkillers are just a few feet away. But relief may be on the way. President Bush helped ensure that Americans would pop even more pills when he created the New Freedom Commission on Mental Health in 2002, a move critics say was engineered by drug companies. The commission of mental health experts controversially called for psychological screening of schoolchildren and eventually all Americans, opening the door to the state mandating drug use for those branded mentally ill. Congress awarded an initial $20 million to the program in 2004, while Rep. Ron Paul, MD, likening it to a Soviet brainwashing program, unsuccessfully tried to block it, warning that, in the future, government psychiatrists could drug Americans "whose religious, social or political values do not comport with those of the politically correct, secular state."[8] The mental health screening plan also alarms the Association of American Physicians and Surgeons, which opposes it partly because screening of children does not require parental consent.

BEATING AIDS—WITH ABSTINENCE

It sure sounded big-hearted when President George W. Bush announced in 2003 that he was initiating a five-year $15 billion plan to tackle AIDS in Africa and the Caribbean. But the plan began deteriorating about the minute the words came out of his mouth. Congress wouldn't approve the whole amount and some believe it was just a PR stunt to make the United States look better when it shortly thereafter invaded Iraq.

Bush's program is controversial on several fronts:

- It pulls money away from the proven effective AIDS funds.
- Abstinence-pushing religious organizations have won grants from the program.
- About 8 percent of the budget is devoted solely to promoting abstinence and fidelity.
- Condom distribution has been curtailed by governments receiving funding, such as Uganda, which recalled all government-funded prophylactics.
- Funding amounts have not lived up to the promises, with far less than $3 billion a year thus far being devoted to the program.

Bush's appointment to head the President's Emergency Plan for AIDS Relief also elicited protest. From 1993 to 1999, Randall Tobias, now "global AIDS coordinator," was the chairman of U.S. drug maker Eli Lilly, one of the loudest opponents of allowing generic drugs to treat AIDS into Africa.

As part of the Homeland Security Act of 2002, Senator Bill Frist—blindly respected because he is a doctor—tacked on an addendum that made Eli Lilly mighty happy. The legislation protected Eli Lilly from liability for using vaccines preserved with thimerosal, a mercury derivative believed to be linked to autism.

7. FDA:

A Failed Experiment?

Agency: U.S. Food and Drug Administration
Description: Oversees food safety and drug safety in addition to other duties
Headquarters: Washington, DC
Head: Lester Crawford, acting commissioner since March 2004
Created: 1906 in response to *The Jungle*—a novel about meat-packing horrors—and patent medicine hoaxes
Budget: $1.8 billion
Employees: 9,000

Notable Numbers

- Over 106,000: Number of people who die each year from adverse reactions to drugs (some 2 million are seriously sickened)[1]
- Over 76 million: Number of Americans who get sick from their food every year

Snapshot
The FDA and Drugs

The American food and drug biz appears to be as well-regulated, above-board, and under control as ever. Helpful calorie charts and nutritional pyramids still adorn our food packages, and our candy-colored pills are still packaged in sterile, childproof containers along with illustrations of the molecular structure of the active ingredients—all giving the impression of a highly scientific, organized affair. It's not.

The U.S. Food and Drug Administration, the hallowed guardian of the country's edibles and pharmaceuticals, is seriously screwing up, and critics—from politicians to the FDA's own scientists—are charging that the protectorate of the people has transformed from a fierce public watchdog to a drooling industry lap-dog. Thanks to changes in laws, which now make the drug industry a paying "client," the FDA appears to be little more than a head-nodding green-light machine stamping approval for new pills and novel forms of food and not monitoring them for unforeseen effects. The once powerful agency now is more responsive to demands of the drug and biotech industries—who increasingly control it—than to the consumer it was designed to protect.

"[I]t was pretty well understood that if you were advocating turning a drug down—particularly if it was from a large pharmaceutical company—that that wouldn't be good for your career."

—FORMER FDA SCIENTIST MICHAEL ELASHOFF, ON HIS YEARS
AS AN FDA DRUG REVIEWER FROM 1995 TO 2000[2]

1992: THE YEAR THE FDA BECAME A JOKE

If you want to know what the heck is wrong with today's FDA, point a finger at former vice president Dan Quayle. In the early 1990s, he headed up a powerful task force of industry insiders that kicked all the current problems into effect. Called the Council on Competitiveness, the group gathered together biotech and Big Pharma representatives for their thoughts and advice. And then, the council made a number of weighty recommendations on how the federal government could help out business. And its advice, which wasn't designed with the consumer in mind, was heeded.

Two of the most important recommendations:

- That all impediments be removed for developing biotechnology. The man who could not spell *potato* correctly also very questionably spelled out the federal take on genetically modified (GM) food: Namely, GM food was to be considered identical to its natural counterpart—thus doing away with any need for special tests. That "food equivalence" policy was officially adopted the next year—meaning that most GM food has never been tested for safety on humans.
- That the FDA create a speedy drug approval process so drugs could hit the market more quickly. In 1992, Congress passed the Prescription Drug User Fee Act, which has since meant that a huge chunk of the FDA budget has been footed by the pharmaceutical industry, and the drug companies are now looked upon as the FDA's clients. The money is used to hire more medical reviewers to hasten the FDA's review process.

To ensure that drugs are approved more quickly, pharmaceutical companies now fork over a hefty "user fee" of $500,000 each time they submit a new drug for FDA approval; in 2002 these drug company fees kicked in over $170 million, more than half of the FDA's drug approval budget, to the agency's drug review piggy bank. That financial arrangement speeds up drug approval time but, say critics, it makes the independent agency beholden to Big Pharma.

- The average time for "priority" drugs to be approved was six months in 2001, compared to twenty-one months in 1993.
- The average time for "nonpriority" drugs was fourteen months in 2001, compared to twenty-seven months in 1993.
- The percentage of drugs approved also jumped from 60 percent in the early 1990s to 80 percent by the end of the decade.[3]
- The number of drugs recalled has risen as well: 1.5 percent of approved drugs were pulled between 1993 and 1996 while 5.3 percent were given the hook between 1997 and 2000.[4]

"Americans need to recognize that every time they put a pill in their mouth, especially a new pill that they've never taken before, it's an experiment. How big an experiment depends on the pill and how well it's been studied. Unfortunately, many of the pills we take have not been studied adequately."

—RAYMOND WOOSLEY, MD, RECENT CANDIDATE FOR FDA COMMISSIONER[5]

We are paying for the FDA's new laxness: Over 106,000 die every year from reactions to the drugs that are supposed to cure them or make them better. Depending on the year, that makes reactions to prescribed pharmaceutical drugs between the fourth and the sixth leading killers in the United States.[6]

Prescription drugs, or rather, fatal reactions to them, are the fifth leading cause of death in the United States on average.

Before a pharmaceutical drug gains FDA approval, thousands of individuals are paid to take it during clinical trials. But the real test comes once it's being prescribed and millions are taking it. Oddly, once drugs are on the market, there is little monitoring of the new releases. The pharmaceutical industry doesn't want to know if there's something wrong and the FDA doesn't have the budget to track most drugs; absurdly, physicians' reporting of adverse reactions is entirely voluntary, with reports coming in from between 1 percent and 10 percent of doctors—even when their patients die from reactions. Thus, when the FDA gives numbers on actual deaths, they often reflect but a tiny fraction of those who actually died from their medicine.

Vioxx was a record breaker. The FDA estimates that Vioxx, manufactured by Merck, caused 27,000 heart attacks, some of them fatal, between 1999 and 2004. David Graham, a veteran FDA drug safety researcher who studied the cardiac problems associated with Vioxx and says his superiors tried to suppress his findings, said the real number is far higher: He estimates that Vioxx triggered between 88,000 and 139,000 heart attacks, causing between 27,000 and 56,000 deaths—the largest ever drug catastrophe in U.S. history. "The FDA as currently configured is incapable of protecting America against another Vioxx," he told the Senate Finance Committee in November 2004.[7]

> In February 2005, an expert panel looking into the Vioxx nightmare recommended that the FDA put Vioxx back on the market. The New York Times revealed that nine of the seventeen on the board had monetary links to the pharmaceutical industry, which often funded their research or paid them handsome consulting fees.

The pharmaceutical industry is generous to its friends: It funds university research and it woos physicians, sending them on luxury vacations, during which they spend a few hours learning about a new drug. The industry's money makes it difficult to find impartial reviewers from the private sector or academia. As noted in the *Journal of the American Medical Association*, recent investigations have shown that more than half of the experts sitting on the FDA's advisory panels were getting checks from the very companies who manufactured the drug that they were reviewing.[8]

The FDA and Food

The FDA, along with the U.S. Department of Agriculture that oversees meat and poultry, is also doing a loathsome job protecting our food, complain consumer groups. The number of diseases lurking in our victuals is steadily rising: Annually, 76 million Americans fall ill from E. coli, Listeria, salmonella, and hepatitis A carried in food; over 300,000 end up in hospitals, and some 5,000 die from their dinner.[9] While the FDA trips over itself to maintain that the food supply is entirely safe, there is absolutely no reason to assume such is the case. Between our beef being shot up with drugs, the government's lax safeguards against mad cow disease,[10] and our questionable policy of regarding genetically modified food as safe, other countries—including those whose people are starving—often don't want American food.

Close-up

Until the early 1900s, food and drugs were a free-for-all: Anybody could peddle anything—Fatoff Obesity Cream, Freckle Eater, Dr. Bonker's Celebrated Egyptian Oil for Cholera, and Johnson's Mild Combination Treatment for Cancer being but a few of the patent medicines that were peddled with false claims about contents and effects. At the turn of the twentieth century, however, Congress passed new legislation that slapped regulations upon purveyors of miracle cures and preserved food to ensure that the American food and drug supply was as safe as it could be. For quite a few decades of the past century, thanks to the FDA, it was.

The catalysts for the laws were two writers: Investigative reporter Samuel Hopkins Adams rummaged through the medicine cabinet, exposing the patent hoaxes and slow poisons sold in elegant glass bottles and painted tins, which often contained cocaine, opium, or even radioactive radon. But Sinclair Lewis—whose reality-inspired novel *The Jungle* told the revolting tale of meat-packing factories—disgusted the masses even more. "I aimed for America's heart and hit it in the stomach," wrote Lewis, who later became a socialist politician. The images that he and Hopkins served up for public inspection were so horrifying that Congress passed the 1906 Food and Drug Act, creating a special Food and Drug Administration to take a good look at the food being chomped and medicines being swallowed.

FDA HEROINE: FRANCES KELSEY

It was just an ordinary sedative, the Cincinnati-based drug manufacturer told Frances Kelsey, a former pharmacology professor who had just been handed her first drug review assignment for the FDA. It was quite similar to sedatives already on the market, the William S. Merrell Company insisted, adding that it had been sold in Germany since 1957. The year was 1960, and the drug was thalidomide, at that moment being prescribed to thousands of pregnant women across Europe to fight off morning sickness. Kelsey saw anomalies in the studies and asked for more tests. The Merrell Company complained to her superiors that the green researcher was being too finicky. Kelsey received additional studies, but still wasn't convinced thalidomide was safe. The company continued resisting and still Kelsey would not back down. In 1961, a German physician reported a rash of new cases of babies born with malformed limbs; soon studies confirmed that some ten thousand newborns in Europe whose mothers had taken thalidomide had the same mangled limbs. Although Kelsey, presented the President's Award for Distinguished Federal Civilian Service by President Kennedy, had effectively banned the tetragenic drug's entry into the United States, "thalidomide babies" were born here as well: The Merrell Company had conducted clinical studies in the United States and given out a million free samples to American doctors, who'd passed them on to their pregnant patients, who usually had no idea they were guinea pigs swallowing an unapproved drug.

Thalidomide led to a new law in 1962: All clinical drug studies henceforth were to be authorized by the FDA, and patients had to be informed they were taking an experimental chemical.

Now, thanks to the continuing kinky marriage between government and business, this sort of foresight and strict regulation has gone the way of Kennedy himself. The FDA has been stripped of much of its power, its desks are filled with industry insiders—and some are trying to delete this important agency from the government directory altogether. Along with Congress, the White House—through the administrations of Bush Sr., Clinton, and Bush Jr.—ordered the

FDA into bed with the companies it is supposed to be babysitting. Is it any wonder that the FDA appears to be a sellout, when pharmaceutical companies pay for much of the drug approval budget, as they have since 1993? Is it a surprise that the agency appears scatterbrained, when the White House often neglects to give the FDA a full time commissioner? Why should it be a shock that the FDA is so pro-industry, when

President Kennedy presented the FDA's Frances Kelsey with the Distinguished Service Award in 1962.

so many of its top people are appointed or hired from the very companies that it regulates?

> *Throughout most of the Bush administration, the FDA has had only an "acting commissioner"—another move some see as keeping the FDA wobbly and weak.*

The historical hero of the FDA, chief chemist Harvey Wiley, was a food purist who loathed unnecessary additives. In the era following World War II, as food manufacturers began adding flavors and colors that had been concocted in labs, the FDA gave an okay to thousands of synthetic additives—artificial colorings and flavorings that often outnumber the identifiable real food ingredients in a box. Certainly you can't fault the FDA for American food manufacturers' love affair with chemicals. But you can question if these artificial additives are nutritious—or even safe. Although the FDA has banned a few faux ingredients here and there, consumer groups today still warn about the effects of eating the chemicals that flavor, scent, and color our food. One of those chemicals is particularly controversial: aspartame, the sweetener brought to the American consumer by none other than Donald Rumsfeld, current secretary of defense.

> *The FDA has received at least ten thousand complaints about adverse reactions to aspartame. Ongoing lawsuits assert that it is unsafe and are demanding that it be ejected from our grocery stores.*

NOT SO SWEET NUTRASWEET[11]

Was it a power play, greed, the biggest food conspiracy theory ever—or all three? In 1965, when a chemist licked his thumb, he had no idea of the controversy he was about to kick off. But when James Schlatter of the G. D. Searle drug company discovered that the chemical he was working with (phenylalimine) tasted sweet, he launched a debate that's gone on for decades—and one that illustrates the twisted politics of food. At least those on both sides of the spectrum—the FDA, which now staunchly defends the safety of aspartame, and "aspartame activists"—agree on one thing: Approval for aspartame (later sold as NutraSweet and Equal, among other names) did not come quickly or easily. The activists, some of whom are taking their charges to the courts, say that when aspartame was first sent in for approval, the research was so shoddy that not only did the FDA reject aspartame, it planned to file criminal proceedings because the research looked bogus. Using information obtained under the Freedom of Information Act, activists have produced memos saying that studies conducted by Searle showed that aspartame caused brain tumors in mice.

Aspartame may have remained unapproved for the rest of time, except for one thing: Donald Rumsfeld, who was crawling with government connections, took over as head of Searle in 1977. Rumsfeld saw a blockbuster in the synthetic sweetener and in 1980 sent the submission for aspartame's approval back to the FDA. As aspartame was already highly controversial, the FDA formed an independent board in 1981 to look into it. The board gave a thumbs-down and would not approve it, but the new commissioner of the FDA, Dr. Arthur Hayes, overturned the board findings and in 1981 gave aspartame the green light. Funny thing: Shortly thereafter, say the activists, when Hayes left the FDA (over charges of receiving improper gifts from companies), he went to work for Searle's PR firm, Burston-Marsteller.[12]

A number of lawsuits concerning aspartame are currently in the courts. Among them is a September 2004 racketeering suit filed in California against Nutra-Sweet and Monsanto (which bought G. D. Searle), charging that the companies "knowingly marketed a deadly neurotoxin for human consumption."

Behind the Scenes

Given that FDA icon Harvey Wiley was such a stickler about proper labeling that it's said he wanted to ban the name "ladyfingers" for cookies unless indeed a woman had given her hand to them,[13] one can only imagine that he would be kicking on his coffin trying to get out if he knew about the food facsimiles and adulterants hidden away in our modern edibles. The problem is, many aren't properly identified.

For instance, in 2000 the FDA approved irradiation to meat, poultry, and other food to help kill bacteria that might cause E. coli. While irradiated whole foods— say, strawberries or spices—must be identified as such, the irradiated strawberries or spices don't need to be labeled as such if the irradiated food is merely an ingredient in a processed edible. New laws allow clever euphemisms as well: Irradiation can now be called "cold pasteurization."

> *The FDA considers irradiation entirely safe, but recent research, including from Germany's Federal Research Center for Nutrition in Karlsruhe, indicates that irradiation may cause tumor-causing by-products.*[14]

The hazards inherent in food and drugs in the United States today are not all a result of the actions or inaction of the FDA, which appears to be a sacrificial lamb being offered up to private industry by government. But this agency, now staffed with many from biotech and pharmaceutical companies, is certainly due for a cleanup. Perhaps it's time to give those revolving doors between government and the private sector a hard spin, and then lock them—keeping private industry shut out.

8. PFIZER:

The Hungry Giant

Company: Pfizer
Headquarters: New York City
CEO: Hank McKinnell (since 2001)
Founded: 1849 as a citric acid company
Revenues: $50.9 billion (2004)[1]

Notable Numbers

- $410 billion: World drug sales in 2004
- 10 percent: Pfizer's take of the world's total drug sales in 2004
- $228 billion: Amount U.S. residents spent on drugs in 2004
- $7.7 billion: Amount Pfizer made from cholesterol drug Lipitor in United States in 2004[2]
- 44 percent: Proportion of U.S. residents taking at least one prescription drug

Snapshot

Pfizer is a whale of a pharmaceutical company that keeps swallowing schools of the competition and is now the reigning beast in the ocean of prescription drugs. Pulling down more in revenue in one year than do the top one hundred movies watched worldwide combined, Pfizer peddles over two dozen pharmaceutical products on the U.S. market—far more than any of its competitors—including the king of the pill hill, cholesterol-eating Lipitor. Pfizer's golden goose grossed more in 2004—$12 billion of sales worldwide—than any drug in the history of mankind.

> With 122,000 employees, Pfizer is the largest corporation this side of Wal-Mart and General Electric.

Pfizer gobbled up Warner-Lambert (including Parke-Davis) in 2000 and Pharmacia (including Searle and Upjohn) in 2002, giving Pfizer plenty of new goodies to stock on shelves.

PFIZER'S PFARMACY

- Cholesterol-killer Lipitor
- Blood pressure drug Norvasc (world's fourth best seller in 2004)
- Antidepressant Zoloft (world's tenth best seller in 2004)
- Antibiotic Zithromax
- COX 2 painkillers Celebrex and Bextra
- Libido-pepper-upper Viagra
- Birth control shot Depo-Provera
- Antianxiety pill Xanax
- Over-the-counter products, such as Listerine, Rolaids, Nicotrol, Bengay, and Neosporin, including some you might not want to be seen buying: e.p.t. early pregnancy test, Effergrip, Rogaine, Tucks, Anusol, Hemorid, and Wart-off

This drug company didn't arouse much attention until the 1998 introduction of the so-called Pfizer Riser, Viagra. But Pfizer now stands out for more than that. Pfizer hands over more money for advertising (such as Viagra's "He's back!" campaign) than any other company. It commands the biggest sales force, over fifteen thousand worldwide, to woo doctors with free dinners, paid vacations, and luxurious gifts to help ensure that a Pfizer brand name appears whenever they scrawl out their prescriptions. Pfizer also throws the most money on lobbying—over $54.8 million from 1998 to 2004[3]—and it dropped a hefty $1.6 million on political contributions in 2004 alone.[4]

CEO Hank McKinnell forked over the highest contributable amount—$200,000—in the 2004 Bush reelection campaign, boosting him to the elite "Ranger" status, while other pharmaceutical CEOs looked chintzy as lesser-donating "Pioneers."

And whether working with the competition in the drug industry's well-muscled lobby group, PhRMA, of which CEO McKinnell is chairman emeritus, or working alone, Pfizer uses its clout to shape U.S. prescription drug laws and policies.

What that means to the consumer: Drug prices will continue heading in the direction of Pfizer's recent Viagra-swelled revenues, which is to say up, up, up.

> *A quarter of U.S. residents don't have health insurance that pays for pharmaceutical drugs. To offset criticisms that the poor, elderly, and self-employed can't afford their drugs, Pfizer recently introduced a program that offers reduced prices to families making less than $30,000 a year. Under some programs, Pfizer's drugs are provided free of charge. Being generous is smart business: The drug company gets tax breaks, while doing face-saving PR and keeping its products dominant in the marketplace.*

Close-up

Being at the head of the drug class, today's Pfizer is quite image-conscious. After being named by British aid group Oxfam the "industry leader in pricing drugs beyond the reach of the poor in developing countries," Pfizer began giving away millions of dollars' worth of antibiotics each year to treat African river blindness and the company has sunk millions into establishing AIDS clinics in Africa as well. Calls within the United States that Pfizer is greedy have been greeted with new programs that discount or give away drugs. And Pfizer led corporate America in its contributions to the countries hit by the December 2004 tsunami: Pfizer donated $10 million and shipped out $25 million in drugs.

Presumably, since it has a high profile, Pfizer was not dumping expired and useless medications, a practice for which the industry is sometimes known.

> *Whenever catastrophe strikes, many drug companies clean out their warehouses. They donate tons of drugs, for which they are rewarded with substantial U.S. tax credits. Emergency aid workers say that often less than a third of the donations are useful, many being drugs that expired years before or are entirely inappropriate, such as horse tranquilizers or diet pills, in starving countries. The problem was so bad in Bosnia that the mountains of drugs required buying a $34 million incinerator to torch the old and unneeded medicine.[5] Villagers, however, sometimes enjoy the gifts from abroad. When a British firm dropped supplies into a rural village in Africa, aid workers were surprised when the village elders profusely thanked the workers for their new "jewelry": The old men had tampons hanging from their ears.[6]*

Despite its charity, Pfizer is still considered by some a corporate slimester. When the Big Pharma druglords were worried in 2004 that Congress would pass a law allowing importation of drugs from Canada, nobody fretted more than Pfizer's CEO McKinnell: He took out a full-page ad in Capitol Hill's newspaper, *Roll Call*, and went on TV to plead his case. McKinnell argued that the issue wasn't really about losing profits—he just didn't want to see his fellow Americans being ripped off by foreigners hawking counterfeit drugs. The company also relied on lobbying giant PhRMA to steamroll through the version of the Medicare Bill that made big drug companies the most money (which of course passed).

He's a whiz, but he ain't exactly volunteering his time. Hank McKinnell pulls down a sweet $2.5 million or so every year.[7]

Coincidentally, a very similar proposal to the Medicare Bill that passed had been made by conservative think tank Cato, to which Pfizer donates heavily. Pfizer also contributes to the Hudson Institute, another right-wing think tank, which recommended against Congress's passing the drug reimportation bill.

And, as is the trend with pharmaceutical firms, the company flies out researchers to tropical jungles and faraway lands to study ancient medical practices and pluck rare plants for drug investigations in labs back home. At least Pfizer hasn't just snagged the samples and run, going on to develop patents on the actual plants. Instead, to gain exclusive access to almost all the plants in Ecuador, the company paid a measly $1 million to the Ecuadorian government and a 2 percent royalty for any developed drug.

BIOPIRACY

Over the past two decades, scientists have embarked on a furious scramble over intellectual rights. In moves that strike many as absurd, assorted scientists and science-based companies hold patents on things that seem inherently unpatentable, such as elements and genes. Now they even hold the patents for exotic plants. The University of Cincinnati holds the patent on the genome of Brazil's guarana seed; the popular Asian spice turmeric is patented by the University of Mississippi; L'Oréal holds the patent for certain uses of kava; and medical teams are scouring remote villages, hot springs, and dense jungles looking for more flora and microorganisms that may hold the cures for diabetes and cancer. Practitioners of modern medicine who have long scoffed at ancient methods of healing, and what they call "old wives' remedies," are now trailing Chinese physicians and village healers, hoping to glean new insights for their multinational medical corporations. Laden with boxes of plants and samples of soil, they unravel the genomes of these unrecorded organisms and patent them, often going on to develop medicines that yield billions of dollars—without tossing the countries a dime, and preventing traditional healers from using the newly patented elixirs. The widescale plundering—called biopiracy—is leading to one of the most heated ongoing geopolitical controversies. The underlying question is this: When does a seed, or a plant's genetic structure, belong to a country and when does its genetic makeup belong to the firm that unraveled it? The 1992 UN Convention on Biological Diversity says that countries own the genomes of the flora and fauna on their land and provides a legal framework for them to demand compensation from companies who pluck and run. But under pressure from drug companies who want it blocked, U.S. Congress has yet to ratify it. Governments in developing countries are so livid at the exploitation by Western companies that many are now demanding exploration rights from visiting scientific research teams, as well bioroyalties if the discoveries yield products that are brought to market.

But Pfizer's most questionable move of late has been its behavior with Celebrex, a painkiller prescribed for rheumatoid arthritis that brought in upwards of $3 billion in sales a year. When competitor Merck was forced to pull its COX 2 painkiller Vioxx in September 2004, Pfizer was all but jigging with joy as Celebrex, also a COX 2 painkiller, picked up the slack. With sales soaring, Pfizer smugly maintained in ads and in interviews that unlike Vioxx, which caused heart attacks, Celebrex was absolutely safe. Apparently those making the claims hadn't read the company's 2003 financial report: Buried in its back pages was mention of a 2001 class action lawsuit brought by users of Celebrex who suffered heart attacks—a suit which Pfizer lost. By mid-December, Pfizer had changed its tune: Celebrex, it admitted, indeed could trigger heart attacks. But even with the admission, Pfizer didn't yank the drug as Merck voluntarily had. Instead Pfizer agreed to stop advertising for it, giving the impression that the company was trying to squeeze every last drop of profit from the drug before its patent ran out.

The FDA remained tight-lipped on the matter until January 2005, when it sent a letter to Pfizer recommending that the company pull several ads, which the FDA said overstated Celebrex's case. By then, the point was moot: Weeks before, Pfizer had stopped running the ads.

Behind the Scenes

Despite the company's confident public behavior, Pfizer must be knocking at the knees. With the 2004 admission that Celebrex is linked to heart attacks and the reprimand from the FDA, its do-gooder appearance was tarnished, and the company's stock plummeted by 25 percent. What's more, the swallowing up of companies such as Warner-Lambert and Pharmacia has brought some indigestion. Warner-Lambert had released a diabetes drug, Rezulin, which shortly thereafter was linked with at least sixty deaths and recalled; Pfizer put aside $1 billion to pay for associated legal suits. Warner-Lambert's Parke-Davis division was also slapped by the Massachusetts district attorney: The company had flown physicians to resorts to illegally inform them about the off-label uses of epilepsy drug Neurotrin, which the company said could be used to treat such disorders as manic depression. That cost Pfizer another $430 million to settle. Also cause for nail-biting: Patents on several of its biggest cash cows are drying up. Zithromax goes bye-bye in 2005 and Zoloft takes off in 2006, but at least Pfizer has until 2010 to milk its last billions from Lipitor. And handily there's no patent on products like Anusol and Listerine.

> Swiss pharmaceutical company Novartis has recently done some buying up of its own, and now threatens to topple Pfizer from the throne.

So while Pfizer moans and groans about the staggering costs of development that force it to charge so much for its elixirs and does everything in its power to block those drugs flooding in from Canada, the company's well-stocked medicine cabinet certainly doesn't worry us that Pfizer will be crushed by debt anytime soon. Thanks to Pfizer and the rest of the pack who won't cut us a break, the only one who has to dig through his pockets is the consumer.

9. MONSANTO:

The Revolutionary

Company: Monsanto
Headquarters: St. Louis, Missouri
CEO: Hugh Grant (since 2003)
Founded: 1901 as chemical company that first produced saccharin in the
    United States
Revenues: $5.5 billion[1]

Notable Numbers

- 167 million acres worldwide: Amount of land devoted to growing genetically modified (GM) food[2]
- 91 percent: Proportion of GM crops in the world from Monsanto seeds
- 58 percent: Proportion of Americans in 2003 who had no idea they were
  eating GM food[3]
- 14: Number of seed companies Monsanto has recently purchased
- One-third: Proportion of world's corn seeds that Monsanto owns or controls
- One-fourth: Proportion of world's soybean seeds that Monsanto owns or
  controls
- 1: Monsanto's place on the list of the world's largest sellers of commercial
  seed
- 0: Number of studies FDA and Monsanto have conducted on the actual
  effects on humans of eating genetically modified food

Snapshot

Whenever you shake out a bowl of cereal, pop open a soft drink, or chop a chunk
of cheese, you are probably staring at the latest—and most controversial—

creations of Monsanto. The chemical giant that brought us such environmental nightmares as Agent Orange and PCBs is now fiddling with our food. Monsanto's genetic tinkering with everything from corn to milk, say detractors, is making guinea pigs of American consumers, most of whom have no clue that they are eating genetically modified (GM) food, since no warning labels identify them as such. Consequently, with a nod from federal agencies, most GM comestibles have slipped into the market with little fanfare and less public debate.[4]

"Critics continue to claim that [genetically modified] foods are unsafe, despite the fact that millions of Americans, Canadians, Australians, Argentines and other people have been eating genetically modified food for nearly a decade—without one proven case of an illness, allergic reaction or even the hiccups."

—JIM NICHOLSON, U.S. AMBASSADOR TO THE VATICAN.[5] DESPITE THE AMBASSADOR'S ASSERTIONS, NEITHER THE U.S. GOVERNMENT NOR ANYONE ELSE HAS CONDUCTED IN-DEPTH STUDIES ON HUMANS INVESTIGATING THE ACTUAL EFFECTS OF EATING THE DNA-DOCTORED EDIBLES, NOR HAVE THEY CLOSELY MONITORED "ILLNESS, ALLERGIC REACTIONS OR EVEN THE HICCUPS" AMONG THE MILLIONS UNKNOWINGLY CHOMPING FOOD FROM BIOENGINEERED PLANTS.

Monsanto—the global giant of genetically modified seeds—is stealthily pushing more and more bioengineered food onto store shelves, where most corn syrup, canola oil, and soybean products already originate with Monsanto's genetically modified seeds. Now a whopping 70 percent of processed food in the United States contains GM ingredients.

In 2005, Monsanto acquired Seminis, a fruit and vegetable seed company that controls 20 percent of the world market and nearly 40 percent of the U.S. market. That move makes Monsanto the single biggest seller of commercial seed in the world.

Monsanto has also stampeded into the corral brandishing Posilac—a bioengineered bovine growth hormone that pumps up cows to produce more milk. Banned in Canada, the European Union, Australia, and Japan, Posilac lassoed FDA approval in 1993, and currently a third of dairy cattle in the United States are injected with the artificial growth hormone; many consumer groups are trying to convince the FDA to toss Posilac from the approved drug list for animals, believing that it poisons the milk from cattle injected with Posilac. Watchdogs point to the questionable manner in which Posilac gained approval from the U.S. Food and Drug Administration as one example of how Monsanto has far too snuggly of a relationship with the feds.

SOMETHING FISHY?

In the 1980s, Monsanto approached the FDA with a novel product. Posilac—a recombinant bovine growth hormone that was the first genetically manipulated drug for animals—promised to be a boon to dairy farmers: Cows shot up with the drug could increase their milk-producing potential by 15 percent. FDA researcher and veterinarian Dr. Richard Burroughs wasn't convinced it was acceptable: Burroughs believed it increased risks of udder infection and caused reproduction problems and unknown effects on humans, and he demanded more tests. Consumer groups protested that the drug was unnecessary (the United States has plenty of milk), unhealthy (it greatly increases the cow's risk of infection, leading to more antibiotic use and pus in the milk), and possibly carcinogenic (European studies have linked the insulinlike substance it produces to assorted cancers, including breast and prostate[6]).

The FDA ignored the consumer protests, fired Burroughs, and, in 1989, hired scientist Margaret Miller. A Monsanto employee who had written up the company's studies on Posilac, Miller became deputy director of the Office of New Animal Drugs. The FDA also hired a new deputy commissioner on policy: lawyer Michael Taylor, who had previously represented Monsanto and would later become vice president of Monsanto's public policy. The FDA gave Posilac a green light. To prevent any distinction from milk produced with help from Posilac and regular old milk, the FDA also went so far as to prohibit dairy farmers from labeling their milk as being from Posilac cows. Consumer groups protested that this shows that the FDA is protecting Monsanto over the consumer; the groups also claim that Miller and Taylor were involved in those controversial decisions, but the FDA denies it.[7] A GAO investigation into the Posilac controversy also cleared Miller and Taylor of serious wrongdoing.

Whether Monsanto's new biotech empire of genetically tweaked seeds and hormones are, as the company claims, the agriculture of the future—providing more food that requires less work and fewer chemicals to grow—or whether it represents self-serving monopolistic moves opening the door to horrors on a global scale (including scenarios where Monsanto dominates the global seed stock), depends on who you talk to. But one thing is for sure: Monsanto has found a good buddy in the U.S. government—which appears just as determined as Monsanto to ram GM food down the throat of the world, whether the world wants it or not.

LOOK WHAT THEY'VE DONE TO OUR FOOD, MA

Most of the genetically modified food under cultivation comes from Monsanto's seeds, and the majority currently sprouts in the United States, where farmers have quickly signed on: Genetically engineered varieties make up one-third of the nation's corn yield and three-quarters of its soybeans. Western Europe, Japan, South Korea, and other countries, however, don't want to play ball, being loath to accept these foreign species of plants. These countries' refusal to import much GM food has slammed U.S. agricultural earnings, down more than $300 million a year since 1996, in corn exports alone. Attempting to stimulate demand for more GM food, the United States filed a suit with the WTO in 2003 over the European Union's hesitation over biotech food, saying the EU had erected an unfair trade barrier. It is also demanding that the EU compensate the United States $1.8 billion in lost sales. Much of the excess genetically engineered corn now goes for American food aid, a move which is politically loaded, since many African countries don't want GM food either. They have been forced to accept it: A requirement to be eligible for medication in the U.S. program to combat HIV is that the countries also take U.S. food aid.

Even the American Corn Growers Association asked the feds to lighten up on their demands on foreign governments, reminding them in a 2000 statement that "the customer is always right" and asking the government to "respect the wishes of our overseas customers" as well as to "not impose trade sanctions against any country refusing to accept [GM food]." The Corn Growers Association also requested that the feds "investigate the relationship between the U.S. Department of Agriculture and the biotechnology industry" to ensure that the USDA wasn't in the biotech industry's pocket.[8]

Close-up

Monsanto would like you to know that it has a new image. The Missouri-based enterprise that once concerned itself with making plastics, synthetic fibers, and poisons is now a "life sciences company" with beautiful greenhouses, lush experimental fields, and gleaming biotech labs. Never mind that Monsanto is still paying out millions of dollars in compensation for the illnesses and birth defects that its chemicals previously caused; now the company is the self-appointed biotech messiah of the planet.

"We're doing God's work. The world will think we're saviors."

—MONSANTO CEO ROBERT SHAPIRO TO FORMER
U.S. DEPUTY SECRETARY RICHARD ROMINGER IN 1996[9]

Monsanto's enemies, of which there are many—particularly in Europe, where Monsanto's GM offerings are referred to as "Frankenfoods"—certainly don't buy the company's recently spruced-up image. They pooh-pooh Monsanto's feel-good ads promising to feed the world's hungry and to save the environment while doing it, and aren't mesmerized by the shots of kindly CEOs and state-of-the-art labs where geneticists are unraveling and addressing all of agriculture's woes. For them, Monsanto is the emblem of corporate evil, and in countries from England to India, Monsanto GM crops are routinely burned down and pulled up.

BIOTECH'S PROMISES

When scientists began inserting foreign materials into the DNA of seeds back in the 1980s, it marked a mind-boggling leap in the evolution of agriculture. While crossbreeding of plants has been common for over a century, this was different: Scientists could inject genes from entirely different plants—or even animals—into the DNA of a seed, attempting to give it new qualities. Scientists designed potatoes that require less oil for frying; they created rice that is prefortified with vitamin A. Experiments are under way to grow coffee beans that are decaffeinated on the bush, tobacco that is nicotine-free, and cotton that is precolored to pop out in blues or yellows, as well as drought-resistant plants. The initial GM seeds that were marketed, however, focused on making life easier for the farmer: Monsanto's Roundup Ready line, for instance, is specifically matched to Monsanto's popular Roundup herbicide, allowing crops to be drenched with the chemical with no harm to the plant. The theory was that by making the plants "herbicide-tolerant," farmers could more effectively get rid of weeds with fewer applications of Roundup, and yields would improve. However, studies reveal that use of herbicide for GM crops is actually way up, yields of GM plants are often lower than normal plants,[10] and the GM plants' pollen is drifting, contaminating non-GM fields, and breeding with wild species: There are reports of weeds reproducing with the herbicide-tolerant plants and creating super-weeds that just don't want to die.

"It's a very traditional system. When [a farmer] buys seed, he also enters into a licensing agreement with Monsanto for the use of that particular gene. . . . That's a license fee that he pays on an annual basis."

—MONSANTO CEO HUGH GRANT, IN 2003, GIVING AN INTERESTING
INTERPRETATION TO THE CONCEPT OF "TRADITIONAL"[11]

The problem, as the company's foes see it, isn't just that Monsanto is cooking up new gene combos that could threaten the environment. Just as disturbing is the company's protectionist policy toward its patented seeds. In a move that revolutionizes agriculture, Monsanto's genetically engineered seeds aren't purchased outright. Their "genetic information" is leased for one growing season: Farmers are forced to sign contracts that say they won't hold on to the kernels of DNA or collect seeds that result from the crops—an idea that is anathema in developing countries, and ticks off plenty of farmers in the United States as well. If a farmer does cling to Monsanto seed, he is sued. If pollen blows over and contaminates his land, he is sued. Even if his competitor plants some Monsanto seeds on his land, or simply calls the Monsanto hotline with a false tip, he might be sued.

SEED SPIES

Across the heartland of America, Monsanto spies are traipsing, snapping photos, jotting notes, and snipping samples slipped into plastic bags. To ensure that everybody who is growing crops from Monsanto seeds has paid that season's seed "rent," Monsanto sends out private investigators and also encourages farmers to turn in their neighbors via a toll-free hotline. The company has initiated legal proceedings against hundreds of farmers, many of whom claim they did not plant the seeds and did not want them in their fields. Take the case of Percy Schmeiser, a Canadian farmer who was dragged to court when some plants from Monsanto canola seeds were discovered in his field in 1998. Although Schmeiser wasn't charged with stealing Monsanto's seeds per se, it was alleged that some of the canola seeds he'd planted from his previous year's crop had been contaminated with Monsanto seeds—and that he should have noticed when he planted them. He was required to pay a licensing fee, a portion of his profits, as well as legal fees, for a grand total of over $500,000.[12] Same goes for Indiana farmer Troy Roush, a former advocate of Monsanto's GM products. In 2001, Monsanto slapped him with a suit claiming he was saving his seed; even though Monsanto ultimately dropped the charge, it cost Roush nearly $400,000 in lawyer fees.

"What you are seeing is not just a consolidation of seed companies, it's really a consolidation of the entire food chain."

—ROBERT FRALEY, COPRESIDENT OF MONSANTO[13]

Furthering the critics' case that Monsanto is on a quest for world domination of the agro market is Monsanto's recent seed company shopping spree. After buying out such global giants as Seminis, DeKalb, Asgrow, and Holden Seed—

as well as seed giants in Brazil, India, and Indonesia—Monsanto now controls over 30 percent of the global corn seed market, along with 29 percent of the global soybean seed market.

Monsanto also holds the patent on Terminator seeds: These seeds produce plants with infertile seeds that won't yield anything if planted. The very idea of the "suicide seeds" caused furor in developing countries, where seeds are saved as a valuable resource and farmers can't typically afford to buy new ones each year. Farmers in India were so infuriated that many attacked Monsanto's greenhouses and offices. Monsanto postponed introduction of the Terminator seeds as a result, but still has that trick up its sleeve.

FRIENDS IN HIGH PLACES

Being a former employee for Monsanto doesn't seem to hurt when it comes to getting a job in DC and vice versa: High-ranking government employees have a way of showing up on Monsanto's board of directors. Here are a few examples of Monsanto's "revolving doors" with the U.S. government:

- **Charles Burson:** Currently Monsanto's executive vice president, secretary, and chief counsel, Burson served as assistant to the president as well as chief of staff and legal counsel to the vice president during the Clinton administration.
- **Rufus Yerxa** (2002–present): Formerly Monsanto's chief legal counsel on international affairs, Yerxa is the WTO's deputy director-general, the number two position.
- USDA head **Ann Veneman** (2000–04): A former board member of Calgene—the biotech outfit that lost its shirt on the bioengineered Flavr Savr tomato and which Monsanto soon thereafter bought—Veneman rah-rahed for bioengineered agriculture throughout her term.
- Supreme Court Justice **Clarence Thomas:** After serving as assistant attorney general of Missouri, became in-house attorney for Monsanto in 1977.
- **Linda Fisher:** Second-in-command at the Environmental Protection Agency, Fisher was Monsanto's governmental strategist in charge of countering public concerns about GM food.
- **William Ruckelshaus:** Two-time administrator of the EPA, sat on Monsanto's board of directors between his two EPA terms.
- **Marcia Hale:** Former assistant to the president and director of intergovernmental affairs, Hale works as Monsanto's director of international affairs.
- **Mickey Kantor:** U.S. trade representative (1993–97) and U.S. Secretary of Commerce (1996–97), Kantor tried to steamroll EU concerns about U.S. hormone-riddled beef and filed complaints with the WTO on the matter. Welcomed onto Monsanto's board of directors in 1997.

Whatever the reason, whether the U.S. government truly believes that GM foods are the key to human survival or that they're a way for American companies to increase the country's dominance on the planet, there is no mistaking that the federal government, supportive of biotech foods from the start, is positively churlish about the matter lately. Never mind that idea that the consumer is always right: The U.S. government is apparently trying to force acceptance of Monsanto's controversial products, making the United States look as much a bully as Monsanto itself.

> President Bush, like President Clinton before him, has demanded that the EU learn to love GM food or at least stop spreading the word about its concerns. "For the sake of a continent threatened by famine [Africa], I urge the European governments to end their opposition to biotechnology," he pleaded in 2003. "We should encourage the spread of safe, effective biotechnology to win the fight against global hunger." European fears about the matter, he added, were "unfounded" and "unscientific."

Behind the Scenes

Not all is coming up genetically modified roses for Monsanto. The company, until recently at least, was scared. Monsanto has been such a hot potato that it went through three CEOs in four years. The biotech food business is at a critical, make-or-break juncture, and some enterprises just aren't panning out. In 2004, Monsanto announced that after years of research, it would not release its GM wheat: U.S. farmers said they didn't want to risk GM being rejected by foreign countries the same way their GM corn has been. Monsanto ditched plans for its low-oil frying potato because fast food restaurants said they didn't want it. The company gave up on Europe, and shut down most operations there. Rather than risk the possibility of arrests, in 2004 the company contacted the Department of Justice and confessed that a company rep in Indonesia had bribed an official with $50,000 to ease the entry for GM crops—an admission that was costly: The Department of Justice slapped Monsanto with a $1.5 million fine. Its much publicized marriage with Pharmacia in 1999 was a bitter romance: The drug giant tossed a crippled Monsanto back six months later, and ran off with Monsanto's pharmaceutical division, Searle. The Department of Justice blocked Monsanto's move to buy up cottonseed company Delta and Pine Land in 2000, and then Delta and Pine Land sued Monsanto unsuccessfully for breach of contract. And then Friends of the Earth got ahold of some information about Starlink corn that made the entire food industry buckle at the knees.

STARLINK

Not all GM food growing in fields across America is alike. Some fields yield crops for humans. Some lesser-quality crops, such as ones that may contain allergens, yield crops for animal feed. And some fields are growing GM plants used to make drugs. The problem is, they sometimes get mixed up. Starlink corn, a GM brand sold by Aventis, a competitor in the life sciences industry, was supposed to be animal feed. But it ended up in such foodstuffs as Frito-Lay corn chips and Taco Bell taco shells. Nobody knows exactly how it happened: Perhaps wind blew pollen into cornfields meant for humans. Maybe somebody mixed up the cargos. But in September 2000, when Friends of the Earth got a hot tip and a testing machine for genes, they discovered that 1 percent of certain corn products on grocery store shelves contained Starlink corn, and demanded a recall. From there, it turned into chaos: Corn growers sued Aventis for contaminating their crops. Consumers sued Taco Bell and Frito-Lay. Taco Bell sued corn growers and Aventis. Lawyers grew rich as millions were shucked out from all sides, and even the federal government was forced to dole out millions to help farmers replant crops. Aventis sold off its biotech unit to Bayer CropSciences. For a few months, it looked liked the whole industry was doomed. But an answer was just around the corner: Its name was Cargill.

Cargill, the largest grain hauler in the world, stepped in to save Monsanto's day. Because it held overseas market captive, it could deliver whatever it wanted, including GM corn, to Europe. And it offered a market for GM corn and soybeans, which Cargill itself made into syrup and oil. Plus it developed new Monsanto products, such as a transgenic oil from canola seeds. In short, Cargill saved the GM industry by saving Monsanto when it was just about to do a major nosedive. And by 2005, the aphids were dropping off and Monsanto began blooming: Sales shot up over 25 percent from the year before, and the purchase of Seminis Seeds boosted Monsanto even higher, making it an ever fiercer giant whose steps make many farmers shudder wherever it stomps.

Monsanto has a few lingering woes, however.

- The company is still paying damages for the use of Agent Orange in Vietnam. Since the 1980s, Monsanto has been paying millions of dollars in compensation to settle class action suits brought by Vietnam vets who have suffered health effects from exposure to Agent Orange—and more cases are being filed.
- Forty years of chemical spills and PCB pollution in Anniston, Alabama, have caught up with Monsanto. The company's pollution from the 1930s to 1971 has caused assorted health ailments in residents, including cancers.

More than 20,000 Anniston residents filed a class action suit against Monsanto, which in 2002 was slapped with more than $600 million in fines.

The company is now breaking new ground, moving into Argentina, Brazil, India, and Indonesia. Monsanto is intent on expansion and bringing its panacea to the world, like it or not. Wherever you live, whether you know it or not, food from Monsanto's continuing bioengineering experiment will probably soon be coming to a grocery store or a restaurant near you.

 Cargill: The Invisible Link

Notable Numbers

▶ $62.9 billion: Revenues (2004)[14]
▶ 59: Number of countries where Cargill has operations
▶ 42 percent: Proportion of U.S. corn Cargill exports in a typical year
▶ #1: Cargill ranking among those awarded contracts to deliver U.S. food aid

No American company better illustrates the problem of concentration—holding too much power in one sector of the economy—than Cargill, an agricultural giant that has swallowed up most of its competition. Cargill serves not only as an international food conveyor belt, hauling grain from farms in the United States, Canada, and South America to destinations abroad, it also manufactures food staples along the way. Never mind that much of its business is unglamorous—from beef rendering to making mystery filler foods like lecithin, "soy protein," "palm kernel oil," and emulsifiers. It is the most powerful company you've probably never noticed. This lone company commands so much clout that if Cargill makes a decision about our food—for example, that genetically modified food is desirable—then the rest of us can just eat it, so to speak.

Secretive Cargill is the largest private company in the United States.

HOGGING THE MARKET

Industry analysts often wince when they report on the grip Cargill has on global food markets. This company alone provides 10 percent of the world's salt, nearly one-third of Europe's sweeteners, and has virtually cornered the market on starch additives in food and drugs. But that's diddly in the mind of Cargill, which strives "to have market dominance [and] leadership in the [food and agricultural] business." Cargill is:

- #1 global oilseed manufacturer
- #2 U.S. beef and turkey processor
- #3 U.S. pork processor
- #2 global supplier of corn meal, flour, and grits
- #3 global supplier of wheat flour and pasta
- #2 global animal feed producer

Cargill, in short, controls far too many aspects of the food industry, warn analysts, making other links in the food chain respond to its demands and giving it plenty of opportunities for price manipulations.

Always in a mood to shop, Cargill bought out one of its main competitors, Continental Grain, in 1999. To do so, Cargill was forced to give up a grain storage unit here and there by the Department of Justice, but the acquisition went through—greatly alarming farmers and industry watchers, who noted that the merged company would control over half of the domestic corn market alone, giving it the ability to dictate what prices it pays farmers.

The Minnesota-based company that started in the grain storage business 140 years ago is still family-owned and plays up its Midwestern friend-of-the-farmer image, but its heart is coldly corporate. Given its operations all along the food chain, Cargill has the muscle to call for changes in the industry to make it healthier or at least more sustainable, but Cargill snuggles up to many a cause that consumer groups oppose.

> ► As a corporate farmer that alone controls the majority of the different meats on our plates, the company endorses the cram-them-in and shoot-them-up-with-growth-drugs style of industrial animal farming—that is both unethical and unhealthy for the environment and the consumer.
> ► This company, obviously believing that size does matter, makes its biggest U.S. deals with the corporate farmers that drench their crops in chemicals and shove the little guys out of the picture.

▶ Likewise, Cargill ignores consumer concerns about genetically modified food and enthusiastically embraces the biotech companies, launching joint ventures with them to develop designer seeds that require Cargill-manufactured fertilizers.

"For the 2005 growing season, Cargill will be contracting with Iowa growers for up to 50,000 acres of [Monsanto's genetically modified] VISTIVE soybean production. Cargill will pay a premium to producers who grow VISTIVE soybeans under contract, then it will crush and sell the processed soybean oil to food companies."

—MONSANTO PRESS RELEASE, OFFERING A HANDY OVERVIEW
OF HOW CARGILL SERVES AS MIDDLEMAN[15]

THE GENETICALLY MODIFIED ENTRY POINT

If you're wondering how it is that most food in the United States contains genetically modified products, look to Cargill. In the course of creating its generic foodstuff like canola oil and corn syrup, Cargill is the conduit for introducing genetically modified food to our tables in gravy and ketchup, canned soup and bread. A partner in assorted Monsanto ventures, Cargill enthusiastically buys genetically altered corn, soybeans, and canola—saying it's up to the FDA to ensure such products are safe. (The FDA meanwhile shirks responsibility for testing, saying it is up to the producer to ensure they are safe.) The company has also been crucial in getting genetically modified products to the international market. Never mind that many consumers worldwide don't want GM products in their food: Manufacturers who buy from Cargill (and most do) find themselves facing Cargill's pro-GM policy. If they don't want GM corn or soybeans, they have to pay more or hire another shipper. And with that same bullyish attitude, Cargill also pushed GM food into Africa. Cargill was the agent behind the 2002 controversy in which genetically modified corn, supplied and shipped by Cargill—as the major shipper of U.S. food aid, as well as a supplier of the grain for that aid—was rejected by several African countries.

The most disheartening aspect of Cargill, which rose to the top via the bread belt, is its seemingly uncaring treatment of farmers, particularly the small farmer, whom it gouges—strong-arming them to sell at painfully low prices while ignoring the effects the company's food dumping have on the local market. The company's control on nearly every facet of food production and its compulsive chomping up of companies has many complaining that this monster needs to be broken up. In the meantime, Cargill only seems to grow fatter and more influential—

dictating what Americans and the rest of the world will eat, whether it is good for us or not.

> Given that so many in agriculture equate Cargill with "rip-off," many were galled that Daniel Pearson—Cargill's assistant vice president for public affairs—was appointed by President Bush to represent farmers on the International Trade Commission.

PART III

SHADOWY STUFF

10. BRIEFING:

Spooks, Sneaks, and Snitches

They're watching us, peering at us from streets lined with so many hidden video cameras that a New Yorker makes taped appearances hundreds of times every day. They're tracing our movements via our phones, now loaded with satellite tracking devices that spell out our precise locations. They're taking notes on our bank accounts, they're monitoring our credit cards, they're studying where we stop on the Internet and how long we stay; they can read our private e-mails and instant messages; they can view all the innards of our computers via spyware—unsolicited software that surreptitiously latches onto our computers, worming its way into our files and sending reports back to its "owner"—gaining access to correspondence, reports, Social Security numbers, and any numbers of secrets.

> Federal authorities "gag" our banks from telling us, but anyone receiving a wire deposit of over $10,000 is now subject to a security review. Wire deposits from foreign countries are also regarded as potentially suspicious.

> Every time we fly, are stopped by highway patrol, or cross a border in or out of the country, our names are checked against a federal "watch list." Kept by the FBI's Terrorist Screening Center, the list holds over 120,000 names of Americans and foreigners—people who may or may not be terrorists. The government won't tell us if we are on the list, or what criteria they use to place people on the "watch list."[1]

They know what we're wheeling around in our grocery carts, and the restaurants where we dine; they follow us when we fly and track our destinations; they even want to color-code our personal "terrorist risk factor." Whether through chips in our passports or retinal imaging for security, they are constantly developing new ways to keep tabs on us and what we're doing, even if we don't leave the house. They are our employers, our bankers, our retailers, but most of all they are our new post-9/11 government, which is fast becoming the biggest info-Peeping Tom of all.

The USA Patriot Act, passed October 2001, gave government authorities the right to peek at our e-mails and demand that libraries, hospitals, and banks hand over our records without having to convince a judge that there was a "probable cause" to do so. In June 2005, the House of Representatives voted to snip investigators' abilities to demand personal records.

The government keeps on increasing its power to snoop on us. In May 2005, for instance, Congress passed the Real ID Act, which mandates a new format for state driver's licenses, creating what is essentially a national identity card. Drivers now need to provide a birth certificate, Social Security number, and proof of residence to get a license. These cards will also carry encoded data able to be read by a machine—which means they will probably carry a radio frequency ID (RFID) chip. Given the controversy surrounding the idea of an encoded card and a national ID, sneaky legislators tacked the measure onto a "must-pass" bill authorizing an additional $82 billion for Iraq.[2]

 ## Machines That Snitch

Why are government agencies, and other interested parties, spying on us so much? Because they can. The latest tools that shadow us, revealing our whereabouts and everyday lives:

Global Positioning Systems (For Locating Us)

The GPS chips now in late-model cars and cellular phones transmit radio waves to satellites, which beam back information telling us—and anyone else who cares to know—our precise location. The same GPS trackers that allow modern 911 centers to pick up our geographical markers can also be used by stalkers, jealous spouses, curious bosses, and even police, who can just slap a GPS chip on our cars and follow every turn in our day. The U.S. military likes them too:

They've used GPS to locate suspected al-Qaeda and to target them with missile-firing drones.

Rental car customers may find hefty fines slapped onto their bills for speeding or crossing state lines, thanks to blabbing black boxes that record location and speed in the vehicles. Small print on the rental contract may prohibit crossing state lines and exceeding the speed limit—and that information shows up when the car is turned in.[3]

Backscatters (For Seeing Our Bodies)

It's the comic book promise of X-ray vision come true. Backscatters, essentially low-radiation X-rays, peer through garments. Forget the idea of "private parts" being private anymore: If all goes as planned by Homeland Security, airline security will soon be able to see the size of our nipples, our cellulite dimples, the shape and/or length of our genitalia, as well as any "personal" items worn under clothes. These machines show so much that airports are considering curtaining them off so fellow passengers don't get a free peep show. With the machines' downloadable records, celebrities are at special risk: It won't take long, imagines privacy activist Bill Scannell, before the details about Mel Gibson's "gibson" or Madonna's "maternal gear" are floating around on the Internet.

Radio Frequency Identification (RFID) (For Reading Our Records)

Already used in the E-Z pass system on toll roads, where they scan the records of the vehicles that pass (as well as the name and address of the registrant), information-laden RFID tags are also common in shipping, where they keep tabs on the location and contents of containers. Retailers, such as Wal-Mart, are trying out products, such as razors or clothes, with embedded RFID tags that allow them to track the product through the distribution network—and through the store aisles.

Plans are under way for U.S. passports to soon be ornamented with info-rich RFID chips. They may also be required on foreign visas to visit the United States. Allowing officials to know when their holders enter and leave, IDs with RFID devices also provide names, addresses, and vital statistics with the quick wave of a scanner. What's creepy: Anybody who passes by within a few feet with an RFID reader can peek at our records, too.

Biometrics (For Identifying Us)

To ensure that we are indeed whom we claim to be, biometric measures such as hand shape, digital fingerprints, and the intricate designs of our irises are being adopted by companies as "biometric ID"; they're already used in some corporations for employee entry and are voluntary additions for "quick pass" border crossings to Canada. Biometric measures will probably also be added to our upcoming national ID cards.

Physical Readers (For Tracking and Identifying Us)

Surveillance technology, including face recognition technology, is scanning us in U.S. cities; face recognition is frequently used in sports arenas and airports. More of these citizen surveillance systems are being deployed in cities across the country, thanks to increased funding from the Homeland Security Agency.[4] Researchers for the Pentagon's experimental DARPA program are working on means to identify us by recognizing our gait, and in the future, sensors may deduce who we are just by our smell. Also on the drawing board: machines that can detect brain waves, to ferret out those who may be threatening or capable of violence (or who may be simply in a cranky mood).

"Clicking on a link in a spam email is the equivalent of handing a burglar the keys to your house."

—DAVID ROBERTS, CHIEF EXECUTIVE AT TIF[5]

E-Mail "Sniffers" and Spyware (For Reading Our Communications)

The FBI has been "sniffing" e-mail—to investigate possible terrorism, fraud, and child pornography activities—since the late 1990s, although back then a court order was required;[6] now, thanks to the Patriot Act, the agency has far more freedom. The agency also employs keystroke-reading devices that allow agents to know what we are writing. The FBI, however, is not alone in this snooping activity: Spyware and keystroke-logging viruses can invade our computers from any number of sources. They may:

▶ Be attached to downloads
▶ Be introduced from a link
▶ Invade on their own, prying into cyberspace "holes" on DSL and stealthily entering our computers
▶ Lurk in normal-seeming e-mail sent from someone who wants to log your computer activity

And anybody can buy it—you can download spyware from the Internet for as little as seventy-nine dollars.

Even though spyware dangerously intrudes into our privacy, and may lead to identity theft (it can log passwords and banking information), the purchase and use of spyware is currently entirely legal.[7]

> *A recent survey of AOL users showed that 80 percent of their computers were infected with spyware—although very few of the users knew it.*[8]

September 11 made one thing clear: U.S. intelligence agencies were not connecting all the dots, and to the extent that they were, the White House wasn't listening. Even though much of the information portending what would happen was actually there—pilots that don't want to learn how to land was one clue—there was no framework to pull it all together and give it urgent meaning. In the race to prevent another attack, government agencies not only wanted to amass mountains of information on everyone in the country, and quite a few overseas, they also began looking at novel ways to rope this random information into one tidy package. To achieve this they looked to data mining—harvesting huge amounts of records—to draw portraits of individuals and predict their future behavior.

THE MATRIX FORMULA: DANGEROUS DEDUCTIONS?

Self-admitted former cocaine smuggler, ex–skyscraper painter, and general computer genius Hank Asher helped launch the national data-mining debate. In the hours after the September 2001 attacks, the then-owner of data-mining firm Seisint (since sold to LexisNexis) plugged in assorted "terrorist profile" parameters for the over 450 million individuals for whom his company had compiled detailed records.[9]

Asher created loose portraits of potential terrorists using such measures as:

- Foreign-born Muslim men
- Entered the United States within previous two years
- Recently received driver's licenses
- Studied at pilot schools

He came up with a list of 419 names. Of those, one of them indeed was listed as a September 11 terrorist, Marwan al-Shehhi, the pilot of the second plane. Five others on the list of names Asher generated had also been red-flagged by the government. However, many of the other 413 men on Asher's list—who may have shared little in common with the hijackers, except for being new Muslim arrivals—were investigated, arrested, detained, and/or deported.[10]

Asher's profiling system, soon known as MATRIX—for Multi-State Anti-Terrorism Information Exchange—was officially launched in 2003 as an $8 million Homeland Security test project in sixteen states. By 2005, all sixteen had dropped out due to protests over privacy. Rest assured, however, that whether it's using the MATRIX system or not, the government will continue its data-mining activities.

"The government is outsourcing our constitutional rights. They are hiring private data-mining companies to collect and keep information on us because it would be highly illegal if the government did it. These private companies now decide if we will get a job, can board a plane, or have the right to vote."

—BILL SCANNELL, PRIVACY ACTIVIST (DONTSPYONUS.COM)[11]

Once the treasured information of marketers, retailers, insurers, banks, and potential employers wanting background checks, these private profiles of us—showing our credit ratings, purchasing habits, court records, and belongings (guns, planes, boats, cars, and houses)—are now going into the hands of the federal government, where at least five dozen agencies rely on outside firms, such as ChoicePoint, to dig up the info for their records. The problem isn't simply that these data miners dig deep trying to pry the skeletons out of our closets, it's that their information is frequently dead wrong.[12] But even if the profile about us from a data-mining company is erroneous, once we've been branded by these guys—whether they've falsely rapped us for a bad driving record or a felony conviction—setting the record straight can be a difficult feat.

"ChoicePoint supported the U.S. Marshals Service in Operation Falcon, which served approximately 10,000 warrants in a single day for crimes ranging from murder to white collar fraud."

—CHOICEPOINT VICE PRESIDENT DON McGUFFEY[13]

CHOICEPOINT: THE GOVERNMENT'S TOP CHOICE FOR FLAWED INFORMATION?

A data-mining firm helped George Bush win his controversial 2000 election. As reported by investigative journalist Greg Palast, that data-mining firm (now part of ChoicePoint) was hired by the state of Florida to "purge" its voting list and determine who was not eligible to vote for the 2000 elections. The firm handed over a list of fifty-seven thousand names that had been red-flagged due to such things as criminal records and voter registration in more than one county. Problem: At least fifty thousand of those voters were listed in error, says Palast.[14,15] (ChoicePoint disputes that figure, but says only the state of Florida knows for sure.) And Palast says a large percentage of the voters who were disqualified were also black Democrats[16] (who may have tilted the vote to Gore in this presidential election, where George W. Bush "won" by a few hundred votes). The data-mining company confused names and information, including outdated records and those that had been expunged: There are reports that the company also used parameters such as misdemeanor crimes and unpaid parking tickets as reasons to prohibit residents from casting their votes.[17]

More recently, ChoicePoint, which admits that it does not verify or update information such as criminal records, made another bad call. The Georgia-based company sold its information—including names, addresses, and credit card numbers of 145,000 U.S. citizens—to members of an organized crime outfit.[18,19] Even though it realized the goof in 2004, ChoicePoint didn't notify the endangered parties for over six months. At least 5,000 of those became victims of fraud and/or identity theft. And ChoicePoint has made such blunders before.

11. POST-9/11 WORLD:

Securing the Patriots

Agencies: FBI, Homeland Security
Movers: John Ashcroft, John Negroponte, Alberto Gonzales,
Michael Chertoff
Instruments: USA Patriot Act, executive orders

Notable Numbers

- 5,000: Number of suspects rounded up and detained after 9/11 attacks
- 39: Number of those suspects convicted for terrorism[1]

Snapshot

Yes, Americans were panicked. In the days when Ground Zero still smoldered, most Americans were willing to kiss off a few rights to prevent another terrorist attack. But no, it has not been proven that Americans and national security have benefited from the hysterical banter or questionable actions of the U.S. government since the fall of 2001, which perhaps needlessly transformed an open society into a quasi–police state. Whether signed by executive order, passed into law by Congress, amended in the Constitution, or simply cleared by White House legal counsel, the many dubious new policies put into place in the months following the September 11 attacks include:

- The concept of applying the status of right-less "enemy combatants" to thousands of foreign nationals simply suspected (but not proven) of having information and/or terrorists links, allowing the United States to imprison them indefinitely without charge and without releasing their names (520 still held at Guantánamo Bay without charge as of June 2005).

- An executive order allowing military tribunals with proceedings closed to the public (not used in the United States since World War II).
- The secretly authorized practice of releasing Iraqi prisoners of war or suspected "enemy combatants" to countries where they would be tortured while in custody (Jordan, Syria, and Uzbekistan among them).
- The secretly authorized practice of U.S. officials using interrogation techniques such as hooding, military attack dogs, and "stress positions" on prisoners.[2]
- A Justice Department rule allowing eavesdropping between attorney and client.
- The passage of laws, including the USA Patriot Act, which gave the government the right to wiretap our phone conversations, read our e-mail, demand sales records of our purchases, monitor our computer activity, and in other ways spy on U.S. citizens (and foreigners) without having to get a warrant or prove justifiable grounds for suspicion.
- The creation of the Information Awareness Office to run a creepy program called Total Information Awareness, to put all information it can get its mitts on—IQ and grades from high school, psychiatric records and pharmaceutical purchases, home ownership and delinquent bill paying—into a data-mining program. The privacy-shredding TIA program was ostensibly killed in 2004—but it is reportedly now tucked away as a classified "black project," and still collecting data.
- A revamped Transportation Security Agency, now under the auspices of Homeland Security, which tried to implement an airline traveler prescreening program regarded by many as Nazi-like—CAPPS II.

RED FLAG
Security Extremes in the Air

What Next—a Yellow Star?

Nobody questions the need for airline security, but the system that Homeland Security's Transportation Security Agency got very close to implementing in spring 2004 struck many as preposterous. For months, the transportation agency that oversees airline security had hemmed, hawed, and out-and-out lied about the passenger prescreening program it had in the works, which was developed in part by Lockheed Martin. In the weeks leading up to the launch of the new flight security program, TSA director Asa Hutchinson declined to reveal what sources the airlines would be using in background checks, while assuring the public in January 2004 that, wherever the information came from, passengers need not worry—no information would stay on a permanent record. That, like so much of the program, called CAPPS II (Computer-Assisted Passenger Prescreening System II), was apparently hogwash. Press reports later revealed that initial plans called for keeping records on passengers for fifty years. In fact so much of what TSA has said is so far from the truth that its own agency issued a report slamming it for near-constant deceit.

The CAPPS II system planned to work like this:

▶ A customer provides name, address, telephone number, and Social Security number when he or she books an airline ticket.

▶ That information is relayed to a commercial data-mining company, which can bring credit records, home ownership, medical records, promptness in paying utility bills, and any number of other parameters into the mix. Data-mining companies, which have proven that they make numerous errors and questionable assumptions, then issues a number—say, from 1 to 100—of each passenger's perceived security risk.

▶ Based on the data-mining number, the Transportation Security Agency then runs additional checks from government databases—which can draw on anything from high school grades to unpaid parking tickets to classified information. TSA then color-codes each passenger, along with the number. Green is all clear, yellow means additional security required, and red means call the police. And passengers have no idea of their standing until they show up at the airport, possibly facing arrest.

Without notifying their loyal customers, several airlines, including Delta, JetBlue, and Northwest, voluntarily handed over their passengers' information in 2002 to the government or to a number of data-mining companies, some of whom were competing for the CAPPS II contract, resulting in an uproar, boycotts, and a few class action lawsuits.

When the General Accountability Office released a report in February 2004 saying seven out of eight privacy issues had not been addressed in the Transportation Security Agency's plan, Congress roared, and essentially put a lid on CAPPS II, at least temporarily. Another extensive information-gathering prescreening system is in the works, and TSA is trying to get it off the ground for fall 2005, though many are already concerned that it too lacks transparency.

> *No hijacking attempts on U.S. airlines have been reported since 2001, leading some to believe that the system we currently have in place works well enough.*

The paranoia about passengers, however, isn't focused solely on those getting on planes. Who gets off planes is just as big a concern, and foreigners and U.S. citizens alike have been harassed and sometimes prevented entry to the country on unusual grounds:

- Kathryn Karrington, a fifty-two-year-old special education teacher from Florida, was arrested at the Tampa International Airport in fall 2004, where her bookmark—which had small lead weights sewn in the ends—was seized as a security threat. She initially faced criminal charges and a $10,000 fine for carrying a concealed weapon, though charges were dropped several months later.
- Australian reporter Sue Smethurst, who'd come to the United States to interview singer Olivia Newton-John for women's magazine *New Idea,* was red-flagged as a threat in 2003. Although she had entered the United States via Los Angeles's airport eight times previously with no problems, her 2003 entry was denied, and she was fingerprinted, handcuffed, subjected to several body searches, and detained for fourteen hours before being shoved back on a flight to Australia. U.S. Immigration, which questioned her, said that she lacked the correct paperwork.
- Greek professor Eugene "Venios" Angelopoulos, scheduled to speak at New York University in 2003, was handcuffed, put in leg chains, and detained for over five hours at JFK while questioned by the FBI about his attitudes about the United States and his knowledge about the Greek November 17 group. He was finally allowed in.
- Singer Cat Stevens, aka Yusuf Islam, famous in the UK for his charitable work, was sent packing back to Britain, apparently for fitting a dangerous profile: He was a converted Muslim. (Even British Foreign Secretary Jack Straw balked at the inhospitable treatment toward a man who had done nothing, and called Colin Powell to complain.)
- Canadian telecommunications engineer Maher Arar, en route from Tunisia to his home in Ottawa, was changing planes in New York's JFK Airport in 2002 when he was stopped, detained, and soon put on a plane to Syria, where he had been born. In Syria, he was imprisoned and beaten for the next eleven months—and nobody can tell him why. According to the *New York Times*, Arar was on a watch list, but he was never charged with a

crime and investigations have yielded no explanation—except that he was deemed suspicious.[3]

Agent of Change
Bill Scannell: Fighting the Government's Demand to Know All

It was just a short Associated Press item posted on the Internet on a late Friday afternoon, that time of the week when news items are slipped in for minimum effect. When Bill Scannell, vice president of communications at an East Coast software company, read those three paragraphs in March 2003, they so upset him that his first impulse was to hightail it out of the country. His second impulse, after his wife vetoed the first, was to stay in the United States and fight a change in airline security screening that struck him as fascist. Homeland Security's new Transportation Security Agency had just announced that the color-coding system used for that day's terrorism forecast would now be applied to every person who stepped on a plane. This "green, yellow, red" plan would be determined by

Privacy rights activist Bill Scannell. "How did nineteen mass murderers turn the nation I love into frothing lunatics who are willing to sell off their birthrights to live in a cage?"

credit records and home ownership as well as federal, state, and local criminal records, which meant that anything from a parking ticket to lipstick ripped off in high school might keep a person from flying. And the group making the initial calls on who might be dangerous and who might not were private data-mining companies, infamous for their incorrect and outdated records. Worse, this privacy-invading concept, put together by Lockheed Martin, wasn't just on some drawing board: Delta Airlines had been selected to launch a trial of this security measure, called CAPPS II.

"I'd seen this bad movie before," says Scannell, who had worked as a military intelligence agent in West Berlin and a journalist in Communist Czechoslovakia, the Balkans under dictator Tito, and South Africa under apartheid. Keeping files on the citizenry smacked to him of the repression he'd previously associated only with foreign regimes. "A totalitarian government," Scannell says he'd discovered abroad, "does not inform its citizens that it is a totalitarian government." The privacy-stripping security change so alarmed Scannell that over the weekend he launched a Web site to protest it—striking out specifically at Delta. Within forty-eight hours of launching www.BoycottDelta.com (with the motto "Delta: Less legroom, no privacy"), Scannell's likeness was beaming across the country on CNN, hundreds of thousands were hitting the Web site, and coast to coast the media were spotlighting the CAPPS II security measure that days before had been poised to slip under the radar. Within weeks, Delta's name had disappeared from the CAPPS II volunteer program.

> "I'm just a guy with a cell phone, a laptop, and a big mouth."
>
> —BILL SCANNELL, WHO QUIT HIS PUBLIC RELATIONS JOB TO
> BECOME A FULL-TIME VOLUNTEER PRIVACY RIGHTS ACTIVIST

Scannell's work wasn't over, however. JetBlue was stepping in to take the program for a trial spin. Scannell discovered that, unbeknownst to the media, JetBlue—and several other airlines—had handed over detailed lists on millions of its passengers to the army—and a bevy of private contractors vying for Homeland Security jobs. Scannell drew up a new game plan: He launched Dontspyonus.com—another sarcasm-infused site, this one calling for concerned Americans to pressure their congressmen to kill the CAPPS II program, scheduled for takeoff in spring 2004. Several months later CAPPS II was dead—and the involved airlines were facing class action suits from irate passengers.

These measures to use data mining to assess our threat haven't gone away. The soon-to-launch "Secure Flight" program unveiled by the Transportation Security Agency is nearly as extreme: Scannell calls it "the corpse of CAPPS II with a big yellow smiley face stapled to its chest." He launched another Web site, Unsecureflight.com—and congressmen may block this program too. And when the State Department announced new RFID chips in passports, Scannell made such a stink that the passport project was postponed.

Some of Scannell's biggest support has come from conservatives: Architect of the Right movement Paul Weyrich, a privacy rights supporter, called to say Scannell was a fine, upstanding American, and Scannell is now a regular on "End Times" religious radio shows, where RFID passports and national ID cards are feared as the mark of the beast.

Scannell says what is happening, and what he is fighting, stems from fear, and the government is stirring it up to grab more control and keep hold of the reins. "The Constitution doesn't cease to exist when we are scared," says Scannell, who tried to block Congressional passage of the national "Real ID" program—calling for chips in our driver's licenses—with his site UnrealID.com. "There are people both in and out of government that want us to remain scared—either to make money off of us or so they keep their political power." His recommendation is that we don't buy into their manipulations, and that we don't kiss off our rights. "There are smart security measures and there are stupid security measures," he adds. And extremist, privacy-invading moves, he believes, fall squarely into the latter category. "These measures have nothing to do with security," he says. "They are about control."

Close-up

Perhaps there should be a law that Congress shall pass no law when it is quivering in its boots. Perhaps the president should sign an executive order barring all presidents from signing executive orders when the country is suffering a collective panic attack. The mood after September 11 opened the door to creating a total, all-seeing surveillance state in the name of protecting the citizens that it now victimizes by spying on.

"We have no privacy anymore."

—Former intelligence employee on the post-9/11 reality for Americans

And now the much more wary citizens of the United States are trying to deal with not only the implications of these invasive measures, but how to turn them back. One of the biggest pushes right now—coming from conservative Republicans as well as progressive left-wingers—is how to modify, or erase, the USA Patriot Act. Over four hundred towns and cities and four state legislatures have already passed ordinances affirming their constitutional rights and prohibiting implementation of the act in their communities. Nevertheless, in July 2005, Congress voted to extend most of its sunset provisions.

The media was barred from Senate hearings on the "enhanced" Patriot Act, but it is believed that one new measure of the act would be to punish any hos-

pital, bank, or library employee who informs a citizen that the FBI is looking at his or her records with imprisonment of up to five years.

The USA Patriot Act (a snappy acronym for "Uniting and Strengthening America by Providing Appropriate Tools Required to Intercept and Obstruct Terrorism") was passed by a panicky Congress, without debate, in October 2001. Legislators now widely acknowledge that prior to passage they didn't really have time to read the act. This civil-rights-stripping law gives the government the right to:

- Snoop at our medical, hospital, and mental health records
- Access our library records
- Take note of our church-going habits
- Wiretap and search our property without probable cause
- Detain non-Americans indefinitely without charge and without notification to their relatives
- Break into our houses and search anything they wish and plant bugs to "tap" our computers, follow our Internet travels, and read our e-mails

2001: END OF AN ERA ONCE KNOWN AS DEMOCRATIC

Constitutional rights that were gutted, damaged, and otherwise sent to the recycling bin by the Patriot Act and executive orders from President George W. Bush include:

- First Amendment: Right to free speech and to assemble without being monitored
- Fourth Amendment: Right to be secure in own house without unreasonable searches
- Fifth and Fourteenth Amendments: Right to due process of law—including, if detained, being formally charged with a crime
- Sixth: Right to speedy and public trial
- Eight: Right to be protected against cruel and unusual punishment

Good news for gun owners: The Patriot Act didn't touch the Second Amendment right to bear arms.

What made many of the new laws even more alarming was that they were designed and ramrodded through Congress by the overzealous U.S. attorney general, John Ashcroft, an ultraright, extremely religious former senator from Missouri who, in his fervor to increase security for the country, showed little regard for upholding basic constitutional rights. In fall 2001, for example, Ashcroft instructed FBI and INS to investigate males with Muslim names, some of which were found simply by looking through phone books.[4]

Fear-mongering, camera-loving, wild-proclamation-prone Ashcroft appeared to have his finger perma-glued to the panic button as he hit the already jittery country with scare campaign after scare campaign, most of which were exaggerated at best, and often enough simply hot air. Besides prompting ulcers and involuntary twitches across the country, Ashcroft created the perfect environment for the passage of his USA Patriot Act. In mid-October 2001, the squat attorney paraded around on the weekend talk show circuit gushing about how his new soon-to-be-passed law would protect the United States from future attacks. In typical puffed-up, loose-cannon style, Ashcroft made those announcements before he had even notified the White House or Congress that he had penned this voluminous, incomprehensible bill.[5]

Since stepping down as attorney general in 2005, supposedly due to health reasons, the fireball Ashcroft is now teaching in the Law School of Regent University, the religious educational institution founded by televangelist Pat Robertson.

Ashcroft, who'd condemned the Clinton administration's 1997 move to extend monitoring of citizens (writing in the *Washington Times* that there "is no reason to hand Big Brother the keys to unlock our e-mail diaries, open our ATM records or translate our international communications")[6] was indignant when the Patriot Act's rights-shredding and privacy-stripping measures elicited protests from those concerned about privacy. Those who didn't swallow his ideas for an all-knowing totalitarian state were the real enemies of freedom, he maintained.

"To those who scare peace-loving people with phantoms of lost liberty, my message is this: Your tactics only aid terrorists—for they erode our national unity and diminish our resolve. They give ammunition to America's enemies, and pause to America's friends. They encourage people of goodwill to remain silent in the face of evil."

—JOHN ASHCROFT IN TESTIMONY BEFORE THE
SENATE JUDICIARY COMMITTEE, DEC. 2001

Ashcroft went on to announce the formation of TIPS, which stood for Terrorism Information and Prevention System, although some speculated it really stood for "Turn In People, Suck-up." Ashcroft believed that the program, wherein he encouraged Americans to spy on and turn in their neighbors, would be readily adopted by the postal service, for one. Postal workers chucked that idea into the dead letter bin, observing that TIPS appeared to have fallen out of a Soviet rule book. Congress killed funding for it in 2003.

ZOOM   John Ashcroft

Member of Council on National Policy
Member of Federalist Society (conservative lawyers group)
Governor of Missouri (1984–92)
U.S. Senator (R-Missouri) (1995–99)
U.S. Attorney General (2001–05)

They preferred a dead man. Missouri voters were so unenthusiastic about John Ashcroft, the Republican candidate for U.S. Senate in 2000, that the majority instead voted for Democrat Mel Carnahan, even though the governor had died in a plane crash two weeks before the election; Carnahan's wife ultimately filled his Senate seat. Ashcroft's stunning defeat, however, freed him up for another far more important position: In 2001, he was appointed U.S. attorney general. The Senate warily confirmed him with a vote of 58 to 42, the lowest senate yea rate in the history of the attorney general job.

> Bush political strategist Karl Rove was an election advisor to Ashcroft in 1994, when the man from Missouri succeeded in grabbing a Senate seat.

In the Department of Justice building, where he reportedly demanded that the bare chest of the twelve-foot statue of Lady Justice be clothed, Ashcroft, a member of the Pentecostal Assembly of God Church, introduced daily prayer meetings and encouraged staff to belt out "Let the Eagle Soar," the rousing anthem that he'd personally penned and set to music. Initially his focus was enforcing drug policy. Favoring mandatory minimum sentences for all drug charges, a return to prayer in schools, and criminalizing abortion even in cases of rape and incest, Ashcroft also demanded that clinics and hospitals turn over names of women who had late-term terminations (request denied).

But it was in the hours after the September 11 attack, when President Bush turned to the attorney general, saying "John, don't let this happen again,"[7] that Ashcroft saw his new calling as the defender of liberty and slayer of evil. His ill-conceived Patriot Act and TIPS programs have ensured that well-meaning Ashcroft will go down along with Joe McCarthy as having created an era as frightening as the evils it was meant to conquer.

"In apprehending Al Muhajir [Jose Padilla] as he sought entry into the United States, we have disrupted an unfolding terrorist plot to attack the United States by exploding a radioactive dirty bomb . . . [thus avoiding] mass death and injury."

—ASHCROFT SHOOTING OFF HIS MOUTH IN RUSSIA, JULY 2002

"I don't think there was actually a plot beyond some fairly loose talk."

—U.S. DEPUTY SECRETARY PAUL WOLFOWITZ, PRONE TO
WILD ASSERTIONS HIMSELF, BUT SUDDENLY SOUNDING LIKE THE
VOICE OF REASON SEVERAL DAYS AFTER ASHCROFT MISSPOKE[8]

While the jury is still out on how effective the new Homeland Security Agency really is, there is little doubt that it was high time to upgrade the intelligence community—and to toss it more funding. The horrifying reality is that prior to 9/11, intelligence was scarcely Internet-savvy—with many FBI agents working on old computers that didn't even offer Internet access.[9]

Believing that the end of the Cold War negated the need for so much overseas intelligence, Congress slashed the intelligence community's budget by 20 percent during the 1990s.

Behind the Scenes

Despite frequent scares, as of July 2005 there has not yet been another major al-Qaeda attack in the United States. While we nervously await some unknown tragedy, we're stuck with a system that now treats its own as terror suspects, and officials who have been happy to pass laws that already seem outdated and draconian. In fact, while we're psychologically sequestered in the land that is feeling increasingly totalitarian, the only thing we may have to fear is our leaders themselves. The new batch of Bush appointees sure hasn't given the country any reason to relax.

- **John Negroponte** (director of national intelligence, 2005–present): The former ambassador to the United Nations, a foreign secret service agent for four decades, and now the head honcho of all spies as director of National Intelligence (a newly created position), Negroponte has shown his abilities to deceive. Among his many dark deeds: During the years he was the ambassador to Honduras (1981–85), he not only ignored the death squads and torture under the hands of military dictator Gen. Álvarez Martínez, he helped further militarize that government, boosting military aid from $4 million to $77 million and setting up so many U.S. military bases that the nation was nicknamed the USS *Honduras*.[10] The reason: to aid and train contras to fight in Nicaragua as part of the Iran-Contra activities, to which he was linked.
- **Alberto Gonzales** (attorney general, 2005–present): Chief counsel to Bush when he was Texas governor, Gonzales wrote up the memos summarizing the cases of those on death row, overlooking and underplaying pertinent facts such as mental retardation or incompetent counsel. In DC, he's demonstrated that same lack of compassion, approving torture for enemy combatants and waving off the Geneva Conventions as "quaint" and "obsolete." While he seemed like Ashcroft lite walking in, he may soon make us miss good ole Johnny Boy. As of July 2005, he is being eyed as a possible Supreme Court judge.
- **Michael Chertoff** (secretary of homeland security, 2005–present): Known as an aggressive political hit man with Democrats and liberals in his sights during his stint as attorney for New Jersey, lawyer Chertoff helped to devise and pen many of the more restrictive acts regarding post-9/11 terror suspects, including working on the legal rulings that the use of torture on suspected terrorists was justified.

RED FLAG
Torture

"I have never ordered torture. I will never order torture. The values of this country are such that torture is not a part of our soul and our being."

—President George W. Bush in June 2004[11]

It should have been obvious what they were going to do, back in fall 2001, when the Bush administration announced that prisoners from the invasion of Afghanistan were going to be flown to a little-used military base in Cuba—Guantánamo Bay. It should have been clear what lay ahead when the administration's legal department, including White House counsel Alberto Gonzales, announced in 2002 that the Geneva Conventions—the international agreements that forbid torture—would not apply to these fighters without uniforms, who would be considered "enemy combatants." We should have known what was happening to the orange-suited prisoners chained and kneeling before barbed wire at Cuba's newly revamped prison, Camp X-Ray.

> "On a couple of occasions, I entered interview rooms to find a detainee chained hand at foot in a fetal position to the floor, with no chair, food, or water. Most times they had urinated or defecated on themselves and had been left there for 18, 24 hours or more. . . . On another occasion, the A/C had been turned off, making the temperature in the unventilated room probably well over 100 degrees. The detainee was almost unconscious on the floor with a pile of hair next to him. He had apparently been literally pulling his own hair out throughout the night."
>
> —FROM AN FBI AGENT REPORT OBTAINED BY THE ACLU UNDER
> THE FREEDOM OF INFORMATION ACT.[12] THE FBI WAS PROTESTING
> AGAINST PRISONER ABUSE LONG BEFORE IT CAME OUT IN THE PRESS.

But the picture wasn't clear. Many Americans didn't know that the use of highly aggressive manners of questioning prisoners had been cleared legally by the Department of Justice. Few would have guessed that these extreme measures of interrogation had apparently been approved from the very top—via secret executive order.[13]

Interpreting Torture

Torture, as defined by the Department of Justice under John Ashcroft in August 2002, "must be equivalent in intensity to the pain accompanying serious physical injury, such as organ failure, impairment of bodily function or even death. For purely mental pain or suffering to amount to torture under section 2340, it must result in significant psychological harm of significant duration, e.g. lasting for months or even years."[14] In fact, the use of torture might be justified, said the Justice Department: If an interrogator used torture, "he would be doing so in order to prevent further attacks on the United States by the Al Qaeda terrorist network."[15]

"December 2, 2002

[Defense Secretary] Rumsfeld prescribes new interrogation policy for Guantánamo, authorizing 'stress positions,' hooding, 20-hour interrogations, removal of clothing, exploiting phobias to induce stress (e.g., fear of dogs), prolonged isolation, sensory deprivation, and forced grooming. These techniques soon spread to Afghanistan and later to Iraq."

—"THE CASE AGAINST RUMSFELD," HARD FACTS TIMELINE, ACLU

The interrogation methods—such as letting guard dogs loose on naked men, a game once favored by Nazis—were extreme, but the aggressive interrogation techniques didn't stop there. Female interviewers sexually taunted the chained detainees, stripping and rubbing the prisoner's face with ink that they claimed was menstrual blood. Hooded prisoners were strung by their hands from the ceiling for days. Detainees were leashed, burned, and electrocuted. They were sexually humiliated and raped.

As of July 2004, there were at least ninety-four confirmed cases of prisoner abuse by U.S. military personnel and contractors at Abu Ghraib and other prisons. Many of the sodomized victims were children.

There was an outcry. In April 2004, *60 Minutes* aired a horrifying segment on the abuses at Abu Ghraib almost the same day the story broke in *The New Yorker.* *Newsweek* and *Time* ran pages of the disturbing photos; *The Economist* ran a photo on its cover of a hooded prisoner attached to wires, with the large caption "Resign, Rumsfeld"—a call that was echoed in Congress and across the world. Many across the United States and the world went into a silent shock, surprised it had gone this far. Abu Ghraib, President Bush assured us, was a fluke, a ghastly crime committed by only "a few American troops who dishonored our country." And meanwhile, the Department of Defense played dumb, with Secretary Rumsfeld repeatedly telling reporters he hadn't read the scathing reports or even seen the photos from the Iraq prison that had the rest of the world aghast.[16]

REPORTER (at May 4, 2004, press briefing): . . . [G]iven the ramifications of not only what is in [the Taguba] report, the findings specifically, but the pictures, the photographs that you knew . . . were going to be broadcast [on 60 Minutes], why did you not feel it incumbent upon you at that time to ask for the findings, to take a look at the pictures beforehand, so you could perhaps be prepared to deal with some of the world reaction?

> SEC. RUMSFELD: *I think I did inquire about the pictures and was told that we didn't have copies.*

The initial outrage dimmed, but classified government-appointed investigations that were leaked to the press showed that the extent was wider than the president indicated. The Taguba report, snuck to the media in spring 2005, slammed the interrogators, reporting "numerous incidents of sadistic, blatant, and wanton criminal abuses" against detainees in Abu Ghraib prison in the fall of 2003. The Schlesinger report condemned the "brutality and purposeless sadism" that was "unacceptable even in wartime," but the report didn't stop there. It asserted that abuses had occurred outside Abu Ghraib, adding, "There is both institutional and personal responsibility at higher levels."

By January 2005, over 130 U.S. military personnel had been charged with crimes related to prisoner abuse and many believe that was still only the start.[17] Army Reserve Spc. Charles Graner, accused of leading the torture ring at Abu Ghraib, was hit with a ten-year sentence, but many of those found guilty of abuse received a fine, perhaps a demotion, or a day in prison.

> *Newsweek reported that when the Taguba report showed up in the hands of the media in May 2005, Douglas Feith, the undersecretary of defense who is in charge of prisoners, sent an e-mail ordering officials to protect themselves by not reading the report and by never referring to it.*[18]

The torture wasn't confined to Abu Ghraib; it was documented in Afghanistan and Cuba as well. And many of these prisoners—the fifty thousand "enemy combatants" rounded up in Afghanistan and Iraq—were not al-Qaeda or terrorists of any persuasion. Many were just everyday Afghans or Iraqis, sidewalk vendors, farmers, local zealots, or just village kids; some had been nabbed by warlords and sold as terrorists to the Americans forces. And locked in the darkest parts of the U.S.-run prisoner camps (as well as those in Egypt and Uzbekistan) were hundreds of the "disappeared" who'd been abducted or sometimes flown in from around the world by secret CIA "rendition" teams.[19] Reports surfaced of hundreds of "ghost detainees" whose identities were not revealed and who were kept hidden away in prisons, in isolation, unsure what country they are in.

"We've documented that the U.S. government is a leading purveyor and practitioner of this odious human rights violation [torture]. And the refusal of the U.S.

government to conduct a truly independent investigation into the abuses at Abu Ghraib prison and other detention centers is tantamount to a whitewash, if not a cover-up, of these disgraceful events."

—AMNESTY INTERNATIONAL USA EXECUTIVE DIRECTOR WILLIAM SHULTZ,
MAY 25, 2005, IN A SPEECH INTRODUCING THE 2005 AMNESTY INTERNATIONAL
REPORT ON HUMAN RIGHTS BEFORE THE NATIONAL PRESS CLUB

In early 2005, the ACLU, which is suing the U.S. government to turn over records and investigations into the treatment of its prisoners, won a victory: The FBI declassified dozens of documents. The organization posted on its Web site numerous FBI e-mails that showed FBI agents were concerned that what was happening was illegal. And one of those e-mails indicated that authorization for at least some of the actions that the FBI considered anathema had come from the president himself.

". . . [A]n Executive Order signed by President Bush authorized the following interrogation techniques among others: sleep 'management,' use of MWD (military working dogs), 'stress positions' such as half squats, 'environmental manipulation' such as the use of loud music, sensory deprivation through the use of hoods, etc."

—MAY 22, 2004, E-MAIL FROM FBI AGENT (NAME REDACTED) ASKING
WHETHER FBI WAS SUPPOSED TO REPORT THE ABUSE IN IRAQ.[20] (NOTE THAT
THIS E-MAIL WAS SENT A MONTH AFTER THE STORY OF THE SUPPOSED ISOLATED
TORTURE INCIDENT AT ABU GHRAIB HAD BEEN REPORTED, SUGGESTING THAT
EVEN IN THE FACE OF THE MEDIA SPOTLIGHT, THE TORTURE WAS CONTINUING.)

The ACLU announcements—including that Department of Defense officials had impersonated FBI agents and State Department officials[21]—weren't the force that brought the focus back to what was happening, and may be still happening, at U.S. detention camps across the world. When *Newsweek* ran a short piece in early May 2005 that talked about the Koran being flushed down the john, the reported desecration helped fuel riots across the Muslim world—all the more when the Bush administration denied it and pressured the magazine to apologize and retract the report. (One political cartoonist in India drew a cartoon of Bush flushing *Newsweek*.) The air was still charged when in late May, Amnesty International released its fifth annual report on torture across the world. The country of gravest concern, the nonprofit human rights organization said, was the United States.

"Guantánamo has become the gulag of our times, entrenching the notion that people can be detained without any recourse to the law."

—AMNESTY INTERNATIONAL SECRETARY GENERAL IRENE KHAN, MAY 25, 2005

"It's an absurd allegation. The United States is a country that promotes freedom around the world."

—President George W. Bush, May 31, 2005[22]

The Bush administration loudly denied it; Vice President Cheney called AI's analogy comparing the U.S. detention centers with the Soviet prison camp system "offensive," and Defense Secretary Donald Rumsfeld said it was "reprehensible." Even the editorial board at the *Washington Post*, which frequently investigates the torture scandal, called the harsh words from the nonprofit another cry in the "partisan fracas"—and it damned the fiery introductions by Amnesty International's heads as "turning a report on prisoner detention into another excuse for Bush-bashing."[23] The *Post* was correct in saying the gulag description didn't fit: In the Soviet Union there was little that citizens could do. In the United States, the people are free, theoretically, to protest and put an end to the practice. But until recently, the abuse at U.S.-run detention centers has been just another quickly turned page in the news.

12. FOREIGN INTELLIGENCE:

Stirring Up the World

Prominent international intelligence outfits:

Central Intelligence Agency (United States)
Mossad (Israel)
Inter-Services Intelligence (Pakistan)

Notable Number

- Unknown billions of dollars: Nobody really knows the size of the CIA budget, which the agency will not disclose.

Snapshot

They eavesdrop. They bribe. They run weapons and drugs, arm guerrillas, and start insurgency groups. They torture, trigger government rebellions, train rebels to kill. They assassinate—those who threaten their countries and those who threaten their countries' corporate interests. And they usually deny all of their subversive activities. Meet the international intelligence agencies—the United States' CIA, Israel's Mossad, and Pakistan's ISI among them—who in the course of protecting their countries have altered the shape of the world.

For all the criticisms of the CIA, there is at least one service they provide for which they should be highly commended. They publish the handy CIA World Factbook, complete with maps and statistics of the world's countries, and offer the information online for free. See http://www.cia.gov/cia/publications/factbook/.

In this nefarious world, agents are never really sure who is their friend; double crosses and backstabs are more common than at a sorority house when there's only one cute guy in the room. Diplomats and business sorts may pass along hot tips to agents, but the cleaner the fingernails, the less likely they'll give any good dirt. In the name of digging up good information, agents have to jump into the cesspool and mingle with the guys who know the word on the street, and if the word is valid or not. That means that much of the information that shapes our world is coming from the drug dealers and gunrunners, dictators and rebels, pimps and other shady characters. Since they're often dealing with scum buckets, it's no big shock that intelligence agents are often slammed by "blowback"—when the situation they've dreamed up turns into a nightmare. Whether Manuel Noriega, Saddam Hussein, or Osama bin Laden, most who have topped our enemy lists were once good chums with the CIA. The CIA is not alone in this tendency. Some say that Israel's Mossad may have had a hand in creating the anti-PLO and Arafat-loathing Hamas, which became one of its most hated foes.

BLOWBACK MAXIMUS

President Carter's national security advisor Zbigniew Brzezinski claims credit for the brilliant idea, but in 1981, the CIA was called in to implement what was in retrospect one of the United States' most grievous errors. The plan was to zap the Soviets' strength and finances by engaging them in an unwinnable guerrilla war in Afghanistan, where the Soviets had invaded in 1979 to install a Communist government. The scheme involved:

- Saudi Arabia, which supplied zealous young mujahideen warriors to fight against the religionless Communists
- Pakistan's secret service, the ISI (Inter-Services Intelligence), which trained the mujahideen
- The CIA, which supplied covert arms funded by the United States, and training

The plan worked: The Soviets were ensnared in a pointless, violent war that dragged on for ten years, sucking them of money and energy. The Soviet-Afghan war is seen as one of the final nails in the Soviet coffin, leading to its downfall in 1991.

The plan backfired: It armed and created a force of well-trained angry young Muslims who saw themselves as Islam's saviors and weren't done fighting when the war wrapped up in 1989. They've been causing major problems—in Saudi Arabia, in Kashmir, in Egypt, and in the United States—ever since. Many of these warriors, including their leader, Osama bin Laden, gave birth to al-Qaeda and other radical militant Muslim groups.

Close-up

In the world of intelligence, no name packs more punch than the CIA. The United States' agency of international espionage is the world's best funded (director John Deutch once allowed that its annual "white budget" of legitimate activities was over $27 billion—and that was back in 1997) and the most aggressive on the planet. It has helped to overthrow democratically elected popular governments and install dictatorships from Chile to Indonesia, Iran to Iraq. It has engaged in shady deals including running heroin out of Asia. In short, its dirty work has extended to all corners of the globe, but lately it has specialized in screwing up. At least that's what the revisionists at the White House would like us to believe.

TRIP TO TORTURELAND

"Renditions" is such a dry, bureaucratic word, but its meaning is ugly. Renditions of prisoners, which the CIA reportedly does quite frequently, means that they are taken to countries where they will be tortured. The CIA has reportedly been involved in transporting Iraqi prisoners (in violation of the Geneva Conventions) to countries including Jordan, Syria, and Uzbekistan—and dropping them off to see if the torturers can knock any information out of them. Since fall 2001, CIA jets have been picking up and dropping off prisoners at military airports all over the world—from Sweden and Scotland to Morocco and Pakistan.[1]

CIA (United States)

Agency: Central Intelligence Agency
Director: Porter Goss (2004–present)
Headquarters: Langley, Virginia
Number of employees: Undisclosed
Budget: Undisclosed but large

"The CIA has the unique legal ability among all US government departments and agencies to . . . [pull funds from] other federal government agencies and other sources 'without regard to any provisions of law' and without regard to the intent behind Congressional appropriations. Every year, billions of dollars of Congressional appropriations are diverted from their Congressionally sanctioned purposes . . . to intelligence agencies without knowledge of the public and with the collusion of Congressional leaders."

—MICHAEL E. SALLA, "AN INVESTIGATION INTO THE CIA'S 'BLACK BUDGET'"[2]

Forget for a moment that some believe that President Franklin D. Roosevelt allowed the attack on Pearl Harbor to happen to rouse the previously isolationist masses to war. Whether he knew or he didn't, FDR wanted new intel—and he created the CIA theoretically at least to address the failure of advance knowledge about the Pearl Harbor attack in 1942, although it took five years to get this new agency formed. A slap in the face to the FBI, the agency was controversial from the moment it pulled up its collar and slipped on some sunglasses in 1947, with the passage of the National Security Act. And it was all the more so in 1948, when international "covert activities" became part of its mission. The most radical of the U.S. intelligence agencies and the one with the least oversight (usually) has been busy.

Clandestine vs. Covert

Clandestine missions are supposed to be secret, but somebody someday might admit to them. Covert activities are those that, if discovered, will be denied, disavowed, and covered up.

CHANGING TIMES: A CIA SAMPLER

- 1953: Overthrew Iranian Prime Minister Mohammed Mossedegh to place U.S.-friendly Shah of Iran in power; also reportedly trained Shah's brutal secret police, SAVAK, teaching them numerous torture techniques.[3]
- 1954: Toppled (via CIA-trained rebels) Guatemala's president Jacobo Arbenz, who was pushing U.S. banana interests out of the country.
- 1950s–1970s: In the MK Ultra program, carried out assorted mind control experiments, including many involving LSD. In one trial, San Francisco prostitutes dosed their unwitting clients with the hallucinogen.
- 1960: Overthrew Zaire's (now Democratic Republic of Congo) prime minister Patrice Lumumba, who was getting chummy with Communists. He was taken prisoner by new leader, Gen. Joseph Mobutu, tortured, and killed.
- 1960s: Launched numerous assassination and overthrow attempts against Fidel Castro, from exploding cigars to the thwarted Bay of Pigs operation in 1961.
- 1960s–1970s: During Vietnam War, trained insurgents and operated Air America, running arms and Southeast Asian heroin to U.S. troops.

- 1965: Helped provide Indonesian dictator Suharto with lists of suspected Chinese Communists in Indonesia, leading to massacre of up to a million.
- 1972: Former CIA employees, among them Howard Hunt, involved in Watergate break-in. (Note: Nixon canned CIA director Richard Helms because he wouldn't cover up Watergate.)
- 1973: Planned overthrow and successful assassination of Chilean President Salvador Allende and brought Pinochet into power.
- 1980s: Helped organize Nicaraguan contras in attempted overthrow of Sandanista government. Helped train Islamist guerrillas in Afghanistan. Ran equipment and arms to Iraq.
- 1990s to present: Theoretically tracked bin Laden, watched China, and busted organized crime, but mostly missed the boat—or so the story goes.

It's hard to imagine a more dreadful time to be a spook, especially one with the Central Intelligence Agency. And the irony is, it was supposed to be easy. The Cold War was over, and the CIA had machines—spy satellites, electronic bugs to filter the "chatter," and e-mail readers—to do their spying for them. When the Soviet threat evaporated, the budget for intelligence was slashed and nearly 20 percent of intelligence agents were laid off and the agents that remained were machine monitors, required less to work overseas. Granted, there were warnings that it wouldn't be a "kick your feet up on the desk" era for long. The World Trade Center bombing in 1993 scattered the dust. Ditto with the Bojinka plot of 1995—a diabolical plan to blow up eleven planes simultaneously while they were high over the Pacific. And in 1998 the CIA screwed up badly—twice. In May, India and Pakistan had a pissing match with the two countries testing nuclear devices for two weeks. Embarrassingly, the CIA hadn't even known that Pakistan had a nuclear program. Neither did President Clinton, who wasn't really pleased to find out about it in the papers. Three months later, the CIA was humiliated again: The U.S. embassies in Tanzania and Kenya were bombed almost simultaneously, killing over two hundred. The CIA pointed at bin Laden, who was then in Sudan. And then they pointed at a pharmaceutical factory just outside Sudan's capital, Khartoum. They believed it was a front for a bin Laden business, and that the factory actually made biochemical weapons and explosives. That very night, missiles ripped the pharmaceutical factory apart. Big problem: It turned out to have been a legitimate pharmaceutical factory.

A weak spot of both the American people in general and the CIA in specific has been a nearly nationalistic refusal to learn languages—that's what translators are for, right? With the Cold War over, the russki yazik, which at least a few had

> *sunk years into mastering, was about as useful as carrying a Communist card.*
> *Few were interested in learning another language with a bizarre alphabet, like*
> *Arabic.*

"The CIA probably doesn't have a single truly qualified Arabic-speaking officer of Middle Eastern background who can play a believable Muslim fundamentalist who would volunteer to spend years of his life with shitty food and no women in the mountains of Afghanistan. For Christ's sake, most case officers live in the suburbs of Virginia."

—ANONYMOUS CIA OFFICER[4]

More terrorist plots were hatched, and they seemed to be growing closer: A plan by several Algerians to blow up Seattle's Space Needle on New Year's 2000 was thwarted, although there were hints that the plot was to entail something much bigger. The elevation in terrorist activities brought an equal rise in government funds and awareness. By the time George W. Bush wandered in, the CIA was far more tuned into terrorism than they had been in years. But the Vulcans had their own plans and didn't much want to listen. In fact, considering that Bush Sr. once headed the agency, it's ironic that with this administration, the CIA gets so little respect.

THE CIA AND THE VULCANS

The Bush administration was warned. The system was "blinking red," as CIA director George Tenet would later describe the weeks leading up to 9/11. Tenet was banging on tables, yelling that an unprecedented number of warnings were coming in about al-Qaeda and something was going to happen. He wasn't alone in the attempts to get the Bush team to think beyond Iraq. Infuriated that the Vulcans nearly yawned when counterterrorism experts brought the subject back up, the intelligence community inserted a chilling report in the Daily Presidential Briefing, warning again that bin Laden was determined to attack in the United States. The matter again was nearly shrugged off.[5] Five weeks later, when al-Qaeda struck, blame was heaped on the CIA for not preventing it. The Vulcans immediately turned the topic back to Iraq: How could the CIA link Saddam to the attacks? The Vulcans didn't like the CIA's answer: They couldn't. Vice President Cheney kept dropping by Langley, putting on the heat to come up with something, and the CIA kept warning the administration not to make exaggerated claims. Defense Secretary Rumsfeld was so teed off, he formed his own intelligence unit to find the "right" answers. Finally, under pressure, the CIA came up with something: There might be mobile biochemical units that traveled around

Iraq, making detection near impossible. It was "a slam dunk," said Tenet. Not that it mattered if the CIA had unearthed anything or not. By then the word of Ahmed Chalabi was made golden (see "Neocon Whopper," page 62), and the war machine was already revved up.

When WMDs weren't discovered, and still weren't discovered, and weren't discovered again, there was a new phrase on the Vulcans' lips: "intelligence failure." Bush appointed a commission to explore the intelligence breakdown leading up to the war. The commission answered the Bush administration's two new favorite words with two more: "dead wrong." A more accurate two-word description with regard to the CIA's role in the lead-up to war might have been "set up."

"We conclude that the Intelligence Community was dead wrong in almost all of its pre-war judgments about Iraq's weapons of mass destruction. This was a major intelligence failure. . . . We simply cannot afford failures of this magnitude."

—COMMISSION ON THE INTELLIGENCE CAPABILITIES OF THE UNITED STATES REGARDING
WEAPONS OF MASS DESTRUCTION, REPORT TO THE PRESIDENT,
MAR. 31, 2005.[6] AMAZINGLY, THE COMMISSION DIDN'T FIND ANYTHING
QUESTIONABLE ABOUT THE BUSH ADMINISTRATION'S BEHAVIOR.

The CIA was yet again made a scapegoat and George Tenet fell on his sword, resigning in June 2004. Bush yanked his father's friend and former CIA agent Porter Goss out of Congress and put him in Langley's hot seat. Seen as an administration suck-up, his arrival prompted two new words to echo through the agency's halls: "I quit."

"We don't do torture."

—CIA DIRECTOR PORTER GOSS TESTIFYING BEFORE SENATE ARMED SERVICE
COMMITTEE.[7] GOSS'S WORDS RANG HOLLOW, CONSIDERING HE WAS LOOKING INTO
THE DEATHS OF FOUR PRISONERS WHO HAD POSSIBLY DIED AT THE HANDS OF CIA
PERSONNEL. THEN AGAIN PERHAPS THE DIRECTOR MEANT THAT THE CIA DOESN'T
PERSONALLY TORTURE; AS IS THEIR TREND THESE DAYS, THEY FARM IT OUT.

The whole truth of what shook down inside the CIA before and after the September 11 attacks, however, still hasn't been told—but there are whispers and a sudden onslaught of leaked reports to the press. And now when administration jaws start flapping out more misinformation—the CIA immediately issues statements that they don't have a shred of proof to back up the claims.

Currently, the two words to describe the CIA are "confused" and "competitive." Designed to concern itself with foreign affairs, the agency was loaded up with more power to act domestically through the Patriot Act, and now it competes with the FBI for at-home power. Until 2005, the director of the CIA was the head of all U.S. intelligence. Now that role is filled by the new National Intelligence director, John Negroponte. A council looking into the matter emerged scratching its head, with some intelligence analysts saying moves to bring intelligence agencies into tandem is simply blurring the collective intelligence mission. [8]

The CIA isn't the only trouble-making intelligence agency on the planet. There are certainly others who make huge international waves. Among the best-known agencies is Israel's intelligence group, Mossad.

Mossad (Israel)

Agency: Mossad
Director: Gen. Meir Dagan
Headquarters: Tel Aviv, Israel
Number of members: 1,200 (estimated)
Budget: $230 million (estimated)

A Few Classic Mossad Moments

- 1960: Nabbed Nazi war criminal Adolph Eichmann in Argentina and hauled him back for trial in Israel; found guilty in 1961, he was executed the next year.
- 1961: Traded information about assassination plot on French president Charles de Gaulle for technology to build nuclear bombs.
- 1972: Taken by surprise when PLO raided Munich Olympics, killing eleven Israeli athletes.
- 1973: Surprised again when Egypt and Syria invaded Israel during Yom Kippur.
- 1976: Raided a hijacked Air France jet (on the ground) in Uganda, getting passengers safely out of plane with only one death.
- 1986: Arrested Israeli scientist Mordechai Vanunu for telling world about Israel's secret nuclear weapons program.

Mordechai Vanunu, the scientist who spilled the beans on Israel's nuclear weapons (which Israel is still trying to keep secret), was found guilty of treason and locked up for eighteen years, most spent in solitary confinement. He was finally released from Israeli prison in 2004, under conditions that he not talk to the press. Vanunu not only talked to the press, claiming among other things that he'd been nabbed by the CIA, not Mossad, he also was reported by the BBC as having previously opined that there shouldn't be a Jewish state. In 2005, Vanunu was hauled back to court, purportedly for violating his no-talk agreement, and slapped with twenty-one counts of ignoring the government's demand to shut up. He's now looking at a possible four-decade imprisonment.

Israel isn't just a state. It's a state of mind. For much of recent history it has suffered a well-based fear that others are trying to destroy Israel and exterminate Jews. Mossad—the name means "the Institution"—was formed by the Israeli government in 1951 to help battle the forces trying to take Israel down. Arguably the brainiest of all the world's intelligence agencies, Mossad certainly knows the most about Islamic terrorists, as so many have blown themselves up in Israel. Mossad, and other Israeli experts, definitely had input—and a very sympathetic ear—when the United States was trying to pull itself together after the al-Qaeda attacks. In fact, depending on whose story you wish to believe, Mossad might have been in the United States at the time, trying to track al-Qaeda down. Some say that Mossad tried to warn American officials of the impending doom.[9]

"It is rather strange that the U.S. media . . . seems to be ignoring what may well prove to be the most explosive story since the 11 September attacks—the alleged break-up of a major Israeli espionage operation in the United States which aimed to infiltrate both the Justice and Defense departments and which may also have been tracking Al-Qaeda terrorists before the aircraft hijackings took place."

—*JANE'S INTELLIGENCE DIGEST*[10]

THE CASE OF THE MYSTERIOUS ISRAELI ART STUDENTS

Who they were and what they were actually up to is a big question mark, but even prestigious British defense publication *Jane's Intelligence Digest* remarked that something seemed odd, including that the media wasn't covering it much, and that U.S. officials dismissed it as myth. The story goes along these lines: Around 1999, a group of Israeli college students showed up in the United States and began going around selling artwork door to door. They often tried to sell their paintings at U.S. government offices, including intelligence and enforcement agencies—and then they began showing up at agents' houses again trying to sell art.[11] After they were reportedly seen taking pictures and snooping about, a DEA agent wrote up an advisory, speculating that they might be spies. The art students, however, weren't simply selling door to door in New York and

DC. They reportedly showed up in other cities, including Hollywood, Florida, the temporary home of several of the hijackers, such as ringleader Mohammad Atta. The U.S. government has laughed off the stories, despite the DEA report, and the Israeli government has denied that the students were spies, or had anything to do with Mossad.

America and Israel are usually close friends—the United States gives Israel (and Egypt) billions in free arms annually, and the two almost always vote in tandem at the UN. But spies plague the relationship. The U.S. government occasionally deports suspected Israeli spies and has busted a number of its government employees for leaking information to Mossad or Israeli government agents. The most recent is Department of Defense Iran expert Larry Frankin, who passed confidential info about U.S. military plans in Iran to the American Israeli Public Affairs Committee. Some wonder if AIPAC, which let two of its top men go in the scandal, is actually a front for Mossad; "America's pro-Israel lobby," as it refers to itself, is currently under investigation by the FBI, which has been hauling computers out of its DC office. Leading neocons are being questioned as part of the Franklin-AIPAC flap. Something strange is definitely afoot, but nobody has yet unraveled it, although the bloggers are definitely trying.

Given Israel's background, including the fact that it was invaded by other countries three times in its first twenty-five years of existence and is a victim of frequent suicide bombers, Mossad isn't shy about assassinating Israel's enemies. They are widely believed to have shot Gerald Bull, a Canadian astrophysicist who was developing a "supergun"—essentially a high-tech cannon—for Iraq, when he was killed in Belgium in 1990.[12] Mossad has slipped up a few times: In 1974, for example, Mossad agents killed innocent Ahmed Boushiki, an Algerian in Norway, whom the agents mistook for the mastermind of the 1972 PLO attack on Israeli athletes at the Munich Olympics. Sweden tried the agents for the murder, finding them guilty, and Israel, while never copping to the murder, later agreed to financially help out his family.

On the other side of the spectrum is Pakistan's ISI, previously one of the least-mentioned intel agencies in the U.S. media, and still one of the least understood.

ISI (Pakistan)

Agency: Inter-Services Intelligence (ISI)
Director: Lt. Gen. Ehsan ul-Haq
Headquarters: Islamabad, Pakistan

Number of agents: 6,000 to 10,000
Budget: $45 million (estimated)[13]
Founded: 1948

For most of its existence, the ISI had but one enemy: India. The ISI, active in battles with India in the Kashmir region, also keenly tracked developments of India's nuclear program, helping to quickly develop one for Pakistan too. Since being strong-armed into the War on Terror—lured by the promise of a ban being lifted so the country could purchase Lockheed F-16s—Pakistan declared a new enemy: al-Qaeda. There was a small hitch with that 2001 announcement. The ISI, in bed with the Taliban, was chummy with Osama bin Laden as well.

Upon signing Pakistan on as a member of the U.S.-led anti-terror coalition, Pakistan's president, Pervez Musharraf, immediately fired several key figures at the ISI, including its director, Muslim fundamentalist Lt. Gen. Mahmoud Ahmad. The director certainly left several unanswered questions when he huffed out. Among them:

- What exactly was Ahmad doing in the United States in the week leading up to the 9/11 attacks, and what exactly was he talking about with the CIA and White House on September 11 and 12?
- Was Ahmad, as reported, a good friend of the hijackers' ringleader, Mohammad Atta?
- Did Ahmad, as reported, wire $100,000 to Mohammad Atta in the days before the attacks?[14]

Ahmad's angry departure has led some to believe that he may try to stage a comeback by forming an alternative to the ISI, and otherwise do all he can to deflate the group's power.

Whether with Ahmad at its head or not, the ISI has been accused of plenty of dirty work. India suspected the ISI may have been behind the December 2001 bombing of its parliament in New Delhi that killed twelve, and says that the ISI still stirs up violence in Kashmir. The decapitation of American journalist Daniel Pearl may have likewise been linked to the agency,[15] which for decades has had strong radical Islamist roots.

In a *New York Times* op-ed piece, Sarah Chayes, a development worker in Afghanistan who formerly reported for National Public Radio, says that the ISI is moving Pakistani student operatives into Afghanistan, in an effort to fight U.S. control. She believes that the ISI was actually the force that stirred up the May

2005 riots in reaction to the *Newsweek* article about guards and interrogators at the U.S. detention facility in Guantánamo Bay mistreating the Koran.

While the Pakistani president maintains he has control of the ISI, it's rather hard to believe. After all, the president barely has control of one huge chunk of his country—the Northwest Frontier, where it's said you can find anything that you want from automatic weapons to plutonium. In that lawless region of village tribes, many believe, Osama bin Laden has found his new home. And some believe that the ISI is helping him stay there undetected.

Behind the Scenes

Even though intelligence agencies often hate to work together—the lack of information sharing between the CIA and FBI was cited as one cause of the 9/11 intelligence failure—there is at least one case where several international spy groups have worked together for decades. It's called Echelon, and it has brought the spy network to nearly every inch of the planet.

Big Bro Int'l
Echelon

It doesn't matter where we go. Even if we're deep in a jungle or atop a faraway mountain, Big Brother can tap in if we're using telephone, e-mail, or fax. "Echelon" is the code name for what is believed to be the world's biggest spy network, one that monitors communications across the planet.

> *Interceptors that look like giant golf balls are hidden across the planet, from Yakima, Washington, to Waihopai, New Zealand.*

Run through UKUSA, a joint U.S.-British intelligence operation that sprang out of the two countries' World War II work deciphering Nazi codes, Echelon was originally designed to listen to Soviet and Chinese communications. The network expanded in the 1980s, however, and now any old body may be the victim or object of eavesdropping. Canada, Australia, and New Zealand are also part of the network, which intercepts some 3 billion telephone, fax, and e-mail messages a day, using high-orbit satellites and earth-based receivers. This "signals intelligence"

(SIGINT) program also relies on sophisticated supercomputers, called "dictionaries," that have extraordinary capabilities: The computers are programmed to listen into communications and recognize words such as "bomb" or "attack" and they can even recognize voices. Osama bin Laden's conversations were routinely monitored from Afghanistan—at least until late 2001 when he switched to an "encrypted" system that is harder to detect and decode.

> *Much of the expanded Echelon system was designed by Raytheon and Lockheed Martin.*

Overseen by the National Security Agency in the United States and GDHQ in Britain, the existence of the project was long denied by both those agencies. However, in 1999 Australia admitted to it and shortly thereafter Echelon's existence was confirmed in declassified National Security Agency documents. Echelon has provided information about such important matters as Iran's attempts to make sophisticated missiles and the whereabouts of suspected terrorists. However, it poses substantial threats to the privacy of individuals and businesses. Problems include:

▶ It can be used for industrial spying; the government agencies deny they do so, but no law prohibits it.

▶ It can provide incorrect information about us—a message taken out of context may be misleading, for instance—and the source of the erroneous information is often not revealed so we have no way to fight it.[16]

▶ There's little oversight on Echelon.

The European Union was so upset when news broke about the world's biggest ears that representatives of the European Parliament traveled to the United States in 2000 on an Echelon fact-finding mission. Both the National Security Agency and the CIA (which often instructs the NSA on who or what to listen in on) refused to meet with them.

"Yes, my continental European friends, we have spied on you. And it's true that we use computers to sort through data by using keywords. . . . We have spied on you, because you bribe."

—FORMER CIA DIRECTOR JAMES WOOLSEY IN 2000 ADMITTING ECHELON'S EXISTENCE AS WELL AS ILLUSTRATING ONE OF ITS USES.[17] THE U.S. GOVERNMENT USES ECHELON-INTERCEPTED INFORMATION ABOUT OTHER COUNTRIES' BRIBES TO ELBOW ITS WAY INTO DEALS. IT HOLDS THE INFO OVER THE COUNTRY'S HEADS, AND THREATENS TO GO PUBLIC IF THAT COUNTRY ACCEPTS THE BRIBERY-GREASED OFFER.

▶▶ ◀◀

PART IV

CONSUMERISM

13. WAL-MART:

The Slave Driver

Company: Wal-Mart
Headquarters: Bentonville, Arkansas
CEO: H. Lee Scott (since 2000)
Founded: First Wal-Mart built in 1962
Revenues: $258 billion (2004)

Notable Numbers

- 138 million: Number of shoppers at Wal-Mart each week[1]
- $1 billion+: Frequent daily Wal-Mart sales total
- 12 percent: Amount of total imports from China that end up at Wal-Mart
- 24: Number of lawsuits Wal-Mart slapped with daily in 2002[2]
- 38: Number of Wal-Mart stores in 1970
- 276: Number of Wal-Mart stores in 1980
- 1,500+: Number of Wal-Mart stores in 1990
- 5,300+: Number of Wal-Mart stores in 2004

Snapshot

With its giggling smiley-face logo bouncing down the aisles slashing prices, Wal-Mart appears utterly innocuous. But nothing impacts daily life in the United States more than the megaretailer that is obsessed with ensuring that it provides "Low prices everyday"—regardless of the costs borne by society. Lately few except Mr. Smiley are laughing at what Wal-Mart is doing. Some are horrified at the power one company can exert: They blame Wal-Mart, now the biggest purveyor of the country's groceries, for the bankruptcies of over two dozen supermarket

chains and other closures that have wiped out thousands of jobs.[3] Some maintain that the company demands slavish devotion of its employees, resembling a
brainwashing cult.

> *Economists say that Wal-Mart saves consumers $20 billion every year. Labor*
> *analysts say that the opening of every Wal-Mart results in the loss of some*
> *two hundred local jobs.*

Many are simply openmouthed at how the country bumpkin from Arkansas that
obsessively hacks prices has slashed its way to the top: Wal-Mart is now the
biggest moneymaker on the planet, pulling in over a quarter of a trillion dollars a
year, and sitting at the number one spot on the Fortune 500 list. Of every $100 a
consumer spends, nearly $9 is spent here, and the company accounts for al-
most two-thirds of retail sales in the United States.[4] And that gives the corporation that now has over 5,300 stores in ten countries incredible clout—including
the ability to force suppliers to set up operations abroad, where labor costs are
a fraction of those in the United States.

> *When he passed away in 1992, Sam Walton was the second richest man in*
> *the country. Only Bill Gates was richer.*

SUPERLATIVE CITY

It's hard to understate Wal-Mart: The retail giant's name rarely appears without
the words "biggest," "largest," or "most."

Biggest retailer in the world (employs 1.2 million)
Biggest food retailer (over 14 percent of groceries in America sold here)
Biggest single seller in the United States of toys, diamonds, CDs, prescription
    eyeglasses, and film developing,[5] as well as:

Dog food: 36 percent sold at Wal-Mart[6]
Disposable diapers: 32 percent sold at Wal-Mart
Toothpaste: 26 percent sold at Wal-Mart
Pain remedies: 21 percent sold at Wal-Mart

> *Wal-Mart alone kicked in over 2 percent of the U.S. gross national product in 2004.*

Consumers may go ga-ga at the rock-bottom prices—sometimes a third cheaper than anywhere else—but Wal-Mart gouges everybody from its workers to manufacturers to keep it that way. Critics say that Wal-Mart is a quickly spreading black hole, sucking the economic vitality out of every community where it appears, creating traffic jams, and strangling mom-and-pop stores and regional chains whenever the retail behemoth rolls into town.

Wal-Mart's newest stores and superstores are sprawling monoliths. They contain grocery stores, pharmacies, lawn and garden departments, bakeries, and optical centers, and sell products from wedding rings and vacation packages to corporate attire and rifles. They've become an omnipresent fixture dotting the landscape; in some places in the South, they spring up every four miles.

The company that not long ago led a "Made in the U.S.A." campaign, now imports 60 percent or more of its goods from overseas. And that's only part of the reason why Wal-Mart—which *Fortune* named the most admired company in 2003 and 2004—is suddenly the most controversial name in the history of shopping, with activists, workers, and politicians leading movements from California to Vermont trying to keep the corporation from taking over another square inch.

Cities across California, where Wal-Mart plans to set up dozens of new superstores, are enacting ordinances preventing and limiting the construction of "big box stores." Vermont had its entire state declared one of the most endangered "Historical Places" to block future Wal-Marts from setting up there.[7] Other grass roots resistance is spreading across the country.

Another factor in the recent popularity slide of the consumer wonderland: Employees, some of whom are tired of commanding wages lower than sixteen-year-old babysitters get, are slapping lawsuits on the company, charging everything from sexual discrimination to being locked inside their stores and coerced to work overtime for no pay.

"Locked-in workers have had to wait for hours off-the-clock for a manager to show up to let them go home after they completed their shift. One worker claims to have broken his foot on the job and had to wait four hours for someone to open the door. Another worker alleges she cut her hand with box cutters one night and was forced to wait until morning to go to the hospital, where she received thirteen stitches."

—Rep. George Miller[8]

COURTING DISASTER

Wal-Mart, the largest single employer in almost a dozen states (with twice the number of workers as GM and Ford combined) doesn't have union members working in its five-thousand-plus stores, and most of its employees make less than $1,300 a month before taxes[9]—which is about $1,600 less than workers might make per month at many comparable stores. But that isn't what prompted the largest class action suit in U.S. suing history: In 2001, six female Wal-Mart employees filed a legal complaint that the company doesn't promote women at the rate that it should, and that the stores routinely pay females less. They say that while two-thirds of the company is female, women represent less than a third of store managers and 15 percent of senior managers, and that the company routinely pays male employees more. Wal-Mart employees say their bosses have told them that men get paid better because they have families to support—a response that doesn't play well to Wal-Mart's single mothers; at least one manager explained the discrepancy by reportedly saying, "God made Adam first," a response that played worse. In 2004, a San Francisco judge allowed the suit to extend to another 1.6 million women employees, past and present. But that is only one migraine that Wal-Mart is experiencing; in 2002, the company was hit with over six thousand lawsuits.

So much merchandise flies out of Wal-Mart stores—a quarter of all Clorox bleach in the country is sold here, for example, as is a fifth of all Revlon products—that the corporation has single-handedly transformed the retail dynamic. Manufacturers don't tell Wal-Mart what they are charging—Wal-Mart tells them; if suppliers can't sell at that price, there is plenty of competition to fill their space on the shelf. Facing the prospect of being the next Rubbermaid (that company had to sell itself to a competitor after Wal-Mart refused to allow Rubbermaid to raise prices when its costs rose), thousands of manufacturers have opened up operations in Asia, where workers, who often live on-site in tiny shanties, are often paid less than twenty-five cents an hour to be part of Wal-Mart's new supply chain.

Wal-Mart imported $18 billion worth of goods from China in 2004: The retailer is the largest single source in helping to multiply the $150 billion trade deficit between the United States and China.

BREAKING CHINA

It doesn't take too many humiliating visits to "Vendor Alley"—the row of glass cubicles in Wal-Mart corporate headquarters where store buyers dictate prices and put the screws to sellers, conducting "reverse auctions"—for some manufacturers to realize that to turn a profit they have to outsource to Asia. This job flight outrages U.S. workers; it also deeply concerns human rights campaigners. They say that Chinese workers in factories supplying Wal-Mart are dying from *guolaosi*—"overwork death"—from working upwards of fifteen hours a day, seven days a week, for months on end in a frenzy to quickly and cheaply fill demand for items going to Wal-Mart stores. The National Labor Committee looked into the burgeoning Chinese toy industry that supplies Wal-Mart, Disney, and Toys-R-Us among others and reported that during the months leading up to Christmas "some three million toy workers—mostly young women—will be locked inside 2,800 factories . . . handling toxic chemicals with their bare hands, while they are paid wages as low as 12 cents an hour."[10]

Close-up

Wal-Mart, where all employees from CEOs to cashiers are called "associates," resembles a personality cult, with all faithful paying homage to company founder Sam Walton—simply known by all employees as Sam—whose presence seems to haunt Wal-Mart aisles. The man who transformed a five-and-dime in Bentonville, Arkansas, into a low-price-obsessed chain before dying in 1992, had plenty of rules, such as the Ten Foot Rule, wherein employees must make eye contact and talk with any customer who comes within ten feet. Offices are lined with pictures of the hallowed founder and employees are instructed to think, "Now, what would Sam do in this situation?"

Sam's Ten Commandments[11]

1.	Commit to your goals	6.	Celebrate your success
2.	Share your rewards	7.	Listen to everyone
3.	Energize your colleagues	8.	Deliver more than you promise
4.	Communicate all you know	9.	Work smarter than others
5.	Value your associates	10.	Blaze your own path

THE WAL-MART CHEER!

Give me a W! Give me an A! Give me an L! Give me a Squiggly!
Give me an M! Give me an A! Give me an R! Give me a T!
What's that spell? Wal-Mart! Whose Wal-Mart is it? My Wal-Mart!
Who's number one? The Customer! Always!

While visiting a tennis ball factory in Korea, Sam Walton was so charmed by their morning cheer, that he brought the concept back home. The Wal-Mart cheer can be heard at annual meetings and store pep rallies, which have been likened to religious revivals, complete with the prayers.

High-level "associates" gather at 7:30 A.M. each Saturday for sales pep rallies in the company auditorium filled with thousands; following a prayer, they belt out the cheer. Those managers not in attendance (they must fly in several times a year), join in the fervor via videoconferencing, and they too must present their weekly sales figures to cheers or jeers, as the employees trace, step by step, where they went wrong and examine how they may do better. Emotions run high, and public humiliation is part of the formula; in a 2002 class action case won by 290 plaintiffs in Oregon, who had been forced into working overtime for free, store managers confessed their rationale: They had been chastised at weekly meetings for their store's high labor costs and were desperate to cut them.

Wal-Mart not only demands devotion from its employees, but its suppliers as well, who are heavily pressured into making a spirited offering to the weekly meetings. Quarterback Joe Montana pitched Kraft Foods at one, DreamWorks sent along a customized video of Shrek leading the Wal-Mart cheer at another, and during 2002, Coke was persuaded to reroute its Olympic Torch run from L.A. to Atlanta to pass numerous Wal-Mart stores.

BARCODE: THE DNA OF MARKETING

Part of Wal-Mart's formula for success is keeping a twenty-four-hour accounting of its inventory, and that's made possible by its heavy reliance on the bar code, which automatically reorders supplies from the warehouse as they are sold. Nobody uses it as efficiently as Wal-Mart: Those little black stripes are examined as though messages from above, yielding info on which hours of which days sales are at a peak, exactly how many items of a particular brand are selling, what prices are most attractive, how many goods are left in the warehouse, and what is in transit. Now Wal-Mart wants to more thoroughly monitor its products—

and the behavior of customers who toss them into the cart. It has requested that many suppliers embed a radio frequency chip in their products: The RFID chip in the products allows tracking of all the customer's in-store travels.

Like the products they sell, Wal-Mart employees are routinely monitored via video cameras, and any hint of talk about unions or union activity is called into Bentonville via a special hotline; hours later, corporate jets swoop down to investigate, and give the store employees another dose of antiunion pep talks and videos.

The AFL-CIO and other unions are launching a campaign in 2005 to inform Americans about the maltreatment of Wal-Mart employees. One area of concern is worker safety and health care. Some say that if they are injured on the job, they are shamed into not reporting it or making a fuss over the matter and that injuries are downplayed: A worker in Little Rock says that after losing his knuckles in a meat grinder, he was handed $600 and told the matter was ended.[12] What's more, the low wages that Wal-Mart pays prevent many employees from signing up for an insurance program without huge deductibles—and it doesn't kick in for six months. From the east coast to the west, counties are complaining that Wal-Mart employees and their children are the ones most frequently showing up in public health clinics, forcing the taxpayer to foot the bill.

"The Democratic Staff of the Committee on Education and the Workforce estimates that one 200-person Wal-Mart store may result in a cost to federal taxpayers of $420,750 per year—about $2,103 per employee [including free lunches for families, federal health care, housing assistance, and low income energy assistance]."

—REP. GEORGE MILLER[13]

Between national television shows asking the question "Is Wal-Mart good for America?"[14] and a spate of critical articles from the *Los Angeles Times* to the *New York Times,* as well as the thousands of lawsuits, union campaigns, and protests whenever Wal-Mart tries to open another store, the heat is seriously on. The company is so panicked that in January 2005, it took out full-page ads in over one hundred U.S. papers assuring consumers that it is a responsible company, concerned about worker welfare and one that brings numerous benefits to communities where it sets up. No one questions the savings that Wal-Mart brings, but increasingly consumers are wondering if the hidden costs to society are worth it.

GIVE CONTRIBUTIONS—GET RESULTS!

Although not a big political contributor in the 1990s, Wal-Mart has been shower-ing politicians lately. In 2003, the company contributed $1 million to federal candidates—making it one of the top contributors in the country. In 2004, it had contributed over $1.1 million,[15] making it the second biggest campaign donor in the nation. In April 2005, the Bush administration moved to ban class action suits, on the state level at least. Federal courts tend not to be as generous to plaintiffs.[16]

Certainly, the president and legislators did not make the class-action-restricting bill into law simply to please Wal-Mart. Other huge corporations demanded it, too (Halliburton, for one, is getting hammered with asbestos suits).

Behind the Scenes

When old Sam Walton left us in 1992, he left more than morale-boosting em-ployee exercises and customer relations rules. The man who opened up the first Wal-Mart in 1962 left billions to his five offspring, making them the richest family in the United States (move over, Cargills). Although most of his children have at assorted points worked with the company—and Rob Walton keeps an office in Bentonville—the family sometimes appears clueless as to the effects their com-pany is having worldwide.

In 2003, when Rob Walton spoke before the American Antitrust Institute, he said that the concern about Wal-Mart was based on misinformation. "Frankly, one of the misconceptions about Wal-Mart today is that we arrive at low prices because of our size and our ability to get the best deals from suppliers. . . . I've seen articles suggesting that Wal-Mart buys at prices lower than our competi-tors' and that this gives Wal-Mart an unfair advantage. I don't believe it."[17]

Despite Rob's disbelief, Wal-Mart's ability to destroy companies and change the face of world labor—all in the name of obsessively aiding the consumer—is registering on plenty of other people's radar. Still, the company may have nothing to fear: When it comes to shopping, consumers may decide that the ultimate good is lower prices, despite the burden that this retail monster puts on society. As they wheel down the aisles, shoppers probably aren't calculating in the hidden costs deducted from their tax dollars, which, thanks to Wal-Mart, may be shoveled out to pay for public health care to Wal-Mart's poor workers, or for the unemployment check to those whose jobs Wal-Mart caused to be shipped out to China.

14. CREDIT CARD COMPANIES:

The Corporate Loan Sharks

Company: Credit card companies in general
Headquarters: Many in South Dakota and Delaware
Founded: First credit card was Diner's Club in 1950
Total American credit card debt: $750 billion[1]

Notable Numbers

- 1.3 billion: Number of credit cards in the United States
- $8,000: Average credit card debt of families in the United States
- $11,000+: Average credit card debt of individuals in the United States
- 53 percent: Amount average American family saw its credit card debt rise during the 1990s (middle-class families saw an increase of 75 percent)[2]
- 1.6 million: Number of American families that declared bankruptcy in 2003[3]

Snapshot

They run the biggest corporate racket going in the United States today—yielding some $30 billion a year—and it's entirely legal. Snaring us with promises such as 0 percent interest rates, then smacking us with nasty surprises—embedded in the fine print and encrypted in high legalese that most consumers can't decipher—credit card companies just aren't what they used to be. Thanks to recent Supreme Court rulings and lax federal oversight, having credit cards is now a risky business—and we the consumer are paying for far more than our purchases.

The credit card industry is now essentially unregulated: Credit card companies don't have a federal cap on what they can charge for interest, they are not restricted by what they can charges for fees, and, quite legally, they can send our interest rates soaring whenever they please.

As some of the 144 million Americans who use cards may suspect, today's power plastic is designed to entrap us: These companies hope we mess up, because when we do that means more profits for them.

> "[Credit card companies are] raising interest rates, adding new fees, making the due date for your payment a holiday or a Sunday on the hopes that maybe you'll trip up and get a payment in late. It's become a very anticonsumer marketplace."
>
> —ROBERT MCKINLEY, FOUNDER OF RAM RESEARCH AND CARDWEB.COM[4]

Banking companies can jack up our interest rates overnight, say from 9 percent to 29 percent, if they wish, for any reason, regardless of our history with them. Thanks to a new practice called universal default, a late payment or missed payment with one credit card company can cause our interest rates with *all* the cards we hold to shoot sky high. There is nothing a consumer can do to fight it, and states are hand-tied as well. All power for overseeing the credit card industry—the most lucrative sector in banking today—is held by the mysterious Office of the Comptroller of the Currency.

The OCC, a bureau in the Department of the Treasury, regulates and supervises over 2,500 national banks. It is largely funded by the banks themselves, who, for example, pay $25,000 to charter a new bank. Some of that money goes for FDIC insurance to safeguard customer accounts.

And even though the OCC receives some eighty thousand complaints a year— a surprising number, given that so few consumers even know the office exists— it rarely takes action against the industry. Despite dozens of highly stinky practices that are now routine in this rotten business, the Office of the Comptroller of the Currency in its entire existence has only really gone after one credit card company—Providian, whom it ultimately fined $300 million.

In a sea of sleazemongers, Providian (now merged with Washington Mutual) stood out for deceiving beyond even what the OCC could tolerate. In its three-page June 2000 fact sheet[5] of Providian's slimy practices, the OCC highlights many of the company's questionable advertising techniques to potential suckers, including:

- Telemarketers pitched "maximum savings" for balance credit transfers to certain Providian credit cards, saying their rates were far lower than whatever the consumer was then paying. The reality was the Providian rate was at most 0.7 percent lower, and telemarketers were prohibited from telling that fact. Those that signed on had to prove what their old rates were: If customers did not show proof within ninety days of signing up or if Providian did not agree with the information that consumers provided about previous accounts, card holders were slammed with interest rates of up to 21.99 percent.

- Providian advertised a "No Annual Fee" credit card, not mentioning that purchase of a $156 a year credit protection service was mandatory to waive the annual fee. The credit protection plan also came with numerous strings and loopholes, sometimes not covering those who, for instance, used a different company's credit card.

Americans paid for $1.5 trillion of their goods with credit cards in 2004. That year, credit card companies experienced their biggest profits ever.

These wheelers and dealers of plastic are armed with a whole new arsenal of money-making devices, all charged with the blessings of the OCC. Forget that old-fashioned concept of grace period: If you're an hour—yes, an hour—late with your payment, you are slapped with a late fee—the average is twenty-nine dollars, although they can be higher. Go over your limit? Never mind that the company approved the purchase: Hand over another twenty-five to fifty dollars for your miscalculation. You probably rely on credit cards when traveling out of the country, but now your hotel, food, and mementos cost more if you charge them: Banks are hitting us with a foreign currency fee—5 percent of the total or more. And annual fees for membership are rising too.

Credit card companies now make over $21.5 billion annually on fees alone.

The expanded fees are only one way these credit card companies are reshaping their business plans to maximize profits. Now these financial wolves are beckoning a different consumer. Shying away from those with substantial savings who wipe clean their monthly slate, credit card companies are targeting customers who pay back more slowly by often making only the minimum payments. And credit card companies are devising new ways to keep these 90 million "revolvers" huffing on their financial treadmill and going nowhere for years—thirty, maybe forty—which is what it may take for many to pay off a simple $5,000 credit card balance.

> *In this warped world, those who pay off their whole balance each month in one fell swoop are derogatorily called "deadbeats." Counterintuitively, credit card companies don't much like them, since deadbeats deprive the companies of their lucrative fees.*

MINIMUM PAYMENTS, MAXIMUM PAIN

Credit card companies recently unveiled a new trick to attract more "revolvers": They lowered minimum payments and simultaneously increased credit lines. That may sound alluring, but ultimately it is about as attractive as being dropped into quicksand with lead weights. With minimum payments comprising only 2 or 3 percent of the balance, revolvers may be burdened with paying off relatively small debts for the rest of their lives.

Credit card balance	Interest	Years to pay off, with min. payments	Interest paid
$5,000	15%	32	$ 7,665
$5,000	18%	45	$13,531
$8,000	15%	37	$12,581
$8,000	18%	52	$22,260

Source: Demos, "Borrowing to Make Ends Meet," 8 Sept. 2003.[6]

> *In 2004, over 1 million consumers filed for Chapter 7—which sells off assets, pays off creditors, and forgives most of the rest of the debt.*

In 2001, nearly twelve out of every one thousand young adults filed for bankruptcy.[7] Older Americans are being hit by overwhelming credit card debt too: Since 1990, the number of American seniors filing for bankruptcy has tripled.

However, consumers won't need to worry about looking bankruptcy in the face anymore. The Bush administration has pretty much taken the option away. In April 2005, President Bush signed a bill severely limiting the ability to file for Chapter 7, and toughening up the rate of paybacks when individuals file for the slower repay option of Chapter 13. Credit card companies were elated.

> *MBNA, the second largest credit card company, is certainly a good friend to President George W. Bush, giving him the most financial support for his 2000 election. In fact, according to the Center for Public Integrity, MBNA holds the number one spot on the list of who's given most to George W. Bush over his entire career. The credit card company has coughed up over $605,000.*[8]

Close-up

If you are feeling a pinch in the credit card department, you are not alone. The amount of debt carried by the typical American family soared at least 53 percent in the 1990s to about $8,000, says consumer group Demos. And 70 percent of Americans say that their debt is becoming so unmanageable that it is causing substantial unhappiness in their families.[9]

THE REVOLVERS

Don't believe the hype put out by creditors that all those who run into credit card problems are just irresponsible losers. Credit cards are the number one source of financing for launching small businesses, says Robert D. Manning, author of *Credit Card Nation*, and it's helped the likes of Jeff Bezos start up Amazon.com; the downside is that plenty of small businesses get bogged down in paying the ongoing debt. Many people with huge debts aren't buying luxury items, either. Harvard Professor Elizabeth Warren, who specializes in bankruptcies, says single moms, whose ex-husbands or boyfriends may not help pay expenses, are one group that often lean on their credit cards to charge their groceries, the kids' doctors' visits, or for cash advances. And food and doctors are usually how people who are suddenly laid off use their cards as well.

Painfully high interest rates, ridiculous fees, and keeping consumers on the slow-pay program is terribly profitable for banks, whose credit card divisions are posting record-high profits. And with the wheelbarrows of money they dump to politicians and the high-powered lobbyists they unleash whenever a consumer-friendly bill is introduced, we may not see any changes any time soon. For millions of Americans, drowning in debt and tripped up, it's making life unbearable and now even many consumer credit groups who are supposed to help bail debtors out are charging such high fees for their services that some watchdogs are saying these groups are no longer not for profit.

- If you die with credit card debt the company will go after your estate.

Behind the Scenes

During the 1990s, some fifteen million Americans were so burdened by their bills that they declared bankruptcy. Meanwhile, bills that would protect the consumer—by capping interest rates or by including a box that clearly shows bill payers the trap they are getting into with minimum payments—are routinely killed in Congress thanks to the industry's power lobby machine; those plentiful political contributions don't hurt either.

"[The credit card] industry's become very, very powerful, and it's very successful in defeating every legislative attempt that's been made over the last several years to inject some responsibility on the part of this credit card industry."

—SENATOR CHRIS DODD, MEMBER OF THE SENATE
BANKING COMMITTEE, IN NOVEMBER 2004[10]

Banks nearly lost their shirts on their plastic in the 1970s when interest rates on their cards could keep up with the ballooning inflation rate. During the 1990s, however, banks devised schemes such as cash rebates and teaser rates, and began turning astounding profits, making the credit card department the most lucrative service of modern banking. There's only one way consumers might profit from the banks' many techniques for ripping us off: Buy stock in the credit card companies. Alas, we can't charge it.

PART V

PERSUADERS

15. PUBLIC RELATIONS COMPANIES:

The Propagandists

Companies: The Rendon Group, Hill & Knowlton, Ketchum, Burson-Marsteller, and others
Headquarters: Washington, DC
Leading CEO: John Rendon (heads the Rendon Group)
Answer to: Pretty much nobody

Notable Numbers

- $100,000: Amount the federal government pays the Rendon Group per month
- $88 million: Amount the federal government spent on PR firms in 2004[1]

Snapshot

Nobody wants to believe that they are being hoodwinked or brainwashed—especially by their government in whom they trust. But our thoughts and attitudes about our elected officials in the capital as well as our perceptions of the world are being professionally shaped. Lies and propaganda are so mixed up with headline news that it's hard to discern the truth anymore. And the parties behind what has become an information blur are getting very well paid with taxpayer dollars for their ability to deceive the American public. Tip your hat to the PR firms (once known as "publicists") for becoming the greasy wheels of the government's propaganda machine.

Ever since DC began farming out its PR in the 1980s, the results have been flashier, wider-reaching, and more alarming than ever before. Under contract with government agencies, PR firms have prepared slick videos endorsing government programs—and millions of viewers watching them are unaware that these are canned propagandist campaigns.[2]

- A video that aired as a news story on at least forty stations in May 2004 was surreptitiously funded by the Department of Health and Human Services and scripted by a PR firm.[3] In it, an actor—posing as a reporter—"examined" the Medicare issue then before Congress. The video was distinctly in support of the controversial government proposal; as part of the faux piece, a pharmacist calls the Medicare plan "a very good idea."
- In a video aired minutes before the 2004 Super Bowl game, another actor playing a journalist gave a thumbs-up to the government's drug policy. That video news release, also scripted by a public relations firm, was paid for by the Office of National Drug Control Policy. It too was aired with no notification that what viewers were seeing had been commissioned by the feds.

"The use of video news releases [i.e., fake news videos passed off as independent reports] is a common, routine practice in government. . . . Anyone who has questions about this practice needs to do some research on modern public information tools."

—KEVIN KEANE, DEPARTMENT OF HEALTH AND HUMAN SERVICES.[4] MAYBE MR. KEANE
NEEDS TO DO SOME RESEARCH ON U.S. LAW: THE GOVERNMENT ACCOUNTABILITY
OFFICE, FOR ONE, FINDS THE PRACTICE OF USING TAXPAYER DOLLARS TO
DECEPTIVELY PROMOTE GOVERNMENT AGENDAS HIGHLY ILLEGAL.

"We conclude that the prepackaged news stories in these video news releases constitute covert propaganda."

—GOVERNMENT ACCOUNTABILITY OFFICE REPORT, 4 JAN. 2005[5]

Helped along by PR "perception managers," the federal government is actively molding our thoughts, using practices that range from sleazy to illegal. Government-contracted public relations firms have hired columnists and talk show hosts to plug government policies without acknowledging they were being paid to do so. In January 2005, several of these relationships came to light:

- TV and radio broadcaster Armstrong Williams admitted accepting $241,000 from the government to promote the "No Child Left Behind" education program, when the proposal was sitting before Congress.
- Right-wing columnist Maggie Gallagher admitted she had been paid over $40,000 in consulting fees regarding the administration's marriage policy,

which pushes unwed parents to take a trot down the aisle; she later wrote a *National Review* article applauding the marriage program.

*   Conservative marriage counselor Michael McManus confessed that he too had a thicker wallet thanks to this practice: He was paid $10,000 to coo about the benefits of the fed's betrothal initiative, and his foundation snagged $49,000 in federal grants.

PR firms now help sell and manage perceptions about wars, too. But that didn't start with the administration of George W. Bush. The textbook example, reported on by the editor in chief of *Harper's* magazine and such watchdogs as Center for Media and Democracy, occurred during his father's administration.

In the lead-up to the 1991 war, the Kuwait government engaged the help of numerous public relations firms to prepare fake "video news releases" with faux reporters telling of the action of Iraqis in Kuwait, producing them to look like news releases. Run on hundreds of stations, these slickly produced spots did not inform viewers that they were in fact watching an advertisement and not a news report.

THE MARKETING OF DESERT STORM

It was a hard sell. The royal family of Kuwait wanted the United States to attack Iraq, which had taken their land. Run out by Saddam Hussein, whose Iraqi soldiers had marched into Kuwait in August 1990, and now living in exile, they'd asked the United States to invade. One problem: Most Americans didn't know whore Kuwait was. And if they actually knew that the tiny oil-rich Kuwait was squeezed between Iraq and Saudi Arabia, they probably didn't care about the fate of wealthy sheiks. To convince Congress and the American people to support this sort of military endeavor wouldn't be easy. An invasion of Iraqi-occupied Kuwait wouldn't be a quick military action like those into Panama or Grenada, which were nearly over by the time the evening news broadcast stories about them. This would mark the first major military deployment since the unpopular Vietnam War.

Only weeks before, the U.S. ambassador to Iraq, April Glaspie, had assured Saddam Hussein, when he'd asked her what she thought of Iraq invading Kuwait, that the United States would have no objections to it—no opinion whatsoever on an "Arab-Arab" war. Now that Iraq had marched on Kuwait, however, the White House sure had very strong opinions. President George H. W. Bush was all for a military action—he immediately sent Secretary of Defense Dick Cheney to Saudi Arabia that August to talk Saudi King Fahd into allowing U.S. troops to base in his kingdom to launch an attack. (Cheney may have used another propaganda technique—doctored photos—to make his sell.) But this invasion would take a few hundred thousand troops, some serious money, some serious time. Bush knew that at that point, he didn't have enough support in the Democrat-dominated Congress to approve such a war.

And that's where a young Kuwaiti girl revealed only as Nayirah entered the picture. In October 1990, on Capitol Hill, congressmen were called to a special Congressional Human Rights Caucus investigating the human rights abuses of Iraqi troops in Kuwait. As the hearing opened, the fifteen-year-old Kuwaiti took the stand. She said she'd worked as a volunteer in the al-Addan hospital in Kuwait City. A few weeks before, she testified, she had been tending to premature infants in the pediatrics wing of the hospital, when suddenly Iraqi soldiers stormed into the hospital and burst into the room. There, she said, they ripped the defenseless babies from their incubators. "They took the babies out of the incubators, took the incubators, and left the babies on the cold floor to die," Nayirah testified, breaking into sobs.[6] The congressmen in attendance were stunned, so were the press people in attendence (those that weren't present were given a media pack with notes on the testimony); Amnesty International condemned Hussein for the display of heartlessness and reported that 312 babies had died at the hands of the Iraqi soldiers. And President George Bush Sr. worked those 312 dead babies into numerous speeches selling his war plan to the American people and Congress. Bush ultimately won Senate approval for his war by a mere five votes. But there was one problem with Nayirah's testimony: That grim tale was a load of horse puckey. Five months after the war had been officially wrapped up, ABC reporter John Martin tried to corroborate the story in Kuwait. According to the physicians Martin interviewed, there weren't 312 incubators in all of Kuwait. The heart-wrenching testimony, it turned out, had been given by the daughter of royal family member Saud Nasir al-Sabah, the Kuwaiti ambassador to the United States; it's believed she wasn't even in Kuwait when Iraq invaded in August 1990. The hoax was the work of Hill & Knowlton, one of the world's largest PR firms, whose Washington office back then was headed by Craig Fuller, George Bush Sr.'s good friend and former chief of staff. As for the congressmen who'd chaired the hearing—Reps. Tom Lantos and John Edward Porter—their Congressional Human Rights Foundation received a $50,000 donation from the Kuwaiti royal family.[7]

The invasion of Kuwait and Baghdad in 1991 itself became a PR vehicle. If you believe that after being liberated in 1991, Kuwaitis loved Americans, that's because PR maestro John Rendon of the Rendon Group orchestrated the image: Minutes before CNN cameras came rolling through the streets, he thrust American flags into the hands of Kuwaitis.[8]

The New York Times *reported in 2002 that the Pentagon had opened a new "Office of Strategic Influence"—specifically set up to peddle disinformation abroad. Pentagon officials admitted it would include propaganda and covert information campaigns, reported the* Times.[9] *John Rendon of the Rendon Group was called in to head it. The public was outraged and the Pentagon shortly thereafter announced it was closing the office—which critics say was itself the office's first act of disinformation, for in fact, Rendon continued consulting for the U.S. government and embroidering the truth.*

The fingerprints of John Rendon were all over the selling of the 2003 invasion of Iraq as well. As a prelude to the blitz of fibs that was woven into the selling of the Iraq War, the Rendon Group cobbled together the perfect disinformation machine: the Iraqi National Congress. Headed by Iraqi Ahmed Chalabi, a Jordanian banker who hadn't been in Iraq for four decades, the ragtag team of Iraqis and Kurds was paid millions of U.S. taxpayer dollars to trumpet unproven allegations, including that Saddam Hussein possessed weapons of mass destruction. The disinformation factory found an ally in the *New York Times,* particularly star reporter Judith Miller: In the months leading up to the 2003 invasion, she was provided with heaps of "leaked" information and fed numerous half-truths and untruths. Miller ran with them, regurgitating the spin and giving the impression of irrefutable evidence of Saddam's lethal weapons and evil intent; once her articles appeared in that veritable bible of news, they were de facto fact. To complete the circle, the administration would then gallop around to the news shows and cite what they'd read in the *New York Times* as proof of their false claims.[10]

MASTER MOLDER: JOHN RENDON

The Renoir of PR, stylishly touching up reality's flaws, John Rendon has worked for governments and politicians from Panama to Aruba (where he famously dreamed up a scheme to beam the logo of the Christian Democrat Party into the night sky), but his most devoted employer is the U.S. government, which previously hired the Rendon Group to run a smear campaign of Saddam in the Middle East, including anti-Hussein radio and a traveling photo exhibit of the violence wrought by the Iraqis. The Defense Department, which paid (and still pays) his firm some $100,000 a month to ensure the public was (and is) swallowing the War on Terror plan, hired the self-described "information warrior" to run the Coalition Information Center—to control information about war-time operations, including countering enemy information, such as the Taliban's claim that it shot down American choppers in Afghanistan. Although the extent of the tangled webs he's weaved still aren't fully known, many suspect Rendon used his sleight of hand to give the appearance that September 11 and Saddam were inextricably linked.

> "Since forming [the Rendon Group], Mr. Rendon has served as senior communications consultant to the White House . . . the Department of Defense, Government of Kuwait, the Government of Zambia, the Government of Panama, Government of Aruba, the Government of Argentina, Bosnia and Herzegovina Privatization, and numerous members of the U.S. Congress, among others. He has developed comprehensive strategic communications training programs in the Caribbean, North and South America, Africa, the Middle East and Europe. . . . Mr. Rendon [also] has served as an analyst for CBS News."
>
> —FROM THE BIOGRAPHY OF JOHN RENDON ON THE
> RENDON GROUP'S INTERNET SITE

In the months leading up to the Iraq war in 2003, 68 percent of Americans erroneously believed that Iraq was behind the September 11 attacks. After the war, over half of Americans erroneously believed that a definitive link between Iraq and al-Qaeda had been established and a quarter mistakenly believed that weapons of mass destruction had been found in Iraq.[11]

Close-up

The 2003 war in Iraq was the most tightly controlled and censored to date: Pentagon-approved reporters were "embedded"; living with the troops, they were forbidden to interview Iraqis or the troops themselves and their stories were sometimes subjected to military censoring. To judge by what the American public was allowed to see and read, the Iraq War was bloodless, even though 20,000 Iraqis died during it—and another 100,000 have since—figures that likewise disappeared from most reporting in the United States. Rarely does the image of a bloodied soldier even show up on American news. As for the 1,500 Americans who have given their lives in Iraq, their countrymen rarely see those body bags returning home. Until recently it was illegal to show them.

ERASE THE DEATH

Like his father during the Persian Gulf War, President George W. Bush called for a ban on media coverage of dead soldiers arriving or being buried at Dover, the air force base to which corpses of U.S. troops are flown. The mainstream media didn't question it, merely swallowing the order—just as they had the government "request" on showing videos of Osama bin Laden. Suddenly, in 2004, the first images of dead soldiers were shown on TV and in the papers—but it took a Freedom of Information Act request to unleash them. The request hadn't come from the mainstream media. It had come from an obscure freelance writer, Russ Kick, who runs an Internet site, www.thememoryhole.org. Forcing the Pentagon to release photos of the war dead, Kick ran the pictures of three hundred dead American soldiers on his site in May. The mainstream media quickly followed suit, breaking the Bush-inflicted taboo.

"This is the most extensive effort at spinning a war that the Department of Defense has ever undertaken in this country."

—AMERICAN UNIVERSITY COMMUNICATIONS PROFESSOR CHRISTOPHER SIMPSON[12]

The Los Angeles Times *reported that the dramatic scene of the noosed statue of Saddam crashing to the ground in post-invasion Baghdad had been engineered by the U.S. Army, who rounded up Iraqis to drag it around for the camera.[13] Contrary to the image presented, some witnesses say the square was nearly empty[14] and that those who were chanting reportedly weren't just saying, "Down with Saddam"—plenty were saying, "Screw the U.S."[15]*

The government is paying journalists to support its views; PR companies are illegally placing false images in the news; TV stations are broadcasting pro-government videos as though they are independent news reports, while knowing that they are funded by the feds and prepared by PR firms. Even the writers of television dramas have been forced to incorporate government-picked themes—such as the hazards of smoking pot—into their plots.[16] With an eye to image control, flacks are planting stories and supplying premade images the government wants us to see, while blurring or deleting the rest. Is it any wonder Americans are confused? Thanks to the interference of government-funded spinmeisters and pressures from DC, we're not getting a clear view of reality—and analysts say that is very much the intended effect.

Behind the Scenes

Psychological operations—psyops—and spreading disinformation are nothing new: Americans have been exposed to propaganda since at least World War I, when fake news reports of Germans bayoneting babies helped drum up support for entering the war from a previously apathetic public. What is new is that public relations firms, such as the Rendon Group, Hill & Knowlton, Burson-Marsteller, and Ketchum have a much slicker bag of tricks to work with in routinely mass marketing disinformation: Among the ploys these days is using "front companies" and biased reports from partisan think tanks to drive home the desired message.

Front companies typically give the impression of backing something that they do not. For instance, to aid its cigarette manufacturer clients in California, Hill & Knowlton devised a group deceptively named Californians for Statewide Smoking Restrictions: The group was actually funded by the tobacco lobby and was actually against passage of the California law prohibiting smoking in all public places. Burson-Marsteller created the organization Keep America Beautiful: It is a lobby for companies opposed to recycling and a national bottle-return bill—namely, it includes trash hauling companies that fear they will lose business if consumers recycle, or that they will be forced to deal with collecting recyclables. Using these front groups, PR firms conduct surveys, release reports, and raise money—all the while confusing us about what they are really representing.[17]

PR companies have clients beyond the U.S. government: They work magic for corporations such as Monsanto, as well as Big Pharma, the nuclear industry, and the beef association, to name but a few. Much of their money comes from governments abroad: Hill & Knowlton was called in to manage the China account after the Tiananmen Square crisis, and to brighten the images of governments from Indonesia to Peru. The ethics of such companies as these have been questioned numerous times, but Hill & Knowlton was never more damned than in a report by the U.S. Senate Committee on Foreign Relations, which investigated the PR firm's role in the BCCI banking scandal. After the bank was indicted for attempting to launder $32 million for the Medellin cocaine cartel, Hill & Knowlton launched a cover-up. The committee found that "Hill and Knowlton ended up providing information to the Congress and to the press and public that was not merely misleading or distorted, but actually false. Hill and Knowlton assisted in discrediting people who were providing accurate information about the underlying situation, including a former BCCI officer, an investigative journalist and his publisher. Given Hill and Knowlton's close ties to both political parties, and its influence in Washington, this was especially unfortunate."[18]

The U.S. has long been an international master of propaganda in all media, but its most brilliant propaganda campaigns were broadcast over the radio waves.

During and after World War II, Radio Free Europe and Voice of America broadcast to countries behind the Iron Curtain and did more than provide a cultural understanding and explain the policies of the United States. They painted a picture of Uncle Sam as a cross between Jesus and Superman, prompting listeners in such countries as Hungary and Poland to rise up against their leaders. Journalists in Hungary today say Radio Free Europe promised that the United States would swoop in and back up their rebellions, but they never came, instilling a lingering resentment when 100,000 or so died for naught when they rose up against the Communists in 1954. In countries across Eastern Europe, the locals still talk about the hope and promises instilled by Radio Free Europe— that were never fulfilled. That, of course, may be news to most U.S. residents: Broadcasts from these propaganda stations or reports about them were forbidden in the United States. American journalists are also prohibited from attending press conferences of U.S. officials held for the foreign press.

The U.S. government recently launched al-Hurra—a new radio program à la Voice of America that broadcasts from Virginia—geared to Arabs living in Europe. One of its aims is to feed pro-U.S. views and counter information from al-Jazeera, the Arab world's equivalent to CNN. Given that the CIA has been forced to cede much of its propaganda work to public relations companies, such as the Rendon company, it isn't surprising that the agency often works closely with American PR firms. In fact, some say that higher-ups in companies such as Hill & Knowlton actually are agents for the CIA.[19] Whatever their connection to the spy world, public relations groups continue to weave lies into the fabric of our media, creating an environment where it is increasingly difficult to discern what is really going on. The Internet, while certainly capable of publicizing disinformation itself, is also one powerful antidote to this routine duping of Americans via the conventional media.

Agent of Change
Russ Kick: Digging Up What's Disappeared

In an era when the truth seems to have fallen into a black pit, Russ Kick keeps reaching into that darkness, retrieving pieces of reality, and posting them on his Internet site (thememoryhole.com)—funding the massive archive of lost facts mostly from his own "shallow pockets." "I'm fascinated by things that have disappeared in some way, extinct languages, lost works of art and literature, forgotten history," says the blogger and author of numerous books, including *Fifty Things You're Not Supposed to Know*—a compendium of facts including that ge-

netic research shows that about 10 percent
of kids are fathered by those who aren't their
"daddy." "I also have a problem with authority," admits Kick. "We're constantly being
lied to and led astray by the self-serving
people and institutions that have power over
our lives." Kick fights back by publishing
their buried facts: the deleted map from government documents that used to show "important caribou calving areas" in the Arctic
National Wildlife Refuge that the Bush administration is opening up for oil exploration; the transcripts of 9/11 with police
telling workers to stay put in the World
Trade Center; those articles that appear, but
quickly disappear—like the news story saying the CIA was considering sending SWAT
teams to yank the computers of journalists.

Russ Kick, alternative archivist,
"rescuing knowledge, freeing
information"

Kick has filed over eight hundred Freedom of Information Act requests. His
first was to the FBI, requesting its file on the Columbine High School shootings.
"They wanted a huge amount of money for the whole thing," says Kick, who
has spent thousands purchasing government files, "so I ended up getting
about two hundred pages of it."

An anthology editor by day, Kick is an underground investigator by night,
whose tools are Freedom of Information Act requests and a seemingly boundless
energy for filling out forms and scouring Internet sites. Kick is best known for
his FOIA request for photos of the war dead from Iraq—a matter ignored by the
conventional press, which heeded the Bush ban on war photos. After he posted
the three hundred photos the night they arrived, he jotted off a few messages to
the media, figuring that he might get a small item on the back pages of newspapers. "When I woke up the next morning," Kick recalls, "CBS was calling to set
up an interview for the evening news. While the camera crew was setting up in
our apartment, ABC called and wanted me to be on *Good Morning America* the
next morning, so they flew my girlfriend and me to Manhattan on two hours'
notice. During all this, I was doing interviews via cell phone with other news
outlets." The story of the daring freelancer was snatched up by cable news, where
it played in heavy rotation. And the next morning the photos were splashed

across newspapers worldwide, including the front page of the *New York Times*. "I had no idea it would explode like it did." The independent writer with an obsession with all that's hidden may himself go down in history—for pulling out the truths and the facts that have been swallowed up into a dark information hole. (www.thememoryhole.com)

"How are you going to work with people [the Democrats] who seem to have divorced themselves from reality?" That was the last question that fake White House reporter "Jeffrey Gannon" aka James Guckert asked before being revealed as a Republican party plant. Nobody is quite sure how an inexperienced "writer" for Talon News—affiliated with GOPUSA—rated a White House press pass, but one suspects that Karl Rove, who is good pals with Talon's executive editor Bobby Eberle, may have played a role in bringing in the man who was called on during tough press conferences, and whose cooing questions were so softball they came off as loving. House Republicans prevented an investigation of the matter.

▶▶ ◀◀

16. RUPERT MURDOCH:

The Mightiest Media Magnate

Powermonger: Rupert Murdoch
Headquarters: New York City (but jets around everywhere)
Founded: Murdoch inherited newspaper in Adelaide, Australia,
   in 1952
Net worth: About $7 billion[1]

Notable Numbers

- $10 million: Amount Murdoch spent on lobbying from 1999–2002[2]
- 1000+: Number of Murdoch media outlets[3]

Snapshot

Not since Walt Disney has a media magnate been as universally identifiable as Australian-born billionaire Rupert Murdoch, and never has one—not even his rival Ted Turner—been as controversial. The man whose face is as deeply lined as a bulldog's stormed onto six continents, launching television networks, newspapers, TV channels, and programs that are often the most popular in their market and that typically snag more media attention than they give. His globe-wrapping empire of beaming satellites, cable networks, and high-tech printing presses offered a home to the revolutionary: Here he welcomed rule-breaking entertainment including *The Simpsons* and *X-Files* and interactive TV that allows viewers to bet on horse races, as well as such journalistic abominations as London's "topless girlie" newspaper, the *Sun,* and America's loudest and most grating network, Fox News.

> Murdoch's News Corporation is the second largest media empire in the world, trailing only Time-Warner.

Visionary in his strategies and insatiable in his Napoleanic desire to expand, Murdoch possesses one quality that overshadows all others: His communication kingdom epitomizes all that is dicey, worrisome, and out-and-out wrong with the media today—from concentration of media clenched in one hand to the unethical use of that network to plug his own businesses and further his political agendas. Formidable in global reach and powerful in altering views, his kingdom of words written and spoken is downright alarming in its potential conflicts of interest and proven ability to misinform and warp public perception of facts.

"Fox was the news source whose viewers had the most misperceptions."

—CONCLUSION OF PROGRAM ON INTERNATIONAL POLICY ATTITUDES
AFTER AN EXTENSIVE SURVEY REGARDING UNDERSTANDING OF FOREIGN
EVENTS AND MEDIA SOURCES IN THE UNITED STATES[4]

Close-up

Murdoch seems incapable of playing by the rules and has a knack for creating markets where nobody thinks they exist, even knocking down the walls in Communist China. Whether through the cajoling of his well-moneyed lobbying machine, the calling in of political favors from those politicians whom his newspapers helped to elect, or the smooth talking of the baron himself, investigations into his business affairs are snapped shut and doors are opened for Murdoch.

CRACKING CHINA

Things didn't start off so smoothly in Asia. When Rupert Murdoch bought a controlling share in 1993 of Hong Kong–based satellite network Star, he did so with an observation that would haunt him. Upon buying into the network that shoots television programming from Turkey to Taiwan, he announced, "Advances in the technology of telecommunication have proved an unambiguous threat to totalitarian regimes everywhere." That didn't play well with China's totalitarian government, which quickly yanked down satellite dishes all over the mainland

and outlawed the Communism-threatening devices, while adding the name Murdoch to its enemy list. Realizing his gaffe, Murdoch backpedaled. To make amends to the Chinese powers that be, Murdoch approached the government with an offer to shove BBC News—which had shown a documentary on Mao that commented on the leader's fondness for nymphettes—off of Star's programming lineup.[5] The next year, 1995, he heaped on more honey: Murdoch's publishing house HarperCollins forked over $1 million for a biography of Chinese Premier Deng Xiaoping written by a rather biased source—Deng Rong, the premier's daughter. Soon thereafter HarperCollins made news again: The publisher canceled a contract for a book written by Hong Kong Governor Chris Patten that criticized the government in Beijing. Even Murdoch's son James, previously CEO at Star TV, got in to the routine: In 2001, he made a speech at a California think tank condemning Falun Gong—branding the religious group persecuted by the Chinese government as "dangerous" and an "apocalyptic cult." Murdoch Sr. didn't hurt Chinese business either when he told *Vanity Fair* that Beijing's other perceived enemy—the Dalai Lama—was "a very political old monk shuffling around in Gucci shoes." In 1999, Murdoch took a Chinese woman as his third wife: actress and reporter Wendi Deng handily serves as liaison between Murdoch and Beijing. All the song-and-dancing paid off: Star, once banned by China, now shoots into Chinese hotels and some 42 million Chinese households, and Murdoch is now involved in new ventures with Chinese state TV.

Murdoch gives up control of all content to China's state censors, but Chinese officials are still worried about the revolutionary potential of TV networks: The Red Guard is set up in the parking lot of the state network, and armed guards keep watch at the doors of broadcast studios.

The vast number of media outlets alone held by the seventy-four-year-old—over one thousand—gives some the heebie-jeebies, but eyebrows really raise when Murdoch uses his media properties to promote one another's businesses. Reviewers in Murdoch's newspapers frequently rave about his other companies' TV shows and movies, and news stories plug his latest business ventures, even suggesting that readers buy stock in them. The *New York Post* and the London-based tabloid *Sun* are vehicles for electing politicians who aid his business interests—and whom he often calls upon to change laws that obstruct his endeavors.[6] And it sure must be handy to own *TV Guide*, which runs cover stories on his networks' programs and highlights which shows viewers should watch.

MEDIA MOGUL EATS ENEMIES!

Able to crush his foes more readily than can most heads of state, Rupert Murdoch is not above broadcasting his personal vendettas and roasting his adversaries on the public rotisserie. When competitor Ted Turner likened Murdoch to Hitler, Murdoch's *New York Post* responded via its front-page headline "Is Ted Nuts?" When the Clinton government nixed a Murdoch satellite project, the *Post* lashed out at poor Chelsea Clinton, running an embarrassing front-page story about her visit to a clinic after a romance soured.[7] When former London *Times* editor Harold Evans (who became Random House publisher after Murdoch fired him) jumped to the *Daily News,* the *Post* flayed him, calling Evans a "poster boy for high-spending perks and excessive book deals that flopped." Murdoch uses his vast holdings for rewards and charm offensives as well. After Mayor Giuliani gave Murdoch a $20 million tax break on a new Manhattan office, the *Post* gurgled and cooed for the rest of Giuliani's first term. When the FCC announced it would investigate Murdoch's holdings in 1994, Murdoch's publishing house HarperCollins soon coincidentally offered House Speaker Newt Gingrich a whopping $4.5 million two-book deal. Gingrich was later pressured to turn down the book deal. In any case, Murdoch's woes with the FCC regarding foreign ownership soon vanished.[8]

Harpooning in print has been Murdoch's trademark since he first entered the publishing race in Australia. After helping to elect the Labor Party's Dolph Whitman prime minister in 1972, he demanded a favor in return: He wanted Whitman to appoint him as ambassador to Britain. When Whitman refused, Murdoch so continuously and heatedly thrashed the premier that thousands of Australians demonstrated, burning Murdoch's newspaper in the streets. Murdoch endorsed Whitman's opponent in the next election, who subsequently granted Murdoch special rights.

Where Murdoch is most revolutionary is in his ability to shake up tired industries and sniff out new markets where none existed before. In 1986, Murdoch charged into the national television scene in the United States, creating a fourth network—Fox—in a stale environment where the three biggies had dominated for fifty years. Fox rattled the big boys with "alternative" and underground programming, and its popularity took off. But Murdoch really got the networks shook up when Fox intercepted the NFL contract that for years had gone to CBS. Fox also revitalized entertainment, giving a venue to unconventional talents as it unleashed such programs as *The Simpsons, X-Files, King of the Hill,* and *America's Most Wanted*—shows that defined American pop culture in the 1990s. Fox hasn't stopped churning out hits, even if the quality is now highly dubious: The number one show in the country—*American Idol*—is one of Fox's more recent smashes.

For his innovations in amusing us and revitalizing television, Rupert Murdoch deserves a warm round of applause. For parading out pejorative-laden reports and dressing up screaming nationalist sentiments as news, Murdoch deserves to be ejected from his power seat and shot into orbit alongside one of his satellites.

Behind the Scenes

Look for future power plays behind those closed doors. Murdoch's designated heir—son Lachlan, who runs *The New York Post*—is appearing a bit lackluster compared to his thirty-year-old type A brother, James, who turned a profit for StarTV and is now expanding operations as CEO of British satellite TV company bSkyb. Things could get even more interesting if rival John Malone, of Liberty Cable, continues buying up voting shares of Murdoch's News Corporation stock.

17. THINK TANKS:

Questionable Sources

Powermongers: Right-wing think tanks, including the Heritage Foundation
  (religion-based, social conservative)
Headquarters: Most are in Washington, DC

Notable Numbers

- $38 million: Heritage Foundation's 2000 budget[1]
- $24.4 million: American Enterprise Institute's 2000 budget[2]
- $15 million: Cato Institute's 2004 income[3]

Snapshot

Ever wonder who planted the idea in George W. Bush's head to privatize Social Security? Or who launched the notion of Reagan's Strategic Defense Initiative ("Star Wars") and helped to blast off the arms race with Russia? That would be the work of nonprofit think tanks, those vastly influential idea machines that plant seeds of changes, forecast the future, and almost invisibly sculpt government policies with their statistic-laden studies and heady reports.

The term "think tank" was first whispered during World War II: It initially referred to a top-secret, secured room where scientists and military strategists plotted battle plans and dreamed up worst-case scenarios. Early think tanks were the hatching grounds for the Manhattan Project, which created the first nuclear bomb, and conceptualized such "far-out" inventions as the "world-circling space ship" presented by RAND in 1945. But before they even had the name "think tanks" some of these intellectual institutions were taking shape during World War I, starting as political discussion groups funded by philanthropists looking into how to broker peace, or best help put back together a war-torn Europe.

Think-tank scholars are those insight-giving eggheads that we see on TV, the brains to whom the press turns for numbers and highbrow quotes, the experts called in to explain issues to the Senate. These cerebral types are sent out to foster dialogue between warring factions in foreign countries and hired to look at issues from the medical use of pot to how to reorganize the UN. Their thoughts and findings, whether revealed in reports, opinion briefs, or essays, are taken quite seriously: Published as articles, op-ed pieces, and books, these ideas, when circulated to politicians and the media, often lead to new programs and changes in laws.

Some of the original think tanks, whose reports have shaped everything from war plans and weapons to water management and Social Security, include:

- **Brookings Institution:** Its roots stem back to the Institute for Government Research in 1916, and Brookings is still the most quoted in the U.S. media.
- **RAND Corporation:** Started in 1948, the think test is best known for its theoretical "war games" projects and serving as the brains of the U.S. military, essentially inventing such concepts as aerial refueling.
- **Center for Strategic and International Studies (CSIS):** Hatched from Georgetown University's School of Foreign Service in the 1960s, and publisher of the *Washington Quarterly,* CSIS spotlights defense and security matters, and this is where many former government bigwigs, including former secretary of state Madeline Albright, take a desk.
- **American Enterprise Institute:** Founded in 1943 as an offshoot of the U.S. Chamber of Commerce, American Enterprise Institute has never hidden its business ties, but it has recently been overtaken by neocons, among them former UN ambassador (under Reagan) Jeane Kirkpatrick. Other notable fellows: Richard Perle and John Bolton.

Given their profound influence on how government officials frame issues and solve problems, what has recently happened to these mighty institutions is cause for openmouthed alarm. Disguising themselves as think tanks, a new wave of conservative political reformers have galloped onto the scene and are shooting fountains of misinformation, twisting facts to serve their purposes and making no effort whatsoever at giving an impartial look at reality: Whether their goals are to bolster defense or bring right-wing Christian leaders and values into the government, they have predefined plans, and they use their supposedly unbiased "reports" and "briefings" to push them forward.

In the realm of biased pseudo-reports, the Heritage Foundation leads the way. Its reach is vast and its impact great, particularly with Christian conservatives. Despite being blatantly biased, it wielded such formidable political-religious muscle during the Reagan administration that some considered the Heritage Foundation to be a shadow government: It was Heritage that first launched the idea of "Star Wars," and after Reagan left office, it continued hard-pedaling the idea for two decades. Under Bush Jr. it was finally seriously relaunched as the financial black hole, National Missile Defense. That's merely one show of how powerful these ideologues are, and how the ideas of think tanks can drain hundreds of billions of tax dollars from the federal budget.

THE HERITAGE FOUNDATION: THE FAUX TANKERS

They have money, they have reports, and oh, they have ideas, which they blanket Congress with in the form of statistic-laden briefings instructing congressmen on how to vote. This institution, formed in 1973 by right-winger Paul Weyrich (who was also instrumental in founding the Moral Majority), is less a research organization and more an ultraconservative advocacy group that for thirty years has been unswerving in its desires.

In 1994, the Heritage Foundation influenced Newt Gingrich's "Contract with America," which helped Republicans with congressional majorities for the first time in decades.[4]

Prior to that, the Heritage Foundation greeted the incoming Reagan administration in 1980 with a weighty present: Called Mandate for Leadership, the twenty-volume monstrosity of recommendations became the policy bible for the administration. Highlights of its plan to erase liberal influence from government included a $35 billion boost to defense, manipulating food aid as a foreign policy weapon, debilitating the FDA and Environmental Protection Agency, slashing minority programs, and infusing Christian values in public education. According to the Interhemispheric Resource Center, in 1985 "the foundation estimated the [Reagan] administration had acted upon 60 to 65 percent of the recommendations in the Mandate."[5]

The Heritage Foundation wants Christianity as our moral guide, a National Missile Defense system guarding the land, and "traditional family values" firmly in place. "A radical feminist agenda has taken hold of the U.N. process!" Heritage experts concluded after a recent UN conference considered how to prevent teen pregnancies. "Is Prayer Good for Your Health?" and "Giving Thanks to God" are two of the group's reports that betray its religious bent. That's just fine for a Bible group newsletter, but with morality-infused reports extolling the benefits of "virginity pledges for teens," and exploring how same-sex nuptials in the Netherlands have ruined marriage, this frighteningly powerful "research institution" that claims to provide nonpartisan analysis is making a mockery of what think tanks used to stand for. (www.heritage.org)

If you want to quickly identify a right-wing, Christian-oriented think tank, look at how it regards womens' rights. When "experts" from the Heritage Foundation attended the 2005 UN Commission on the Status of Women, they skewed their report thusly: "What benefits women more: promoting healthy family life or asserting new privacy rights for teens? It's clearly the former, experts Jennifer Marshall, Melissa Pardue and Grace Smith write in a new paper from The Heritage Foundation. Decades of social science research suggest that the family centered on marriage offers tremendous economic and social welfare advantages to women and children. Yet many attendees at the annual meetings of the U.N. Commission on the Status of Women . . . don't seem to agree. . . . Women would be far better served if the delegates worked to protect marriage and the family as the fundamental building block of society. . . . Few things are better than healthy family life at preventing women from suffering the many ill effects of poverty." (From a March 2005 Heritage Foundation press release.)

MR. MONEY BAGS: RICHARD MELLON SCAIFE

When Bill and Hillary Clinton hinted at a right-wing conspiracy against them, they were talking about billionaire Richard Mellon Scaife—who handed *The American Spectator* magazine $2.3 million to dig up Clinton dirt, and who is rumored to have believed that the Clintons had killed some sixty people in their rise to power. The publisher of the *Pittsburgh Tribune-Review*, which he uses to skewer his enemies, Scaife (who inherited his money from the Mellon oil and banking empire) is considered to be the financial godfather of the modern conservative movement donating some $200 million to right-wing causes over the years. He first threw himself into politics during the Nixon years by donating $1 million to Nixon's election (disguised as 3,300 checks of $3,000 each to bogus fronts). Believing that the right was underrepresented in U.S. government and American society, he financed the building of an empire of conservatism: Much of his funds went to pseudo think tanks such as the Heritage Foundation and right-wing magazines and shrill advocacy groups, although some does end up at more trustworthy sources such as CSIS. Surprisingly, Scaife may not be as right as he is made out to be. To the dismay of his ultraconservative colleagues, he is pro-choice on the abortion issue, and has also given millions to Planned Parenthood over the years.[6] Well, what do you expect from a loose cannon?

The venerable brain trusts that wield tremendous clout in DC are themselves now being studied: Some observers say think tanks are far too influential, sometimes writing government policy, and that some are little more than lobbying groups, with political conclusions drawn long before scholars start their research or pick up their pens. The new wave of right-wing think tanks—brought to life mostly by billionaire Richard Scaife—seem to be incapable of independent, nonpartisan thinking: Many of the young'uns (as well as the older Heritage Foundation) write reports that resemble advertising campaigns, and only champion the causes and the views dictated by their conservative benefactors, their corporate donors, their church leaders, and the Republican Party.

The latest arrivals on the think tank scene are heavily funded by corporations. Their thinkers often appear on TV, but they mostly spew whatever information their corporate sponsors would like you to hear. They offer yet more proof that even though the administration may change, the powers that be never really go away: Many just take a desk as a fellow, expert, or consultant at a think tank. A few of the notables:

- **Hudson Institute:** It's taken the World Health Organization to task—for approving generic HIV-fighting drugs—while announcing that antibiotic- and-hormone-soaked beef is actually good for us (helps the economy), as is genetically modified food. We can only assume that cigarettes and heroin would be acclaimed by Hudson as well if their producers donated as much as biotech food growers and drug makers do—nearly $8 million last year. That its board of directors includes Craig Fuller—who led the Hill & Knowlton propaganda blitz about Kuwait in 1990—and James Dowling from PR whitewasher Burson-Marsteller (which represents Monsanto, among others) makes this think tank's credentials even more dubious. (www.hudson.org)

- **Center for Security Policy:** Created in 1988 by "I-Heart-Arms" neocon Frank Gaffney, a columnist for Sun Myung Moon's *Washington Times*, this think tank, with the motto "Promoting Peace through Strength," cheers for a bolstered military and attacks all who oppose missile defense or support such silly notions as arms controls and bans on nuclear testing. The ros- ter of directors and advisors is a Who's Who of Defense—from Lockheed and Boeing VIPs to ex–CIA directors and Pentagon officials. Its newslet- ter, which goes to the White House, Pentagon, and Congress, and its on- site collection of articles, provides the best roundup of international stories on security and military matters and gives anxious types new things to worry about, like how electromagnetic energy pulsing from a nu- clear blast in the atmosphere could knock out the entire communications system of the country. (www.centerforsecuritypolicy.org)

- **Competitive Enterprise Institute:** Cobbled together in 1984, this anti- environmental, pro-business think tank is great for soothing jangled nerves. The FDA may worry about mercury levels in fish, but CEI's envi- ronmental experts say there's absolutely no reason to worry, levels are negligible. Food activists criticize the biotech industry, but CEI informs us that the activists are simply fearmongers: "Not a single person has been harmed or an ecosystem disrupted" from eating genetically modified food, it asserts.[7] (Never mind the fact nobody has ever tested the effects on human health, and that the Union of Concerned Scientists documents that the ecosystem is indeed being contaminated.) CEI applauds the Bush administration for pulling out of the Kyoto Protocol on reducing air pollution—the treaty is flawed, they say, plus the idea of global warming is bogus. And that merger between Verizon and MCI, says CEI, is actually "good for consumers." The tank that advocates dropping air quality standards for automobiles—it causes more people to die because consumers buy smaller cars that sustain more severe damage in crashes, they claim—is, not surprisingly, heavily funded by the auto and oil industries.[8] Too bad that this bunch of jokers is so media-friendly that its so-called experts are regularly quoted in papers from the *Wall Street Journal* to *USA Today:* When you see the name CEI, raise an eyebrow. (www.cei.org)

Close-up

A handful of foundations run by wealthy families who are pumping hundreds of millions into conservative think tanks each year are fueling the shift to the Right: Progressives call it "the buying of a movement."[9] The financial boost from the (brewmeister) Adolph Coors Foundation helped launch the movement and the Heritage Foundation; the foundations of John M. Olin, the Koch Family, and Lynde and Harry Bradley are three others that kick in barrels of money to fuel the Right's spectacular rise. But Richard Mellon Scaife truly revved up the conservative think tank machine—and the conservative momentum in general. He's handed out more than $340 million ($600 million in today's dollars) to right-wing causes in the past three decades.

Centrist and progressive groups point out that with their right-wing agendas in hand, these politically driven think tanks are cogs in an information-cranking machine that is crafting conservative U.S. policies including privatizing Social Security, disempowering government agencies, increasing military defense expenditures, and handing over social agency powers to religious organizations. The might of the new Right's institutions and their affiliated advocacy groups grows as they harness everything from the Internet and satellite TV to speakers' bureaus to broadcast their views. While some thinkers continue to shape policy by honestly trying to assess facts, implicitly promoting neither Right nor Left, the emergence of these well-funded ideological institutions on the political scene is co-opting the collective cerebral establishment. More than ever we're watching the slow death of the true think tank and with it any semblance of impartial, objective thought.

Behind the Scenes

In the same way that many right-wing think tanks sprang up to balance the power of the Council on Foreign Relations and think tanks that they considered liberal, such as the Brookings Institution (which many consider moderate to right-leaning), an even newer wave of centrist and progressive think tanks is shooting up. Among them: "think tank without walls" Foreign Policy in Focus (www.foreignpolicy-infocus.org), the Progressive Policy Institute (www.ppionline.org), the Center for American Progress (www.americanprogress.org), and the Institute of Policy Studies (www.ips-dc.org)—all further politicizing institutions that used to be nonpartisan, theoretically.

> *The media use far more conservative experts when they interview think-tank spokespeople, but it is not usually deliberate: Right-wing think tanks have signed on with powerful public relations firms and speakers' bureaus, so the media is likely to hear from their speaking agents whenever a relevant issue arises.*

Meanwhile, numerous nonpartisan professional alliances—such as the Union of Concerned Scientists (www.ucsusa.org) and the Federation of Atomic Scientists (www.fas.org) are churning out their own slick reports and books—on issues from the control of seed banks to the inner workings of the war machine and the politics of oil—as are citizen activist groups such as the Polaris Institute (www.polarisinstitute.org), Public Citizen (www.citizen.org), the Center for Public Integrity (www.publicintegrity.org), and Political Research Associates (www.publiceye.org). The truth *is* out there, somewhere, but increasingly, we have to be motivated to find it.

18. COUNCIL ON FOREIGN RELATIONS:

Powerful Whispers

Organization: Council on Foreign Relations (CFR)
Headquarters: New York City
Membership: 4,000

Notable Number

- $30 million: CFR's annual budget, mostly from foundations and membership dues

Snapshot

It's powerful, that we all agree on. The Council on Foreign Relations has molded U.S. policy for the past eighty years. CFR's journal, *Foreign Affairs,* is so influential that it's said if you want to read tomorrow's laws, read today's *Foreign Affairs.* But trying to get a handle on exactly what this bipartisan, nonprofit organization is can be a tough task. It wears many hats, including:

- A think tank: CFR's big-name fellows and researchers regularly expound on weighty issues in highbrow opinion papers read by the world's governing elite.
- A policy forum: Its members are invited to exclusive lunches where they can talk with the most influential movers of the day.
- A private social club for high-IQ types: Almost anybody who is anybody in the world of government and media, or plans to be in the future, clamors for membership in this prestigious cadre.

- A public service agency: The council puts up numerous guides to current events, foreign affairs, and terrorism on its Web sites. Don't know the difference between Hamas and Hezbollah? Not sure why China and Japan are spatting? Check out CFR's easy-to-understand Web sites (cfr.org and terrorismanswers.org).
- An unofficial job placement agency: It's said that high-powered CEOs go through the CFR phone book when looking for qualified brains to fill job positions.
- A publisher: The council's journal, *Foreign Affairs,* routinely contains many of the most influential ideas to see the ink of a printing press.

Recent speakers at private CFR meetings include:

- U.S. Secretary of Defense Donald Rumsfeld
- Prime minister of Japan Junichiro Koizumi
- Former U.S. secretary of state Henry Kissinger
- UN weapons inspector Hans Blix
- President of Colombia Alvaro Uribe
- President of Afghanistan Hamid Karzai
- Former U.S. secretary of state Madeleine Albright

Whatever you wish to call it, the Council on Foreign Relations is terribly cerebral and Ivy Leaguish. With its membership by invitation only, CFR exerts a vast, and often unpublicized, impact on the world, particularly with regard to the United States and the face it puts forward on the overseas stage. CFR meddles in every area from foreign relations to security, economics to trade, news coverage to wars. Even though it operates outside of government, this power player in fact flexes huge muscles with both the U.S. government and the international community, since many of its members are government leaders or become part of government. It is also horribly threatening to conservative groups—even though CFR is neither a liberal nor a political organization and its members have been deeply polarized over issues such as the war in Iraq. In fact, faux think tanks such as the Heritage Foundation and boards such as the Council for National Policy openly state that they are the right-wing's answer to CFR.

THE BEGINNINGS OF THE COUNCIL ON FOREIGN RELATIONS

The group that would later become known as the United States' most powerful organization was born during World War I. Col. Edward M. House, advisor to President Woodrow Wilson, pulled together bright young thinkers of the day

to provide background briefings about Europe and to suggest ideas for recon-
structing Europe once the war ground to a halt. This group of Americans, known
as "the Inquiry," and headed by soon-to-be-famous columnist Walter Lippman,
set sail for France in 1919 where the *très* important Paris Peace Conference
was reorganizing postwar Europe. While abroad, the Inquiry met up with other
intellectuals, strongly bonding with those of the British delegation, with whom
they formed the Anglo-American Institute of International Affairs. From that organization, the Council on Foreign Affairs was ultimately conceived in 1921 with
a few million dollars from the Rockefeller and Carnegie Foundations as well as
funding from banker J. P. Morgan. It was first headed by former secretary of state
and Nobel Peace Prize–winner Elihu Root while their British counterparts
founded the Royal Institute of International Affairs. The goal of the new American
group, whose members were mostly wealthy bankers, lawyers, professors, and
government sorts was to keep up an ongoing discussion on international affairs.

During World War II, a group from CFR presented the U.S. State Department
with postwar planning ideas called "the War and Peace Studies"—650 reports
funded with $350,000 from the Rockefeller Foundation—and secretly circulated
through the State Department. "The matter is strictly confidential," wrote CFR director Isaiah Bowman, "because the whole plan would be 'ditched' if it became
generally known that the State Department is working in collaboration with any
outside group."[1] The studies were one factor leading to the hugely important
Marshall Plan, when the United States loaned European countries billions of
dollars to rebuild after World War II.

---

*Typically, both the Republican and Democratic presidential candidates are
members of CFR. George W. Bush is one of the few presidents in the past
eighty years who wasn't a CFR member. (His father was on the roster.)*

The main reason that right-wingers regard CFR suspiciously, and why it
causes raised eyebrows even among some progressives, is that CFR greatly
shapes and shades government policy, whether the council's thinkers are called
in as official consultants or not. Granted, their effects aren't so obvious within the
current administration, but they nonetheless still guide U.S. foreign policies and
regulations. Thanks to CFR, for instance, the United States has a new practice
of screening container ships for explosives and weapons of mass destruction—
before they ever leave foreign ports.

The group's greatest effect, however, may have been during the Cold War,
when CFR—or rather its member diplomat George Kennan—accidentally triggered an arms race.

THE RUSSIANS AREN'T COMING, THE RUSSIANS AREN'T COMING

In 1947, *Foreign Affairs* published an article called "The Sources of Soviet Conduct" by "X"—later identified as diplomat George Kennan—which presented a concept that would launch a new way of thinking about enemies as well as a huge arms buildup. Referred to as communist "containment," the article suggested that the United States try to restrict the ideological flow of communism in other parts of the world. Reflecting how seriously *Foreign Affairs* and its publisher, the Council on Foreign Relations, was (and still is) regarded, this postwar suggestion kicked off the Cold War and the Red Scare as though a sickle-wielding Satan were approaching the Statue of Liberty. As a result of the article's inference, the U.S. government launched a war to militarily "contain" communism before it struck our shores: Billions of dollars were shoveled into arms and handed out to foreign countries who promised not to succumb to the Evil One's call; the United States plotted the toppling of "damn Commies" (or those believed to be) everywhere. The idea of the communistic contagion itself was contagious, growing like maniacal obsession, unleashing the McCarthy era and a wave of bomb-shelter-building paranoia. Horribly, this perception of a direct threat from the Soviet Union was altogether exaggerated—at least at the beginning, according to the article's author. It was a "misunderstanding almost tragic in its dimensions," George Kennan would later lament.[2] "It all came down to one sentence in the 'X' article," he told *NewsHour with Jim Lehrer* in 1996, half a century after his article planted the misunderstood "containment" idea, "where I said that wherever [the Soviets] confronted us with dangerous hostility anywhere in the world, we should do everything possible to contain it and not let them expand any further. I should have explained that I didn't suspect them of any desire to launch an attack on us. This was right after the [second world] war, and it was absurd to suppose that they were going to turn around and attack the United States. I didn't think I needed to explain that, but I obviously should have done it."[3] Yes indeed, sir, that might have been really helpful.

Close-up

Today, the Council on Foreign Relations' backdrop logo is often seen when television networks show clips of speeches by VIP officials such as Donald Rumsfeld and Paul Wolfowitz, who make a point of personally explaining their policies to this mighty bunch that includes powerful Republican and Democratic politicians and well as the top players of the media. CFR members are often called to be part of task groups or to make recommendations on such matters as homeland security and terrorism. While the country was still scratching its head after the 2001 al-Qaeda attacks, for example, CFR was busy posting explanations of terrorist groups and their motives on its Web sites.

> *With members including Condoleezza Rice, Colin Powell, Bill Clinton, Dan Rather, Sandra Day O'Connor, Dick Cheney, Diane Sawyer, and thousands of other big-name Americans, the nonpartisan group is accused of being elitist: Members must be sponsored to join and once in the club, they are privy to intimate lectures by the leading powermongers of the day, gaining an understanding of world issues that rarely filters down to the common man.*

The group's influence is only one factor that rankles some right-wingers. They also suspect that CFR, like the United Nations, which extreme conservatives also loathe, is pushing for a global government. Recycled John Birchers and other ultraconservatives have long believed CFR is the playpen of the communist devil: They regard the very origins of the Council on Foreign Relations as a cause for alarm. Woodrow Wilson's advisor and CFR founder, Col. Edward House, an admirer of Marx, later wrote a novel called *Philip Dru: Administrator.* In the fictional work, the protagonist sought to establish a socialist, one-world government; the book also mentioned tax-free foundations and the graduated income tax. This has been fodder for conspiracists to assert that the Council on Foreign Relations, which takes advantage of funding from tax-free organizations, is, like Philip Dru, also pushing for an integrated global government.

Behind the Scenes

The Council on Foreign Relations isn't the only "policy forum" that pushes its ideas on the government. The Trilateral Commission and the secretive Bilderberg Group have serious clout as well, although it is more difficult to see their specific effects. One member they all have in common: David Rockefeller.

The Council on Foreign Relations, while arguably the most powerful and certainly the most open and helpful of the bunch, is but one of several policy groups that issue reports, make recommendations, and have a hand in stirring world events. And like the Council on Foreign Relations, the Trilateral Commission and the Bilderbergers were all funded by Rockefeller funds.

Born of World War I, World War II, and the Cold War, CFR represents the clout of the concerned citizen at the extreme: It presents a means for its members to stay abreast of foreign policy matters, sway decision makers, and network with the power players of the day, all in one. Then again, that's the same thing the Heritage Foundation is doing.

19. GEORGE SOROS:

The Meddler

Powermonger: George Soros
Headquarters: New York City
Founded: Quantum Fund in 1969
Net worth: $7.2 billion

Notable Numbers

- $5 billion: Amount Soros has donated to promote "open societies" world-wide
- 50: Number of countries where his foundations have tried to foster democracies

Snapshot

George Soros likes to meddle, and when Soros meddles the impact is huge. The financial whiz, whose Manhattan-based Quantum Fund was the most successful investment firm ever, meddles in several arenas, starting with foreign cash: His 1992 speculating on the British pound netted Quantum Fund a couple of billion dollars and earned him the name "the Man Who Broke the Bank of England"; some say his gambling on the Thai baht kick-started the 1997 Asian financial crisis.

Many analysts say it is unfair to blame Soros for the devaluation of the British pound or the Asian financial market: He merely predicted what would happen and successfully and legally gambled on it. They say he should not be held responsible for whatever effects that speculation had on those economies. As for his take on his role in those financial crises, Soros says he was playing by the rules. But he also thinks international finance rules should be tightened to prevent people like him from being able to take advantage of vulnerabilities.

Soros is far more than a simple financial opportunist, however. He is better known as a billionaire philanthropist meddling in global affairs. The man who loathes dictators, propagandists, and idealogues donated millions to Soviet dissidents during the 1980s, helping to pull down the Communist regime. He also helped build up democracies in post-Communist Eastern Europe, giving away billions to fund projects from education to bringing electricity to villages.

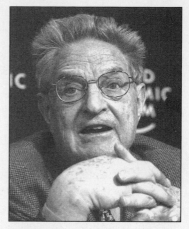

George Soros guarding democracy—
even in the United States

"He's been described as the only private citizen with his own foreign policy."

—STEVE INSKEEP, ON NPR'S *MORNING EDITION,* MAY 9, 2005[1]

Donating some $450 million a year to projects to better the planet, George Soros is one of the world's largest donors; some say that with regard to percentage of income, he is the top donor. Considered by the editor of *The American Benefactor* to be "the only American who rivals the great philanthropists of the 1890s,"[2] such as Andrew Carnegie and John D. Rockefeller, he typically gives away more than the Ford Foundation every year.

BACKGROUND

Born a Hungarian Jew in Budapest in 1930, George Soros was first known as George Schwartz. His father, a promoter of Esperanto, changed the family name to Soros—which means "to soar" in that "medley language"—but there were political reasons as well. As Nazis moved into Hungary, Soros's father broke up the family, hiding them in the homes of sympathetic Hungarians. Hidden away, the Soros family survived World War II and the Holocaust, but Communists marched in and steamrolled democracy at war's end. Shipped off to England, Soros studied at the London School of Economics, but it was when he jumped to the United States that he launched his fortune. Starting the Quantum Fund, he showed a talent for slick international finance maneuvers, quickly grasping how to manipulate foreign currencies and betting against their rise or fall with hedge funds. Watching what was happening in Eastern Europe from across the Atlantic, he financially backed resistance groups, including Solidarity in Poland and Vaclav Havel's Chapter 77 in Czechoslovakia. In 1991, when the Soviet Union fell, he founded the Open Society Institute, which donates hundreds of millions each year to promote "open societies"—democracies where discussion is fostered and a free market is in place. And that includes fighting tyranny and funding those who try to bring it down—from Georgia and the Ukraine to the United States.

Having invested over $5 billion to overthrowing dictatorships in Africa and Asia, Soros never thought he'd have to fight totalitarianism at home. Rightly fearing that democracy is disappearing in the United States, Soros is now meddling in a whole different field: American politics. He's not running for office, though. He's simply been riling things up—holding up a mirror and showing what the United States has become in a few short years. Not long after 9/11, Soros began giving speeches at political rallies warning that the U.S. government has been hijacked by extremists who are shoving our rights out the window and turning the land of the free into the home of the afraid. But he gave more than speeches, his time, and advice. He gave millions trying to defeat George W. Bush in the 2004 election.

"America, under Bush, is a danger to the world. And I'm willing to put my money where my mouth is."

—GEORGE SOROS IN NOVEMBER 2003, WHEN HE HAD ALREADY DONATED
OVER $15 MILLION TO THE DEFEAT-BUSH CAUSE[3]

All told, Soros donated over $27 million to defeat the president, saying it was the "most important cause I'm involved in" and the "central focus of my life."

Close-up

One simple sentence turned Soros into a political animal in the United States: "Either you are with us or you are with the terrorists." Uttered in September 2001 by President George W. Bush, the words struck a very raw nerve with Soros. "It reminded me of the Germans," he told the *Guardian*. "My experiences under Nazi and Soviet rule have sensitized me." When Attorney General John Ashcroft condemned those who questioned his Patriot Act, saying those who opposed him "give ammunition to America's enemies," it reminded Soros of the propaganda the Communists churned out in every broadcast on TV and in every copy of the news.

Starting in 2003, Soros mounted a loud, controversial campaign against the reelection of George Bush, whom he believes is guided by a mean, militaristic, neoconservative political machine, which came into power to assert American dominance over the world and to increase military spending in the process. Soros took out full-page ads imploring Americans not to cave in to "the politics of fear," pointing out how the Bush administration was "shamelessly exploiting the fears of 9/11," conjuring up images of "mushroom clouds over our cities" while simultaneously "suppress[ing] all dissent by calling it unpatriotic." The horrors of September 11, Soros said, had "been hijacked by a bunch of extremists to put into effect policies that they were advocating before—such as the invasion of Iraq."[4] He painted the Iraqi war as a disaster that has "endangered our security and our troops" and brought worldwide condemnation, particularly as the United States couldn't find weapons of mass destruction or a link between Saddam and al-Qaeda, or even establish democracy in a country that is now overrun with insurgents.

> "We went to war in Iraq on false pretences. There was no connection between Saddam Hussein and al-Qaeda. There were no weapons of mass destruction. . . . And what I find most galling is the final argument of justification that we went for the sake of the Iraqi people."
>
> —GEORGE SOROS, IN A JUNE 3, 2004, SPEECH IN NEW YORK

The backlash to his anti-Bush stance was predictable. Fox's Bill O'Reilly called Soros a "left-wing loonie" and "a crusading atheist." Right-wing pundits sneered that he was "a socialist billionaire" and "a soft-money Marxist," and the rabid Republicans at GOPUSA sniped that he was "Satan." Speaker of the House Dennis Hastert even went on to dangerously slander Soros on Fox TV, insinuating that Soros was involved in drug cartels—a slap for which Soros demanded an apology, and could have hauled Hastert's hiney to court.

Soros has had direct dealings with the Bush family. In 1986, Harken, an oil company partly owned by Soros, bought up Spectrum 7, a troubled oil company run by George W. Bush, who was briefly installed on the board before Harken went belly up. Soros also is an investor in the Carlyle Group— a private equity firm—in which George Bush Sr. also invests (and worked as a consultant).

In the end, Soros's efforts appeared to be for naught. Despite Soros's hefty donations to organizations such as America Coming Together, the Center for

American Progress, and Moveon.org, and despite the philanthropist's passionate articles and speeches, President George W. Bush took the 2004 election.

Behind the Scenes

Now that Soros has identified himself as a political force, he's dodging more bullets from the Republican Party. Lawmakers loudly point out that Soros supports euthanasia, medical marijuana, and a needle exchange program for junkies, insinuating that these are all un-American activities. The extremists are now painting Soros as a radical, referring to him as a convicted felon[5] because of a French court ruling on insider trading.

JUDICIAL SLAP

Although Soros keeps his nose clean in most financial operations, in 2002 he was fined $2 million by a French court after being found guilty of insider trading, a decision that Soros is appealing. Soros says he was asked to join a takeover of a French bank in 1988, an offer he declined. However, he bought the bank's stock. Others who were tried in France for doing the same were acquitted; the book was thrown only at Soros.

One of Soros's more controversial ideas: He wants more regulation of international financial markets, and the way to do that, he has said, is to give more power to the World Bank. No word on if his views have been modified now that neocon Paul Wolfowitz—one of Soros's idealogical foes—is heading the institution.

Soros's plan to defeat Bush's reelection may have been shot down, but Soros is not shutting up. He still implores Americans to guard the democracy that is slipping out the back door, and the man who survived the Nazis and the Soviets continues to urge citizens to stand up and be critical of the state.

20. REV. SUN MYUNG MOON:

Still Rising

Zealot: Rev. Sun Myung Moon
Estimated worth: In the billions of dollars
Followers: Believed to number in the millions worldwide

Notable Number

- 1,000: Estimated number of Moon front organizations[1]

Snapshot

Most people thought he went the way of the wide tie and got lost somewhere in the 1980s. But Rev. Sun Myung Moon is back. Once accused of running his Unification Church like a brainwashing cult, the man who was tossed in U.S. federal prison for tax evasion, and was once suspected of being Korean intelligence, is more powerful and richer than ever with assets believed to be in the billions of dollars. These days the round-faced octogenarian and self-proclaimed Messiah holds court with powerful politicians and religious leaders, owns vast holdings of real estate in the United States and South America, and runs companies across the planet—from chinchilla farms and small weapons businesses to fishing fleets in Alaska and the wire service UPI (which he bought in May 2000).

Moon owns dozens of publications worldwide—from Japan to Africa, Latin America to the Middle East—including Insight *magazine and* The World and I. *In DC, his hard right* Washington Times, *has gained respect in some conservative circles.*

LOVE IN THE LIGHT OF THE MOON

Traditionally, the Unification Church mandated that all marriage mates be chosen by Rev. Moon, known as "Father," who coupled complete strangers in weddings that some speculated were more about providing U.S. citizenship to Koreans than about producing long-lasting marriages; some former members have sued Moon for throwing them into unhappy relationships. Although not all of his ideas about sex are known—the church keeps the details of many of his teachings under wraps—they do include elaborate rituals, including:

* All sex acts must be performed near a photo of him, perhaps for its aphrodisiacal qualities.
* Three days of man on top are followed by three days of woman on top.
* Specific procedures must be observed for using the holy, church-provided washcloth, and it should never be washed.

Extramarital affairs are anathema, and he's referred to gays as "dung-eating dogs"; he condemns American women as coming from "a line of prostitutes." Rape so defiles the victim that he has urged women to kill themselves—by biting off their tongue if need be—rather than submit to the attack. And who knows how many of these ideas are slipping into his government-funded programs on marriage counseling and celibacy for youth.

The man known for his "mass marriages"—he has wed thousands of couples simultaneously in such venues as Madison Square Garden—is now deemed so respectable that several of his Unification Church front groups, such as Free Teens USA, are being tossed millions of dollars by the Bush administration to teach couples how to stay married and to teach teenagers how to stay celibate until that special time.

MOON: THE STAMP OF FEDERAL APPROVAL

Top Moonies have snatched plum jobs in the Bush administration and several Moon front groups are being handsomely funded through Bush's Faith-Based Initiative program.[2] The short list:

* David Caprara, once president of Moon's American Family Coalition, now oversees VISTA, the government agency that funds projects in low-income areas and doles out millions of dollars for funding of "faith-based" programs.

- Josephine Hauer, who graduated from Rev. Moon's Unification Theological Seminary, works for the U.S. Department of Health and Human Services as a marriage specialist.
- Free Teens USA: The Moon-backed group, which teaches "no sex" education, recently received $475,000 to run celibacy programs for teens. (One of its lessons to illustrate sex's intimacy involves passing around a cup of warm spit.)
- The California State Healthy Marriage Initiative, which funds Moon marriage counseling front groups, received a $336,000 federal grant in 2004.

After George H. W. Bush left office, Moon hired him (and the Mrs.) to speak at conventions for Moon front groups, reportedly paying $100,000 per speech.[3] *At one, Bush praised Moon for being "a man of vision"—words that may have been more powerful than a pardon.*

George Bush Sr. so believes in the Korean-born preacher that the former president now jaunts around the world to laud him—being paid handsomely by Moon to speak at conventions where thousands turn up. And Moon is apparently held in such high esteem that he was recently "crowned" by a member of Congress—in a Senate building no less.

MOON'S CONGRESSIONAL CORONATION

In one of the more absurd acts in congressional history, Rev. Sun Myung Moon was "crowned" in March 2004 by Sen. Danny K. Davis, in front of some eighty congress members in an event staged in the Dirksen Senate Office Building. The ceremony was officially part of Moon's Ambassadors for Peace program, which awarded dozens of civic leaders and politicians for their acts to promote peace. But the showstopper was when the senator from Illinois placed shimmering, jewel-encrusted crowns atop the heads of Moon and his wife, Hak Ja Han, both decked out in embroidered velvet robes befitting the royalty that, last time we checked, they aren't. In his following speech, Moon went on to modestly declare himself the savior of the planet, as is his wont. Nearly as bizarre as the ceremony itself was that the media ignored the fact that a man who is trying to turn the world into a theocracy united under him had drawn so many bigwigs together to seemingly endorse his plan. Several months later freelancer John

Gorenfeld broke the story in Salon.com, forcing the *Washington Post* to belatedly cover the event—and then there was some explaining to do. Most of the congressmen in attendance said they had been tricked—having had no idea what Moon had planned right there on Capitol Hill.[4]

The University of Bridgeport in Connecticut is another Moon holding. Professors World Peace Academy, a Moon front group, bought it out in 1992.

MOON MEDIUM

But those are only his connections on this planet. He really has some high-placed friends in the netherworld, he says. In fact, Moon says he's been meeting regularly with everybody from Jesus to John F. Kennedy and Dwight D. Eisenhower. They all adore him, according to Moon, who claims that all the dead VIPs, every last one of them, agree that Moon is our savior.[5] In a 2002 advertising blitz, Moon took out full-page newspaper ads explaining to Americans that he had been tapped as the new religious leader of the world. Jesus, the campaign said, had recently hailed Moon as the new Messiah, and Mohammed himself was so thrilled at the idea that he led a cheer for Moon[6] at a conference of the dead where the usual suspects—Confucius, Thomas Jefferson, Abe Lincoln, and even university founder John Harvard showed up, along with numerous other deceased leaders. (God, alas, was unable to attend, but sent along a message saying he agreed with Jesus' call.) Earthly forces, however, conspired to keep the word from fully reaching the masses: The full-page ad was nixed coast to coast—from the *New York Times* to *The Oregonian*.[7]

"There is something that people must fulfill for the sake of their eternal lives in the spirit world. All the people of America must follow the teachings in the Unification Thought and Divine Principle of Rev. Sun Myung Moon, who is the returning Lord in this age and the Messiah."

—JAMES MADISON, AS QUOTED BY MOON IN 2003[8]

What Moon is actually up to isn't entirely clear,[9,10] but he's focusing not just on the political establishment but powerful religious leaders as well: He's thrown money at Christian ultraright strategist/*Left Behind* author Tim LaHaye[11] and by at least one report he is funding the ultraright-wing Council for National Policy, believed to be the core of the Republican Party. And like LaHaye and other members of the Council for National Policy, Moon envisions a world where the law of the land is the law of God. What he neglects to mention widely is that in his world the only accepted language may be Korean.

"We must have an autocratic theocracy to rule the world."

—REV. SUN MYUNG MOON[12]

Close-up

Bit by bit, piece by piece, Moon is successfully wooing—some would say buying—evangelicals, Muslim leaders, and world politicians over to his team. His groups sponsor prayer breakfasts and luncheons attended by U.S. congressmen and former attorney general John Ashcroft, and his Interreligious and Interfaith Federation for World Peace conferences have pulled in hundreds of thousands as speakers and attendees, including the Bushes and the powerful Tim and Beverly LaHaye. He has been buttering up religious leaders of all faiths—one of his front groups bailed out Jerry Falwell's financially floundering Liberty University, handing over several million dollars to keep the religious institution in Lynchburg, Virginia, afloat—and he worked with Louis Farrakhan in a Muslim-Christian Million Family March in October 2000.

Moon recently launched a campaign to yank crosses from churches: The American Clergy Leadership Conference—backed by Moon—promotes the idea that the crosses divide religions that he wants to come together as one religious kingdom headed by him. Some churches actually pulled them.

Whether religious leaders take him seriously or they just like his dough is a matter of debate, but Moon's pull with politicians is cause for concern. Perhaps they are just paying him back for past shows of faithfulness to their causes. After all, Moon has shown his support in many ways:

- Launched pro-war rallies during the Persian Gulf War of 1991.
- Funneled at least $100,000 to covertly fund the contras in Nicaragua.
- Moon's American Freedom Coalition produced *Oliver North: Fight for Freedom* (a video heaping praise on North) and the *Washington Times* loudly supported North during the Iran-Contra hearings.

- Moon's *Washington Times* promoted Reagan's Strategic Defense Initiative, the precursor of today's National Missile Defense.
- The American Freedom Coalition reportedly produced a pro-SDI documentary, "One Incoming," partly written by Tom Clancy and narrated by Charlton Heston. The propaganda pieces were shown numerous times on hundreds of American TV stations.[13]

In 1977, Moon was named in an investigation known as "Koreagate"—a congressional probe into influence peddling, the Korean intelligence service, and the activities of Sun Myung Moon. The investigation concluded that Moon had been on the South Korean CIA's payroll[14] and found that Moon was implicated in violating assorted laws from immigration to banking. The 1978 House of Representatives subcommittee report, "Investigation of Korean-American Relations" found "evidence that [Moon organizations] had systematically violated U.S. tax, immigration, banking, currency, and Foreign Agents Registration Act laws."[15] It also raised more questions, and recommended that the White House probe Moon more thoroughly. Instead, Moon became a VIP in the Reagan administration, invited as a star to the presidential inauguration. Throughout Reagan's two terms, Moon used his media organs to broadcast support for Reagan and many of his foreign policies.

Although it isn't clear exactly how close Moon is to George W. Bush's ear— the president did green-light a White House–backed and Moon-hosted Inaugural Prayer Luncheon in January 2001—he certainly had pull with George Bush Sr. Some believe their acquaintanceship may go back to Bush's days as head of the CIA in 1976. At that point, Moon is believed to have been running covert anticommunist outfits in North Korea, and he also appeared to be linked to South Korea's intelligence service.[16] After he was imprisoned in 1982 for tax evasion, Moon unsuccessfully song-and-danced to receive a presidential pardon. But at least he (or rather his head man, Bo Hi Pak) was given opportunity to rub elbows with then vice president Bush. According to PBS's *Frontline,* former CIA deputy director Max Hugel, who'd been forced to resign from the agency in a financial scandal,[17] went on to help develop Moon's media empire: He reportedly offered to arrange a photo session between Bo Hi Pak and Bush Sr.—for a cool $50,000. Now Moon pays Bush Sr. at least double that amount to commend him.

Behind the Scenes

Always a controversial religious leader, Moon is just as controversial a financial figure—as evidenced in his 1982 conviction on tax evasion. He owns a huge number of business operations including real estate holdings along boardwalks in American cities. He reportedly has very close ties with Japanese organized crime,[18] and former followers, including an ex-daughter-in-law, say he is running a big-time money-laundering racket.[19] He also owns huge land tracts in South America, reportedly runs a hotel complex in North Korea, and is involved in everything from car manufacturing to arms dealing overseas.

> Born in North Korea in 1920, Moon claims that Jesus came to him over Easter in 1935 with a request: He wanted Moon, then a young preacher, to resume the work he had left off with two millennia before. A decade later, Moon had pulled his ideas together in the Divine Principle—a philosophy which concludes that the Holocaust occurred because Jews had turned Jesus over to the Romans.

Moon regards his marriage with his (third) wife Hak Ja Han to be so blessed and sin-free that he demands that they be referred to as the Perfect (sin-free) Couple, and their family (they have thirteen offspring) as the Perfect Family. At least a few of his kids and in-laws are casting aspersions at Pa for being a philandering hoax involved in shady financial deals. Worse: No one is volunteering to take over his holy kingdom. Who knows what will happen to his billions when the eighty-five-year-old kicks, but before he leaves the planet, Moon reportedly is hell-bent on creating a holy land in North Korea, dedicated to him.

MOON AND THE LOON

Conspiracy theorists could have hours of fun if they ran with reports from investigative reporter Robert Parry. The journalist, citing information from the U.S. Defense Intelligence Agency, says that Moon—an avowed anticommunist—has given tens of millions of dollars to North Korea's Communist regime, including to Kim Jong Il and his father, Kim Il Sung, both of whom developed North Korea's nuclear capabilities.[20] While that money may simply have gone to lubricate business deals—Moon reportedly has real estate holdings in North Korea, including a hotel complex in capital Pyongyang—Moon's money may have also gone to acquire the requirements for nuclear missiles. And those nuclear missiles are the main justification to build the costly National Missile Defense system, so heavily peddled by Defense Secretary Donald Rumsfeld and the Bush administration, with whom Moon seeks to curry favor. You fill in the blanks.

21. MEDIA MATTERS:

Losing Focus

Notable Numbers

- 74 percent: Proportion of U.S. residents who get news from television[1]
- 44 percent: Proportion who get news from newspapers
- 24 percent: Proportion who get news from the Internet
- 22 percent: Proportion who get news from radio

Snapshot

"There is a crisis regarding truth and democracy in the United States right now. It's very serious."

> —CHARLES LEWIS, FOUNDER OF CENTER FOR PUBLIC INTEGRITY, A TEAM OF INVESTIGATIVE JOURNALISTS THAT REPORTS ON CORRUPTION, CONFLICTS OF INTEREST, AND ALL THE THINGS THE GOVERNMENT DOESN'T WANT YOU TO KNOW AND THE MAINSTREAM MEDIA WON'T INVESTIGATE ON ITS OWN[2]

Somewhere out there is the truth. Somewhere buried under the public relations and advertising, the political spin, and the web of untruths, lie the bare facts. Every good reporter is trying to pierce a hole in the fog of deception and gather those facts. In a democratic society, which we still pretend to be, the media is handed the crucial role of telling us that truth, and just as importantly they are supposed to tell us when we are being taken for a ride. Not long ago, they used to be able to report on their findings. Not anymore. In the corporate mainstream media, at least, it is becoming increasingly difficult to tell the truth—and the right-wing media aren't even trying.

President George W. Bush admits he rarely reads the newspaper. "I glance at
the headlines just to kind of [get] a flavor of what's moving," he told Fox TV's
Brit Hume in October 2003. "I rarely read the stories." Bush probably missed it
when Hearst papers published his words shortly after his TV appearance.[3]

"It's hard, even painful, to believe that your government lies to you. Human nature
is to trust authority figures—we don't want to believe that they don't have our
best interests at heart. But they don't. If everybody truly realized this and let
themselves get as pissed off as they should be, we'd have real change quickly."

—INVESTIGATIVE REPORTER RUSS KICK[4]

A Lie Is a Lie Is an Inaccurate Fact

"You can't say George Bush is wrong here. There's no way you can say that in
the New York Times. . . . You can't just say the president is lying. . . . You can
in an editorial, but I'm sorry, you can't in a news column."—New York Times
political reporter Elizabeth Bumiller in a November 2004 panel discussion
sponsored by the Medill School of Journalism at Northwestern University,
as reported by Fairness and Accuracy in Reporting.[5]

After 9/11, censorship, self-censorship, and propaganda became everyday routine and anything but flag-waving support of every government move was cause
for epithet-tossing and harsh reprisal. In the blitz of untruths leading up to the
war, the New York Times's unquestioning writing about Iraq's weapons of mass
destruction engraved into stone the erroneous idea that Iraq had some.
Reporters embedded among troops in the Iraq War had little access to anything
the government didn't want them to see—and were frequently arrested, deported, or shot if they poked around on their own.[6] The Defense Department
not only snapped blinders onto the media during the war, it went so far as to
feed the giants such as CNN disinformation about, for instance, the attack on
Fallujah (CNN was informed, and reported, that the attack had begun three weeks
before it did, because the DoD wanted the Iraqi insurgents to be confused about
the timing).[7]

SHOOT, WE GOOFED!

It's not as if the alternative press and millions of protesters weren't scream-ing about their uneven and questionable coverage at the time, but the main-stream media have recently confessed that—oops—they didn't do so great of a job covering the "debate" about the government's allegations and the Iraq War. As Daniel Okrent, *New York Times*'s "public editor," noted in May 2004, "To any-one who read the paper between September 2002 and June 2003, the impres-sion that Saddam Hussein possessed, or was acquiring, a frightening arsenal of WMD seemed unmistakable. Except of course, it appears to have been mis-taken." And it wasn't a matter of a little error here and there, the editor added: The *New York Times* was played. "The *Times*'s flawed journalism continued in the weeks after the war began," Okrent wrote, "when writers might have broken free from the cloaked government sources who had insinuated themselves and their agendas into the prewar coverage."[8] The *Washington Post* publicly kicked itself as well in August 2004. "We should have warned readers we had information that the basis for this [war in Iraq] was shakier," lamented former investigative hero Bob Woodward.[9] Added executive editor Leonard Downie Jr., "We were not giving the same play to people who said it wouldn't be a good idea to go to war and were questioning the administration's rationale."[10] Well, it is honorable that the two most powerful papers in the country—and arguably, the world—admit their coverage was lame. But it doesn't excuse the fact that because of their flawed information—echoed in nearly all corners of the mainstream media—the American public was misled, many buying the misportrayal of facts and giving a green light to a ridiculously costly war that appears to have largely been moti-vated by oil and a strategic real estate grab—as protesters and the alternative press were reporting at the time.

Meanwhile, more venues are being swallowed by a tiny handful of corporations, most of them not originally in the news business. The risks reach beyond unifor-mity of views and that we won't be seeing investigations into the corporations that own the media. The biggest danger is they don't see the need for in-depth research. "When a corporate chain like Gannett buys a paper they want to see a profit margin of 25 percent," says Paul Waldman of Media Matters. "The first thing they do is cut costs [for investigative reporting] and start pulling more items off the wire."[11]

OWNERSHIP INTERFERENCE: SINCLAIR BROADCASTING

Eyebrows raised nationwide in October 2004, when Sinclair Broadcasting, a Maryland-headquartered company that owns sixty-two TV stations, including affiliates of Fox, NBC, CBS, and ABC, made a startling announcement. It mandated that all of its stations show a documentary, "Stolen History," that slammed presidential candidate John Kerry. In earlier elections, such a move would have required free airtime for Kerry to respond—but the FCC's "Fairness Doctrine" was tossed out in 1987. Pundits were nevertheless openmouthed at what was considered a brazen attempt to engineer the election's outcome and it wasn't the first time that Sinclair—a staunchly Republican company—has dictated what network affiliates must and must not show. In April 2004, the broadcaster yanked a special *Nightline* broadcast (which did air on ABC stations not owned by Sinclair). The reason: The show gave all the names of the soldiers who had died in Iraq. The company is negotiating with Comcast, the biggest cable TV company, to expand operations—and media groups are monitoring its every step. Some have even gathered into a coalition—the Sinclair Action campaign—to protest what they believe is an increasingly powerful company that is aggressively pushing its own political and business agenda.

RED FLAG
Media Conglomerates

European royals weakened their regal blood by insisting on marrying their kin—producing mental deficients and stutterers. Our news media appear to be going the same way. Our chances of getting independent news reporting and analysis shrink by the day: A handful of corporations are chomping up the competition. Helped along by FCC rulings that have eased the number of media outlets they can own in a given market, the Big Boys' include:

General Electric
2004 revenues: $152.6 billion

General Electric holdings include: NBC, MSNBC, Telemundo, Universal Pictures, CNBC, Bravo, fourteen NBC stations, fourteen Telemundo stations, and vast holdings in other sectors, including defense and appliances.

Time Warner
2004 revenues: $42 billion

Time Warner holdings include: Warner Bros., America Online, CNN, HBO, Time Warner Cable, Turner (TNT, TBS), Cartoon Network, Hanna-Barbera Cartoons, New Line Cinema, Castle Rock Entertainment, Atlantic Recordings, Elektra/Sire, Time-Life Books, DC Comics, *Time, Fortune, Life, Sports Illustrated, Money, People, Entertainment Weekly,* and Netscape.

Disney
2004 revenues: $30.8 billion

The Walt Disney Company holdings include: ABC, Disney Channel, ESPN, A&E, History Channel, E!, Buena Vista, Touchstone Pictures, ten television stations, over sixty radio stations, ESPN Radio, Miramax Films, Hyperion Books, and theme parks.

Viacom
2004 revenues: $22.5 billion

Viacom holdings include: CBS and UPN networks, MTV, Nickelodeon, Nick at Nite, TNN, VII1, Comedy Central, Showtime, The Movie Channel, Sundance Channel, over thirty-five local television stations, Infinity Radio Broadcasting (over 175 AM and FM stations in twenty-two states), Paramount Pictures, Simon & Schuster, Pocket Books, Scribner, The Free Press, Fireside, Touchstone, Washington Square Press, Blockbuster Video, United Cinemas International (50 percent ownership).

News Corporation
2004 revenues: $21.8 billion

News Corporation holdings include: FOX Network, Fox News Channel, FX, DirecTV, National Geographic Channel, 20th Century Fox, the *New York Post, TV Guide* (partial), *The Weekly Standard,* HarperCollins Publishers, Regan Books, thirty-four local television stations.

As corporate owners clamp on their editorial handcuffs, those who advertise in the media are subtly and not so subtly dictating content. Our communicators are now often beholden to those who throw them big money to take out big ads, providing far more revenue than the small percentage kicked in by subscriptions and newsstand sales. When revenues from advertising began to decrease in the 1990s, the size of news staffs shrank right along with them. The media began to cater to advertisers, killing articles that might cause them to yank their ads, even working with them to produce "advertising special sections" in which reporters write "pseudo articles" that look like real articles but are devoted to shilling products.

For a 1998 AIDS conference in Geneva, *USA Today* turned out a "fake" special edition of the paper—distributed to hotels where those attending the conference stayed. It looked like *USA Today* and was written by *USA Today* writers, but nearly all the articles covered advertiser Glaxo Wellcome's drugs.[12] Shows from Barbara Walter's *20/20* to radio programs have been criticized for casually "plugging" an advertiser's products while on air, and now TV is riddled with "fake news" segments that use well-known broadcasters such as Walter Cronkite to hawk products under the guise of reporting on them as news items.

Pat Kingsley of PMK is the queen of star management in celebrity journalism circles. If editors print an unflattering article about one of her clients—say, Courtney Love—in a magazine like People *or* Entertainment Weekly, *they risk never getting an interview with the likes of Gwyneth Paltrow or Matt Damon. Such ball-busting tactics are common throughout the industry. Ditto for the White House: Critical reporters find that after writing unflattering articles, they are "black listed."*

Lately we've been hearing about rising gas prices, the problems of oil dependency, and what guzzlers SUVs are. That's a change: For decades, the mainstream media avoided publishing any article criticizing our dependence on cars—and they still downplay them. Editors confess that they rarely run pieces that may anger automobile manufacturers, a main source of revenue for the media. Even food critics are gagged from dishing out the dirt on restaurants that advertise with their paper. In the Chicago area, one reviewer found that her critiques had been rewritten—by the restaurant's public relations firm.[13] Medical journals are facing the same problem. Now the pharmaceutical companies often hire outside public relations agents to write stories about their drugs—and then they ask well-known researchers and academics simply to sign their name to it, submit it to one of the prestigious journals, and collect a huge check.

Close-up

To top it off, the media itself has been making headlines for numerous scandals. Sometimes the organization may have done nothing wrong per se—as with *Newsweek*'s reporting on Koran mistreatment at Guantánamo Bay.

In a short item in its May 9, 2005 issue, *Newsweek* reported that interrogators at the U.S. detention facility at Guantánamo Bay had flushed the Muslim holy book down the toilet, an allegation that has been made repeatedly by detainees and reported by the American and British press. *Newsweek* had previously shown the anonymous official who had been the source of the info—a controversial move in itself—and the official had not denied the story. Eleven days after the story ran, the Pakistani press picked it up. The desecration of the Koran is a grave offense in Islam, and riots broke out all over the Muslim world, particularly in Afghanistan, the homeland of most of Guantánamo's detainees. During the rioting, at least fourteen were killed by police and private security guards. The Bush administration responded by attacking *Newsweek*—demanding that the magazine apologize for reporting what looked to be the truth. When the magazine went back to the source, he hemmed and hawwed and said he couldn't be sure if it was true. The magazine retracted the story and, under heat from DC, indeed apologized. The Bush administration continued attacking the magazine, saying this showed the danger of anonymous new sources, while maintaining that its interrogation logs had no reports of flushing the Koran. Here's betting the logs don't mention the extent of the routine torture at Guantánamo either.

Note: Author is an occasional freelance contributor to *Newsweek*.

The Media-Making Headline News

The role of the media is to rip back the curtain, but lately its pursuit of truth and transparency keeps leading back to its own newsroom. Beyond the furor that ensued after several journalists were exposed for taking government money to cheerlead administration programs, the Big Players have been hit hard in a number of shocking brouhahas. In some cases their misdeeds were obvious, in others they were telling the truth, based on the information they had been given, in some cases they were canned simply for stating opinion.

▶ **Dan Rather:** The CBS news anchor of twenty-four years pushed back from his desk in 2005, after a controversial *60 Minutes* piece reported by Rather that aired in fall 2004 claimed that President George W. Bush had been shown favoritism while he was a Texas Air National Guard. The White House, shown the memo upon which the assertions were based before the *60 Minutes* segment aired,[14] lashed out after it was shown, questioning the story's validity and saying it was a preelection smear tactic. Shortly thereafter, the National Guard official who had supplied *60 Minutes* with memos admitted he had lied about where they had originated; ultimately, they appeared to be forgeries. Four CBS VIPs, including *60 Minutes*'s executive producer and a CBS vice president, came tumbling down in the Memogate crash. Rather, however, was not fired: In March 2005 he resigned.

▶ **Jayson Blair:** Was he shy, inept, or broke—or truly schizophrenic as his new memoir maintains? Whatever the reason, Jayson Blair rarely left New York to research the stories that his *New York Times* editors believed involved in-person interviews all over the country. Instead he simply snatched quotes and information from other articles without citation—and passed them on as his own. He got the heave-ho in 2003 for fabrications in at least thirty-six of his last seventy-two articles. Blair's downfall also took down dictatorial editor in chief Howell Raines—credited with the comprehensive 9/11 coverage that won the *Times* six Pulitzers.

▶ **David Kelley:** *USA Today*'s star reporter, who'd pounded out articles for over two decades, had been stealing and fabricating some of them since 1991. A seven-month investigation revealed that he had bilked his employer for tens of thousands in fake expenses and had inserted fabrications in at least twenty of his fourteen hundred stories. Among his reports that were unable to be confirmed: an article about a 2001 Israeli attack on Palestinians, a 1999 article referring to a notebook ordering an ethnic cleansing of a Kosovar enclave, and an article about Cubans being tortured. His fall brought down several top editors as well.

▶ **Stephen Glass:** This gifted twenty-five-year-old writer, who penned brilliant articles for *The New Republic, Harper's,* and the *New York Times Magazine,* was busted in 1998 when it was discovered that a stellar piece he'd written for *Forbes Digital Tool* about a fifteen-year-old hacker extortionist was fabricated. It turned out most of what Glass had been writing was whipped up from thin air. Ironically, Glass had previously headed the fact-checking department at *The New Republic.*[15]

▶ **Eason Jordan:** The CNN exec admitted that the network had ignored Saddam Hussein's poor treatment of his people in 1990 to ensure that CNN had access to the Iraqi government, and he also allowed that he'd heaped gifts on North Korea's Kim Jong Il to lubricate relations with the dictator. He slithered out the door in 2005 after he suggested that the U.S. military was targeting journalists—an assertion made first at a conference in Portugal, and then at a closed session at the World Economic Forum in Davos. Right-wing bloggers ran with it, causing such a ballyhoo that he was forced to resign, saying his words had been misunderstood.

Lost in the uproar over CNN's Jordan was the legitimate question of why so many journalists perished in Iraq.

▶ **Pat Mitchell:** President and CEO of PBS, Mitchell resigned over the flap caused by the cartoon rabbit star of *Buster.* In one 2005 episode, the cotton-tailed creature—who visits real-life families all over the country, including Mormons, born-again Christians, and Orthodox Jews—hopped over to Vermont to interview two children of lesbian mothers. That caused a huge stink—so much so that PBS opted not to distribute the piece—and Mitchell hit the trail.

▶ **Bill Maher:** When the host of *Politically Incorrect* questioned the Bush administration's calling the 9/11 attackers cowardly, Maher paid big. "We have been the cowards lobbing *cruise missiles* from two thousand miles away," Maher said on a fall 2001 broadcast. "Staying in the airplane when it hits the building, say what you want about it, it's not cowardly." Sponsors yanked their ads, and in 2002, ABC pulled the plug. Maher walked to HBO, where he now hosts *Real Time with Bill Maher.*

▶ **Phil Donahue:** He had the highest-rated show on MSNBC, but was canned in 2003 for apparently allowing antiwar sentiments to be heard on his TV talk show.[16]

▶ **Howard Stern:** With some 8 million listeners and some sixty-five stations broadcasting his lewdities of the day, perhaps shock jock Stern thought he was immune, but his shield was pierced around the time Janet Jackson showed that her nipple was, too: Clear Channel, which broadcast Stern's show on six of its stations, woke up and noticed Stern's program was "vulgar, offensive and insulting." Conveniently, the company made that observation mere hours before it was due to testify before Congress about indecency. Clear Channel was slammed with a fine for multiple millions (some $455,000 for Stern's alleged "indecency" alone) and booted the jock from Clear Channel stations, but big whoop—he's still on some forty-five other ones.

> *Janet Jackson's breast, which flopped out during the 2004 Super Bowl game in front of nearly 89 million TV viewers, may be the world's most costly teat: CBS paid $550,000 for airing it.*

▶ Also ejected from Clear Channel: Radio personality Bubba the Love Sponge. Popular in Florida for such live stunts as staging "drink your pee" and goldfish-swallowing contests, the three-hundred-pound Bubba performed his most disgusting act when he castrated and slaughtered a screaming pig on air. He was last seen trying to squeeze into Sirius satellite radio.

Behind the Scenes

The secretive Bush administration, which is notably hostile to the press, couldn't be happier at the media mess. Between its selling out to advertisers, its bowing down to the almighty Vulcans, and its recent behavior, the media is nearly invalidating itself. And that's unfortunate. Because with a government that can't distinguish between wishful thinking and fact, we need accurate news and more of it. As surveys are showing, we are dreadfully confused.

> *Only 36 percent of Americans now believe the news from the U.S. media.*

A HIGHLY MISINFORMED PUBLIC

In the months leading up to and following the 2003 invasion of Iraq, a national polling group overseen by the University of Maryland conducted seven polls, which gave frightening insight into the confused state of the American public.[17]

When asked whether a link was clearly established between Saddam Hussein and al-Qaeda:

67 percent of Fox viewers said yes
56 percent of CBS viewers said yes
49 percent of NBC viewers said yes

48 percent of CNN viewers said yes
45 percent of ABC viewers said yes
40 percent of those who rely on print media said yes
16 percent of PBS viewers and NPR listeners said yes

When asked if weapons of mass destruction had been found in Iraq during the 2003 war:

33 percent of Fox viewers said yes
23 percent of CBS viewers said yes
20 percent of NBC viewers said yes
20 percent of CNN viewers said yes
19 percent of ABC viewers said yes
17 percent of those who rely on print media said yes
11 percent of percent of PBS viewers and NPR listeners said yes

When asked if the majority of the world supported the United States in the Iraq war:

35 percent of Fox viewers said yes
28 percent of CBS viewers said yes
27 percent of ABC viewers said yes
24 percent of CNN viewers said yes
20 percent of NBC viewers said yes
17 percent of those who rely on print media said yes
5 percent of PBS viewers and NPR listeners said yes

Of all respondents, those who relied on Fox News for information showed the highest level of misperception: 80 percent of Fox News devotees believed at least one of the three non-truths was true.[18] Those who turned to public media—PBS or NPR—for their news were most likely to have their facts straight: Only 23 percent had misperceptions about the three issues.

Only 3 percent of the public tunes into PBS and NPR as news sources.[19]

According to TV Free America, the average American spends four hours a day watching TV. At that rate, by the time we've reached age sixty-five, says the organization, we'll have spent nearly nine years in front of the tube.

Along with National Public Radio, the government-funded Public Broadcasting System is illustrating how crucial it is in giving us the straight facts. That may soon come to a halt. In spring 2005, the conservative chairman of PBS announced that he might be making some changes and was calling in a review team to assess if PBS was showing a liberal bias. The "think tank" making that call is the conservative Center for Media and Public Affairs, which according to Fairness and Accuracy in Reporting, has shown considerable conservative bias in its reports.[20]

For all the media's faults and its wimpy performance in the past few years, there may be cracks in the veneer. From online media roundups such as Commondreams.org and Air America Radio, the alternative media that filled in when the mainstream press took a nap is going gung ho and often lending more of an international perspective than the usual suspects on a hot news day. The mainstream media, realizing its role its threatened, is suddenly getting tougher—and more Internet savvy. Now on the *New York Times* site, for example, you can download classified reports, such as the Taguba investigation on Abu Ghraib abuses, that were leaked to the press. Well, it's a start at getting back where we used to be before those planes hit.

Agent of Change
Charles Lewis: Cutting Through the Lies

After eleven years Charles Lewis was sick of the whole shebang. Being a TV producer—whether for ABC News or *60 Minutes*—felt artificial. The whole reality of TV reporting—rushing for a quick sound bite, waiting around until an interviewee finally cried, galloping off to another story, and condensing news stories to thirty seconds—seemed contrived. Stories that he thought were crucial didn't get reported, and he was sick of "suits" telling him what he could and couldn't cover. One day in 1996 he walked out of a four-year contract with *60 Minutes*. "I had a mortgage, a family, and no savings," he says, but he had a thirst to do deep investigative reporting "unfettered by time and space." A few days later, along with two journalist friends, he'd set up a new venture in the guest room of his house: the Center for Public Integrity, a bastion

Charles Lewis of the Center for Public Integrity. "The level of lying in our society is out of control."

of investigative reporting (a venture no longer considered "cost-effective for the corporate media") that would uncover misdeeds and secret deals, track lobbying efforts, and simply document the truth.

Now a clearinghouse of information, with reports on topics from media ownership to private military companies, the Center for Public Integrity is an investigative news-breaking machine that does the "heavy lifting" and deep reporting for the time-strapped media. Among its accomplishments:

- Broke stories about Clinton fund-raising scandals
- Was the first organization to reveal that Enron had been George W. Bush's top political contributor for years
- Was the first to direct the spotlight on Halliburton's contracts in Iraq—pointing out that Vice President Cheney's former employer was receiving billions in no-bid contracts
- Published the best-selling "The Buying of the President 2004," which documents the political contributions to the presidential campaign
- Pointed out the $76 billion worth of financial links between nine members of the Defense Policy Board, which advises the Defense Department on when to go to war, and the defense contractors they work and lobby for
- Over the pleas of the Department of Justice, published online the government's plans for Patriot Act II, which would further increase government snooping powers (while Attorney General John Ashcroft was denying such plans existed, a copy of the plan happened to show up on Charles Lewis's desk)
- In its massive report "Outsourcing the Pentagon," revealed where $900 billion of Defense Department spending had gone—pointing out that $362 billion was handed over to contractors without competitive bidding
- Has won over two dozen major awards in the past nine years, and received plenty of threats, subtle and not so subtle

---

"Over the years, those unhappy with my investigations have tried just about everything to discourage our work. They have issued subpoenas, stalked my hotel room, escorted me off military bases, threatened physical arrest, suggested I leave via a second-story window, made a death threat personally communicated by concerned state troopers who asked that we leave the area immediately (we didn't), hired public relations people to infiltrate my news conferences and pose as "reporters" to ask distracting questions, attempted to pressure the Center's donors, and even brought expensive, frivolous libel litigation that takes years and costs millions of dollars to defend."

—CHARLES LEWIS, CENTER FOR PUBLIC INTEGRITY, FEBRUARY 2005[21]

Lewis says it's increasingly difficult for journalists to tell the straight truth these days, because it's increasingly difficult to even find it—lies from the powers that be are told without so much as the batting of an eye. "We've never before seen anything like the audacity in this administration," he says. The level of deceit from this government is unprecedented, he adds, pointing out that on top of all the fibs, "The government spent $250 million producing counterfeit news— they're using taxpayer money to put out propaganda." And like veteran reporters nationwide, he faces previously unknown levels of hostility and the threat of being frozen out.

"It's thrilling that a small scrappy group of investigative reporters can make a difference. You don't have to be the *New York Times*."

—CHARLES LEWIS

The public is not understanding how it is being routinely deceived, Lewis says. "Since 9/11 the public is more malleable [and gullible] with regards to the White House." And they've never distrusted the media more. Meanwhile, the issues are crucial to understand: "Politics and religion are mixed up in a way we've never seen," he says. Propaganda is floating through mainstream channels, deregulated companies and a rich political elite are dictating policies and laws, and the public is being shut out of the debate. His advice to us: Speak up, dig up the facts, and become "citizen muckrakers"—including at the local level. "As Tip O'Neill said, 'All politics is local.' And when citizens show up at community meeting and ask questions, they are serving as investigative journalists themselves."

As one last show of absurdity, New York Times *reporter Judy Miller was sent to jail for shielding the identity of a government source, whose information she never used. She was imprisoned as part of the investigation into who revealed the identity of CIA agent Valerie Plame.*

With its six main stories a night, TV news often fails us, but a few mainstream shows are surprisingly informative. Viewers of Jon Stewart's *Daily Show,* for instance, came in tops on preelection knowledge in a recent survey—higher than readers of highbrow newspapers or viewers of any news shows. And in the post-9/11 era, Oprah Winfrey sensed that Americans were so confused that the talk show hostess aired programs devoted to geopolitics.

The Self-Helpster Oprah Winfrey

She's the queen of the media and, arguably, the most influential person beaming down from the satellites. With a wave of her wand (or rather, a word into her mic), she can transform books by unknowns into chart-topping best sellers, solicit millions in donations, or cause public opinion to shift. Oprah Winfrey is more than simply a talk show hostess. She's a nonstop make-a-difference machine who fulfills the role of educator, counselor, and everyday inspiration for 22 million in a country suffering from a dearth of female mentors, or heroes of any sort.

> The Oprah Winfrey Show *is shown in 160 countries across the world.*

Most Popular TV Personalities in 2004[22]

1. Oprah Winfrey

2. David Letterman

3. Jon Stewart

Matching donations put up by the public, her Angel Network builds dozens of schools in developing nations and her show sometimes turns into a classroom; when Americans were baffled about September 11, Oprah gave them a hand with a roundup of geopolitics in "World 101," giving each audience member a globe. Open about her less-than-wholesome beginning—born of unmarried parents, she was raised on a Mississippi farm that lacked indoor plumbing, and later became a victim of abuse, a runaway, and a pregnant teen—and startlingly honest in an arena best known for botox smiles and faux sincerity, Winfrey has helped spawn a national conscience. Tackling unsavory issues that the media has largely ignored—such as genital mutilation of women in Africa, or the frequency of incest—gutsy Oprah even dared to comment on the state of American beef.

"[I have just been] stopped cold from eating another burger."

—OPRAH WINFREY, UPON LEARNING ON HER APRIL 16, 1996, SHOW THAT CATTLE WERE BEING FED THE REMAINS OF OTHER CATTLE, SICK ANIMALS, AND ROADKILL

BIG BEEF'S BIG BEEF

It can be dangerous business having an honest reaction on air these days, especially when you're Oprah Winfrey and you've just alarmed the National Cattlemen's Beef Association, a wealthy, well-muscled lobby. When Oprah broadcast a segment in 1996 about mad cow disease, knees were knocking before the show even aired: The beef futures market began dropping at the very announcement that she was tackling the issue of bovine spongiform encephalopathy right on daytime TV. When a former cattleman-turned-activist described the practice that created mad cow disease—feeding the remains of sick cows, roadkill, and euthanized animals to cattle—the audience groaned and Oprah publicly swore off burgers right in front of the camera. Cattle futures plummeted to lows not seen for nearly a decade—based mostly on the fear that if Winfrey stopped eating beef, so would America. The program caused such a flap that Winfrey invited beef industry spokespeople to appear the next week—but still the cattlemen weren't happy. "I don't think it repaired the damage," said Bill O'Brien, head of Texas Cattle Producers. "She didn't go on the program and eat a hamburger before the world." The National Cattlemen's Beef Association, which claimed the show had cost millions in damage, yanked $600,000 in advertising from Oprah's network[23] and Paul Engler, who runs the largest U.S. cattle feedlot company, and other cattlemen promptly slapped the celebrity with a lawsuit, claiming "food disparagement laws" (protecting food from false claims) had been broken. During her trial in Texas (Oprah filmed the show from Amarillo that week), the defendants argued that the information on her show was false, misleading, sensationalized, and that it hurt the family farmer in the name of pumping up ratings. The jury didn't buy it: Oprah won.

A book selected by Oprah's Book Club sells hundreds of thousands of copies— her recommendations have sold some $80 million worth of books[24]—and as she guided Americans away from the TV and into print, Oprah single-handedly revitalized the publishing industry. She launched her club in 1996; when she announced seven years later that the club had come to its last chapter, publishers nearly broke into tears.

Oprah's Book Club relaunched in 2003, and this time it focuses on classics of world literature by the likes of Leo Tolstoy, Gabriel García Márquez, John Steinbeck, and Pearl Buck.

Criticize Oprah as one may—for her fondness of celebrities, her obsession with her weight, and her habit of forcing employees to sign a lifetime confidentiality contract—in a medium where most fill the air with empty words before and after cutting to the break, Oprah has pulled off many a good deed. Now a billionaire, the woman who has given away millions illustrates the power of the individual when teamed with self-motivation.

▶▶◀◀

PART VI

WAR MACHINE

22. BRIEFING:

Defense Maneuverings

Humans have not yet been able to make the evolutionary jump and toss out that nasty habit of warring from our collective skill kit. But for all the millennia we've been clobbering each other—over land, resources, historical grudges, the local Helens of Troy as well as simply wanting an opportunity to test-drive new war toys—we've never had so many novel ways to attack, so many potential targets, or so many possible arenas in which to fight, nor has the United States ever believed that it legitimately had so many reasons for doing so. With perceived enemies and hazards lurking everywhere, no wonder that the federal government is stuffing the Defense Department's pockets with over $400 billion a year.

> *In 2002, the U.S. government named China, Iran, Iraq, Syria, Libya, North Korea, and Russia as countries where it might launch a nuclear attack. Those making the short list reacted indignantly, but none was more rattled than China, where officials immediately conveyed the message that they were "deeply shocked."*

MUSHROOM CLOUDS

Forget that idea of keeping nuclear weapons locked away as a last resort on a very bad day. Stating that the Pentagon should adopt a more "flexible" attitude about using these weapons of mass destruction, the 2002 Nuclear Posture Review outlined five scenarios where the United States would respond with nuclear weapons:[1,2]

- If U.S. troops or U.S. citizens are attacked with biological or chemical weapons
- If Iraq attacks Israel

- If China attacks Taiwan
- If North Korea attacks South Korea
- Any other time the United States feels like it—in response to a military surprise

The defense industry is so lucrative—it brings in revenues in the hundreds of billions a year—that it sometimes appears that certain organizations[3] and individuals amplify feelings of insecurity and perhaps even agitate unrest, simply because they profit handsomely whenever the United States goes on another arms-buying spree.

 Defense Policy Board

Formed: 1987
Purpose: Advise Defense Secretary on military matters
Membership: 31
Big names: James Woolsey, Newt Gingrich, Henry Kissinger, Dan Quayle, and
    formerly Richard Perle

Who decides when and where we go to war? Well, the members of the Defense Policy Board have a loud say in the matter. Handpicked by the Defense Department to share their insights without compensation, this weighty bipartisan advisory group of military brass, former government agency heads, think tank scholars, professors, and defense industry reps gave a bright green light to the idea of attacking Iraq in 2003. In fact, some board members, including Richard Perle and James Woolsey, were so gung ho on the "take down Saddam" idea that they song-and-danced across TV shows and front pages helping to sell the Iraq war campaign, just as they've previously tapped across the TV screens selling missile defense. Too bad that, as with so many government-appointed policy boards, these government advisors often have outside interests that might cloud their judgment. As revealed by the Center for Public Integrity in 2003, nine of the Board's thirty-one members were closely linked (as board members, presidents, employees, or lobbyists) to defense companies that had snagged over $76 billion of Pentagon money since 2001.[4]

> The proposed 2006 budget for the Department of Defense is 40 percent larger than the 2001 defense budget.[5]

We are frighteningly well armed and unleashing a mind-boggling parade of novel weaponry: U.S. taxpayers are now footing the $420 billion bill for the 2006 budget of the Department of Defense—the biggest single budget of the federal government outside of the Social Security Administration.[6] No other country comes close to the amount the increasingly paranoid United States is pumping into defense. But despite our military dominance, hawks—especially of the neocon variety—keep demanding more and more be thrown into the kitty as they point out new threats coming from all directions, often exaggerating their potential for disaster. The new frontiers to protect, attack, and fret about include:

- Cyberspace: Hackers could wreak havoc on the computers that control nuclear weapons, nuclear plants, and dams, as well as zap banks of money, erase corporate records, tap confidential government plans, and strangle everyday Internet communication.

- Space: The outer limits are the battleground of the near future (says the United States, at least), and the American military wants to dominate it. Between the space-based laser weapons being developed as part of National Missile Defense and the weapons being launched that can destroy enemy satellites, the United States is weaponizing space, a move that may lead to a space arms race.

- The skies: Somewhere over the rainbow is where antiballistic missile interceptors would (theoretically) explode incoming aerial threats. Another threat: An electromagnetic pulse, from a nuclear blast high in the sky, could wipe out our electronics and communication systems.

- Subterranean: Deep bunkers and underground military centers are used by both the United States and its foes; while the United States needs to protect its own underground installations, such as those below Colorado's Cheyenne Mountain, it is developing new nuclear weapons to obliterate the subterranean hiding places of its enemies.

The Defense Department's mammoth budget, however, doesn't reflect the total money allocated to maintain the United States' position as the world's most fearsome force. When you add up defense-related expenditures from other

PROPOSED 2006 FEDERAL BUDGET

Total federal budget:	$ 2.3 trillion	100.0%
Dept. of Defense:	$419.3 billion	19.0%
Homeland Security:	$ 34.2 billion	1.4%
Dept. of Education:	$ 56.0 billion	2.4%
Environmental Protection:	$ 7.6 billion	0.3%

agencies—including the billions of dollars' worth of grants for free weapons the U.S. State Department hands out to foreign pals each year—the figure is closer to $800 billion annually.[7] In other words, over one-third of the entire federal budget is currently going to wars, defense, security, and military grants to other countries.

Accounting for almost a quarter of all foreign aid, some $5 billion in U.S. military grants are handed over each year to certain foreign countries. These grants are essentially gift certificates to go shopping at U.S. arms companies. Each year, Israel gets about $2.2 billion and Egypt about $1.3 billion in military grants—a lingering legacy of the peace-making Camp David Agreement. Until recently, Greece and Turkey were also on the U.S. weaponry gift list.

2003's BIGGEST MILITARY SPENDERS

	National expenditure (in $billions)	Dollars spent per resident	Percentage of global military spending
1. United States	$417.4	$1,419	47%
2. Japan	$ 46.9	$ 367	5%
3. UK	$ 37.1	$ 627	4%
4. France	$ 35.0	$ 583	4%
5. China[a]	$ 32.8	$ 25	4%
6. Germany	$ 27.2	$ 329	3%
7. Italy	$ 20.8	$ 362	2%
8. Iran[a]	$ 19.2	$ 279	2%
9. Saudi Arabia[a]	$ 19.1	$ 789	2%
10. South Korea	$ 13.9	$ 292	2%

[a] Estimated.
Source: SIPRI, "The Major Spenders in 2003."
These figures use the market exchange rate for 2003.

These ten countries spent over $669.3 billion in 2003, accounting for 76 percent of the $880 billion spent that year on defense worldwide.

A FEW NEW WAR TOYS

Some got a test-drive in Afghanistan and Iraq, some are still in development. A few goodies in the war chest:

- Machine-gun-toting robots on wheels[8] (in use in Iraq)
- Unmanned spy vehicles—aerial drones—that hone in on enemies and shoot missiles (in use in Iraq)
- Aircraft equipped with laser rays (in development)
- Lighter tanks that are more easily transported (in use)
- Master map system that interfaces satellites, drones, digital pictures, and computers to allow commanders to see and diagram all the pieces of the overseas war fields while they are sitting on their tushes at CENTCOM in Tampa, Florida (in use)
- Mininukes: Bunker Busters that blast open deep targets in conventional war (in development)
- Antisatellite weapons to guard satellites and destroy enemy satellites (in use)
- Space-based laser weapons to zap enemies from outer space (in development)
- Missile-intercept systems in Alaska, along the coasts, and in Hawaii (being tested)
- Unmanned ambulances to haul the wounded[9] (being tested)

So when we see social programs slashed, low-cost clinics pull down their shutters, and regulatory agencies such as the FDA and EPA become ineffective and crippled, we know where that money has gone:

- The occupation of Iraq
- Babysitting in Afghanistan
- A bursting treasure trove of weapons
- Missile defense systems
- Tests of high-tech weaponry
- Development of space weapons
- Assorted secret activities of the Pentagon—which tells us that all this is absolutely necessary for our security

The reality is that for the most part these projects are making us less secure, as the United States becomes a target of more rage, and the object of charges that it is trying to dictatorially dominate the planet—and space.

> Created in 1982, the Air Force Space Command's mission is "to defend the
> United States through the control and exploitation of space."[10]

Control of Space

"Right now, the air force in particular is pushing a strategy of space warfare that
would see the United States fighting in, from, and through space. And it's my be-
lief that this is an extremely dangerous strategy. It's one that will undercut and
not enhance U.S. national security. It will create a situation where all of our satellites are targets, whereas right now, no one is threatening us in space. Simply de-
ploying any satellite weapons or space weapons—not even using them—could
increase the odds of accidental war, including accidental nuclear war, and esca-
late conflicts into a crisis situation."

—THERESA HITCHENS, DIRECTOR OF CENTER FOR DEFENSE INFORMATION, APRIL 2005

Beyond the billowing clouds, a constellation of thousands of satellites is spinning around the earth. More than simply providing graphic images of weather
fronts for TV news, these paneled contraptions and the information they beam
back to earth connect our global system: Credit card approvals, ATM withdrawals, telephone calls, and TV transmissions are but a few of the operations
that make satellites integral components of our twenty-first-century life; commercial use of satellites now generates $90 billion of business a year.

> The farthest satellites are some 22,000 miles above earth. By way of compari-
> son, the moon is 240,000 miles away.

OUT THERE

Thousands of satellites are circling overhead, but not all satellites are the
same, nor are they circling us from the same orbits.

• Low earth orbit (LEO): Miles above earth: 400–1,600. Satellites in low earth
orbit fight off gravity's pull by traveling at extremely rapid speeds—about sixteen thousand miles an hour, so fast that they completely orbit the earth in
ninety minutes or so. Used for telecommunications, broadband Internet.

• Medium earth orbit (MEO): Miles above earth: 1,500–6,000. Among the
satellites in this orbit belt, you can find the Department of Defense's Global

Positioning System (GPS), which works on the theory of triangulation. A receiver—for example, a cell phone—receives a signal from the two nearest GPS satellites, and the difference in the time it takes the signals to reach the receivers is used to calculate where the receiver is located—within one hundred feet.

- Geostationary earth orbit (GEO): Miles above earth: 22,000. Traveling at the same speed as earth (hence its name), geostationary satellites focus on one spot on earth. This is where you might find weather satellites, spy satellites, and other military projects.

Global Positioning System (GPS) satellites serve as the location grid for the entire world. GPS not only allows soldiers, hikers, and sailors to know their exact location on earth within a few feet, the satellites are the compasses that pilots and air traffickers use for navigation. Owned and operated exclusively by the U.S. military, which can shut it off to all but select users, the global reliance on GPS makes other countries nervous. Europe is planning to launch its own Galileo satellite navigation system. The Americans don't much like that idea, particularly as the Europeans want to use a wave band that the U.S. military was planning to exploit for secret communications.

What's more, the military has its own fleet of satellites—some snapping spy photos as they whiz past other countries and others linking up special military communications or conducting experiments—which have made space integral to modern warfare.

When Saddam Hussein briefly jammed information beaming from U.S. military satellites during the 2003 invasion, some U.S. military regarded it as the first act of space warfare.

Given the American dependence on satellites, the United States doesn't want to risk an enemy shooting up a weapon that can knock out our satellites in what the 2001 Rumsfeld Space Commission called a "space Pearl Harbor." Many also worried when China recently launched a small nanosatellite, which could theoretically attach to other countries' satellites like a parasite and cause them to malfunction.

At least $22.5 billion of the 2006 defense budget is going to space—for both classified and unclassified projects.

To the consternation of other countries, the U.S. military is currently developing assorted weapon-containing antisatellite satellites (ASATs) to protect existing satellites or ward off an enemy attack. When the United States recently shot up a microsatellite called the XSS-11, it proclaimed that the tiny orb could help "fix" malfunctioning satellites. What they neglected to mention was that if the XSS-11 could "fix" a satellite, it could also "destroy" one, as Theresa Hitchens from the Center for Defense Information quickly pointed out to the press. Critics say that while satellite safety is an issue, ASATs are a dangerous way to try to solve the problem, as they are introducing a form of weaponry to space.

ASATs are small stuff compared with the space-based laser weapons that the United States is planning to introduce as part of its antiballistic missile defense. Some envision these space weapons, which are currently being developed by U.S. defense companies such as Boeing and Lockheed Martin, as capable of frying missiles heading toward the United States, and of targeting sites and individuals on the ground; some scenarios forecast a ring of thousands of these weapons (some also perhaps with radio wave or microwave weapons) in space aiming down at earth, with everyone in their line of fire. Other countries, including China, Russia, and Canada, are livid: After four decades of agreements not to weaponize space, they don't want the United States to turn our last frontier into a battleground.

Pressure is on the U.S. government to sign a treaty for the Prevention of an Arms Race in Outer Space (PAROS), which essentially every country in the world except the United States and Israel supports, but the Americans don't want to touch it. It's a huge issue, causing countries around the world to once again call the United States a hegemon, but as usual, the Bush administration doesn't much care.

> One thing most everybody wants to avoid: a nuclear explosion in space or even in the high atmosphere. Even small nuclear explosions sizzle satellites.

With so much money coming out of the Defense Department's ears and so many exciting projects, arms manufacturers and other Pentagon contractors are marching in to take advantage of the lucrative contracts. In their urgency to score jobs that might pull in a few spare billion, top contenders (typically Lockheed Martin, Boeing, and Northrop Grumman) use lobbyists, political contributions, revolving-door contacts, placement on advisory boards, corporate spying, and sometimes even bribing to try to nab a contract.

Defense companies also make a fortune from selling arms—from fighter jets to missiles—to foreign countries. Most deals officially go through the State Department, but they are often initiated by presidents and secretaries of state and defense when they visit overseas. When trying to get a foreign leader to sign on for a military coalition or to swing their vote on political matters, officials often lubricate the decision by dangling the offer of a discounted arms deal.

> *To lure Pakistan into joining the War on Terror in 2001, the Bush administration promised to sell that country a number of F-16 fighter planes. Just to be fair, the United States may also sell F-16s to Pakistan's foe India, a move some believe will trigger another arms race between these two nuclear powers.*

Thank goodness the United States is keeping arms makers plenty busy, because global arms sales to developing countries are slipping—they were a mere $25 billion in 2003 compared to $29 billion the year before. As always, U.S. arms makers took most of the pot, being responsible for 57 percent of arms sales to the countries that we once called the "third world." The biggest arms pushers to developing countries (2003):[11]

1. United States	$14.5 billion
2. Russia	$4.3 billion
3. Germany	$1.4 billion
4. France	$1 billion
5. Italy	$500 million

ZOOM

RED FLAG
Missile Defense
National Missile Defense

"For the first time in its history, the United States today has a limited capability to defend our people against long-range ballistic missile attack."

—DIRECTOR OF MISSILE DEFENSE AGENCY LT. GEN. HENRY OBERING, TO THE HOUSE ARMED SERVICES SUBCOMMITTEE ON STRATEGIC FORCES IN 2005.[12]
EMBARRASSINGLY, THE PREVIOUS TWO MISSILE DEFENSE TESTS HAD FLUNKED.

"I don't think that you can say the [the National Missile Defense] system is operationally ready today. . . . We don't have a demonstrated capability—from detec-

tion [of missiles barreling toward the United States] through negating the incoming [missile] threat."

—DAVID DUMA, ACTING DIRECTOR OF THE PENTAGON'S OFFICE OF
OPERATIONAL TEST AND EVALUATION, WHICH OVERSEES EFFECTIVENESS
OF WEAPONS TESTS DISPUTING OBERING'S ASSESSMENT IN 2005[13]

---

*Estimated ultimate costs of missile defense à la Bush: $200 billion to $1.2 tril-
lion. The U.S. government requested $9 billion more for missile defense in the
2006 budget.*

When the Soviet Union unveiled its first intercontinental ballistic missile
(ICBM) in 1957, followed by the United States two years later, the strategic chess-
board changed: For the first time, the countries could lob nuclear weapons at
each other across thousands of miles. Both countries also became obsessed with
the idea of how to shoot down incoming missiles before they hit their targets.

---

*The original ICBMs—the Russian R-7 and American Atlas—were monstrous
contraptions nearly as big as space rockets. Today's versions, such as the
Peacekeeper, are much sleeker, and can carry eight nuclear warheads at a
time—each warhead capable of causing a blast some twenty-five times bigger
than the one at Hiroshima.[14]*

In 1969, the United States had designs in hand for an antiballistic weapons
system, called Safeguard. The system, in which one hundred missile interceptors
could launch out of underground silos from Grand Forks, North Dakota, cost $25
billion in today's dollars.[15] On October 1, 1975, the system was deployed. The
next day, Congress, deeming it unworkable and dangerous, voted to cancel the
program—and the following January, then secretary of defense Donald Rumsfeld
announced the system would be shut down.[16]

Despite that boondoggle, President Reagan—advised by neocons and the
Heritage Foundation—revived the National Missile Defense idea with "Star
Wars," or Strategic Defense Initiative. President George H. W. Bush added a new
twist to the plan: He called for "Brilliant Pebbles"—a sophisticated ring of space
weapons that could shoot down missiles en route. President Clinton didn't support the idea, however. Under pressure from Congress, he called for a report from
the country's intelligence agencies on the matter.[17]

We didn't need it. That was the word from the country's intelligence community on building the missile defense system. The 1995 report said threats of a

long-range intercontinental ballistic missile crashing into the United States were minimal. According to the report, rogue states such as North Korea, Iran, Iraq, and Libya didn't have the capabilities for ICBMs and wouldn't for at least fifteen years. Meanwhile, expensive tests of a fledgling missile defense system to shoot down theoretically incoming ICBMs weren't performing well at all; between the report and the performance, missile defense appeared ready to crash-land. Speaker of the House Newt Gingrich and other congressmen demanded another report. Donald Rumsfeld, who'd stepped out of politics nearly two decades before, was wound back up and wheeled back in. His duty: to head the congressionally appointed Commission to Assess the Ballistic Missile Threat, a group of military experts, including Paul Wolfowitz. The report the Rumsfeld Commission presented to Congress in 1998 was alarming: North Korea, it said, was actively trying to build intercontinental missiles, and could have them within five years or less. Many initially dismissed the Rumsfeld Commission report as exaggerated.

How the commission dug up that info wasn't made clear, but it may have had inside help on the situation within North Korea from Rumsfeld himself. Although he did not mention it, Rumsfeld was then a director on the board of ABB—a Swiss company that had a contract to build nuclear plants in North Korea.[18]

Countries known to have working long-range intercontinental ballistic missiles and the means to launch them:

- ▶ *United States*
- ▶ *China*
- ▶ *Russia*
- ▶ *Britain*
- ▶ *France*
- ▶ *Israel, probably*

India, Pakistan, North Korea, and Iraq under Saddam Hussein have also launched shorter range ballistic missiles.

The Rumsfeld Commission's finding was shockingly underscored when six weeks later, North Korea launched a three-stage rocket that flew over Japan. Never mind that the purpose of the rocket was to launch a satellite—and that the shoddy contraption, put together from old Scud missiles, blew up, destroying the satellite. The mere idea that North Korea might be able to develop an ICBM reinvigorated the missile defense plan. Missile interceptors are now being built in Alaska, Hawaii, on board ships, in aircraft, with projects in the works to set up weapons that can shoot lasers from space.

"God bless you, Kim Jong Il."

—DONALD RUMSFELD COMMENTING ON NORTH KOREA'S 1998 MISSILE LAUNCH
MERE WEEKS AFTER HIS COMMISSION'S REPORT. THE TIMING WAS SO EXTRAORDINARILY
CONVENIENT THAT ONE MIGHT WONDER IF NORTH KOREA HAD ANY HELP FROM THE
MISSILE DEFENSE PROPONENTS IN THE UNITED STATES.

Still, tests for the missile defense system so frequently flopped that the program was again looking like it might be scrapped in 2001. But after the September 11 attacks, Rumsfeld again lobbied for his favorite cause and, yet again, brought it up from the ashes.

"[Missile defense supporters] spin these elaborate—however illogical—scenarios of a madman or a terrorist group or an unknown country or group acquiring an ICBM and using it to attack the United States. And they say that it'd be irresponsible for the president not to provide protection, if we could. And of course, there's the rub. Can we? Is it really feasible? After a good forty years of trying and over $100 billion, we still don't have an answer."

—JOSEPH CIRINCIONE, DIRECTOR, NON-PROLIFERATION CARNEGIE ENDOWMENT
FOR INTERNATIONAL PEACE AND FORMER MEMBER OF THE
HOUSE ARMED SERVICES COMMITTEE[19]

The 1972 Anti-Ballistic Missile Treaty between the United States and Russia allowed for each country to develop one site. In 2002, President George W. Bush binned the Anti-Ballistic Missile Treaty—over Russia's protests—wanting instead to pursue a "layered" scheme to shoot down missiles from land, sea, and space.

THE MISSILE SHIELD DEFENSE THEORY[20]

If an enemy launches an ICBM, it theoretically causes the following:

- The missile is detected by early warning satellites and radar on ships specially equipped with AEGIS equipment; info is relayed to NORAD.
- Early warning radar in California and/or Alaska tracks course.
- Supersensitive radar "locks" on the target, discerns real thing from decoys.
- At least two interceptor missiles are launched by United States, perhaps from Alaska or California or from ships. A Lockheed Martin "kill vehicle" shot from the booster slams into the warhead and destroys it, vaporizing its deadly warhead.
- Aircraft might also attempt to zap the missile with laser rays and some time in the future, lasers might be beamed from space to try to stop it.

> Wild concept, but the program, say numerous scientists, is a costly "stinker." Even in tests where the coordinates of the decoy missile are given, the meeting spot of the missiles is mapped out in advance, and the decoy missile is artificially rigged to attract the intercept missile, the interceptor frequently misses its target.

The right PR campaign can sell any program to the American public, even if it's a loser. To tackle the image problem of missile defense, proponents hired former San Francisco 49er Riki Ellison (also a paid Lockheed Martin "consultant"). The footballer kicked off the Missile Defense Advocacy Alliance, which was given $500,000 to lobby for the cause. With budgets like that, former Doobie Brothers guitarist Jeff Baxter began singing praises for missile defense as well, being handsomely paid by defense industries to harmonize his words with theirs. Baxter, however, sure doesn't sound like a rocket scientist when he notes that "the bad guys . . . [are] trying to get nuclear weapons and a means to deliver them."[21]

Agent of Change
Theresa Hitchens:
Bringing Space to Ground Level

"It is not in the Bush administration's interest to make the issue [of weapons in space] a public debate—witness what happened in the Star Wars era. The American public is extremely queasy about space weapons, and rightly so."

—THERESA HITCHENS

Theresa Hitchens wants us to look up and to look out for what's happening up there. There's a whole world of controversy spinning around in space—one that the air force and Defense Department would prefer we didn't know about and one that's largely been ignored by the media. Until, that is, Hitchens, vice president of the Center for Defense Intelligence, launched the *Space Security* newsletter and started piping up on the scene—debating with air force generals, for instance, on radio and at Council on Foreign Relations forums on the questionable need to send weapons to space. Young, articulate, and knowledgable, Hitchens takes the old guys off guard: They are often reduced to "It's, uh, true that Miss Hitchens makes valuable points . . ." Now when the government says

Space weaponization expert Theresa Hitchens. "Weapons in space won't make us safer. Instead, they will make all of us—the entire globe—less secure."

that it is putting a microsatellite in space that could repair U.S. satellites, Hitchens is there pointing out that if it can fix a satellite that means it could attack an enemy satellite too. And when the government says that our satellites are vulnerable so we should put weapons in space that can attack targets on the ground, Hitchens points out that there is a disconnect in the logic: Satellites in space are vulnerable, she says, but that means that we need to protect them (with backup systems, for instance), not that we need weapons circling us from above. And Hitchens is putting the word out: When it comes to the idea of the United States putting weapons in space—be they satellites that can attack other satellites or weapons that can attack targets on the ground—other countries don't like it at all. "The rest of the world is exceedingly concerned about the U.S. direction in space," she says. And their worries are legitimate. Some within the administration and in the military "argue that the U.S. should take complete control of Low Earth Orbit [the most common orbit for satellites] and not allow any other country to send anything up in space, even communications satellites, without U.S. permission." Just as much a concern is the real potential for an arms race in space—if the United States weaponizes the "space commons," other countries will follow—with a showdown that creates a real-life Star Wars.

"The [Bush administration] decision on space use appears to be driven by the desire to begin testing space-based missile defenses. But the U.S. Air Force has much more than that in mind. For example, there is ongoing research and development on a hypersonic glider with a global strike capability, which would carry munitions or sensors . . . [and would have] the ability to strike anywhere on the planet within ninety minutes. This program has moved forward with no serious public discussion."

—THERESA HITCHENS AND SEAN KAY, IN A *CLEVELAND PLAIN DEALER* OP-ED PIECE, MAY 25, 2005

Regardless of the Bush administration's desire to keep the matter hush-hush—and to imply (honestly for once) that the matter is "over our heads"—other countries are screaming about the issue and Theresa Hitchens is bringing the news straight to us on the Center for Defense Information Web site: cdi.org. What we need to do, she says, is bone up on these important issues, write our congressperson, and publish opinion pieces about government actions in the skies overhead.

> "No other nation on earth is going to accept the U.S. developing something they see as the death star. It's not going to happen. People are going to find ways to target it, and it's going to create a huge problem."

—THERESA HITCHENS, MAY 2005[22]

23. DARPA:

Over the Edge and into the Present

Outfit: Defense Advanced Research Projects Agency
Headquarters: Arlington, Virginia
Director: Tony Tether
Budget: $3 billion (2005)

Notable Numbers

- $1.5 billion: DARPA funds going to "Advanced Research Technology"[1]
- $238 million: DARPA funds acknowledged as going to top secret "black projects"[2]

Snapshot

The windows are black in the DARPA building, a boldly angled granite structure that resembles the armored head of Darth Vader. But what is happening inside the government building in Arlington, Virginia, is more curious: The Defense Advanced Research Projects Agency is creating the future. And what a bizarre future it is.

THE EDGIEST RESEARCH

Funded through the Department of Defense, DARPA hands out billions of dollars to the most off-the-wall, out-of-the-box thinkers on the planet—the kind of people who are happy to spend years unraveling what makes a cockroach so heat-sensitive that it can detect a fire blazing the next city over or how migrating birds flap for days without sleep or exactly what mechanism allows geckos to scamper up walls—all skills that would come in handy for soldiers. DARPA pays scientists to train bees to sniff out explosives or to figure out how dogs smell so well. Their motive isn't merely to better understand science; their goal is to radically transform the U.S. military into a force made stronger and smarter by letting "nature be a guide towards better engineering." Known to conduct experiments in psychic research, such as "remote viewing," in which people try to peer at locales thousands of miles away, projects also forge new frontiers in the "biorevolution"—developing artificial blood (helpful in desolate battlefields), looking into ways that bodies can cut off pain without narcotics, or investigating what genes might be tweaked to produce a supersoldier. Predictably there's a high failure rate—around 85 percent—in these bizarre projects, but there's a high payoff too in allowing imaginations to fly. DARPA projects have already yielded such marvels as unmanned drones, stealth planes, and night goggles, now common on the battlefield. And that's just the start of the new world that DARPA is cooking up.

The future as brought to us by DARPA is littered with spies: Fluttering specks of "intelligent dust" carry sensors that report on microclimate conditions or incoming gases. Rats are controlled by radio waves that allow them to scout, chemicals detect underground bunkers, and sea lions not only notify when enemy divers appear, they snap handcuffs onto these underwater foes. And this future is already here—these scenarios are currently in development—with more appearing around the corner.

Altering Daily Reality

DARPA's research is designed for the military, but inventions from this agency have changed everyday life as well. A few successes:

- The Internet
- Global positioning satellites
- The computer mouse
- Self-correcting writing programs

DARPA projects trigger controversies, whether over treatment of animals who are drafted to fight or concerns that it is unleashing Big Brother. The agency that wants to "track everything that moves" has several projects that are just plain creepy. They include:

- Cities that see: Relying on "smart" surveillance cameras (which recognize faces) and other sensors, including, in the future, miniature flying spies, this system—already being tried out in some cities—not only collects visual information, it tags and follows what it finds. Already computers can identify cars and couple the images with information from data banks; biometric markers such as iris scans and gait recognition will soon allow citizens to be tracked; and that new national ID card that was snuck into law in May 2005 comes with a chip that will reveal identities with the quick wave of a hidden scanner.

- Total Information Awareness (later renamed Terrorist Information Awareness): DARPA calmly assured us that this mother of all computer data-mining programs (purportedly abandoned in 2004) would only be used to monitor suspected terrorists, but some feared that this would be the ultimate snoop, tracking not only shady sorts but the regular Joe. Convicted Iran-Contra felon John Poindexter devised and headed this program.

- Developed in 2003, the Futures Map program turned the ability to predict terrorist acts into a way to make money: Like a futures market on oil or corn, investors gambled on which targets—from buildings to politicians—would be attacked. Planned to yield information on forecasting terrorism, the controversial "game" was quickly shut down after news of the project leaked to the press. That caused the hasty resignation of its director: Perhaps not surprisingly, Poindexter was also behind this DARPA monster.

Close-up

Conceived of in the hours when the U.S. government was still red-faced and furious over Russia beating it into space, with its basketball-sized Sputnik spacecraft, DARPA (then known as ARPA) was created to rev up the technological engine and ensure that the Soviets never beat it in the technology race again. The agency draws its ideas from pretty much anybody: experiments shot down by more rational agencies have a way of showing up here, and even commoners are welcome to take their ideas off the drawing board and into reality in contests that pay winners millions of dollars.

CALLING ALL WOULD-BE INVENTORS

Anybody from a basement inventor to a seventh-grade science student who has a concrete idea and a way to develop it can approach DARPA for possible funding. The agency invites technology whizzes far and wide to partake in its annual unmanned ground vehicle race. Called the Grand Challenge, the competition calls for driverless vehicles to cross 175 miles of an obstacle-littered course in the Mojave Desert—and to roar to the finish line within ten hours. When launched in 2004, the Grand Challenge illustrated how flawed the vehicles were: Crashing into boulders and wiping out around sharp curves, none of the unmanned vehicles made it past the ten-mile marker. The 2005 event, scheduled for October, ups the ante: The award has been doubled to $2 million. As of March, nearly two hundred entrants had signed on—three from foreign countries and several from high schools.

Ongoing DARPA projects:

- *Computers and robots that reason, learn, and accept direction*
- *Origami-like airplanes that fold into different shapes*
- *Flying, hummingbird-sized surveillance cameras*
- *Imperceptible "ghost radio" technology that uses waves that are dissolved by oxygen*
- *Scent detectors that identify humans by their odor*
- *New Internet system designed for top secret military communiqués*
- *A thinking cap to jog human memory*
- *"Ladar" that can peer through dense forest canopies*

Besides sitting around studying bugs, DARPA researchers also study the functions of the brain, figuring out exactly what is involved in thought processes and how to translate it externally. Some of their most sci-fi research involves using thought to manipulate the physical world. The agency has made astounding inroads into decoding brain waves: In one experiment, monkeys were trained to move a cursor to another field on the computer—just by "thinking" it there. DARPA envisions a day when warriors can direct planes from the ground, simply by thinking commands.

SUPERSOLDIERS

Hollywood has nothing on DARPA, where inventors are dreaming up fighters that are self-contained war machines. Experiments are under way to develop cocktails of hormones and stimulants that, along with electric jolts, can keep soldiers awake and alert for days, and soldiers themselves may be genetically modified. Uniforms of the future will include strap-on exoskeleton units that impart mechanical strength and make hundred-pound backpacks seem featherlight, and shoes that allow them to climb walls. The ill will be able to heal themselves through inserted microchips that diagnose what is wrong and self-correct it, and robots may aid in surgeries and clearing land mines. Unmanned vehicles will rove the earth and fly through the air unobtrusively collecting information, and computers will serve as intelligent helpers able to organize and predict what their owners need next.

Behind the Scenes

The research that DARPA openly talks about is already eerie, so one imagines that the numerous classified projects are even more chilling. Very few know what it's really up to, but you can bet that some of its most top secret experiments are being conducted in space.

BLACK PROJECTS

It sounds like something straight out of *The X-Files,* but it isn't: The Pentagon (sometimes through DARPA) funds billions of dollars' worth of hushed-up "black projects" every year, many of the projects awarded to defense contractors such as Lockheed Martin, Northrop Grumman, and Raytheon. Officially denied and blacked out in budgets, these projects were long rumored by conspiracy types, but their existence was not proven until 1983. James Gritz, a retired special forces lieutenant colonel spilled the beans to a Senate subcommittee, referring to one project as "black," a term that took even Congressmen by surprise. The General Accounting Office (as it was then named) was called in and confirmed that such undercover projects existed, and now even the industry's widely respected journal *Jane's Defence Weekly* refers to assorted projects as "black." Nobody knows just how many projects have been funded as black: Inventors and engineers who work on these projects, it's said, are forced to burn plans once their project has ended and take the secrets to their graves. One thing is for sure: The practice of classifying test projects—common during the Cold War (when sometimes over a third of the budget was black)—didn't stop when the Cold War fizzled out. The Center for Strategic and Budgetary Assessment, a defense research group, reported that secret spending by the Pentagon is shooting sky high: During 2003 it was over $23 billion—a figure that hovers near that of the very "black" Reagan years.[2]

While the agency's openness to fresh ideas is laudable, it's nevertheless sad-
dening to see human creativity at its most bold leading once again to warfare
that showcases humanity at its most cruel. It's true that besides creating new
game plans for future wars—where unmanned vehicles are crucial and animals
play starring roles—DARPA opens the doors that private industry follows, modernizing the landscape of everyday life. Perhaps those technological boosts are
a plus. But the lesson that DARPA best illustrates is the bitter one that our ability
to manipulate our external environment is awe-inspiring, but on the mental and
emotional levels, we're simply not that advanced.

24. LOCKHEED MARTIN:

Snoop 'n' Shoot

Company: Lockheed Martin
Headquarters: Bethesda, Maryland
CEO: Robert J. Stevens (2004)
Founded: 1995 (when Lockheed merged with Martin Marietta)
Revenues: $31.8 billion (2003)
Employees: 130,000
Works with: Nearly every agency in the government

Notable Numbers

- 75 percent: Amount of Lockheed Martin's work that is for U.S. government agencies (work ranges from computer programming to developing nano-technology projects for space)
- 10 percent: Proportion of total government contracts (not just military) that are awarded to Lockheed Martin (this is more than any other contractor)[1]
- Over $11.4 million: Amount Lockheed Martin has spent in political contributions since 1990[2]
- $94 billion: Lockheed Martin's contract sales to Pentagon, 1998–2003[3]

Snapshot

These days Lockheed Martin is the government's all-purpose handyman—capable of redesigning everything from the space shuttle to the mail system, and happy to develop privacy-stripping Homeland Security programs for border crossings and security checks. The firm that launched its name in aeronautics now refers to itself as an "advanced technology company," but the new Lockheed Martin, like the old Lockheed Martin, is spooky in every sense of the word. From its smart computers to its futuristic weaponry, this company provides the government with the means to find, follow, and destroy enemies—with machines.

In October 2001, the Pentagon awarded Lockheed Martin the largest military contract of all time: building the new F-35 Joint Strike Fighter that will replace fighter planes in all branches of the military. Price tag for the project: $200 billion. In 2004, the company received more good news: It won the prestigious contract to build the presidential helicopters.

"It's impossible to tell where the government ends and Lockheed begins."

—DANIELLE BRIAN, OF THE PROJECT ON GOVERNMENT OVERSIGHT,
A NONPROFIT WATCHDOG GROUP[4]

The world's number one seller of flashy death toys is unleashing a new generation of creepy weapons: Sleek Darth Vader planes that sneak past radar, laser-guided missiles that blast off from drones, and location-targeting satellites that spell out the precise coordinates of those who are hiding are but a few of Lockheed Martin's terrifying contributions to the War on Terror.

In November 2002, a CIA-operated unmanned aerial vehicle equipped with camera and sensors spotted a car with six suspected al-Qaeda operatives in Yemen; the UAV "drone" fired on the car with one of Lockheed Martin's Hellfire missiles, killing all occupants. Yemen wasn't a war zone, raising questions on the legality of that killing, but in Afghanistan it was: There, the Hellfire proved its capabilities hundreds of times, at $45,000 a missile.

WAR TOYS

There isn't much in the way of competition for Lockheed, one of three fighter plane manufacturers in the United States and the biggest in the world. Granted, Boeing, the number two defense contractor, first introduced AWACS—those blimplike eyes in the skies that allow advanced intelligence monitoring. Boeing also designed the Stratofortress flyer, which made its name carpet-bombing Afghanistan. Northrop Grumman designed the B-2 stealth bomber and assorted elaborate drones. But Lockheed leads the pack and at these prices it's no wonder the company's rolling in dough. A few of Lockheed's favorites:

- Javelin: Shoulder-fired antitank missile

  Price tag: $100,000 per unit

- Guided Bomb Unit-28 (Bunker Buster): Dropped from an F-15 fighter jet or B-2 stealth bomber, this laser-guided 5,000-pound bomb carries a 4,400-pound warhead.

  Price tag: $145,000 per unit

- Trident II: Weighing in at 130,000 pounds, this forty-four-foot long interconti-nental missile can travel over 4,500 miles and would probably be the one sent out on a nuclear mission.

  Price tag: $30.9 million per unit

- F-16 Fighting Falcon: Whether used for air-to-surface attacks or air-to-air fighting, this sleek, compact fighter is the world's most popular—Lockheed sells them everywhere from Chile to Poland.

  Price tag: $50 million per unit

- F/A-22: An elegant long-nosed fighter with such easy maneuvering that it had many believing it would be the most popular fighter of the era; advanced though it may be, the prohibitive price tag helped shoot down its popularity.

  Price tag: $130 million+ per unit

Like the reconnaissance aircraft it designs, Lockheed Martin itself sometimes slips off the screen, with the scope of its operations never really known. Engineers often work on top secret "black projects" that in the past have included such warfare aids as laser guns, robot soldiers, six-inch spy planes, mini nuclear bombs, electromagnetic weapons that reportedly use depleted uranium, and better "bunker buster" bombs. Even hazier is information about what research the company is conducting in the atom-rearranging nanotechnology depart-ment, but some believe the results could be self-repairing planes or footwear that allows soldiers to leap over walls. Even some projects that are currently de-classified—such as Lockheed Martin's space-based laser program—could be reclassified and hidden again if the American public wakes up and notices that the United States is slipping weapons into space and "Star Wars: The Real Thing" could soon be playing overhead.

Aerospace buffs get all misty-eyed about Lockheed's old Skunk Works plant in Burbank, California, where, during World War II, it worked on classified projects including building some of the country's first spy planes at breakneck speed. Essentially a converted shed next to a smelly plastics factory, it was so hur-riedly transformed into a work space that they didn't have time to build a real roof—instead using a circus tent to cap the top-secret work space. Most neigh-bors, however, don't miss the "plant," which closed up and moved out in 1992. Thousands filed lawsuits claiming lingering health problems from the pollution on-site, a factor that resulted in property damage; Lockheed, while admitting no wrongdoing, has coughed up millions to Burbank residents.

Lockheed Martin heavily lobbied for building a National Missile Defense program—for which it is currently building assorted expensive parts, including the "kill vehicle" interceptor missile and high-altitude aircraft for spying. And if its space-based laser gets off the ground, Lockheed Martin may have the honor of being the first company to watch its weapon blast down from space.

"[National Missile Defense has] never been about defense. It's always been about controlling space, dominating space, denying other countries access to space and the U.S. being the master of space. And that isn't a defensive posture."

—BRUCE GAGNON, COORDINATOR OF THE GLOBAL NETWORK
AGAINST WEAPONS AND NUCLEAR POWER IN SPACE

Close-up

These days Lockheed Martin appears to be the golden child—but for a while it was sitting in the corner. Lockheed once charged the government $646 for a toilet seat, and Congress passed the 1977 Foreign Corrupt Practices Act specifically in reaction to Lockheed's palm-greasing maneuvers. In the 1970s, Lockheed was popped trying to financially lubricate business by throwing of millions of dollars to VIPs including Dutch Prince Bernhard; the company "hired" the king of Japanese organized crime to help push through a deal with Air Nippon; and while it was busy handing out money, it also threw a few bags at the former Japanese prime minister and the transportation minister—both of whom were found guilty of taking millions in bribes. The company didn't halt its door-opening practices: Lockheed Martin was also rapped in 1995 for bribing Egyptian officials to place an order with it. Since 2000, the company has shucked out over $50 million in fines for defrauding and overcharging the U.S. government. It also has a troubling relationship with China. In June 2000, the aeronautical giant was fined $13 million by the U.S. government for passing along sensitive state materials to Beijing—apparently the gift ribbon on the satellite package it sold to China in 1994—and for violating over two dozen arms export laws when it gave China advice on which rockets to use to launch it.[5]

   Lockheed Martin can also be a blatant brownnoser: Perhaps as payback for
making Lockheed Martin the government's number one supplier, company vice
president Bruce Jackson headed up the Coalition for the Liberation of Iraq, a
group cheering Bush on when he led the persuasion war to topple Saddam. The
company was so overjoyed at the idea of the Iraqi invasion (which would lead to
more sales) that they reportedly drafted letters for eastern European governments to sign on as part of "the coalition of the willing."[6] Lockheed succeeded in
convincing "New Europe" to sign on, but that too may have been a payback. After
all, Lockheed Martin had heavily lobbied for them to be invited into NATO. The
company wasn't so concerned about the countries' security: It just wanted to sell
them the arms that would be required to join what mostly amounts to an exclusive arms club.

---

*Poland recently bought forty-eight F-16s from Lockheed Martin for a grand total
of $3.5 billion.*

Behind the Scenes

With bombs dropping, fighter planes swooping, and the piggy bank filling up,
Lockheed Martin has been on an acquisitions spree. The company bought information technology company ACS in 2003, a purchase that included all of ACS's
government contracts. It moved toward buying out defense contractor Titan
Corporation that same year, although the status of that purchase is murky: Titan
was slapped for bribing foreign officials, and Lockheed acted as though it was
outraged. Sadly, the apple of Lockheed Martin's eye is Northrop Grumman, the
company that split off from Lockheed in 1928. Too bad the two ever parted ways,
because now their romance is star-crossed. In 1998, the Department of Justice
ruled that a merger between them could not take place. If the two came together,
the resulting company would control over 25 percent of the defense contractor
market. As if, officially or unofficially, Lockheed Martin doesn't control at least
that much already.

25. HALLIBURTON:

Inside Connections

Company: Halliburton
Headquarters: Houston, Texas
CEO: David Lesar (since 2000)
Founded: 1919
Revenues: $16.4 billion (2004)[1]
Employees: 85,000

Notable Numbers

- 100: Number of countries where Halliburton works
- $61 million: Amount Halliburton was accused of overcharging feds for oil in 2003
- 1: Halliburton and subsidiaries' ranking on U.S. military contractors list[2]

Snapshot

Who'd have thought that a company that specializes in something as incredibly boring as lining the insides of oil wells could cause such an uproar? Who knew that our federal government was so masochistic that it would continually reward a contractor that consistently rips it off—to the tune of billions of dollars a year? And how can we not believe that the favors bestowed upon this company aren't a result of its connection to the very bowels of the White House? But Texas-based Halliburton[3] isn't just any old engineering firm, it's the second biggest oil service company in the world. And lately, it's one of the richest, thanks to U.S. vice president and former Halliburton CEO Dick Cheney, who—despite his denials—is still collecting Halliburton paychecks.

"Since I left Halliburton to become George Bush's vice president, I've severed all my ties with the company. . . . I have no financial interest in Halliburton of any kind and haven't had, now, for over three years."

—DICK CHENEY TO MARK RUSSERT OF *MEET THE PRESS* IN SEPTEMBER 2003. CONGRESSIONAL INVESTIGATIONS FOUND CONTRADICTING INFORMATION. CHENEY NOT ONLY HOLDS MASSIVE STOCK OPTIONS IN HALLIBURTON VALUED IN THE TENS OF MILLIONS OF DOLLARS, HE ALSO SNAGS AN ANNUAL SIX-FIGURE CHECK FROM HALLIBURTON—$178,000 IN 2003—IN DEFERRED COMPENSATION, WHICH WILL CONTINUE THROUGH 2005.

Given Cheney's enthusiastic endorsement for the war in Iraq, it's par for the course that his former company landed multibillion-dollar contracts from it. Not only is Halliburton making a tidy profit from the messy occupation, it landed many of its contracts without even having to bid. And if that smells stinky, what the firm did once it got over there was worse.

As of December 2004, Halliburton's engineering and construction subsidiary Kellogg, Brown & Root (KBR) had secured contracts in Iraq valued at more than $10 billion—the largest amount awarded to any company for Iraq's reconstruction. The most lucrative contract concerns feeding and sheltering U.S. soldiers, which rings in at about $8.3 billion, at least when Halliburton and subsidiary KBR are running the show. The company was also tossed a contract for over $2.5 billion to repair Iraqi oil wells.[4]

According to a report from the General Accountability Office, KBR didn't even plan for the housing and food it was supposed to provide to troops in Iraq until May 2003, six weeks after the soldiers had arrived.[5] The company's goof certainly didn't help morale: Troops didn't have showers in 120-degree weather, their bathrooms were ditches, and the food, once KBR finally showed up with it, made them sick, literally. Troops complained that the food was "dirty," salad bars were covered in grime, pans weren't cleaned, and kitchens were actually splattered with blood. It was so revolting, soldiers said, they preferred to risk the food sold by vendors on the street. And to top it off, the company billed out for millions of meals that were never eaten. That merely portended what lay ahead.

The first clue to Halliburton's corrupt accounting was the oil, a matter now being investigated by the FBI. The same oil that cost the U.S. military less than $1.57 a gallon to haul from Kuwait into Iraq cost $2.43 a gallon when delivered by KBR's golden boys. According to congressional testimony, employees were instructed to charge for twelve hours a day, seven days a week, even when they weren't working. Unneeded equipment was purchased to pump up the bill and despite being ordered to move into an air-conditioned tent, the company kept some of its employees lodged in Kuwait's five-star Hilton hotel, a luxury that cost taxpayers nearly $10,000 a day.[6] To top it off, the company admitted that employees had taken bribes of over $6 million from a Kuwaiti subcontractor.

> *The GAO reported that the company also padded expenses and delivered questionable receipts. In a government contracting formula that seems designed to ensure dishonesty, the company takes a 7 percent fee of all its expenses—so it literally pays a contractor to inflate costs.*

In March 2005, the Department of Justice indicted KBR manager Jeff Mazon with "major fraud against the U.S." The government charged Mazon and a subcontractor with billing out $5.5 million for works that should have cost $680,000. The KBR man is accused of making a sweet million off of the deal in which the government was charged absurd prices such as $100 to clean a bag of laundry. And, alas, the buck didn't stop inflating there. By spring 2005, U.S. Rep. Henry Waxman calculated that the company had puffed up its actual costs by over $200 million.

"The entire Halliburton affair represents the worst in government contracts with private companies: influence peddling, kickbacks, overcharging, and no-bid deals."

—SEN. FRANK LAUTENBERG (D-NJ) IN MARCH 2004[7]

And while some were calling for the Defense Department to can the company right then and there, the federal government instead rewarded the misdeeds. Mere weeks after Mazon's indictment, mere days after Waxman's grand total, the Defense Department announced it would be giving the company a bonus—of $72 million. Congress was howling about the misuse of taxpayer money, the media were harping about conflicts of interest, when yet another scandal emerged. Halliburton had somehow convinced the feds to literally "cover up" a defense contract audit questioning Halliburton by redacting the figures with the official black pen. When Congress ordered that the blacked-over numbers be filled in, it showed that of the $875,255,594 for which the company had billed the government, over $105 million was questioned and another $1,255,333 was entirely unresolved.[8]

"When you keep finding problems, you're a damned fool to keep working with the same guy. It seems to me that the Pentagon has been taken for a ride."

—RETIRED ARMY MAJOR GENERAL WILLIAM NASH, NOW AT THE COUNCIL ON FOREIGN RELATIONS, ON THE PROBLEMS WITH HALLIBURTON[9]

Then again, Halliburton's overbilling thus far hasn't come close to the total it wracked up in the 1990s, when it accompanied U.S. troops to the Balkans. Back then the figure was $500 million.

Close-up

Halliburton, like engineering firm Bechtel, had its first big-time dealings with the U.S. government during World War II when it was called upon to deliver ships for the war effort. The fact that a good friend of Halliburton's higher-ups had been appointed secretary of the interior helped seal that deal. But while Bechtel later went on to build up cities, and construct pipelines and energy plants, Halliburton specialized in oil well engineering and in going to war—including building the housing that troops needed. The company first made a name for its military services during the Vietnam War, when it threw up army bases and ripped down jungles, earning some $380 million over the following seven years.[10] Once again that contract smacked of the good old boys' network: The firm was from Texas, and so was the president, Lyndon B. Johnson, who was also a good friend of Halliburton's upper echelon.[11] From the start the company battled reports of its wastefulness: The government later slammed it in a report saying Halliburton's lax operations had resulted in a loss of some $120 million for the army. Halliburton was shortly thereafter involved in a price-fixing scandal involving offshore oil rigs, and a series of misfortunes over the next decade saw it tumble to the brink of bankruptcy.

The Persian Gulf War, initiated by another Texan president, George Bush Sr., put Halliburton back in the playing field. After hiring several companies to extinguish Kuwait's blazing oil fields in 1991, Secretary of Defense Dick Cheney was apparently most impressed with Halliburton's performance in battling the fires. The next year, Cheney made a decision that would reap Halliburton billions of dollars: He put the firm at the head of the pack for private contractors, while setting the Defense Department in motion for heavily outsourcing to Halliburton and other private firms. And then he became Halliburton's CEO in 1995. He quit in July 2000, after cashing in some $30 million in Halliburton stock, to become George W. Bush's running mate.

According to Dan Briody, author of The Halliburton Agenda, *accounting practices during Cheney's reign as CEO were so dodgy that the SEC investigated charges that Halliburton cooked its books, which led to a $7.5 million fine.*

CHENEY AND HALLIBURTON

It was certainly convenient how things worked out for Dick Cheney. In 1992, as secretary of defense, Cheney paid Halliburton's subsidiary Brown & Root $3.9 million to compile a report showing how it would provide services to the U.S. military in assorted parts of the world. Then he paid the company $5 million more to elaborate on it. Once he'd set up the machinery for the Department of Defense to outsource to private firms, he walked into the head seat at Halliburton, and began to take advantage of the very system he had put into place. By paying Halliburton to run through the mock exercises back in 1992, he'd made it the most qualified for nearly all upcoming Pentagon contracts. Hiring his former Defense Department chief of staff as a Halliburton lobbyist, and working his inside connections, Cheney helped the company's government contract business soar: Subsidiary Brown & Root scored $2.2 billion in contracts to set up bases for U.S. troops in the Balkans starting in 1995. Halliburton's pull with the U.S. Export-Import Bank likewise strengthened: The company that previously could warrant a $100 million loan now qualified for $1.5 billion. Stock skyrocketed as it was obvious that Halliburton was back in the saddle. And some say that when Cheney walked into the White House in 2001, Halliburton's competitors dropped in status. Although the government has also awarded contracts to such firms as Bechtel and DynCorp, Halliburton and its subsidiaries have nabbed more than anyone else. Meanwhile, the company and the White House defend the contracts, saying they were awarded on Halliburton's merits and not its close connections with the vice president.

In recent decades, Halliburton has swallowed up several companies. In 1998, under Cheney, it acquired Dresser Industries, a move that was costly: Halliburton was forced to pay out $4.2 billion to plaintiffs who'd been exposed to asbestos in Dresser's previous constructions. Halliburton had also acquired engineering firm Brown & Root in 1962, and through Dresser, a company called Kellogg. While the parent company, Halliburton, specializes in oil drills and restoring wells, Kellogg, Brown & Root is its engineering, construction, and military services arm.

"Go fuck yourself."

—DICK CHENEY TO SEN. PATRICK LEAHY IN JUNE 2004. LEAHY, WHO WAS INVOLVED IN SENATE INVESTIGATIONS CONCERNING HALLIBURTON, TRIGGERED THE PROFANE REMARK WHILE TRYING TO MAKE SMALL TALK WITH THE VP DURING A PHOTO SESSION IN THE SENATE.

Behind the Scenes

Granted, it's hard to find a lily-white corporation anywhere—particularly when it comes to the sleazy oil business. Halliburton's hands, however, appear sootier than most. The company admitted to not only over $6 million in Kuwaiti kickbacks in 2003, but $2.4 million in bribes to a tax official in Nigeria, where according to Corporate Watch, Halliburton was also complicit in the death of a local protester. The company often mucks around in countries that are officially under economic sanction or are considered rogue states—among them Libya, Iran, Burma, and Iraq while Saddam was in power; in the case of Libya it was fined $3.8 million for violating U.S. trade laws and selling six pulse neutron generators that could be used to detonate nuclear devices. Time and time again it has been caught over-billing—in the Balkans, the company charged the United States eighty-six dollars for plywood that it had bought for fourteen dollars, for instance. Why Halliburton and its subsidiaries continue to score military contracts, and especially why they rack up more contracts than anyone else, is baffling; equally mysterious is why the government forks over contracts that have no ceilings on costs and where the company takes a percentage of expenses. Expecting Halliburton and its subsidiaries to play honest when they rarely have in the past is like handing an alcoholic and convicted drunk driver a bottle and the keys and saying, "Gosh, please don't drink and drive."

It's not only the U.S. government that sucks up to Halliburton. The British government, which pays Halliburton to manage the decommissioning of nuclear submarines in English dockyards—where Halliburton has been accused of causing radioactive pollution—announced in January 2005 that it was awarding Halliburton's KBR a $7.4 billion contract to build two aircraft carriers.

Lately, the Halliburton misdeeds have become a partisan issue, with House Minority Leader Henry Waxman among those leading the call for probes into what is going on behind the scenes. The fact is, when a company is leading the government around by its nose, overcharging hundreds of millions of dollars and still getting more work—and big work at that—both the victim and the abuser deserve thorough examination. Beyond needless waste, taxpayer rip-off, and cronyism, this speaks to a government in bed with some seriously greedy, two-timing friends.

With all the hullabaloo about subsidiary KBR, Halliburton is currently talking about putting the subsidiary on the block and divesting itself of the headache-causing sidekick.

The Pentagon announced in July 2005 that it is tossing another $5 billion contract to Halliburton for more of its stellar work in Iraq.

RED FLAG
Private Military Contractors

They've crept into the war machine with little notice from the public, and they've slipped into the Pentagon's budget to the tune of an estimated $100 billion a year.[12] Halliburton is but one high-profile example of a PMC—private military contractor—to whom the U.S. Defense Department, like governments most everywhere, is tossing many of its biggest and sometimes shadiest jobs. While some PMC work is rather mundane (setting up electricity generators or running laundry services, for instance), some of it is seriously dirty—private mercenaries may be hired to spy, trigger riots, stomp out labor disputes, and interrogate prisoners.

> "We are hiring a private army. We are engaging in a secret war, and the American people need to be told why."
>
> —U.S. REP. JANICE SCHAKOWSKY (D-IL) IN JUNE 2001, WHEN THE EXTENT OF PMCS BEING USED TO TRAIN MILITARY AND SOMETIMES FIGHT OPERATIONS IN COLOMBIA AND PERU CAME TO LIGHT[13]

PMCs hold several attractions for the governments around the globe that use them: They free up the military for strategizing and fighting; unlike troops, PMC employees don't require pensions or the other needs of full-time workers, and they can quickly zip across the planet for clandestine operations without media attention. And, since they're not technically the military, PMCs can slip under the wire and through loopholes: They can perform all kinds of tasks that the government might not wish to perform or officially endorse—including training foreign armies, running guns, or even fighting in wars in which the government isn't officially involved. The military isn't usually held responsible for them if they get caught—and they don't qualify for the rights of prisoners of war if they are captured. Since PMCs don't have to answer directly to the military, they may act out of line. In Iraq, they have been known to run amok with stashes of arms—holding up gas stations, brandishing their automatic weapons, to avoid long lines, and acting like general hellions accountable to no one.

> "Just south of Nasiriyah, we stopped for gas....People can wait for days, camped out in their cars, for a full tank....Instead, we commandeered the gas station....Contractors with guns jumped out and stopped traffic from coming in. Others took positions around the perimeter of the station."
>
> —TUCKER CARLSON, WRITING IN *ESQUIRE* IN MARCH 2004 ABOUT HIS ADVENTURES WITH PMC DYNCORP IN IRAQ[14]

Some people simply call PMCs mercenaries or war profiteers, since they are highly lucrative operations. Outsourcing to private companies was supposed to save money, but private firms often get double or triple their typical pay while working for government contracts. Employees are sent to some of the most dangerous places on the planet—Afghanistan and Iraq among them—but they often pull down a cool $15,000 or $21,000 a month; a former Green Beret or special forces fighter may pull down as much as $30,000. That's another problem with PMCs: The wages are so attractive that government soldiers are beginning to defect to PMCs.

PMC professionals are a real grab bag of talents, ranging from retired army officers and highly trained Green Berets or navy SEALs to mall security guards. Even if they are dealing with prisoners, PMC employees may not be familiar with such protocols as the Geneva Conventions covering treatment of prisoners, although they are officially supposed to abide by them.[15] While soldiers face trials and the possibility of court-martials if they become violent or commit rapes, PMC workers are far harder to supervise and discipline.

Employees for PMCs were blamed for:

- *Some of the acts of torture in Iraqi prison Abu Ghraib*
- *The shooting down of a plane carrying missionaries over Peru in April 2001[16]*
- *Crashing unmanned aerial vehicles during 2001 war in Afghanistan*

In the Persian Gulf War of 1991, PMC employees accounted for about 2 percent of the foreigners who'd come in for the war. Now they make up over 10 percent of those involved in military operations, with some fifteen thousand in Iraq alone.[17] As the government minimizes the number of U.S. troops, PMCs will pick up even more of the slack.

PRIVATE MILITARY COMPANIES: A ROUNDUP

Hundreds of PMCs work with the U.S. government alone, and they tend to keep low profiles about their assignments. A few that are well known:

- Vinnell, a PMC (once run by the Carlyle Group and now owned by Northrop Grumman) that some believe is a CIA front,[18] trains the Saudi National Guard (as it has since 1975). It's a difficult assignment: Dozens of Vinnell employees have been killed by insurgents, including in 2003 when a car bomb exploded in the company's housing compound, killing thirty-five, including ten Vinnell employees. Vinnell also raked in $48 million to train the new army in Iraq. That mission bombed: After a few months, half the Iraqi army had deserted.

- DynCorp, a Virginia-based PMC, supplies bodyguards to President Karzai and other politicians in Afghanistan, as well as visiting U.S. emissaries in the Middle East. In Colombia, its employees guard Unocal pipelines and swoop down in helicopters, spraying herbicides over coca crops and unfortunate peasants as part of the U.S.-funded Plan Colombia.

- MPRI, now owned by L-3—a firm run by former U.S. military officers—trained Croatian fighters during the Bosnian War, and delivered arms to Bosnians.

- Executive Outcomes/Sandline International: This PMC owned by South Africans and Brits kicked up all kinds of action in Africa and Asia in the 1990s. Among its misdeeds: running arms to countries under UN sanctions and wreaking havoc from Papua New Guinea to Sierra Leone, occasionally causing local government to collapse.[19]

According to Charles Lewis of the Center for Public Integrity, the Pentagon is using so many PMCs for so many different projects that it couldn't figure out exactly who was doing what. To sort out the matter, the Defense Department called in a PMC.

26. THE CARLYLE GROUP:

Slippery Arms

Company: The Carlyle Group
Headquarters: Washington, DC
Chairman: Louis Gerstner (2003)

Notable Number

- $19 billion: Carlyle's investment fund in 2005

Snapshot

Take a few major shakers from the U.S. government, say George H. W. Bush, James Baker, and Frank Carlucci—a former president, a former secretary of state, and a former secretary of defense. Pay them to hold court with the world's ultrawealthy—Kuwaiti royals, Saudi princes, and the siblings of Osama bin Laden—who loosen their purse strings and hand over billions to invest. Fold in increasing global clout, more world leaders, and high returns, then introduce questionable arms deals and charges of screaming cronyism, war profiteering, and conflicts of interest. Together these elements add up to the Carlyle Group, the world's third largest equity firm and one that is swirling in controversy, despite having really done nothing that's provably wrong.

In 2004, Carlyle became a major investor in Loew's Cineplex. Some wonder if that will prevent the chain's movie theaters from showing films like Michael Moore's Fahrenheit 9/11, which criticized Carlyle and the U.S. government.

Although it is known as a private equity firm, Carlyle's holdings in defense-related companies also make it one of the country's biggest defense contractors—the ninth biggest according to the Center for Public Integrity. Even though Carlyle itself doesn't manufacture any goods or make direct sales, the firm has a controlling interest in a dozen defense companies, which collectively snagged $9.3 billion in deals with the Pentagon from 1998 to 2003.[1]

WHERE FORMER BIGWIGS HANG THEIR HATS

When big-name politicians walked out of office, they used to head to consulting firms, start foundations, or curl up in their dens to write books. Now they seem to be flocking to Carlyle, which may pay them $100,000 for every speech that they give as well as offer them equity in Carlyle funds if they add their weighty names to advisory boards. A few who have happily signed on:

- Former defense secretary Frank Carlucci (chairman emeritus)
- Former secretary of state James Baker (legal counsel)
- Former president George Bush Sr. (advisor, paid speaker 1988–2003)
- Former secretary of state Colin Powell (consultant)
- Former budget chief Richard Darman (partner)
- Former SEC chairman Arthur Leavitt (senior advisor)
- Former FCC chairman William Kennard (managing director Global Telecomm and Media)
- Former British prime minister John Major (former chairman European branch)
- Former president of South Korea Park Tae Joon (international advisor 1998–99)
- Former president of the Philippines Fidel Ramos (advisor until 2004)
- Former Thai prime minister Anand Panyarachun (advisor until 2004)

Specializing in buying up privately held firms—from Texan gas drillers to cable TV companies in South Korea—and reselling them for huge profits (after tweaking their business strategies, tidying up accounting, and revamping management), Carlyle's work doesn't sound particularly glamorous. But the sheer amount of money bulging in its wallet—$19 billion—combined with the collective weight of the names on its roster, gives this group serious muscle as it snatches up real estate as well as energy, telecommunications, and media companies around the globe.

Carlyle, which started in 1987 as a small-time DC-based outfit with a paltry $5 million in its portfolio, now epitomizes globalization: Its six hundred investors

live in fifty-five nations, and the company's multibillion-dollar portfolio repre-
sents businesses in fourteen countries.

To manage investments in a particular field and scout out new opportunities, Carlyle often hires a former head of the U.S. agency that regulates it. Former head of the Federal Communications Commission William Kennard, for instance, is Carlyle's media investor, and former secretary of defense Frank Carlucci was its defense brains. There's nothing illegal about it, although detractors say that the former government employees know their areas too well: They know who to lobby and they can take advantage of the laws they put into effect while in office, perhaps knowing that they could later benefit from them while working the other side of the fence.

As a high-end investment firm, Carlyle can only solicit funds from those who
have millions, or billions, to burn. According to its Web site, "US securities laws
allow firms such as Carlyle to work only with 'accredited' investors. These are
sophisticated investors with considerable financial and legal resources, such
as high net worth individuals and institutional investors. These rules prohibit
Carlyle from offering its products to the general public."

What really gets critics going is how this bunch gets the world's golden crowd to ante up. Big names such as George Bush and James Baker have been wheeled out for speeches to the well-to-do in countries from Kuwait to Korea while Carlyle's sales staff worked the room, essentially using the frontmen as paid endorsements. Again, it isn't illegal, but to many it carries more than a whiff of influence peddling.

On September 11, 2001, Carlyle had gathered together a group of former gov-
ernment officials, defense contractors, and wealthy Arabs at the Ritz-Carlton
in DC for its annual investor conference. They gathered around a TV as the
horror of that morning unfolded, perhaps not realizing the implications. Not
only would that attack boost sales for the many private defense firms Carlyle
held, it would also cause one of those sitting in the room to be crossed off
the Carlyle list—Shafiq bin Laden, brother of Osama, whose family had
invested $200 million in Carlyle's fund (which was soon returned).

Critics have plenty of questions about what borders on conflicts of interest, including:

- Was it unethical that George H. W. Bush was essentially hawking for defense companies while having a direct line to the president's ear—while also having access to all CIA information that might come in handy to Carlyle's investment team?
- What is up with James Baker III—who is sometimes jaunting off to solicit funds for Carlyle in the Middle East, and the next minute jaunting back to the same countries as an official U.S. envoy, making political deals about the reconstruction of Iraq?
- Is it not a bit dangerous that Carlyle's chairman emeritus, Frank Carlucci, is extremely good friends with the secretary of defense, Donald Rumsfeld, who orders arms from companies that Carlyle owns?
- How can we believe that with so many ex-leaders (ex-presidents and ex–prime ministers of the United States, Britain, Thailand, Philippines, and South Korea) and powerful officials that somebody isn't pulling some government strings to help Carlyle earn more money on its investments?

So unseemly were the appearances regarding Carlyle and its link to the White House that even conservative watchdog group Judicial Watch jumped into the debate, and finally, under pressure, George H. W. Bush ceased work as a Carlyle consultant in the fall of 2003.

Close-up

Murky dealings, gray areas, backroom deals that give the feeling that all is not right, but offer little proof—it's no surprise that Carlyle is now epitomized by such descriptions. What else would you expect when Frank Carlucci, one of the more slippery characters to come to power in the twentieth century, is involved? The former secretary of defense, many believe, was a CIA operative starting in the 1960s and he still manipulates behind-the-scenes deals. It was Carlucci, after all, that really put Carlyle on the map—first by directing the firm to buy up defense contractors that had been floundering in the twilight of the Cold War, and later by bringing Baker and Bush over to play for the team.

ZOOM ▶ The Fingerprints of Frank Carlucci

U.S. ambassador to Portugal (1978)
Number two at the CIA (1978–80)
Deputy secretary of defense (1980–82)
National security advisor (1986) (to Reagan)
Secretary of defense (1987–89) (he passed the DoD baton to Dick Cheney)

> *A foreign service agent during the Cold War, Carlucci was stationed in Congo when President Patrice Lumumba was assassinated. According to papers of the intelligence-investigating Church Commission, Eisenhower had given orders to kill Lumumba, although the commission cleared the United States of Lumumba's death. Carlucci reportedly had a fit when a recent movie portrayed him as having a hand in the assassination.*

For the powermonger that he is and has been, Frank Carlucci—college roommate of Donald Rumsfeld, with whom he wrestled on the Princeton team—never really blipped on the common man's radar. He might prefer it that way. The slight, soft-spoken former bureaucrat is said to have been a spook: Some believe that at least a few of the companies he's brought to Carlyle—including BDM and Vinnell, which work out of Saudi Arabia—are fronts for the CIA and serve as covers for arms running.[2] It's not the first time he's been believed to be working behind-the-scenes military magic. When Carlucci was CEO of Sears World Trade in the 1980s, publications including the

Frank Carlucci: the powermonger whose name doesn't register

Washington Post and *Fortune* accused him of running a cover for CIA agents and arms deals—a charge that he never denied. Carlucci now sits on the board of trustees at think tank RAND, which some also believe is riddled with spies.

Carlucci claims he never lobbied buddy Rumsfeld to buy arms, but gee, it would have been easy enough just to casually mention what Carlyle's holdings were peddling when Carlucci and Rumsfeld met for one of their frequent dinners. And besides, Carlucci has certainly put in a few phone calls to other arms buyers in the U.S. government and to help broker deals for Carlyle using his high-placed connections. Now in his seventies, Carlucci flies around the world as a board member, paid hefty sums to attend dozens of board meetings. At one point he sat on thirty-two boards, including drug giant Pharmacia, G2 Satellite Solutions, many telecoms, and several defense contractors. Detractors say he is gaining insider information that may guide Carlyle's investments.

Conspiracy theorists point out that in 1981, as secretary of defense, Carlucci limited the public's access to information available under the Freedom of Information Act. He also cleared out his desk at the CIA a little too well: When he left the office, he carted out dozens of boxes of confidential records.

Until Carlucci was dealt into the game in 1989, Carlyle had been a financial nobody. Sure it had names, or sorta names. It was founded by former Carter aide David Rubenstein; a former chief financial officer at MCI, Daniel D'Anielo; and a Marriot executive, William Conway, but Carlyle didn't pack much punch. Until, that is, Rubenstein hired Carlucci, and saw how to put knowledge gleaned inside the government to work in the investment world. As Carlucci deftly revamped the firm's priorities toward defense—taking advantage of policies for longer and more lucrative contracts that he'd put in place as secretary of defense—Carlyle began its ascent, cashing in on companies that had teetered near failure as the Soviet Union began crumbling, but boomed once Saddam Hussein (and the neocons directing foreign policy and defense) put the United States back on the warpath.

> By the early 1990s, defense-related contracts made up 60 percent of the Carlyle portfolio.[3]

In 1991, an overseas investor boosted Carlyle to front-page news. Saudi Prince Alwaleed—one of the ten richest people on the planet—wanted to save Citibank, which was shivering at the doors of bankruptcy. Carlyle brokered the deal that gave the Saudi a 5 percent share of the company, and suddenly Carlyle was the talk of the financial world. The next step in its rise to superstardom came when Carlucci brought James Baker and George Bush over to bat for the team, both moves that unleashed a flood of Middle Eastern money. Carlyle soon went from a tiny investment firm holding mere millions to a merchant bank flaunting its billions.

Carlyle's handling of United Defense illustrates how the company might be making use of its connections. After Carlyle bought out United Defense for $180 million, the government suddenly started ordering up the Crusader Howitzer series—big clunky guns on wheels—even though it had previously decided they didn't fit in with the concept of a lean mean military machine. While United Defense still had the government contract for the Howitzer—boosting its value—Carlyle launched United Defense as a public company. The stock sales turned a tidy profit, making Carlyle $588 million. However, what the public didn't know was that the Howitzer contract with the Department of Defense was already under fire, and would soon be canceled, bringing stock values down when the news was shortly thereafter announced.

> Carlyle has a whopping $1 billion in its Asia Funds—and billions more set aside for Japanese investment.[4] It is buying up companies across Taiwan, South Korea, and Japan, with a special eye to banks and telecoms.

MAKING INTERNATIONAL WAVES

The potential conflict of interest that hovers around Carlyle came to light in several uncomfortable situations recently:

- The federal government was forced to cancel a $1.1 billion sale of weapons made by United Defense—a company owned by Carlyle—after congressmen and the media howled that the sale would directly financially benefit George H. W. Bush and, indirectly, his son.
- James Baker's fall 2004 mission to the Middle East on behalf of the U.S. government was undermined because of Carlyle: Baker was asking countries to forgive the money owed to them from Iraq. Almost simultaneously Kuwaiti officials were among those to receive a letter from a financial consortium of well-connected Washington players including Carlyle, saying that if the Kuwaitis cut them in, they would ensure that Kuwait got the $45 billion or so owed to them from Iraq. The consortium intimated that they would be able to do so because of their tight ties to the government, including the closeness of Carlyle and its main man James Baker to the administration. In other words, Baker was put in the position of getting countries to forgive the debt, but according to the consortium would make sure that they were paid back. (Carlyle subsequently pulled out of the consortium.)
- Carlyle has prompted angry calls to the U.S. government from the Chinese government in Beijing. The reason: In 2002, the firm's chairman, Frank Carlucci, put together the first meeting between the Taiwanese government

(which wants to secede from China—a very prickly issue in Beijing) and the U.S. government since 1979. He not only introduced members of the Taiwanese government to U.S. Deputy Secretary of Defense Paul Wolfowitz, he also brought along a cadre of American arms dealers, making the Taiwanese feel that stocking up on arms was a prerequisite to introductions to top U.S. officials.[5]

United Defense, then under Carlyle's control, nabbed a $250 million contract with Taiwan in September 2002 for assault vehicles.[6]

James Baker III:

Another Vulture Who Won't Stop Circling

White House chief of staff 1981–85 (Reagan)
Secretary of treasury 1985–88 (Reagan)
Secretary of state 1988–91 (Bush Sr.)

Like Carlucci, lawyer James Baker III has been one of those influential background guys for decades, and like Carlucci, he apparently hasn't looked at his watch long enough to see that he hit retirement age about a decade ago. Although his career doesn't stick out in the collective memory, Baker has actually done quite a lot—a lot that he might prefer would stay under the carpet with the dust bunnies. Heading the State Department under Bush Senior, he initially kept relations cozy with Saddam—who was by then receiving some $1 billion a year in U.S. aid.[7] But in 1990 he did an abrupt about-face, in what was at best a misunderstanding and at worst a "trap." Baker had told U.S. ambassador to Iraq, April Glaspie, in summer 1990, that the United States took a neutral view of Saddam's potential invasion of Kuwait—and she told Hussein that the United States had "no opinion on your Arab-Arab conflicts." Then Baker let Glaspie catch the hell when she was attacked for giving Iraq a "green light" to invade Kuwait.[8] He also cut some iffy deals while assembling the international coalition for the 1991 Persian Gulf War (Desert Storm)—including promising Hafez Assad, the dictator of Syria, that the United States would ignore his moves on neighbor Lebanon, if Syria joined the push-Iraq-out-of-Kuwait club.[9]

But it was his role during the Reagan years that was most curious. Back then Baker was secretary of the treasury during a time of shady transactions. During that era's savings-and-loans scandal, which *Houston Post* writer Pete Brewton reported was very much linked to money laundering by the mafia and CIA, Baker wasn't doing much except whistling and looking in the other direction. No wonder Baker didn't want to crack open the savings-and-loan scandal, since some of the shadowy deals led to the Iran-Contra affair; what's more, a son of then vice president George H. W. Bush—Neil—was deeply implicated in a financial scandal in Colorado that had helped to trigger the savings-and-loan crisis.

If there is one thing the record shows it is that James Baker has a dicey record with elections. He lost the only time he ran for an office (Texas attorney general in 1978), and he was campaign manager for President Ford's 1976 defeat. Baker was orchestrating the show when George H. W. Bush lost his reelection bid in 1992, as well as when Bush lost in his 1970 Senate race. In fact, not only was Baker campaign manager when Bush dropped his presidential bid in the 1984 Republican primaries, Baker—much to Bush's ire—actually threw in the towel for the candidate without telling him. Ironically, he's now credited with saving Bush Sr.'s career by making him jump to the number two spot on Reagan's presidential ticket.

In fact, one of the few times that Baker has overseen a successful election was when George Sr. pushed him in to salvage George Jr.'s presidential votes in Florida in 2000. Baker's Florida team (which included John "Iron Fist" Bolton) blocked the recount ordered by the state Supreme Court, and got the matter redirected to the U.S. Supreme Court, where the judges ruled that George W. had won. George W. has found use for him since, shooting him to the Middle East to sweet-talk the regional power brokers, a role he also plays for Carlyle—which has led some to wonder how many balls he can ethically juggle at one time. That Baker himself brought Bush Sr. into the Carlyle investment club may have been motivated by more than mere friendship: Shrewd Baker also realized that his former boss would only boost status of the firm that has yielded him many millions.

Behind the Scenes

With critical books, articles, and TV programs delving behind the scenes at Carlyle, some VIPs are flapping off: In 2004, former British prime minister John Major gave up his post as chairman of Carlyle Europe, although he stayed on as a consultant. To minimize its reputation as an arms dealer, Carlyle gave Carlucci a new title—chairman emeritus—and called in Louis Gerstner of IBM to head the board. But even if some of the marquis' names aren't so brightly displayed, it doesn't mean the Big Boys are not actually working there. They've merely been tucked away: Carlyle has a policy of not disclosing the names of its investors and many of its consultants. Besides, with the money that can be made at this place, there is no shortage of influential types flocking to Carlyle and bringing more cash with them. The queen of England's personal banker recently gave up his royal post and jumped over to the firm. And Carlyle has sent a personal invitation to another potential partner: former secretary of state Colin Powell, who is a close personal friend of, who else, Frank Carlucci.

> *Billionaire George Soros, who seems antithetical to this cabal of cronies who came out of the White House of the 1980s, is one of the firm's investors—and one of the few whose identities are publicly known.*

Whether you call the Carlyle Group a walking case of screaming cronyism or an example of how wheels turn in the twenty-first century, this DC-based private equity firm marks the overlap between the world's most politically powerful and the globe's ultrarich. And the result of this high-stakes financial gamble of shifting money around is a very loud, multibillioned ka-ching that critics claim increases the desirability of the United States' continuing its marches to war.

27. BECHTEL:

The Master Builder

Company: Bechtel
Headquarters: San Francisco
CEO: Riley Bechtel, fourth generation leader of the family company
Founded: 1898 as railroad building firm
Revenues: $17.4 billion (2004)[1]
Employees: 40,000

Notable Numbers

- 140: Number of countries in which Bechtel operates
- 22,000: Number of Bechtel projects, including 420 fossil fuel plants, 150 nuclear plants, and 85,000 kilometers of pipeline

Snapshot

Bechtel is not a household name, but it should be. After all, who constructed the Metro in DC, built the Bay Area Rapid Transit system in San Francisco, is behind Boston's "Big Dig," and is currently renovating London's Tube? Who laid the pipes that pump out Saudi Arabian and Kuwaiti crude, and who was called in to put out the oil well fires that blazed across Kuwait when Saddam Hussein angrily retreated in 1991? Who built the Hoover Dam, the Bay Bridge from San Francisco to Oakland, the Alaska Pipeline, airports in Las Vegas, Hong Kong, and Peru, the first highway in Croatia, and the Chunnel connecting England and France? And who pioneered the building of nuclear reactors and helped clean up the nuclear disasters at Three Mile Island and Chernobyl? These are only a few of the projects that pump billions of dollars into the accounts of Bechtel, the world's largest engineering and construction firm and the one that—at least until Halliburton butted into the picture—is often closest to the feds.

BECHTEL'S POLITICAL MUSCLE

During the Reagan era, two high-level Bechtel employees took seats in the Cabinet, and the company still yields plenty of clout in matters geopolitical.

- **George Shultz:** Former secretary of state under Reagan, Shultz was previously president of Bechtel, and now sits on Bechtel's board of directors. Bechtel maintains "he did not exert any influence in the awarding of government contracts for work in Iraq to Bechtel," but as chairman of the pro-war Committee for the Liberation of Iraq, Shultz heavily promoted invading Iraq—and rebuilding it.
- **Caspar Weinberger:** Bechtel's former general counsel and director, he left Bechtel and immediately became secretary of defense under Reagan.
- **Gen. Jack Sheehan (Ret.):** Bechtel senior vice president and project operations manager of Bechtel's petroleum business, Sheehan serves on the Defense Policy Board, which advises the secretary of defense on matters such as invasions.
- **Riley Bechtel:** The company's CEO sits on the president's Export Council, advising about international trade.
- **Daniel Chao:** Bechtel senior vice president Chao sit on the board of the U.S. Export-Import Bank, which lavishes taxpayer-funded loans on Bechtel and other multinationals.
- **Donald Rumsfeld:** Current secretary of defense, Rumsfeld lobbied Saddam Hussein in 1983 on Bechtel's behalf for the building of a pipeline to Jordan.[2] (That was the famous visit when Rumsfeld presented Saddam with a pair of golden spurs. If that was the best he could cough up, is it any wonder the pipeline didn't go through?)

The master builder has had decades of high-profile successes building everything from smelters and seaports to oil refineries and telecommunication networks, but until recently Bechtel has been relatively obscure, barely registering on the media charts of who's who. Lately, however, it's been under nearly constant attack: The *Boston Globe* slammed it for the cost overruns of the Big Dig, activist groups paint Bechtel as the face of corporate evil, and demonstrators in macabre masks routinely target its San Francisco headquarters, chaining themselves to the gates to protest the company's global stature and bulging piggy bank, which they regard as war profiteering. They point out that until 1990, Bechtel was building a chemical plant in Iraq, which could have been used to manufacture mustard gas; moreover, they consider Bechtel incompetent, and say that it only gets work because of its friends in high places.

OOPS

A few of Bechtel's big-time bloopers:

- Boston's Big Dig project to build an underground transportation network is grossly over budget and past deadline. What was envisioned to be a $2.5 billion project in 1985 has ballooned into a $14.6 billion boondoogle that has made driving in Boston an even more hellish experience. The state of Massachusetts is suing Bechtel and contractor Parson Brinckerhoff for project mismanagements to the tune of $250 million.
- Bechtel so botched the Alaska Pipeline it was kicked off the project, critics say.
- When Bechtel was brought in to modernize the water system in Cochabamba, Bolivia, the project became so costly that Bechtel hiked water bills to twenty dollars a month—in a country where for many that amount represented a third of the monthly take-home pay. Mass demonstrations and a general work strike resulted—and Bechtel bolted. The company is now suing the Bolivian city for $25 million in lost profits.
- Bechtel's nuclear record is shoddy: The Palisades nuclear plant in Michigan broke down only months after Bechtel had finished constructing it. When Bechtel built California's San Onofre reactor in 1977, the company constructed the reactor backwards, so its entry was where its back was supposed to be. It built the Humboldt Bay reactor directly over a fault line. The Trojan nuclear plant in Oregon developed leaks that caused its closure. A reprocessing plant built in 1966 in West Valley, New York, was such a nightmare it was shut down in 1972 and continues to leak radioactive waste, while the bill for cleanup—scheduled to end in 2041—is estimated to be $4.5 billion.[3]
- Using information from the Nuclear Regulatory Commission's Office of Investigations, critics such as Public Citizen and CorpWatch say that Bechtel did not adequately repair parts of the Three Mile Island plant, "deliberately circumventing safety procedures."

Despite ongoing criticism of its work in Iraq, Bechtel maintains[4] that since 2003, it has:

- Restored the Port of Umm Qasr, opening Iraq to shipping
- Repaired the airports in Baghdad and Basra, opening Iraq to commercial flights

- Fixed more than 1,200 Iraq schools
- Partially restored energy plants, telecommunication systems, and drinking water systems in Iraq
- Subcontracted work to 160 Iraqi companies, employing more than forty thousand Iraqis

The fifth largest privately held company in the United States, Bechtel dismisses charges of cronyism and says that it wins contracts on experience and merit. The only thing that we know for sure is that Bechtel is currently heading up a number of pricey taxpayer-funded projects that can have grave consequences if they foul up. The list includes:

- Hanford, Washington: Bechtel was contracted to tidy up this heavily contaminated nuclear waste repository that for six decades has been leaking radioactive materials into the Columbia River and spewing radioactivity into the air.
- Yucca Mountain: Bechtel won the $3.2 billion contract to develop the controversial new national nuclear waste dump in Yucca Mountain, Nevada, being built in a known earthquake zone.
- Nevada Test Site: Bechtel oversees operations down the road from Yucca Mountain at the top secret Nevada Test Site—a strip of toxic wasteland bigger than the state of Rhode Island—where weapons are tested and counterterrorism operations worked out.
- Missile Shield Defense: In locations from Alaska to the Marshall Islands, Bechtel is working with Lockheed Martin and Boeing to build up the money-sucking Missile Shield Defense.

Close-up

Bechtel has been working hand in hand with the federal government for over a century. The company's founder, Warren Bechtel, created his company laying railroads, then motorways for the government; his son, Stephen, brought Bechtel into the building of the Hoover Dam. But it was World War II that sealed Bechtel's success: The company was commissioned to build hundreds of battleships during the war—impressively sending off some twenty a month. And in the course of that endeavor, Stephen Bechtel formed a partnership with engineer John McCone, who would soon thereafter give Bechtel its biggest boost. Appointed U.S. deputy to the secretary of defense in 1948, McCone was appointed chairman of the Atomic Energy Commission in 1958. He immediately brought in

Bechtel, commissioning his former partner to turn the United States into a show-case for the peaceful use of the atom. Bechtel landed the contract to build the first civilian nuclear reactor in the country, going on to build four dozen more—or nearly half of the reactors in the United States.

> In the 1960s, McCone chastised Caltech scientists who supported the idea of a nuclear test ban. The Atomic Energy Commission chairman sniped that they were needlessly creating "fear in the minds of the uninformed that radioactive fallout from H-bomb tests endangers life."

Bechtel was also commissioned in the 1990s to build nuclear reactors in North Korea, a project currently on the ice due to concerns about the intents of North Korean leader Kim Jong II.

The company has linked arms with corporate big boys in joint ventures that some find dubious. For instance, Intergen—a joint operation with Shell Oil—sets up power plants and pipelines in more than a dozen countries, including nuclear plants built just over the border in Mexico to sell electricity to the United States. Mexico's lax environmental regulations allow for cheaper construction. Bechtel also rolled around under the covers with Enron and General Electric. In Maharashtra, India, the companies jointly erected a $2.8 billion nuclear power plant that was so substandard that it ran for only two years before the cord was pulled.

Behind the Scenes

Conspiracy theorists love to link every major player to spies and shadow governments, but in the case of Bechtel, which is sometimes called "the working arm of the CIA,"[5] that claim may indeed be true. The company reportedly had quite close connections to Allen Dulles, CIA director from 1953 to 1961, but the relationship grew even cozier when John McCone—who had tossed Bechtel numerous nuclear jobs when he was head of the Atomic Energy Commission—plopped into Dulles's chair and became director of the Central Intelligence Agency in 1961. As one of the first companies to barge into the international scene after World War II, Bechtel, which built bridges, power plants, and cities across the Middle East, had the perfect cover: Some say it played roles in political overthrows in Syria and Iran and that the company is still teeming with informants and spies.

After its long entrenchment with the U.S. government, Bechtel isn't really thrilled about the entry of all-purpose military contractor Halliburton into its cushy world. Bechtel was awarded over $2 billion to reconstruct Iraq after being selected out of seven bidders for the job; Halliburton, however, was handed some $10 billion—and it didn't even have to compete, being handpicked by the U.S. Army Corp of Engineers.

While Bechtel is now most associated with the Middle East, its most lasting legacies are on domestic soil: Those nuclear plants it built, which now dot the American landscape, aren't necessarily up to snuff. But that probably won't matter: With a flurry of new interest in developing more nuclear energy plants, you can rest assured that utilities will be picking up the hotline to Bechtel.

PART VII

PRECIOUS LIQUIDS

28. BRIEFING:

Oil and Water

We take gasoline for granted: It's just something we pump into our cars at the service station in exchange for a wad of dollars. But the process of getting from the ground to our wheeled machines is one of the more convoluted journeys on the planet—one involving pumps and pipelines, tankers and trucks, refineries and storage tanks (and often through bribes and arms sales)—its value rising every step of the way.

Oil Terms

Upstream: *Finding oil and pumping it (production)*
Midstream: *Transporting it*
Downstream: *Refining and delivering it*

THE VERY BEGINNINGS

That goo we call petroleum is the remains of previous life forms, mostly one-celled creatures such as plankton, that were trapped, smashed, and heated up over hundreds of millions of years. Petroleum deposits often lie in former seabeds and river deltas that were folded into geological layers, their primitive forms of life decaying into a hydrocarbon-rich ooze, spread between sand and rocks. It seeped up over the millennia; ancient warriors tipped spears with it,

American Indians repaired huts with asphalt, and in ancient Persia a whole religion, Zoroastrianism, celebrated the gases that slipped up from cracks in the earth's crust and magically kept fires ablaze. But until the 1800s, that slime was ignored as a resource. A new illuminant, kerosene, however, first made tapping oil wells a profitable venture.

Canadian geologist Abraham Gesner had discovered how to distill kerosene from petroleum in 1849, and it became a widely popular lantern fuel starting in the 1850s. Even though Edison would make Gesner's ideas irrelevant by the end of the nineteenth century, the Canadian is credited with helping save the whale, which was being harpooned to near extinction for its illuminating whale oil.

THE GEOGRAPHICAL ORIGINS

Gasoline in the United States, as of 2004, typically originates from one of four countries:

- Canada, where much of it is squeezed out of Alberta's tar sands
- Mexico, where the oil fields are located off the coast
- Saudi Arabia, where "Saudi Arabian light" lies just under the desert
- Venezuela, where it is a black viscous material resembling tar

Gasoline in Europe often comes from:

- Russia
- Norway
- Iran
- Libya
- Nigeria

The first piece of the petroleum chain is finding it, a process that for most of the past century was a random game of hide-and-seek that left gaping holes along the way. Even into the 1970s, geologists simply guessed, based on rock formations, where petroleum deposits might be tucked away. Based on their hunches, "wildcatters" bore drills into the earth—and over 90 percent of the time, they found absolutely nothing. Now the process is much more sophisticated. Sound vibrations are the modern key that geologists use to deduce which layers of rock may contain oil. The results are impressive: With "3-D seismic tools" the success rate of striking black gold is about 70 percent.

HEARING OIL

Sound waves are more than a way to transmit language, music, and fra-cases on the street: They are the tools that show where petroleum deposits are lurking. Since the 1980s, geologists have used seismic technology to cause "mini earthquakes" with powerful vibrating "thumper" trucks that violently whack the earth's crust to rattle the rocks miles underneath, studying via computer how long it takes the sound waves to bounce back. When searching out oil under the sea, they use "streamers"—small tanks that are pulled along by ships; once at their destination, streamer tanks blast extremely high-powered compressed air until it wallops the ocean floor. Again, the speed and manner in which waves bounce back can show where oil and natural gas might be found. To determine where they should even bother thumping, prospectors often first fly over land areas with equipment that measures gravity and magnetic qualities to deter-mine densities of rock.

Petroleum—which usually consists of oil, sulfur, and asphaltlike gunk and is often topped by a layer of natural gas—typically isn't found simply in a pool. It's all mixed in with rock and/or sand, residing in the pores and fractures of rocks, such as sandstone and limestone.

Once a petroleum stash has been uncovered, the next ordeal is to get it up to the ground. Giant bits drill down—or sometimes horizontally—occasionally to depths of several miles. These wells are then lined in piping and concrete—the business that made Halliburton rich—and the goo is then pumped out. Sometimes the pressure alone will force it up. Sometimes water (which is heavier than oil) or steam is shot down a nearby column to force the petroleum up. After petroleum starts gurgling up, the main components may be separated: Water is dumped from the brew, and natural gas is siphoned off. The remaining petroleum (which may be a substance that is the color and texture of honey or may be a black lava-like glop) is piped to another destination. Sometimes its travels take it hundreds of miles to a refinery; sometimes it goes to ocean tankers, tanker trucks, or tanker rail cars.

One barrel of oil (containing forty-two gallons) typically yields about:

- Nineteen gallons of gasoline,
- Nine gallons of fuel oil,

- Four gallons of jet fuel, and
- Ten gallons of other products such as butane, kerosene, and asphalt.[1]

> *Spillage is an unfortunate, but common, part of this sloppy operation. Nearly one-tenth of the amount the world uses every day is lost somewhere along the chain of operations, coating oceans or seeping into the ground.[2]*

 ZOOM ▶ **Trouble Areas**

Tankers built since the *Exxon Valdez* fiasco in 1989 are double-hulled—with an extra wall that can trap leaking oil—but plenty of older single-hulled vessels are still in use. The most dangerous are often operated by owners whose identities are lost in a blur of holding companies and paperwork, as evidenced when the *Prestige* sank in 2002 off of Spain, with nobody exactly sure who was responsible. The places where things can go wrong are myriad and include:

▶ Pipelines: The world is crisscrossed with pipes that transport crude oil from source to ship, truck, or refinery. Most of those pipes stand aboveground, making them an easy target for terrorism or tapping by thieves. Iraq and Colombia are the most dramatic examples where sabotage and "leakage" by oil robbers occur along the way, but it's a problem almost everywhere.

▶ Tankers: As of 2004, fewer than three thousand oil tankers were plying the seas—and many aren't up to snuff: Some are "rust buckets" that are falling apart, often flying "flags of convenience"—countries that stamp approval without much inspection—and aren't necessarily going to hold up in storms or collisions.

▶ Choke points: Like cars, ships also experience traffic jams, but when traffic gets blocked along these narrow waterways it affects oil transportation worldwide, adding millions in costs to every shipment. The Strait of Hormuz, where the Persian Gulf makes an intestinelike turn between Iran and Oman, is the most critical of all the geographical bottlenecks, but the Strait of Malacca, which links the Indian Ocean and the Pacific, is another nightmare. This stretch is at points only 1.5 miles wide, and ships are at greater risk of colliding and under constant threat of pirate attacks. Newer bigger ships, such as "very large crude carriers," can't get through the Panama

Canal, which connects the Atlantic and Pacific oceans. And the Houston Ship Channel, lined with refineries, is only two hundred feet wide and forty feet deep. At points in the past decade, an accident occured there nearly once every two days.

▶ Refineries: There are fewer than eighty refineries in the whole world and most are in the United States and Southeast Asia. Not all refineries can refine all types of petroleum: "Sour" or high-sulfur petroleum like that from Venezuela and Russia is relatively new, and many aren't equipped to deal with it. The most commonly used refinery for fuel heading to Asia is located in Singapore, dangling off the end of Malaysia, which requires the dangerous journey through the Strait of Malacca.

TANKERS BY THE NUMBERS

40: Days it takes a typical tanker to carry oil from Saudi Arabia to the United States

$81,000–$100,000: Amount per day paid for a tanker to carry oil from the Middle East to the United States[3]

2 million barrels: Capacity of a "very large crude carrier"

445: Reported cases of piracy attacks in Malacca Strait in 2003[4]

400: People murdered or captured from ships in Malacca Strait 2004[5]

The next step is refining petroleum: Impurities such as sulfur, nitrogen, and oxygen are separated out, and its molecules are "cracked" with heat and/or chemicals to yield various products, including gasoline, premium gasoline, heating oil, butane, and kerosene.

Petroleum yields far more than gasoline for our cars and jet fuel for our aircraft. It provides natural gas used for industry and heating, and butane for our lighters and European heating stoves. Its other uses include:

- Plastics
- Textiles
- Fertilizers
- Pharmaceuticals
- Chemicals

The final step of the journey is getting gasoline—unleaded, antiknock premium, or diesel—from refinery to distributor to our station. That may involve more pipelines, but somewhere along the way it typically makes its way onto a tank truck and zips along the highway. And as it crosses state lines, that globalized product increases in price one more time, when it is slapped with a state tax, often more than twenty cents a gallon. In Europe, the jump is more extreme: Taxes can nearly double the price from distributor to pump.

Water
The New Oil

"The wars of the next century [the twenty-first century] will be about water."

—ISMAIL SERAGELDIN, WORLD BANK VICE PRESIDENT, IN 1995

Imagine turning on the tap, but nothing trickles out. That is already happening in some parts of the world, and thanks to bad water management it may soon be a reality even in the United States, where nearly 5 billion gallons of fresh water is flushed away every day.[6] We treat water like oil, which is to say that our systems waste it—and the problem is worse thanks to old, leaking pipes that crisscross our cities. While upgrades to the water system can help minimize waste—as can low-flow fixtures and appliances—many of our problems are built right into our way of life.

> The average American uses over eighty-six gallons of water a day for bathing, drinking, cooking, washing, and watering the lawn. On a yearly basis, nine thousand gallons per average American goes down the john.

Irrigation, which sucks up 40 percent of the water used in the United States, is also drying up supplies: Water tables are dropping in California's San Joaquin Valley; the High Plains Ogallala Aquifer, which stretches between South Dakota and Texas, is being pumped dry; and water is so tight in parts of Florida, such as Tampa, that they rely on desalinization of seawater.

> Desalinization may be the wave of the future, and thousands of plants worldwide already take salt out of seawater. The downside is that the process—a form of reverse osmosis—is costly and it's not energy efficient: Huge amounts of oil or natural gas are needed to run the plants.

The world's water woes are more extreme: 1.2 billion people—20 percent of the world population—don't have access to clean drinking water. The UN estimates that within twenty years, over 2 billion will be cut off from potable water. When their governments bring in the World Bank–approved companies to address that problem (through privatization), the situation can become even more of a mess, so much so that the masses have rioted in the streets, sending the companies fleeing. (See "Veolia and Suez," page 325.)

Dams are stopping up water to countries downstream, as illustrated in Turkey. The country's $32 billion Southeast Anatolia Development Project—a hydropower complex of nineteen power stations and twenty-two dams—is controversially under way along the Tigris and Euphrates rivers: Valleys of ancient civilations are now lakes, and Syria and Iraq are already screaming, since it cuts into their water supplies, downriver. The project was viewed as so destabilizing to the Middle East that the World Bank refused to fund it.

> Most of the world's water is trapped in polar ice caps or seawater. Only 2.5 percent is freshwater and less than one-half of 1 percent is available as drinking water.

Israel, which, along with Jordan, has so tapped the Jordan River that it is now at points little more than a stream, is meanwhile importing water from water-rich Turkey, trading arms for the precious liquid. Egypt has threatened to aim its arms at Ethiopia and Sudan if they make good on plans to dam the Nile, which is Egypt's lifeblood—yet another example of the world's many ongoing water conflicts, which experts predict we will be seeing plenty more of in the near future.

> The water problem is worsened the more humans pave over land. When rain hits soil, it can trickle down into groundwater and replenish the aquifers and wells. But if it hits asphalt instead, it runs off into a waterway, and often can't be tapped.

▶▶ ◀◀

29. THE OIL BEAST:

An Addiction

Notable Numbers

- 211 million: Number of automobiles registered in the United States (cars and light trucks)
- 82 million: World oil consumption in barrels per day in 2004[1]

Snapshot

Some say it's all Henry Ford's fault for introducing the mass-produced automobile, to which Americans are now beholden. Some blame American urban planners who zoned our houses far away from our work, while others point at Goodyear, who a century ago bought up trolley car tracks only to rip them up and increase demand for their rubber wheels. Whomever you wish to credit for making petroleum hugely important, we're now addicted to the oil that comes from it. It powers every aspect of our life, but the biggest use of petroleum is in its refined form of gasoline, used to run our cars.

> With 5 percent of the world population, the United States consumes 25 percent of the world's oil.

Biggest Oil-Suckers in the United States[2]

Cars	43%
Industry	24%
Trucks	12%
Jets	8%

Homes	6%
Electricity	3%
Farm equip./Other	2%

OIL APPETITES

Of the 82 million barrels of oil used by the world every day, the world's leading consumers:[3]

1. United States	20.5 million barrels per day
2. China	6.3 million barrels per day
3. Japan	5.5 million barrels per day
4. Russia	3.7 million barrels per day
5. Germany	2.6 million barrels per day
6. India	2.5 million barrels per day
7. Canada	2.3 million barrels per day
8. South Korea	2.2 million barrels per day
9. Brazil	2.2 million barrels per day
10. Mexico	2.0 million barrels per day

Car drivers in the United States alone use 8.5 million barrels of oil a day, the biggest single use of oil anywhere in the world.[4]

Unlike other parts of the world, the United States was purposefully developed as a car culture; with the exception of a few cities, such as New York, we are obliged to hop in the car whenever we leave the house. Our cars have done more than make us fat, aggressive, and broke. Now Americans are so hooked on petroleum that we don't control it anymore, it controls us. And our government will do whatever it takes—bribe, sell arms, swing iffy deals, break laws, or take us to war—to ensure that we have more. Meanwhile we'll dig deeper into our pockets, ignoring pollution, our government's shady deeds, and international cries that we are using too much, just to make sure we can get our fix.

DIRTY OIL

They called it the "devil's dukey" or, more officially, "Satan's excrement." The sixteenth-century Spanish who came upon the bubbling crude in Venezuela had no use for the stuff—they were far more interested in gold and silver—but they may have captured the true essence of petroleum with their unflattering name. Oil and the art of mucking around in that business is stinking dirty, and dealing with it tends to corrupt and drive men to vile acts.

Buying oil overseas is a long chain of "baksheesh"—behind-the-back gifts. Never mind the laws dictated by congresses and parliaments: Oil companies blow through mountains of bribes to get their job done. Millions of dollars are slipped to officials to push through business deals, while farther down, smaller wads and cartons of smokes go to the guides who pilot tankers through the Suez Canal. The countries who supply us the most oil can have their pick of our armaments showroom—Saudi Arabia now boasts one of the most modern arsenals in the world and the most high-tech military command centers, thanks to the United States. In Africa, as European companies know well, free rifles and other small arms also lubricate every oil deal. Organized crime is often embroidered into the dirty tapestry that unrolls from refinery to gas station, and the oil spilled and leaked along the way barely elicits a shrug. And we're so tightly bound to our bloody oil, that apparently we'll kill, or look the other way when our government does.

The first priority of the United States during its attack of Iraq was to secure the oil fields and get them pumping again. Oil was flowing out of Iraq within weeks of the March 2003 invasion.

Close-up

As the biggest consumer and the most powerful country in the world, the United States has long had unfettered access to its oil fix; even if we don't control oil prices, we've usually been able to control supply. The United States alone has typically accounted for most of the increased demands, as we've switched to SUVs, and more and more young Americans take the wheel every year, while older Americans won't let go.

In 2000, the United States used 19.6 million barrels per day; in 2004, it had jumped by nearly a million barrels a day to 20.5 million. SUVs played a large part in fueling that jump.

SUVS

"[Americans are] still driving their SUVs to Wal-Mart," squealed the head of Royal Dutch/Shell Jeroen van der Veer at a 2004 dinner for oil executives that was particularly joyous, given that oil had shot to over fifty-five dollars a barrel. Certainly the five-thousand-pound machines have their benefits: better view of the road, more room, a feeling of protection and personal power in a chaotic world, but they chug gasoline—getting a measly fifteen miles per gallon in city driving, for instance. That hasn't had much effect on purchases—thanks in part to congressional legislation, which recently offered tax credits for buying them. While sales of passenger cars dropped nearly 2 percent in 2002, sport-utility vehicle sales soared almost 7 percent. Environmental groups such as the Natural Resources Defense Council say SUV drivers alone are consuming an additional 5 billion gallons of gasoline a year, and some Christian groups are hopping mad too. "What would Jesus drive?" asks the evangelical environmental network. It may not be a matter of religious values or environmental ethics that brings the demise of these beasts. If oil prices keep climbing, these babies may be permanently relegated to the garage for all but the very rich.

But that's changing. Suddenly, China, which has long supplied its own oil, is barreling into the world market in a big way, in part because the Chinese are beginning to trade in their bikes for cars: The demand for cars in China is growing some 20 percent every year. Same for India: In the country with the fastest growing population, more and more are learning to drive.

"Emulating the United States . . . China's long-term goal is to have every household own a car."

—WORLD RESOURCES INSTITUTE[5]

Hubbert's Peak

"Peak oil" is a term that gets bandied around a lot these days, and it's originator, geophysicist M. King Hubbert (1903–89)—who worked for Shell—posthumously has influenced a whole school of thought. Using a bell-shaped curve as his model, Hubbert predicted way back in 1956 that U.S. oil resources would peak around the 1970s. After that, petroleum reserves would dwindle and oil deposits would be more difficult and more expensive to access. Indeed, in the early 1970s known oil supplies in the United States "peaked." Now many are taking his curve and applying it to world oil supplies. Some say global oil supplies will peak as early as 2007, although natural gas can hold out longer.

The question is how much we're willing to pay for the stuff—not only in price per barrels, but in environmental degradation as companies ravage wilderness areas, such as Alaska's National Wildlife Refuge, and drill offshore, cut down forests, and scour prairies in their search for more black gold.

"If you think the price of oil and gasoline has been volatile, you ain't seen nothin' yet."

—BILL O'GRADY, COMMODITIES ANALYST FOR A. G. EDWARDS AND SONS, IN 2005[6]

HAPPY NEWS FOR OIL COMPANIES

Since taking office, President George W. Bush has made barrels of decisions that make his oil buddies mighty happy. These include:

- Reneging on the Kyoto Protocol: President Bush erased U.S. approval for the international agreement that sought to reduce emissions of hydrocarbon gases produced by fossil fuels, such as oil.
- Rewriting energy policy: While nearly ignoring all alternatives such as methane, Bush's National Energy Plan calls for opening up the Alaska's National Wildlife Refuge, where some 6 billion barrels may be lurking. Another important feature: The National Energy Plan relaxes any federal regulations that might hinder building new oil-related infrastructure.
- Dropping sanctions on Libya: Yee-ha, say oil companies, whose investments there have been frozen for over a decade.
- Invading Afghanistan: Although the 2001 act was retribution for September 11 attacks, it also opened up the area for future pipelines, which companies such as Unocal are building.
- Invading Iraq: Ostensibly a move to seize Saddam Hussein's WMD—not found as of this writing—the 2003 invasion opened up Iraq for U.S. oil investments.

Once the largest producer of oil in the world, the car-dependent United States blasted through its reserves, which have been going downhill for the last three decades. The biggest oil deposits now lie in the Middle East, although there could be lots more than meets the eye in Venezuela. Several new areas are also coming into focus:

- North Sea: Oil was first discovered here in the 1960s, but in the past two decades, even more has been found in offshore territory belonging to Norway.

- Abathasca tar sands: Western Canada was once rich with more conventional oil deposits, but the United States helped Canada suck those dry. Now the oil sands in Alberta—which may hold enough oil to last some 165 years—are looking very attractive. Alas, the lands that hold them are a blight once the sands have been ravaged.
- Caspian Sea area: Notice how recently the United States has become very interested in the "Stans," actually noticing where they are on the map? And this is not the only country drooling over the potential oil and gas resources in Kazakhstan, Turkmenistan, and offshore in the nearby Caspian. Several other "Stans," Iran, and Russia are also lining up to get a piece of that action.
- Gulf of Guinea: Nigeria, Angola, and Gabon were already on the map. Tiny São Tomé de Principe is the newest oil-rich land ripe for exploitation.

Behind the Scenes

Sooner rather than later, we're going to have to switch to alternative energies, be they ethanol, methane, or hydrogen, and we will be forced to alter our settlement patterns into more "urban villages" that promote walking rather than firing up the four-wheeled machine every time we need to buy a loaf of bread. Global geopolitics are now based on our addiction to the automobile. Who is running the world? To a large extent we are, and we are making an impact on it, every time we rev up our cars.

30.THE AL-SAUD:

Conflicts of Interest

Country: Saudi Arabia
Capital: Riyadh
Ruler: King Abdullah (August 2005)
Writer of the checks: The late King Fahd's son Abdul Aziz
Population: 26.4 million (includes 5.6 million nonnationals)[1]

Notable Numbers

- $100 billion: 2004 revenue from oil exports[2]
- 15 percent: Proportion of oil in the United States that comes from Saudi Arabia[3]
- 10 percent: Proportion of GDP spent on military[4]
- 25 percent: Unemployment rate in 2004 (estimated)
- $12,000: Per capita income in 2004
- 29 percent: Estimated illiteracy rate for females (versus 15 percent for males)

Snapshot

Rolling in dough, swimming in oil, and clamping down on insurgents to keep hold of the familial reign, the al-Saud—the absolute monarchs who rule Saudi Arabia—are the world's wealthiest and most influential clan. They could throw the whole planet into a tizzy merely by cutting off supplies of their addictive "Saudi Arab Light" (as they did in 1973, causing the American "energy crisis")— or worse, by losing control of their oil to radicals, a growing fear nowadays.

In 1973, the al-Saud rulers demonstrated how easily they could screw up the world system. Furious that the United States had rushed arms to Israel when Egypt and Syria invaded during that year's Yom Kippur War, King Faisal shut off the spigot of oil to the United States and Western Europe. Oil prices quadrupled, Wall Street stocks tumbled, and the economy teetered for the eight months the embargo lasted. Unbeknownst to most Americans, within weeks of being cut off, the United States was plotting to militarily seize Saudi oil fields. Under pressure, King Faisal secretly supplied oil to the U.S. Navy, thus stopping the beating war drums. The inflated price of oil, which never dropped back to pre-embargo prices, helped kick his country into an era of unprecedented wealth.

This extended family of some six thousand males fills all offices of the government, hogs the national piggy bank (even fourth-generation princes qualify for hefty allowances of some $20,000 a month), and now faces its most perilous threats. With a quarter of the kingdom's men unemployed and per capita income in this oil-oozing nation dropping to $12,000, many of the Saud's subjects are ticked: Punished with beheadings for drugs, alcohol, or alleged sorcery, stoned to death if they partake in adultery, their hands chopped off if they steal, the masses view many of the Saud princes as cocaine-snorting, heavy-boozing, prostitute-loving hypocrites who demand cuts of every business transaction in the land and throw billions around buying arms and building lavish new palaces. And many of the country's devout are most unhappy that shiny high-rises and malls now stand where date palms used to sway, and the car has shoved aside the camel.

DUELING RICHES

The ruling family since 1932, when ancestor Abdul Aziz al-Saud stitched together the land of warring tribes with fundamentalist Islamic preacher Mohammad al-Wahhab at his side, the al-Saud suffer the curse of too many riches. The desert of Arabia that Abdul Aziz stamped with his last name is bejeweled with holy cities: Mecca (where Islam's prophet/founder Muhammad was born and wrote the Koran) and Medina (where he was buried), the destinations of millions of Muslims each year making the pilgrimage across Islam's most sacred soil. Hidden below those swirling sands, however, lies another treasure trove: one-quarter of the planet's known petroleum reserves.[5] And the conflict between the two treasures—or more precisely, between the oil wealth that buys the al-Saud their hedonistic comforts and the religion that fueled their rise to power—is the source of the family's thorny problems. The Islamic religious establishment (the ulema), with whom the al-Saud family theoretically co-rule, loathes the modernization and Westerners that exploitation of the black slime brings. In charge of education, the religious elite have indoctrinated Saudi youth with hatred of the infidels, including those hundreds of thousands of infidels who stepped into their hallowed land to fight 1991's Persian Gulf War to push Saddam Hussein out of neighboring Kuwait. Dick Cheney, then defense secretary, had promised the

United States would pull out immediately after "Desert Storm" in 1991. Tens of thousands of American armed forces and private military contractors, however, stayed after the war's end. Some were hired to protect the oil fields and the al-Saud themselves—increasingly, they find themselves targets of religious fanatics, as are the rulers themselves. In November 2004, twenty-six Saudi clerics issued a fatwa ordering the faithful to rise up against the West and attack Westerners and their interests throughout the Persian Gulf.

The Persian Gulf War was costly to the al-Saud in numerous ways: Besides the social, religious, and political ramifications of letting in foreigners, the United States charged them over $50 billion to fight it. It also created the al-Saud's most vociferous enemy: Osama bin Laden. He's despised the monarchy ever since they rejected his offer to fight Saddam Hussein with his holy warriors, the mujahideen, straight from fighting the Soviets in Afghanistan, and instead brought in the modernized forces of the United States and Europe.

The United States finally initiated a serious pullout of troops from Saudi Arabia in April 2003.

If the al-Saud initially downplayed the role of their subjects in the September 11 attacks—with fifteen of the nineteen hijackers believed to be Saudis—they've sure changed their tune recently with al-Qaeda vowing to bring down the house of al-Saud. The kingdom is reeling with the knowledge that militants inspired by Osama bin Laden are rampaging across the land: Since May 2003, a rash of al-Qaeda bombings and shootouts—including of the U.S. consulate in Jedda and the Saudi Ministry of the Interior—have killed over one hundred people, and the government is rounding up dissidents and throwing up roadblocks to check cars for weapons, a measure never needed before.

AL-QAEDA IN THE HOMELAND

Sporadic bombings and attacks on foreigners killed hundreds starting in the mid-1990s, but this is different: Al-Qaeda is setting not only Westerners in its sights, but the Saud family and their government.[6]

• May 12, 2003: Twelve al-Qaeda suicide bombers simultaneously car-bomb three housing compounds in the capital, killing thirty, wounding two hundred.

- November 8, 2003: Two al-Qaeda suicide bombers blow up a van in another residential compound, killing seventeen, wounding 120.
- April 21, 2004: Car bomb explodes outside of Riyadh police headquarters, killing six, wounding 150.
- May 29, 2004: Unknown number of al-Qaeda operatives break into housing complex in Khobar, going from apartment to apartment on a violent twenty-four-hour spree that ends in the deaths of twenty-two.
- December 7, 2004: Al-Qaeda militants storm into U.S. consulate in Jeddah, tossing grenade, blasting automatic weapons, killing guards, and taking eighteen hostage, before Saudi police blast in. Nine killed, four injured.
- December 29, 2004: In the course of two hours, al-Qaeda operatives explode a bomb outside the Ministry of the Interior, killing one, and explode another bomb outside of a military recruitment center, killing two, then battle police in Riyadh, resulting in the deaths of seven.

"The sins the [Saudi] regime committed are great . . . [the Saudi regime is] violating God's rules . . . it practiced injustices against the people, violating their rights, humiliating their pride . . . [the Saudi misspend oil money while] "millions of people are suffering from poverty and deprivation."

—FROM AN AUDIOTAPE BELIEVED TO BE OF OSAMA BIN LADEN SPEAKING
THAT EMERGED IN DECEMBER 2004

While their country is rocking with calls to change—some demanding more religion, some demanding more freedom—the al-Saud princes continue their international gallivanting, stealing the spotlight for being both heroes and hellions: Prince Alwaleed swoops in to save flooded villages and ailing businesses, while the government funds religious schools that mold militant zealots. Crown Prince Abdullah personally hands over $7.2 million in 2004 for tsunami relief; other princes throw parties that cost nearly as much and are so raucous they would make Mick Jagger blush. Prince Ahmed (as owner) won the world's most prestigious horse race, the late King Fahd lost millions in one night playing poker. Talking religion out of one side of their mouth, dealing oil diplomacy out of the other, the princes' reputations often have been forged on excesses, be they reports of beating servants, running booze, using diplomatic immunity to smuggle tons of cocaine,[7] or going on shopping sprees in Marbella, Spain, where the royal entourage racks up hundreds of thousands of dollars of sales every hour.

MEET THE GRANDSONS

When Abdul Aziz al-Saud died in 1953, his thirty-four surviving sons, the youngest now in their seventies, became the contenders for future kings. His Western-educated grandsons, however, frequently dominate the news.

- **Prince Alwaleed bin Talal bin Abdul Aziz:** The sixth richest man in the world and the number one largest foreign investor in the United States, the outspoken Alwaleed bailed out Citibank in 1991, saved EuroDisney in 1994, and owns considerable stakes in Saks Fifth Avenue and the Four Seasons and, previously, the Plaza Hotel. His post–September 11 check for $10 million was tossed back by New York Mayor Rudolph Giuliani in 2001 after Alwaleed lectured that the United States should examine its Middle East posture—but he's also demanded that Saudis examine why fifteen of the nineteen hijackers came from their country.

- **Prince Bandar bin Sultan:** Fun-loving, hard-drinking, flirtatious Bandar is Saudi ambassador to the United States. Beloved by the Bushes, who invite him to the family compound, Bandar is an important link in U.S.-Saudi relations: He convinced Libya's Moammar Qaddafi to send the Lockerbie suspects to trial, and he also arranged for dozens of Saudis, including Osama bin Laden's kin, to fly out of the United States on September 12, 2001—after Bandar promised to keep the country rolling in Saudi Arab Light.[8]

- **Prince Turki bin Faisal bin Abdul Aziz:**[9] Now ambassador to the UK, Turki was Saudi Arabia's head of intelligence for twenty-five years, stepping down a mere ten days before the September 11 attacks. At the behest of the United States, he helped fund and funnel mujahideen into Afghanistan during the 1980s when they fought the Soviets; he also made several attempts to convince Osama bin Laden to give up his guerrilla-training ways and return to Saudi Arabia. Smooth-talking and seriously smart, mysterious Turki seems to know lots more than he's telling.

- **Prince Ahmed bin Salman bin Abdul Aziz:** Charismatic horse fanatic who bought the 2001 Kentucky Derby winner ten days before the race, Ahmed was also a media mogul, running some thirty publications out of London. Died in summer 2002, reportedly from a heart attack; some say the forty-three-year-old was murdered. An American writer alleged that he was a spy for al-Qaeda, but that seems the most far-fetched of all the conspiracies that are a-swirling.

- **Prince Abdul Aziz bin Fahd bin Abdul Aziz:** Even though Crown Prince Abdullah had been running the place since King Fahd had a debilitating stroke in 1995, Abdul Aziz—Fahd's youngest and favorite son—is reportedly signing the kingdom's checks. He controversially signed some $4 billion worth of them to build his new palace, definitely a bad PR move in these testy times.

Close-up

Whether working individually or collectively as the country's government, the al-Saud family has boosted economies everywhere from Afghanistan (where they funded the Taliban's rise to power) to Britain (where they negotiated a $30 billion arms deal in the 1980s that the *Financial Times* called "the biggest sale ever of anything to anyone"[10]).

But nowhere are the al-Saud weightier players than in the United States. Besides guaranteeing affordable supplies of the oil that runs the American machine (and usually coming through on the promise), al-Saud princes and other wealthy Saudis have invested some $420 billion in companies and on Wall Street,[11] and they hold billions in U.S. bank deposits. Saudis also first made a big name of the fledgling private investment firm Carlyle Group, when at the behest of Carlyle advisor George H. W. Bush and firm partner James Baker, they tossed billions into the investment fund.

Rumors were flying after 9/11 that Saudis had pulled $200 billion out of U.S. stocks and banks. Indeed some money was yanked due to hostilities, but the figure was less than $1 billion.[12]

The United States delights in the Saudis' arms buildup—they typically buy at least $2 billion of American arms every year, but Israel isn't thrilled that the neighbors now boast fancy war toys and elaborate spy planes, including radar-carrying AWACS.

The oil-for-protection pact made six decades ago between Abdul Aziz al-Saud and Franklin Roosevelt has for the most part endured, although it's nearly frayed several times over the issue of Middle East peace. Simply put, the al-Saud don't recognize Israel's right to exist—and they may never, unless Israel pulls back to the territory it occupied prior to the Seven-Day War of 1967, when it made significant gains into land previously held by Jordan and Palestine, including claiming all of Jerusalem. In 2002, then Crown Prince Abdullah floated a Saudi peace proposal, promising the Arab world would normalize relations with Israel if it would withdraw to the pre-1967 borders; the response was tepid at best. While the United States pressures the al-Saud to help mend relations between Israelis and Palestinians, the hard-core religious leaders within Saudi Arabia try to prevent it.

King Abdullah is seen as more pious than most of his kin, which doesn't hurt the al-Saud's standing with the powerful religious establishment. Although he took the throne when Fahd died, the strength of his grip is debatable: Several of his half-brothers are also eyeing that chair. Among them: Defense Minister Prince Sultan, respected for privately funding the building of a billion-dollar hospital; powerful Prince Salman, the mayor of Riyadh; and Interior

Abdul Aziz and FDR agreed on "oil for security"

Minister Prince Naif, increasingly anti-Western and accused of blocking investigations into previous bombings.

Reform-minded but cautious, King Abdullah is now walking down a ribbon of land mines: With some factions pulling the al-Saud to open up the country, and others pushing them to close it further, the country may simply rip apart. For all their faults and excesses, should the al-Saud fall from power, the successors will have the means to slam the world economy, and the weapons to engage in a nasty war. Should the royal family seriously start to teeter, however, it won't be surprising to see the United States moving in to escort them back to their throne. To embark on a full-scale democracy experiment at this time is to risk seeing Osama bin Laden at the control board, a possibility neither the al-Saud nor the United States wants to face.

In December 2004, bin Laden demanded via an audiotape that Saudi "oil prices should be at least $100 a barrel," and called upon his followers to prevent the West from accessing Arab oil by attacking oil facilities all over the Persian Gulf region. According to the Jerusalem Center for Public Affairs, this call marked "the first time that al-Qaeda's leadership had openly divulged its strategy of hitting the Western economy by disrupting oil supplies and causing prices to skyrocket."[13]

Behind the Scenes

No situation better reveals the oppression of modern Saudi Arabia than the country's treatment of women. Only half make it to high school, only two-thirds are literate, and only their hands and eyes can be exposed when they are in public. Religious schools teach that they are physically, emotionally, and mentally inferior. Few are permitted to work—and even fewer find jobs because of the problems of segregation in public: Even restaurants are divided into areas for the different sexes. They are not to go out unchaperoned or without their abaya and carrying a note from the man of the house—which must be shown to the religious police who wander the streets—and should they be caught kissing anyone other than their husband they could be stoned to death or drowned by their father in the family swimming pool.[14] And Saudi women know that even when they get married, they may only be one of four wives, although the expense of keeping up a harem is curtailing that practice. (The situation isn't much better for men: With unemployment among young males hovering near 50 percent, they don't have the money to take a wife.)

THE DRIVE-IN

The religious establishment blamed it on Western influence, and indeed maybe it was the impetus. In July 1990, fifty women did the unthinkable: They shoved out their chauffeurs and took the wheel, cruising for half an hour around a parking lot. What sounds innocent to Western eyes was a radical crime in Riyadh, where they were arrested, shamed, and some were beaten; what had merely been banned by cultural customs previously, became illegal both by the king's declaration and religious edict.

A 2005 study of sixteen countries in the Middle East and North Africa, conducted by Freedom House, rated Saudi Arabia the lowest for women's rights.

Slowly, far too slowly say some (and far too quickly say others), the al-Saud are opening up Saudi Arabia. As crown prince, Abdullah okayed municipal elections—the first time Saudis have voted for city councilmen since 1965. And at least one Riyadh candidate caused an uproar—and triggered death threats—when he campaigned to put car keys back into womens' hands. Although al-Suleiman lost, he might have a better chance in 2009. By then, some say, women may actually have the right to vote.

31. OPEC:

Controlling Natural Riches

Organization: Organization of the Petroleum Exporting Countries (OPEC)
Headquarters: Vienna, Austria
Founded: 1960
Member countries: Saudi Arabia, Iran, Iraq, Kuwait, United Arab Emirates,
Venezuela, Libya, Nigeria, Qatar, Algeria, Indonesia
Collective revenues: $338 billion in 2004

Notable Numbers

- 66 percent: Proportion of world oil reserves OPEC represents[1]
- 42 gallons: Amount of oil in a "barrel"
- 34 percent: Saudi Arabia's share of OPEC revenues

OPEC Countries and Their Proven Reserves (in Barrels)

Saudi Arabia	262 billion
Iran	126 billion
Iraq	115 billion
Kuwait	99 billion
United Arab Emirates	98 billion
Venezuela	78 billion
Libya	39 billion
Nigeria	35 billion
Qatar	15 billion
Algeria	12 billion
Indonesia	5 billion

Some estimates say that the top six OPEC producers have enough oil to last through the twenty-first century—at current rates of consumption, at least.[2] There's the catch: Oil demand is on the rise, thanks to the United States—where the rising population means a rising population of drivers, many of them driving longer distances—and to China and India, where many are buying their first cars.

Snapshot

Where can one find two-thirds of the world's proven oil reserves and a dysfunctional clique of ruling families and dictators prone to building grandiose public works projects before their peoples' basic needs are met? That would be Vienna, when the heads of OPEC countries meet at the organization's headquarters to hammer out quotas and supplies to the world market.

THE OIL MEN

The United States inadvertently created it. In 1959, American oil companies had a change of heart: After years of buying their crude from the Persian Gulf countries and Venezuela, they turned their tankers toward Canada and Mexico instead. The sudden switch crippled countries such as Saudi Arabia, Iran, Iraq, and Venezuela, where oil is the main source of filling the coffers. OPEC—or the Oil Producing and Exporting Countries—was born the next year. And the world response was more or less "Who cares?" The countries squabbled among themselves and in terms of negotiating, OPEC was ineffective and weak. In 1973, however, OPEC showed just what a fearsome force it could be. Saudi Arabia, upon whose oil the United States had once again become dependent, turned off the oil spigots: King Faisal, under pressure from the Saudi religious establishment, cut off the United States for arming Israel during that year's Yom Kippur War, which, thanks to the weaponry, Israel won. (Britain was also embargoed.) Most OPEC countries linked arms with the Saudis, and with vastly reduced supplies, the price of world oil shot through the roof. The United States still got its oil, much of it resold from European countries, but the high prices caused shortages, long gas lines, and America's first taste of an "energy crunch." Unknown to the public, the United States seriously considered militarily solving the problem by commandeering Saudi Arabia's oil fields.

The Iranian revolution of 1979 caused world oil prices to spike as most of Iran's oil was temporarily taken off the market, slashing supplies.

The cartel is often viewed as a bunch of greedy, conniving oilmongers, but the truth is oil continues to be the only major source of income to these countries, some of which are quite populous.

THE MAGIC FORMULA

They sound like exotic coffee blends, but Algeria's Saharan Blend, Saudi Arab Light, Venezuela's Tia Juana, Nigeria's Bonny Light, Indonesia's Minas, UAE's Dubai, and Mexico's Isthmus (although Mexico is not part of OPEC)—the so-called OPEC basket—are the seven types of crude oil that OPEC uses for its pricing formula:

- If the average price per barrel is less than twenty-two dollars for ten straight days of trade, then OPEC slashes supplies by 500,000 barrels per day, in the hopes of increasing prices by tightening supply.
- If the average price per barrel rises above twenty-eight dollars for the basket, OPEC is supposed to increase the supply to make the price drop. The problem is that lately, they are all pretty much working at capacity so there's not much more that they can kick out.

Saudi Arabia dominates OPEC—and the Saudis often keep oil prices lower than the more populated members, such as Indonesia (population 239 million, $3,200 per capita income, 27 percent in poverty) and Nigeria (138 million, $900 per capita income, 60 percent in poverty), want them to be. The reason isn't altruistic: What helps push OPEC prices lower than some desire is the fear that high prices will drive oil companies to seek new oil sources to develop. Exploration and new development, after all, are expensive operations, but some costly sources, such as tar sands, look more attractive when prices top thirty dollars a barrel. And with prices soaring past sixty dollars a barrel lately, the move is on to develop Canada's tar sands—and rapidly.

OPEC, whose muscle grew over the years as well as its tendency to flex it, is loved by few, but is particularly scorned by neocons. According to BBC's

Newsnight, *one objective in occupying Iraq is to pump the heck out of the Iraqi fields and flood the world market with oil, thus rendering OPEC powerless and, the neocons hoped, destroying it.*[3] *Like all their other ideas about Iraq, this one hasn't yet materialized.*

Close-up

Every country that is a member of OPEC has its own agenda and its own personal problems, both of which can affect world oil supplies and prices. A two-month oil strike in Venezuela, civil unrest in Nigeria (where the locals rarely see any of the profits from their crude), and separatists' attacks on petroleum companies' operations in Indonesia have all taken their toll on OPEC's recent output.

National Iranian Oil Company: The Old Geezer

Iran's population is 69 million, with 40 percent in poverty and a per capita income of $7,000.

- It is the second largest OPEC producer and fourth biggest producer in the world.
- It has the second largest known world oil reserves (10 percent).
- It is still under some sanctions from the United States.

The National Iranian Oil Company (NIOC) formed in the 1950s in reaction to the British companies that had been dominating the country's oil since before the first world war. The Brits may be long gone but the company is poorly managed and beleaguered by old and rickety infrastructure, and inefficiency abounds, but it manages to pump out some 4 million barrels a day. NIOC could be cranking out far more than that, but Iran—which ran out all the foreigners after the Iranian revolution in 1979, including Britain BP—needs new money to snap it into shape. It is getting some from joint ventures and "payback deals" with French oil company Elf Aquitaine, Italian company ENI/Agip, and China's National Petroleum Company. Russia's Lukoil and French-Belgian Total and British BP are also circling around, but the matter probably won't get entirely sorted out until the religious government takes a bow, ahem, if in fact it ever does.

Iran also holds vast amounts of natural gas. According to the U.S. Department of Energy, it is second only to Russia. Deals are under way to build pipelines to pump Iranian natural gas to China and India.

Iran needs an injection of foreign capital—and knows it. In 2003, the government passed the foreigner-beckoning "Law on the Attraction and Protection of Foreign Investment"—the first time the country has opened widely to outside investment since the ayatollah slammed the door to outsiders in 1979. One area where Iran needs particular help is in building new refineries to produce gasoline: Iran currently spends $2 billion a year importing car fuel into the country. The recently discovered Azadegan oil field, believed to hold some 26 billion barrels, is eliciting some foreign interest. Iran doesn't have the money to tap it, and is luring a Japanese consortium in to develop it. The United States is pressuring the Japanese to drop that idea. China, however, may pursue it.

 ZOOM **Iran**

Iranians are loners in the Persian Gulf neighborhood. They're not Arab, they're Persian, and they're not Sunni Muslim, they're Shiite Muslim, and those factors are hugely important in the local dynamics. The Islamic government that the people—well, the merchants and students, at least—brought into being back in 1979 is getting pretty stifling and boring, and now plenty of Iranians, especially women and college students, want to turn the page and finish that book. The Bush administration loudly supported recent uprisings, but lately hundreds of dissidents have been killed. In 2004, Iranian conservatives and the religious government clamped down hard—removing thousands of reformers from the ballots in the 2005 elections and steamrolling student demonstrations. In the meantime, the economy is going to hell, and Iran's hardheaded insistence that it will continue developing nuclear power—a move the United States insists is about making nuclear weapons—has many fearing that Iran may encounter the hardheaded wrath of the United States in a repeat performance of the Iraq War. The June 2005 election of hardliner Mahmoud Ahmadinejad as president (after hundreds of moderate and reformist candidates were disqualified from running by the religious establishment) does not bode well for smooth resolution of the U.S.-Iranian conflicts.

THE UNITED STATES AND IRAN

Bad blood between the governments of the United States and Iran goes back for decades.

- In the 1950s, the CIA helped take down a prime minister and put in the Shah, who bought billions of dollars of war toys from the United States, and let loose his nasty secret police, who killed thousands of Iranians, all with a shrug from DC, which saw Iran as a strategic gas pump.
- In 1979, things got really ugly during the Iranian revolution, when the people ejected the Shah and installed a religious government, headed by Ayatollah Khomeini. It was alarming enough when the religious leader cut off oil to the United States; when radicals held fifty-two Americans hostage, holding most for 444 days, it caused an international crisis.
- In 1980, the U.S.-backed Saddam Hussein kicked off the eight-year Iran-Iraq War, during which Hussein fought Iranians with chemicals. (Some say that the United States put Saddam up to the invasion, hoping to pry Iran's ayatollah out of power.) Iran turned over the Tehran hostages—Bush Sr. is rumored to have negotiated a behind-the-scenes deal to postpone the handover until Ronald Reagan stepped into office[4]—but Iran would be behind another hostage-taking ordeal in Lebanon.
- In 1988, the last year of the brutal Iran-Iraq War, the USS *Vincennes* shot down a commercial Iranian plane over the Strait of Hormuz—killing 290. Iranians were livid, all the more so when President George Bush Sr. awarded a medal to the shooter and announced, "I will never apologize for what Americans do."
- In 1995, President Bill Clinton slapped sanctions on Iran, when that country was implicated in the 1988 blowing up of Pan Am Flight 103 that killed 270 over Lockerbie, Scotland (some say it was a payback for the USS *Vincennes*).
- In 2002, President George W. Bush named Iran as part of the "Axis of Evil" in his State of the Union Address.
- In 2004, President George W. Bush renewed the economic cuffs that had been clamped on by Clinton for yet another year, noting that Iran posed an "unusual and extraordinary threat to U.S. security." With continued rumors that Iran wants to develop nuclear weapons—a fear of Israel, which holds nuclear weapons itself—the United States started growling again about WMDs. Neocons are urging the United States to stomp in there while its troops are already in the neighborhood.

Iraq National Oil Company: Fragmented but Functioning, Sort Of

Iraq's population is 26 million, with an estimated 30 percent in poverty and a per capita income of $3,500.

- It has the world's third largest oil reserves (115 billion barrels) and is the thirteenth largest oil producer in the world.
- Its oil infrastructure is a chaotic mess under constant attack.
- Oil companies are lining up to develop its oil fields.

Hey, oil lovers, come on down! Should you be able to survive the constant suicide bombings and attacks, it's a real bonanza in Iraq, which has at least eighty known oil fields, only seventeen of which have been developed. The country's State Oil Marketing Organization is busy taking orders for the country's Iraq National Oil Company to fill and the U.S. Army Corp of Engineers and Halliburton are trying to get the wells and infrastructure in working order. One problem: Despite the fourteen thousand hired guards, many of them Iraqis, who are theoretically protecting the oil system, every time something is fixed, insurgents blow it up again. From April 2003 to September 2004 alone, Iraq's pipelines, power lines, refineries, and wells suffered over 120 major attacks, one shutting down the entire pipeline from the Kirkuk oil field to Turkey, and pipelines are tapped to the tune of 2,500 tons a day, reports the U.S. Department of Energy. Nevertheless, enough oil successfully made it out of the country in 2004, says DOE, to ring in some $20 billion of sales—which theoretically is going to the Iraqi government. The chaos that rules in the country spreads to the oil world as well: Russia, China, and France are among those that are waiting to find out the status of the deals they made when Saddam Hussein was in power. Russia's Lukoil alone had committed $3.7 billion to developing new fields.

> *Nobody yet knows for sure how much oil Iraq holds: Since Saddam was in the dog house for most of the past fifteen years, he didn't have the access to new, more sophisticated technology that can more accurately assess reserves.*

Currently the southern Rumaila fields and the northern Kirkuk fields are pumping out the most oil, which is being sold to some twenty oil companies from Greek to Chinese, Exxon to BP. As to who will ultimately develop what, like everything in this black hole, that remains to be seen.

Petróleos de Venezuela SA (PDVSA): South America's Robin Hood

Venezuela's population is 25 million, with 47 percent in poverty and a per capita income of $4,800.

- It is the fifth leading OPEC producer and ninth biggest oil producer in the world.
- Some say offshore and new unexplored areas could hold more oil than Saudi Arabia.
- Its Tia Juana oil is the blackest and most viscous—requiring special refineries.
- Billions of dollars of oil reserves are now funding social welfare.

Loose cannon Hugo Chávez, who as president of Venezuela is de facto owner of the state-run oil company, doesn't much care for the United States—and the feeling is mutual. For one thing, ever since he was pushed out of power for two days in 2002, a coup he blames on the United States, Chávez has been obsessed, perhaps correctly, with the notion that the administration wants to see him dead. "If I am killed," he has warned, "the administration can forget about getting even one drop of oil."[5]

> The Bush administration regards Venezuela's leader as an unreliable, loud-mouthed quasi-rogue. Bushies were none too happy that upon taking power in 1999, he jaunted off to see Cuba's Fidel Castro and Libya's Moammar Qaddafi, and that he's criticized American hegemony in Latin America as well as the U.S.-funded Plan Colombia, which is trying to wipe out both Colombia's coca fields and radical groups. Chávez also blasted the civilian deaths caused by the U.S. invasion of Afghanistan in 2001. Holding up pictures of bloody corpses of Afghan children for the TV camera, he bellowed, "These children were alive yesterday. They were eating dinner with their parents when a bomb fell on them." The United States yanked its ambassador the next day. After Chávez launched a four-hour radio apology, the administration reluctantly sent the ambassador back.

Never mind that the United States buys some 60 percent of Venezuela's exports; when Chávez was ousted from power in a coup in 2002, the Bush administration not only applauded the highly undemocratic move, it even "appointed" a fill-in. Chávez came back after two days, and he's been on a tirade ever since: He's met with Chinese oil companies and signed contracts to allow China to develop oil fields and import Venezuelan oil; he wooed India as a prospective customer; he's selling discount oil to Cuba.

> Recently, Chávez has threatened to sell off Citgo—Venezuelan-owned refineries that are subsidiaries of PDVSA in the United States—a move that signals he'd be happy to shut off his country's oil supplies to the United States.

Chávez has successfully weathered a few other hailstorms: In 2003, he infuriated PDVSA's workers by appointing a political pal to lead the state-owned company. All eighteen thousand workers walked out in protest, not returning for two months. Chávez fired them, but production hasn't reached prestrike levels.

Chávez was screwing around for his first few years in power, talking big and delivering little. After winning a confidence vote, he rewarded the country by coming through on some of his promises. Critics say he is using PDVSA to play Santa Claus, but that he should be allocating more money for new oil development.

Nevertheless, high oil prices have made for a banner year—and Chávez is finally pumping the profits into Venezuelan society: PDVSA's billions have funded new clinics, literacy programs, housing developments, railroads, and a discounted government-subsidized grocery store. The oil wealth has built up new telecommunication systems and TV stations—and funded a new state-owned airline.

The Bush administration isn't thrilled at his latest plan: Chávez is trying to organize an OPEC-like cartel for oil-holding Latin American countries. And if Chávez has his way, the as-yet-unformed cartel would halt all sales to the United States.

Despite his desire to embrace new customers in Asia, Chávez faces logistical problems. Namely:

- Venezuela doesn't have any "very large crude carriers" to ship to Asia.
- The country lacks a Pacific port, and large tankers can't make it through the Panama Canal to the Pacific. At the least, Venezuela needs more pipelines to the Pacific.
- Due to the extremely viscous and sulfuric nature of Venezuela's Tia Juana, many refineries are unable to refine it.

Despite the risks in doing so, Chávez may indeed "eighty-six" the United States, at least while Bush or his colleagues are in power. A heave-ho from Venezuela would be unfortunate, given that some analysts believe that the country might be sitting on a treasure trove of the black gold in its unprospected northeast. In any case, the U.S. Senate is looking into what will happen if Venezuela drops the United States as a customer—or vice versa.

Behind the Scenes

Even though Russia and Mexico aren't members of OPEC, they often show up at the meetings, and Mexico's oil price is averaged into the OPEC basket. So even though they act like they're not subject to OPEC quotas, the two may be being dealt in on the side, at least to some extent. But while those two countries may act as unofficial members, official member Iraq has not been playing by OPEC's rules and quotas for years; the United States will probably try to push the Iraqi government to drop the club in the future. In fact, that's one theory of why the United States invaded—so that private oil companies could buy up the place and dismiss OPEC from the picture entirely.

32. NON-OPEC OIL PRODUCERS:

The Outsiders

Oil suppliers: Canada, Mexico, Russia, Norway

Notable Numbers

- Canada: 178 billion barrels proven reserves (if you count tar sands, that is)
- Russia: 60 billion barrels proven reserves (and organized crime tied up in it)
- Mexico: 15 billion barrels, maybe, proven reserves (Pemex keeps juggling its numbers)
- Norway: 10 billion barrels proven reserves (and squirreling away the profits for future generations)

Snapshot

OPEC isn't the only petroleum show on the planet. Several major oil producers refuse to ante up and join the cartel's poker game: Russia, Canada, Mexico, and Norway are all among the free agents that independently pump up and sell oil from their lands. OPEC doesn't much like it, but the United States sure does: Canada and Mexico are respectively its number one and number three oil suppliers, and Russia and Norway kick in some, too.

GOOD TO THE LAST DROP

The United States imports some 58 percent of its oil, but its single main source of petroleum is still itself—from the Gulf of Mexico, Alaska's North Slope, Texas, California, Montana, and Oklahoma. Across the country, some 500,000 wells are pumping away, although the majority of the fields have gone dry. These tiny operations squeeze out no more than a few barrels a day—each well merely a drop in the bucket toward meeting the country's 20.5-million-barrel-a-day habit, but together there's enough to meet almost half of the U.S. daily oil demand.

Close-up

The non-OPEC countries usually have warmer relations with the United States, but they also tend to be the ones whose oil is far more difficult to get out of the ground. Captured in sticky "tar sands" or located offshore, this oil often costs more to produce. Lately, however, availability counts more than ease of access, and demand for these countries' oil is skyrocketing, as everybody jockeys into position to ensure they continue to have a piece of the oil pie.

Canada

Canada's population is 33 million, and its per capita income is $30,000.

- It is the eighth biggest oil producer and seventh largest energy consumer in the world.
- Canada sells 1.6 million barrels a day to the United States (90 percent of its oil exports).
- It supplies the United States with more oil than any other outside source.
- It is believed to hold the biggest global oil deposits—but much of it is in tar sands.

It's the United States' number one trading partner, providing resources from lumber to hydropower-generated electricity in trades that see $460 billion swinging back and forth across the border each year. And Canada, that fair land to the north that has kindly gone along with just about everything the United States has ever asked it to do (until the 2003 Iraq War and National Missile Defense came along, that is) may be in a position to start dictating a few of the rules in its historically one-sided relationship with the United States. The Canadian province of Alberta is now believed to hold more petroleum resources than anywhere in the world. Unfortunately it comes in the form of tar sand. And if oil is always a messy business, it's far messier when the petroleum is actually a sticky coat on sediment grains.

To get oil from tar sands, the top layer may be ripped off the top of the earth—leaving hideous deep pits. The sands are then essentially "washed" with hot water to dissolve the petroleum off the sand. If the oil sand deposit is deep, however, steam is injected into the earth, which causes the petroleum to break off and gush up. It's not a pretty business in either case, but it's made Alberta the richest Canadian province—and likely to grow far richer. Since oil from tar sands is much more viscous than other oil, it has kicked off new refinery business in Chicago where the gunk is now piped to, using some of Canada's nine thousand miles of pipeline. With the new appreciation of Alberta's once scoffed-at petroleum offering, thousands more miles of pipeline are being put in to send it west to the coast.

> *Sand to oil: Two tons of tar sands yield a mere forty-two gallons of oil (one barrelful).*

If Canada weren't selling oil to the United States, and letting U.S. companies rip up their lands to get it, the States would be even more dependent on Middle Eastern oil, but U.S. residents remain woefully ignorant of how important their northern neighbor is. In fact, many don't even know it's a neighbor.

- In one recent survey, nearly one-third of Americans thought Canada was part of the United States.[1]
- Another poll showed that 60 percent of Canadians regard the United States as Canada's best friend, but a mere 18 percent of Americans consider Canada their country's best pal.[2]

O, CANADA

Canada is the land o' plenty: It's got water, forests, hydropower, oil, and natural gas, and suddenly, Canada, our underrated neighbor with its vast Athabasca oil deposits, exerts huge control over our future energy supplies. Of course, there's no reason to think that the warmongering United States would invade Canada, although it has happened before—in the War of 1812, which, interestingly, both sides claim to have won.[3] It's not inconceivable, however, that the United States might try to buy Canada. Canadians say that politician Michael Dukakis once joked that given his druthers he would purchase the whole country—paying $1 million for every man, woman, and child. Not a bad deal:

There are only 33 million residents, the place is overflowing with natural riches (including water, which the United States now craves), and he was talking $1 million *Canadian*. Rates for (hypothethically) purchasing Canada, however, could be going up: Relations are certainly testier since the Bush administration took over to the south. Prime Minister Paul Martin, despite heavy pressure from the U.S. camp, nixed the idea of signing up for President Bush's missile defense club—throwing a logistical wrench into the "surround North America" plan—and Canada has adamantly pushed a UN treaty to prevent weaponization of outer space, which the United States is happy to ignore. Canada is still peeved that the United States won't sign its anti–land mine treaty, which nearly every other country in the world has signed. And recently, Canada's former foreign minister wrote a letter to Condoleezza Rice that aptly captured the Canadian growing impatience with its bossy neighbor.

"Dear Condi,

"I'm glad you've decided to get over your fit of pique and venture north to visit your closest neighbor. . . . I know it seems improbable to your divinely guided master in the White House that mere mortals might disagree with participating in a missile-defense system that has failed in its last three tests, even though the tests themselves were carefully rigged to show results. But, gosh, we folks above the 49th parallel are somewhat cautious types who can't quite see laying down billions of dollars in a three-dud poker game. . . ."

—Former foreign minister Lloyd Axworthy, current president of University of Winnipeg, in a letter to Condoleezza Rice published in the *Winnipeg Free Press,* March 4, 2005

Russia—Lukoil, Gazprom, Rosneft, and Yukos: Monopoly Gone Awry

Russia's population is 144 million and its per capita income is $9,000.

- It is the second largest oil producer and supplier in the world.
- It has the eighth largest proven oil reserves in the world.
- It has the world's largest reserves of natural gas.
- The world's oil companies are running to tap resource-rich Sakhalin Island.
- Pipelines are being built every which way.
- Caspian Sea resources look promising for the future.

Russians—slapped by their howling winter winds since the beginning of time, stomped down by centuries of tsars, steamrolled by decades of Soviet

Communism, and now largely controlled by their chilling mafia—have a truly twisted sense of drama. And currently that's being played out in the energy field, into which it appears the Russian mob has stuck its grimy hands, and the Russian government may (or may not) be trying to yank them out.

> "Today Russia is on the threshold of a new era. I am convinced that we will become the witnesses of a great renaissance in Russian society."
>
> —FORBES EDITOR PAUL KLEBNIKOV, WRITING IN THE FIRST ISSUE OF THE RUSSIAN FORBES IN APRIL 2004. THEY WERE AMONG THE LAST WORDS HE WROTE: KLEBNIKOV WAS GUNNED DOWN THREE MONTHS LATER IN A MOSCOW SUBURB AFTER PUBLISHING A LIST OF THE ONE HUNDRED RICHEST PEOPLE IN RUSSIA, MANY OF WHOM ARE PART OF RUSSIA'S OIL AND GAS BUSINESS. MANY BELIEVE IT WASN'T A COINCIDENCE.

Russia used to be the leading oil producer in the world—selling more than Saudi Arabia—but when the Soviet Union fell apart in 1991, the state companies that controlled its resources were sold off to a cadre of politically connected young men dubbed the Oligarchs. Lukoil and Yukos became Russia's leading oil companies after they were bought up in auctions that some speculate were rigged. While Lukoil is at the moment still going strong—and trying to figure out what is going on with its investments in Iraq—Yukos stumbled in 2003, when President Putin ordered the arrest of its billionaire CEO Mikhail Khodorkovsky for tax evasion and fraud, though some say his arrest had more to do with Khodorkovsky's reversal of support for the president. Whatever the reason, Khordorkovsky landed nine years in prison, many Yukos executives have fled the country, the company's head of security has been convicted of contracting two murders, and Yukos recently sold 78 percent of its oil production arm to a consortium controlled by Russia's natural gas giant Gazprom, which is now partially government owned.

> In 2003, fears about the possible collapse of Yukos, which supplies about 2 percent of the oil on the world market, briefly shot oil prices up.

Whether it's to turn Russia back into a totalitarian state or to blast off underworld grime, lately Putin is trying to grab back many of the resource companies, sold off and privatized a decade ago, and put them back on a government leash. In the meantime, both the country's state-owned and private companies are cranking out oil and finding even more.

> Recent news that Sakharin Island in Russia's far east holds at least 15 billion barrels and five oil fields has brought an onslaught of foreigners to the former penal colony. Italian and Japanese companies are joining Exxon, BP, and nearly everyone else in sinking drills.

Lukoil, Russia's largest oil company, is snatching up gas stations all over Eastern Europe, including in Hungary, Poland, and Ukraine. In 2001, it bought thousands of gas stations in the northeastern United States from Getty Petroleum. (Around the same time, U.S. investigators began reporting that the Russian mafia in the United States had a complicated new scam involving selling oil to gas stations without being taxed. Predictably, the Italian mafia demanded a cut of the deal.)

> For every barrel that comes out of Russia—and plenty make their way to the United States—you can bet that somewhere along the way, whether it's in the "protection" that must be paid, an illegal transit fee, or bribery required to get anything done, it's somehow benefiting the Russian mob.

When people talk about Moscow becoming the new Riyadh, they miss one thing. Although it is currently pumping away madly, Russia doesn't have all that much oil—and much of what it does have is inconveniently located in the permafrost of Siberia. But what Russia is rolling in is natural gas, holding more than a third of the world's proven reserves. No country on the planet—not even gas-rich Iran or Qatar—has more. And almost all of that resource is controlled by state-run Gazprom, which recently ended up acquiring a vast part of Yukos Oil. The company is already talking about starting its own OPEC—this one for countries rich in natural gas.

Mexico—Petróleos Mexicanos (Pemex): The Screwballs

Mexico's population is 105 million, and its per capita income is $9,000.

- It is the fifth biggest oil producer in the world.[4]
- It is the third biggest oil supplier to the United States.
- It also supplies lots of cocaine and heroin.

- Mexico won't let foreign oil companies tap its oil deposits.
- It does let them play around with natural gas.
- Pemex loses over a billion dollars each year to corruption, secret fuel sales to drug dealers, and checks to "employees" who don't actually work there.[5]

It would be one thing if Mexico's state-owned oil monopoly, Petróleos Mexicanos—Pemex—was merely an outdated, inefficient giant that wastes oceans' worth of pesos a year. But it's more than just that: Pemex is downright dangerous. Its plants explode—catastrophes in Mexico City (1984) and Guadalajara (1992) injured thousands and killed over eight hundred. Its pipelines frequently blow, most recently in December 2004, when fifteen thousand gallons spilled into the Coatzacoalcos River, suffocating the fish; the year before, a natural gas line blasted open, causing a fiery explosion that killed eight and left hundreds injured, blinded, and disfigured.

> Between 2001 and 2004, Pemex operations experienced over 1,400 spills, explosions, leaks, and other "environmental emergencies."[6] Mexicans complain that Pemex always promises compensation but rarely delivers.

The company was nationalized in 1938—when American and British companies were thrown out and their properties seized—and is heavily taxed, with about 60 percent of its $50 billion or so in annual income going to support the needy government, kicking in over a third of the treasury. It's those taxes, some say, that prevent Pemex from making expensive but much-needed improvements to its pipelines, and from sinking billions into further exploration. Others say corruption weakens the system as badly as its corroded pipes. They point to Pemex's numerous shady dealings—thousands pick up paychecks without actually working and jet fuel has a way of secretly making it into the hands of drug runners who fly cocaine and heroin into the United States. Whatever the cause, Pemex had best get on it, and *muy rapido*: Unless new oil deposits are found quickly, the Mexico supply could dry up as early as 2016.[7]

Norway—Statoil: Fishing for Energy

Norway's population is 4.6 million, and its per capita income is $38,000.

- It is the world's seventh largest oil producer and third largest oil exporter (behind Saudi Arabia and Russia).
- It sells almost all of its oil to Europe.
- Its oil resources may only last a few more decades; its natural gas should stretch longer.
- Norway itself eschews major reliance on petroleum.

It must be hard to be Norwegian and not look at your Scandinavian neighbors and secretly think, "Ha, ha, ha." Because had Norwegian oil been found much earlier, the substantial money it is yielding might be going into Denmark's or Sweden's piggy bank, since for the longest time Norway was chained to one or the other. Independent only since 1905, Norwegians discovered some sixty years later that the source of their fishing and shipbuilding economy held more riches than previously imagined. The North Sea also holds vast reserves of oil. The petroleum wealth that so transformed the place—overnight making it one of the world's richest countries—hasn't been wrecklessly squandered, although this is a Scandinavian "welfare state" country where residents are kept pretty cozy. But in the land where, even into the twentieth century, Norwegian fishers were often so poor that some wore only woolen socks in the snow, there's still a sense of disbelief that such wealth is rolling in, and a fear that one day it might all vanish as quickly as it appeared. Most of the billions from oil revenues are squirreled away for future generations in an offshore Government Petroleum Fund, currently valued at about $150 billion.

> *Norway—which is wary of using oil for anything more than producing gas for their cars—is now searching out more sources of alternative energy. Among the experiments: harnessing the power of waves.*

Statoil is no longer fully state owned; more and more, Norway is granting licenses to private companies from around the world to tap the North Sea's oil and natural gas fields and to discover more.

MISTAKEN GEOGRAPHY? OR TICKED AT INTELLIGENCE?

In early 2003 al-Qaeda's number two man, Ayman al-Zawahiri, made a shocking announcement: Norway, he warned, would be a target for future al-Qaeda attacks. Norway? What had Norway done? Norwegians (and the rest of the world) wondered. Was it the Oslo Accords when they tried and failed to bring peace between Palestinians and Israelis? Was al-Qaeda upset by Norwegian hunting of whales? Was bin Laden bummed he hadn't been a recipient of the Nobel Peace Prize the country hands out? Many believed al-Zawahiri was actually confusing Norway with Denmark, where the country's reigning anti-immigrant party targets Muslims and says horribly racists things; some wondered if Osama bin Laden's spokesman was referring to military activity in Afghanistan, where Norway had sent troops, or if perhaps Norway was a target because it is a NATO member and was among the very first to support the Iraq War. Perhaps more likely: Al-Qaeda may have been ticked because savvy Norway's intel told on it. Not long before, Norway had alerted international maritime authorities to the existence of two dozen "phantom" ships—hijacked and repainted—that were actually al-Qaeda's fleet.

33. VEOLIA AND SUEZ:

The New Water Barons

Veolia (Formerly Vivendi Environnement)

- Headquarters: Paris
- Revenues: £28.6 billion (approximately $51 billion) (2003)

Suez

- Headquarters: Paris
- Revenues: £11.4 billion (approximately $20 billion) (2004) (water services only)[1]

Notable Numbers

- 460 million: Number of world residents dependent on private water companies in 2003[2]
- 51 million: Number of world residents dependent on private water companies in 1990[3]
- 1.2 billion+: Number of world residents lacking access to clean water (more than 20 percent of the world population)

Snapshot

The French may be most commonly associated with wine, cheese, and snails, but worldwide they are known for water. We're not talking just Evian or Perrier. The two reigning kings in "water privatization"—French firms Veolia and Suez— are now running water utilities in thousands of communities on five continents, including setting up the infrastructure that delivers and disposes of the essential liquid to hundreds of millions of residents. And critics charge that they are bungling their vitally important job.

Two global problems have brought billions in business for the water barons:

- *Over 20 percent of the people in the world don't have access to clean water.*
- *The water infrastructure that currently exists in developed countries is old and falling apart.*

Developing countries aren't the only ones reliant on the French water barons. Veolia and Suez have rather quietly moved into the U.S. market: They are now working with the governments of over two hundred North American cities, from Tampa to Indianapolis. And when these so-called water barons appear, rates often shoot up, and the quality, say detractors, may go down: In Puerto Rico and Atlanta, Georgia, for instance they so botched operations that they were run out of town.

CUT OFF IN ATLANTA

Across the United States, cities are finding that their water pipes are falling apart. Atlanta's water system was a prime example of one in need of a vast overhaul. Pipes were old and leaky—resulting in water waste and the occasional exploding water main. In 1999, city government called for bids from private companies. Suez and Veolia battled for the contract—a particularly important one since it marked the first time a U.S. city opened up bidding to foreign firms. Suez sealed the deal for a twenty-year contract for $420 million. As work began, many Atlantans experienced things they'd never seen before: When they turned on the water, nothing came out—for days at a time. Other times, the emerging liquid was brown or brackish. Notifications of the need to boil water were frequent, although sometimes they came late, and fire hydrants were known to gush for so many days without being fixed that some sidewalks washed away.[4] Suez maintained that it inherited a nightmare and hadn't known the extent of Atlanta's problems. Besieged by complaints, Atlanta's city government canceled the contract after only four years.

Although there are other transnational private water companies (including the third and fourth biggest, Germany's RWE and Britain's Thames Water Company), as well as those who will build new water systems for communities (including Bechtel), the two French companies Veolia and Suez control the majority of the private water business worldwide and thus are the ones that attract the most news. And they also have wracked up some of the loudest complaints, including:

- Puerto Rico canceled its 1995 contract with Vivendi (now known as Veolia), when after seven years, water supplies still didn't reach many residents—who were nonetheless billed for the service; some residents who had water before Vivendi took over suddenly had empty taps for weeks or months at a time.
- In New Orleans, where Veolia worked under the name US Filter, equipment wasn't fixed—and sewage spilled into neighborhoods and spread into the Mississippi in 2001.
- In Manila, Philippines, and Buenos Aires, Argentina, Suez decided the water infrastructure projects they were working on weren't profitable enough: They simply packed up and pulled out, leaving both cities' systems in disarray.

When these companies work their magic in less developed parts of the world the effects are far more dramatic. In theory it's commendable that they have successfully brought water to houses in communities that have never had indoor running water before, but in practice the development all too often goes haywire and the rates the water barons impose are consistently unaffordable for their customers in developing countries.

In an exposé of private water companies, the International Center for Investigative Journalism concluded that their track records are spotty: "They can be ruthless players, who constantly push for higher rate increases, frequently fail to meet their commitments and abandon waterworks if they are not making enough money."

HOW THE WATER BARONS INADVERTENTLY TRIGGERED A FATAL EPIDEMIC

While lovely South Africa certainly has its wealthy areas, many of the land's villages are poor. In the decades since Apartheid, many of them have successfully connected with clean water, and although it poured out of public spigots, at least it was free. Then, as part of an infrastructure upgrade in the late 1990s,

South Africa brought in private companies to connect homes in the villages. Although after the upgrades many homes could proudly boast indoor plumbing and a water meter, many households couldn't afford to turn it on: The connection fee of five dollars and the monthly bills, which sometimes surged to twenty dollars a month, were simply out of their grasp. The companies responded by shutting off the water to the households—and the villagers went back to their public spigots, only to find that those too were shut off. So the people went back to the water source they didn't have to pay for: the nearby rivers and streams. Across South Africa, a cholera epidemic soon raged: 250,000 people fell sick, and nearly three hundred died. As a result, the government spent millions of dollars to truck in clean water—offering it for free.

In South Africa and other communities today, access to water is often controlled by a coin-operated delivery system. You have to slip in the coins before the water comes out.

Close-up

Now serving almost a ninth of the world's people, private water companies are bound to grow even richer as they compete for the global drinking water market, worth over $1 trillion (some estimate the figure is at least three times that).

Some critics have an issue with the fact that private companies are set up to make profits. They think access to water is a basic human right and it should be supplied by public utilities—for no cost.

Water lords are expanding outside of the traditional municipal pipe business. As the world experiences greater shortages of water, it is becoming as valuable as oil (see "Water," page 290). As a result, Veolia and Suez are going into the water exporting business. Suez, for instance, has plans to build a 140-mile pipeline to divert water from the Rhône River to Barcelona and is involved in a business that delivers water in oversized thirty-ton "water bags" to Greece. Veolia is part of a joint venture planning to ship water from Australia.

Water-bearing supertankers are already plying the seas—carrying water from Turkey to Israel, for example.

THE INTERNATIONAL WATER BUSINESS

Scurry as the private companies might to grab a stake in the upcoming water exporting business, there may soon be a global power shift once water importing goes into full effect. Suez and Veolia are nevertheless trying to jockey into position as those countries holding the most water—Brazil, Russia, China, Canada, Scotland, and Norway among them—have the potential to become tomorrow's water cartel. Canadian firms, for example, are already developing water export plans that may require building huge pipelines, diverting rivers, and using Japanese fleets to ship water worldwide. Norwegian firms are looking at ways to melt glaciers.

Behind the Scenes

The World Bank, which loans out the billions needed to restore or expand water infrastructure, is making water privatization a common phenomenon. Having loaned bagloads of money to governments whose plans for water development never materialized—although some corrupt officials may have received nice new houses and fancy vacations with diverted funds from the loans—the World Bank often favors internationally known and experienced companies, such as Veolia and Suez, to get the operations rolling.

While government-run utilities are frequently inefficient and sometimes corrupt, the private companies who are taking the contracts away from government utilities have also been known to be rather shady; as in the oil business, financial lubrication is just part of the water territory. Even in France, which has had privatized water companies for over 150 years, and where Veolia and Suez control 80 percent of the country's privatized water, the companies have been slammed numerous times for overbilling and lavishly bribing the officials who sign on the dotted line. Those practices have expanded as they've set up in foreign lands—from China and the Philippines to Argentina and Brazil.

The mayor of Grenoble, France, Alain Carignon, got slapped in 1994 when the French courts found him guilty of accepting $3 million in bribes (and over 120

> *free plane tickets) from Suez. Sentenced to five years, Carignon served twenty-nine months.*

Unfortunately, developing countries in Africa, Asia, and Latin America are trapped by their need for development funds. These cash-strapped countries can't develop their economies unless they modernize and build new infrastructure—roads, electric utilities, pipes that move drinking water, and pipelines that funnel their oil to ports. Unable to fund such projects from their treasuries, the desperate often turn to institutional aid institutions, such as the World Bank or IMF, which offer financing and technical assistance, serving as a sort of credit card company to countries—and with many of the same slimy tricks up their sleeves.

> *Over $3 billion, or nearly 15 percent, of the World Bank's $20 billion in loans in 2004 went to water projects.[5]*

RED FLAG
International Financing Woes

World Bank and International Monetary Fund

Headquarters: DC
Founded: 1944

Notable Numbers

▶ $20 billion: Amount loaned in 2004 by World Bank to government and businesses[6]
▶ $90 billion: Amount of outstanding loans to IMF in 2005[7]
▶ $2.5 trillion+: Amount developing nations are in debt to international aid organizations[8]
▶ $375 billion: Amount developing nations pay each year in interest, surcharges, and payments to international aid organizations[9]

The World Bank and IMF were created in 1944 with development financing needs in mind. Back then, the issue was rebuilding Europe, smoldering in the ashes of World War II. Now, however, these institutions have a large hand in developing natural resources, including modernizing water systems in impoverished countries. Founded with the idea that these global lending institutions could help countries get back on their feet, they historically were a boon to countries in need. But something changed: Now these international institutions are in bed with a small number of construction and engineering giants—including Veolia, Suez, Halliburton, and Bechtel—whose pockets are filled whenever the World Bank writes out a check. The problem is so massive and so engrained into the international lending system that some, including "economic hit man" and author John Perkins, say it has created a "corporatocracy"—a power conglomerate of construction firms, international banking institutions, and governments that aims to keep the third world in chronic debt.

> "Economic hit men are highly paid professionals who cheat countries around the globe out of trillions of dollars. They funnel money from the World Bank, the U.S. Agency for International Development (USAID) and other foreign 'aid' organizations into the coffers of huge corporations and the pockets of a few wealthy families who control the planet's natural resources. Their tools include fraudulent financial reports, rigged elections, payoffs, extortion, sex and murder."
>
> —JOHN PERKINS, AUTHOR OF *CONFESSIONS OF AN ECONOMIC HIT MAN*[10]

This corporatocracy works by peddling loans for infrastructure to countries that can't necessarily afford them—but firms have been known to bribe leaders along the way to sign them up for the deal. The lenders, such as the World Bank, then typically approve only certain multinational firms to perform the contracted work. The banks also require the countries to devalue their currency and/or take in more foreign goods—moves that make it harder for the country to pay back the debt.

WORLD BANK VS. IMF

Conceived during a meeting of forty-four countries in Bretton Woods, New Hampshire, during the last days of World War II, the World Bank and its sister institution the IMF share several qualities. They are both headquartered in DC, their money comes from taxpayers in 184 member countries, and they are both dominated by the United States, which kicks in the most money and dominates the voting system, being the only country with veto power. However, the two have differing roles in the international financial world. The World Bank—formally called the International Bank for Reconstruction and Developing—gives technical advice and loans funds for specific projects in developing countries, from roads and water wells to building schools or bringing electricity to the countryside from dams. World Bank loans, a small percentage of which are no-interest, often require repayment between three and seven years, and the World Bank has a major say in approving which companies get the contracts for the project. The International Monetary Fund was created to stabilize the global exchange of money: It keeps tabs on what countries owe to other countries and also oversees currency exchange rates. However, the IMF has two other important roles: It makes short-term loans to countries to pay off outstanding international debt, and it also advises countries on how to handle their money, mandating such programs as bank restructuring, devaluing currencies, opening trade, and putting the country on a tight budget. The president of the World Bank, currently neocon Paul Wolfowitz, is almost always a U.S. citizen; the head of the IMF is almost always a European.

In 2001, the IMF set the stage for disaster in Malawi. To pay off debt, the agency demanded that Malawi sell off most of its emergency reserves of maize. The following year, drought ravaged the country, and thousands that would have been fed had the reserves been kept stock, died from starvation.

Among the controversial practices that make these institutions much maligned by the antiglobalization movement is that the World Bank and IMF attach certain "conditions" to their loans. They often require countries to privatize their government-owned facilities or to at least hire private firms to overhaul the systems—moves that open the door for firms such as Bechtel or Veolia to come in. And privatizing doesn't always mean high-quality results: A private company, especially from another country, is not responsible to the consumer the way a government is; if plans go awry, a private company can simply bolt regardless of the stage of the project. Another problem: The loans often come with demands for "cost recovery"—which means that that country's citizens entirely pick up the tab, without the government subsidization that typically accompanies such things as drinking water in industrialized countries.

According to the Center for Public Integrity, 80 percent of World Bank loans in 2002 came with privatization conditions, requiring full or partial privatizing of state-held programs such as a country's waterworks in order to qualify for the loan.[11]

The result of cost recovery programs, says watchdog Public Citizen, is that locals in Peru may pay six times more for their water than residents of the United States; in parts of India, the poor may be forced to fork over a quarter of their monthly paycheck for such needs as drinking water.

Whether the project succeeds or not—Public Policy in Focus says that over half of the projects the World Bank funds don't come to complete fruition[12]—the country has to pay the debt, sometimes in the billions of dollars even though they aren't making any money from the project. Like a person who is laid off but still is stuck with a crushing credit card debt, a downward spiral soon emerges: More and more of the treasury goes to paying the loan, and the country is forced to borrow more to pay the original debt, often paying interest on both loans, and zapping the national budget simply to pay the minimum payment. Also helping to ensure that countries grow ever broker: "Economic hit men" are hired by consulting companies and engineering firms to draw up reports that look good on paper, while actually being designed with the hopes that they fail. Those who default on their international loans may owe more than money: They may be pressured to cough up oil, turn over land for U.S. military bases, and/or give paybacks in the form of UN votes, in return for the financial reports needed to get more loans.[13]

Detractors are demanding that Bretton Woods institutions drop debt repayment for those countries unable to pay, and eat part of the debt for projects that the World Bank approved, when it was obvious they would fail. Many see these powerful institutions, which distribute billions a year without oversight from outside agencies, as corroded and in need of a major renovation. And few regard the new, Bush-appointed World Bank president, Paul Wolfowitz—known for his bungling and botching of major operations such as Iraq—as the Mr. Fix-It Man needed for the job.

Agent of Change
John Perkins

"People ask me all the time why are people in Bolivia and Peru throwing stones at U.S. embassies after all we do to help them out. The truth is our embassies are not there to help the people: they are there to help our big corporations and commercial interests."

—John Perkins

Murder, seduction, bribes, planes carrying presidents that crash in fiery balls: John Perkins's best-selling book, *Confessions of an Economic Hit Man* reads like a spy thriller. Its not: The nonfiction works give an insider's view into the international wheeling and dealing that is designed to keep first world countries on top and third world countries down. "Most Americans believe foreign aid is altruistic and serving the ends of democracy and liberty around the world. In fact, that isn't true." Working for a financial consulting firm, Perkins traveled to palm-fringed coasts with lapis waters and countries thick with jungle; he hobnobbed with heads of government and CEOs of Fortune 500 companies. And he made millions writing up financial reports that helped countries secure billions of dollars in loans from the World Bank for hydroelectric dams and pipelines. One problem: His work was making him sick. Although well respected in the international community, Perkins was actually a corporate con artist, or an economic hit man, as he calls his former job. He says that his clients and assorted governments hoped that the ambitious projects didn't work out and that the loans given to the countries kept them indebted. "It was like walking into a ghetto," he

Ex-economic hit man
John Perkins

says, "and handing out credit cards with a $50,000 limit, knowing that people couldn't repay it." The reasons for extending the loans were twofold: First, in order to receive the huge loans, the countries often were forced to contract with a corporation on the World Bank's short list—the Halliburtons, the Bechtels, the Veolias—so those corporations immediately cashed in from the loans. Second, if the country was strapped by unmanageable debt—worsened if the project that was supposed to generate income didn't work out—then they would not only have to spend most of the government treasury paying back the loan, but they would owe favors, which they might be asked to pay back with natural resources, by hosting training camps for rebels, or by swinging votes. The World Bank and the United States in particular, he says, set up the loans so the countries would open up their jungles to our oil companies, vote with us, send troops where we tell them to, and become part of our empire.

British Prime Minister Tony Blair, adding his voice to a growing movement, is currently lobbying the United States and the World Bank to forgive third world debt.

Disgusted by what he saw going on, Perkins is now loudly blowing the whistle on what he says is an international aid scam that funnels trillions of dollars into the pockets of the corporatocracy that runs the World Bank and other world lending institutions. "Most Americans don't know how corrupt the international aid system is," he says, and they don't know how much it is controlled by the United States, which donates the most and has veto power. "It's not a World Bank. It's an American bank." Now Perkins is working with the indigenous groups whose cultures his previous actions helped destroy—by bringing in the projects that pushed them off their land. He believes that when Americans understand what is going on—how the United States and a few other countries and institutions are exploiting poor countries' resources and actively trying to keep them impoverished and weak—they will make enough noise to make the system change. "Americans don't see how we are conducting ourselves in the world and what the consequences of our actions are." He says we don't see how American commercial interests are often working against the democracy that we believe the United States is trying to establish. "We think nothing of overthrowing governments if they won't support our commercial interests, or supporting despots if they do." And he thinks we can in fact change the system, and points to other great leaps initiated by individuals who worked together. "Women's right to vote grew out of a small group of individuals," he notes. "Nobody gave a damn about the environment and DDT until Rachel Carson wrote *Silent Spring*. Look at the Soviet Union—the CIA and our military spent billions trying to bring it down, but it crumbled from inside: A few union leaders and poets and playwrights began demanding rights and brought it down. Change always starts with the individual." As for Perkins, himself the catalyst for what could be a vast shake-up, he says he's not afraid of the repercussions of speaking out about the secret "corporatocracy." He says, "It's not in their interests to kill me. If I die a strange death, I'll sell millions of books."

PART VIII

ROGUES

34. NORTH KOREA:

Nuclear Rogue

Capital: Pyongyang
Leader: Kim Jong Il
Population: 22.9 million

Notable Numbers

- $5.2 billion: Amount North Korea spent on military (2002)[1]
- $30 billion: Estimated GDP (2004)[2]

Snapshot

It's understandable why countries around the world crave the idea of owning their very own nuclear weapons. Simply put, you ain't getting dealt into the card game unless you have some chips. The five most powerful countries in the United Nations—namely, the United States, China, Russia, Britain, and France, all of whom sit on the Security Council—aren't there on looks alone: They are the most badass countries on the planet (they like to think) because they anted up and joined the nuclear club. And in doing so, all were rogues at one time or another.

NUCLEAR POWERS

Country	First nuclear test	Number of nuclear weapons (as of 2004)
USA	1945	10,240
Russia	1949	8,400

Britain	1952	300
France	1960	350–450
China	1964	390
Israel (not declared)	Not tested	200+
India	1974	60–90
Pakistan	1998	30–50
North Korea	Not tested?	0–18
Ukraine	Not applicable	0–200 (may have some of Russia's nukes)

A few countries that quit the nasty nuclear habit:

- South Africa
- Argentina
- Iraq

Nuclear arms, deemed necessary and legitimate for mature, responsible countries such as the United States or Britain, become "weapons of mass destruction," however, in the hands of "rogue states"—those countries that the United States believes support terrorism.

Lately, it's not only what a country possesses in its arsenal that poses a threat. Dangerous weapons that the United States simply imagines a country is hiding away can have serious repercussions as well. (See "Team B.S.," page 69.) Prone to hyperbole, UN ambassador John Bolton has previously charged that Cuba and Syria are holding biological and chemical weapons of mass destruction. Suddenly all eyes were peering at those two countries, and one could nearly hear war drums beating faintly in the background. U.S. intelligence agencies, however, yanked the power on that drum machine, immediately making very clear that they possess no information that would support Bolton's claims.

Happily, the list of nuclear rogues *is* shrinking: Not so many months ago Iraq and Libya both held spots on the danger roster. Whether those charges reflected political motives, hype, or faulty intelligence, both Iraq and Libya have been deleted from the list; Iraq apparently hasn't had any WMD since UN inspectors carted off the last in 1994, and Libya claims that it has dropped the idea for a nuclear program. Although it certainly snagged headlines in 1998 when it tested several nuclear weapons, even Pakistan isn't really considered a nuclear rogue since it enlisted in the U.S.-led war on terror. Ditto for neighbor India.

Iran, while not believed to be holding nuclear weapons at the moment, appears to be embarking on a program to develop them. The United States is threatening to go to the UN Security Council to push a plan for how to stop Iran's "enrichment program"—which could yield nuclear bombs. As of May 2005, the noise on the matter had escalated to the point that it was being called a "crisis"—albeit perhaps one brewed up mostly by the powers that be and the media.

The real headache lately is North Korea, the Communist dictatorship so closed off from the world and divorced from reality that it is called "the Hermit Kingdom." And just as disturbing as the fact that the country is led by a man who is crazy is the maddening response from the Bush team, which ignored the problem until it was a shrill nuclear alarm. While there is little doubt that North Korea's dictator—Dear Leader Kim Jong Il—is a certifiable loon, the Bush administration's bungled, oops-changed-our-minds-again posture toward North Korea has itself been schizophrenic. In 2003, while the United States was bellowing its intent to invade Iraq to destroy that country's (nonexistent) weapons of mass destruction, Kim was all but doing cartwheels to announce that North Korea had nuclear weapons ready to go and was developing more. The official U.S. response seemed to alternate between "Yeah, whatever" and "We'll change your regime next, after we're done rearranging Iraq." Perhaps Kim is not being paranoid: Sometimes it certainly appears the Vulcans are out to get him. And by pushing his buttons, which the United States does oh so well, it only increases the chances of him pushing a button himself.

Kim Jong Il occasionally misunderstands what the United States is saying. Among the occasions when Kim believed that the Americans were declaring war:

- January 2002: When George Bush included North Korea as part of his "Axis of Evil"
- Every summer: When U.S. and South Korean military taunt North Korea with "war games"
- April 2005: When President Bush called Kim Jong Il "a tyrant"
- May 2005: When National Security Advisor Stephen Hadley warned that if North Korea tested its nuclear weapons the United States would take "action"
- Possibly every February: When the United States typically doesn't send a card for Kim's birthday, which is a major to-do in Pyongyang

---

Close-up

President George W. Bush loathed North Korea's Kim Jong Il from the start, and he made no effort to disguise it. There are ample reasons for many to dislike the

Korean leader, who took over when his father died in 1994. Kim Jong II is believed to have:

- Used donated food mostly to feed his soldiers, while North Korean civilians ate grass: Over 2 million civilians have died in the decade of Dear
  Leader's rule.
- Set up concentration camps, where those who are caught trying to flee to
  the relative freedom of China are sent for reprogramming
- Been the force behind a 1983 bombing that killed 17 South Korean ministers, and the downing of a South Korean plane in 1987 that killed all 115
  on board
- Launched a multistage missile in 1998 that made some believe that in the
  future North Korea might be capable of hitting the United States (a dubious assumption, but one that helped sell the National Missile Defense
  program in the United States)
- Kidnapped hundreds of South Koreans and Japanese—sometimes sending submarines to grab them from the beach (wanting to make a movie in
  the 1980s, he snatched his favorite South Korean actress and director and
  held them for years)

THE HERMIT KINGDOM: BACKGROUND

Japan moved into Korea in 1911 and wouldn't budge until after World War II.
When the Japanese vacated, the United States was to oversee the transition in
the south, and Russia would supervise from the north. The Russians installed a
Communist leader, Kim II Sung, who tried to militarily convince the south to join
the Communist cause. The result was the Korean War (1950–53), which the
United States and allies got involved in hoping to keep communism out. Instead,
the war, which killed 3 million, resulted in a deeply divided country—North and
South—cleaved by a 150-mile-long demilitarized zone, with half a million soldiers guarding either side.

North Korea was already eccentric and economically dysfunctional when
it was headed by Supreme Leader Kim II Sung, but things got even stranger
when Supreme Leader's son, wacky Kim Jong II—possibly brain-damaged and
alcoholic—took a turn at driving the car. Even though most of the country's
money already went to maintaining the stiffly marching armed forces and their
weapons, for Kim Jong II that wasn't enough. He wanted a nuclear program, and
that was launched during his father's reign.

North Korea has the third biggest military on the planet.

In 1994, months before Kim Il Sung died and his son assumed command, the country's graphite nuclear plant (which produces more weapons-ready pluto- nium than a typical light water nuclear reactor) became a source of alarm when North Korea removed thousands of nuclear fuel rods from it, ostensibly to make nuclear weapons. As a result, an international showdown began brewing be- tween North Korea and the Clinton administration, averted when former presi- dent Jimmy Carter swooped in and negotiated an agreement with Kim Il Sung in 1994. This agreement—in which interested parties would give North Korea en- ergy plants and supplies if the country dropped its nuclear weapons plans—was known as the Agreed Framework.

AGREEING ON THE FRAMEWORK

As part of the 1994 Agreed Framework, the United States, Japan, and South Korea agreed to:

- Supply fuel oil to North Korea
- Build two light water nuclear reactors in North Korea
- Lift any economic sanctions

In return, North Korea agreed to:

- Drop its nuclear weapon program
- Close its graphite nuclear plant
- Lock up its eight thousand fuel rods, so they would not be transformed into plutonium

With the Agreed Framework, the problem appeared to be at least temporarily solved. But in 2000, at the twilight of the Clinton administration, the nuclear reac- tors were slow in showing up, and North Korea was already starting to complain. Then the Bush administration turned an uneasy situation into a global migraine.

Coincidentally, Donald Rumsfeld was sitting on the board of Swiss engineering firm ABB in 2000, which had previously snagged a $200 million contract to oversee the building of North Korea's two nuclear plants.[3]

Beyond simply fearing for his survival, Kim rules a country that is dirt poor, lacking energy resources, and economically unsound—and has no friends, although China maintains a lukewarm relationship. The little money that comes in from trade (often of illegal arms and drugs) goes to maintaining the military and Kim's bon vivant lifestyle. Dependent on the fuel promised by the Agreed Framework to supply much of North Korea's electricity, Kim was already in a tight spot when the Bush administration came to power in 2001, almost immediately saying that it had second thoughts about the Agreed Framework.

If reports that Bush had belittled him for being short didn't make Kim Jong Il happy, the news that the Bush administration was waffling on the Agreed Framework—possibly Kim's only chance to keep his country from collapse—made him furious. The Bush administration said it wasn't sure about building nuclear reactors after all—then, General Electric, which had been contracted to construct them, pulled out. Not only were the plans for the plants suddenly on hold, but promised fuel oil was showing up late, when it showed up at all, claimed North Korea. By June 2001, North Korea was making noises about new missile tests and hinting that perhaps it would break its moratorium on the old nuclear plant. The United States mumbled something about sticking with the original agreement, while rumors circulated that the Defense Department's Donald Rumsfeld and Paul Wolfowitz were pushing the idea of pushing Kim Jong Il out the door. And then in 2002, President Bush included North Korea on his "Axis of Evil."

Kim Jong Il, at best not the most stable of personalities, rightly detected a note of hostility, and really started banging on the table about the United States coming through with its promises and demanding that the country sign a nonaggression pact, saying it would not invade North Korea. No deal, said the Bush administration, which was busy selling an invasion of Iraq. By the late fall of 2002, Kim openly admitted that North Korea was restarting its nuclear program, from the production of electricity to the manufacture of weapons. Kim reiterated that North Korea would drop the program if the United States signed an agreement not to invade and supplied the promised oil and plants. Again, the administration shrugged off the demands. Shortly thereafter, North Korea ripped up all previous deals: Kim kicked out the UN inspectors who'd been ensuring the eight thousand fuel rods stayed locked up and he reopened the shut-down graphite plant. In April 2003, Kim loudly announced that North Korea too had nuclear weapons.

> North Korea hasn't tested any weapons, but analysts suggest that it might already have up to eighteen nuclear weapons, with the plutonium available to make more.

In 2003, the Bush administration appeared to finally notice the noise coming from Pyongyang. The Americans pressured China and South Korea to get North Korea to the negotiating table. North Korea wanted to meet alone with the United States, but that apparently wasn't an option: The United States pushed for talks where it would appear along with China, Japan, and South Korea. Even though the goal was to defuse the escalating situation, the Bush administration laughably sent its resident hard-ass, John Bolton, as representative to the talks. Predictably, Bolton only stirred up North Korea's anxieties: Hours before a meeting in 2003, Bolton trashed Kim Jong Il during a speech in South Korea, replanting the idea that the United States might invade and that the bottom line was regime change. Predictably, North Korea refused to meet with Bolton. Thanks to Bolton's lack of diplomacy and the Bush administration's schizophrenic behavior, it's been harder than ever to get North Korea back to the table—although Secretary of State Condoleezza Rice appears to be thawing the ice, and recently Kim agreed to more talks.

In May 2005, North Korea launched another test missile. It flew a piddly forty-five miles before crashing into the Sea of Japan, making some wonder if North Korea could even strike South Korea, much less Japan or the western United States as the Rumsfeld Commission had postulated in 1998.

Behind the Scenes

Poor Condoleezza Rice has been handed this plate of steaming discontent to deal with as secretary of state. Although the neocons, such as Wolfowitz and Bolton, wanted to knock both the Agreed Framework and the Dear Leader off the table, Rice is backpedaling and trying to get Kim to simmer down. "We have no intention to attack or invade North Korea," Rice now repeats in the direction of Pyongyang as though reciting a chant.

"I'll just restate that the United States, of course, recognizes that North Korea is sovereign. It's obvious . . ."

—CONDOLEEZZA RICE IN MAY 2005 TO JAPANESE PRESS

Despite Secretary Rice's repeated assurances, Kim Jong Il may still feel panicked. For one thing, should he have access to the U.S. Nuclear Posture Review, he might note that his country stands prominently on the list of potential U.S.

nuclear targets. For another, Iraq, one point of the "Axis of Evil," is down, and the second one, Iran, is looking like it may be a future target.

IRAN'S NUCLEAR INTENTIONS

Iran, swimming in oil, has been developing a nuclear energy program since at least the 1990s, with help from Russia and China. Given its petroleum riches, its interest in using nuclear power as an energy source strikes most everybody—and particularly Israel, which would be a likely target of Iranian nuclear bombs if there are any—as a front for manufacturing nuclear weapons. (Then again, maybe Iran is just trying to meet the Kyoto Protocol by using energy sources that don't produce so many greenhouse gases.) Although Iran maintains that it is only interested in the peaceful use of the atom, it insists on developing uranium enrichment facilities—and that's what makes eyebrows raise. While indeed enriched nuclear matter can be used for fuel in nuclear plants, it is also necessary to produce the core of nuclear weapons. The European Union pressured Iran to freeze its enrichment program in late 2004, but as of August 2005, Iran looked poised to start it back up. The Iranian government insists it has a right to pursue not only a nuclear energy program, but a nuclear weapons program as well if it wishes; the Big Boys in Europe and the United States don't much like that idea. Neither does Israel. The country that took it upon itself to destroy Iraq's nuclear facilities in 1981 might do the same with Iran—although Iran has warned that should Israel take out its nuclear plants, Iran will launch a horrific counterattack. Nevertheless, U.S. Vice President Dick Cheney nearly seemed to be calling for Israel to do exactly that in 2005 when he said that "Israel might well decide to act first" and "let the rest of the world worry about cleaning up the diplomatic mess afterwards."

Underlying the current tenseness over Iran is the fact that Israel possesses hundreds of nuclear bombs, and wants to remain the only nuclear power in the Middle East.

35. TERRORISTS:

Aiding the Government?

High-profile examples: al-Qaeda, Hamas, Hezbollah

Notable Number

- $25 million: Osama bin Laden's estimated worth when he launched al-Qaeda

Snapshot

It's not as though young men wake up one morning, look at their face in the mirror, and decide, "Hmmm, perhaps terrorism is my calling!" Couples around the world don't whisper mid-embrace, "Honey, let's create a family of suicide bombers!"

> *Radical groups often find willing recruits in the bored, unemployed, and unmarried youth of their countries.*

Typically what kicks off the actions of terrorist groups are long-harbored grudges that stem back decades, centuries, even millennia. The tales of wars, unfair borders, vicious rapes, and villages destroyed are passed down through the generations along with tales of ancestors who died fighting the cause. Nurtured by political extremists and religious zealots, these unhealed wounds and unaddressed issues are liable to explode whenever a country or group is undergoing "stress"—be it a reaction to a corrupt government, an economic downturn, a war, or all three.

SOURCES OF ANGER

The U.S. State Department posts a list of thirty-seven groups that it considers international terrorists. Including Peru's Shining Path (who want Peru to be communist), Japan's subway terrorists Aum Shinrikyo (religious wackos who attacked with chemical gases), and even Israel's Jewish extremist Kahane Chai (who want Israel to go back to its medieval biblical state), the groups' "issues" and "goals" can be broken down into four broad categories, although their motives may straddle a few.

- Religious extremism: Egypt's Gama'a Islamiyya (held responsible for the 1993 World Trade Center bombings), al-Qaeda, and Lebanon's Hezbollah all have installing a religious Islamic government as their ultimate goal.
- Territorial conflicts: Hamas and Islamic Jihad are a few that want to destroy Israel and create a Palestinian state; the IRA and Real IRA want Britain to give up control of Northern Ireland.
- Separatism: Spain's ETA wants to secede and form a Basque country in northern Spain and southern France; Abu Sayyaf wants several southern Philippine islands to secede.
- Political change: Many of South America's radical groups, including Peru's Shining Path and Colombia's FARC and ELN, were originally inspired by communist ideals.

The underlying issue in some conflicts is actually resource shortage. In the Middle East, one huge problem is scarcity of water—a factor in Israel's annexing of some Palestinian territories, which triggers Palestinian fury. In South and Central America, rich plantation owners shove the peasant out of prime land and into the mountains, fueling a desire for communism.

When the United States simply labels them as "terrorists," it is overlooking one integral part in explaining why these groups attract followers and retain power: They often provide social services that are not available from anyone else, including the government. They essentially step in as a quasi government. In the Palestinian territories, Hamas runs schools, clinics, and ambulance services as well as providing food for the poor. Osama bin Laden wrote out checks for the families of the mujahideen who died in Afghanistan. Colombia's FARC gave coca seeds to secluded peasant farmers, and provided a market for their crops. Lately several Palestinian groups, including Hamas, have been handing over thousands of dollars to the impoverished families whose members have traveled to Israel and died as suicide bombers.

The hard-core Christian Right in the United States wants to take over the social services. And thanks to Bush's Faith-Based Initiative program they are moving in.

Hezbollah may be the most technologically savvy of the bunch. Thanks to Iran, which funds it and gives it new war toys, in 2004 Hezbollah sent a spy drone to hover over Israel, before it crashed into the sea. Israel was outraged, although it was tit for tat: Israel reportedly sends out unmanned aerial snoopers to peek on Lebanon, too.

A FEW TERRORIZING STANDOUTS[1]

- **al-Qaeda** (See page 350.)
- **Hezbollah:** Started in 1982. Estimated members: several hundred.[2] Now such an institution in Lebanon that it has radio stations and newspapers and holds a seat in Parliament, anti-Israel Hezbollah first snagged international headlines in the 1980s for its ghastly deeds against Americans in Lebanon.[3] In 1983, Hezbollah suicide bombers detonated trucks of explosives first at the U.S. embassy in Beirut (killing 63) and then in Marine barracks (killing 241). The group hijacked TWA Flight 847 in 1985 and was probably behind the kidnapping of thirty Americans from 1982 to 1992, including the CIA's William Buckley in 1984. Lately, Hezbollah's favorite activity has been launching rocket attacks on Israel from north of the Israeli border.
- **Al-Jihad** and **Gama'a al Islamiyya:** Started in the 1980s. Members: unknown. Though these Egyptian groups have different methods (for instance, Egypt's Al-Jihad, which assassinated President Anwar Sadat in 1981, specializes in infiltrating the military), they're both ticked off that Egypt kissed off its own culture and embraced the West. Both seek to oust dictator, er, President Hosni Mubarak, both seek to install a religious government, and neither holds the United States in high esteem, thanks to its annual gift of over $2 billion in arms that keeps Mubarak firmly entrenched.
- **Hamas:** Started in 1987. Estimated members: unknown. It hates the PLO and it hated the Palestinian territory's ineffective leader, the late Yasser Arafat, and it especially hates Israel, at whom it has launched militia attacks as well as funded suicide bombers who have killed thousands. Although put together by Egypt's Muslim Brotherhood, which generally pushes for the cre-

ation of Islamic governments, it's unclear whether Hamas actually wants to establish a religious government. What is clear: It wants to create a Palestinian state—including the territory now known as Israel.

Hezbollah's hostage taking in Lebanon during the 1980s led to Reagan's trading of arms for hostage release—the Iran-Contra affair. For the hundreds of millions of dollars sunk into that covert operation, a mere three hostages were freed.

Close-up

Of all the terrorist outfits on the planet, the one most intriguing and frightening to the United States is al-Qaeda, the group behind the 9/11 attacks.

Al-Qaeda

Estimates on the number of al-Qaeda members range from a few hundred core members to some twenty thousand wannabe warriors.

Rarely known for foresight, the U.S. government is partly responsible for creating its current number one enemy. In an attempt to weaken the Soviet Union, the United States launched a plan in the 1980s to use Arab Muslim warriors (mujahideen) to fight in Afghanistan during the Soviet-Afghan War that had started in 1979. (See "Blowback Maximus," page 140.) Thanks to the U.S. efforts, that war proved to be the Soviets' Vietnam, but after the Communists put their tanks into reverse in 1989, the guerrilla mujahideen were still riled up. Typically, their own countries did not want the hellions back, and they wandered off to kick up some more trouble in Kashmir, Chechnya, and wherever else they could find it. In the 1990s, Osama bin Laden gave them a new calling: to fight off the evil United States, supporter of Israel and the force keeping religious governments from being installed in most of their countries.

> More than a decade after the Soviet-Afghan War ended, the United States
> tried to buy back weapons from Afghans and mujahideen to whom it had
> supplied weapons such as the ground-to-air missile launcher. The buyback
> was a dismal failure.

Fronted by Saudi-born Osama bin Laden, with his physician, the Egyptian Ayman al-Zawahiri second in line, al-Qaeda has a habit of changing its stated reasons for attacks, making its motives rather hard to discern. After the devastation of 9/11, al-Qaeda sent out messages to the media that the attacks were a response to:

- U.S. military presence in Saudi Arabia
- U.S. support for Israel
- U.S.-supported economic sanctions on Iraq

Since then, however, Osama bin Laden has added substantially to the list.

In November 2002, apparently Osama bin Laden himself posted a "Letter to America" in which he explained and expanded al-Qaeda's motives. His short answer to the question of "Why are we fighting and opposing you?" is "Because you attacked us and continue to attack us." His short answer to "What are we calling you to and what do we want from you?" is "We are calling you to Islam" and "We call you to stop your oppression, lies, immorality and debauchery."[4]

OSAMA BIN LADEN'S "LETTER TO AMERICA":
THE LONGER VERSION[5]

The letter blames the United States (and the U.S. taxpayers) for:

- The "creation and continuation of Israel"
- The "blood pouring out of Palestine"
- The "Indian oppression in Kashmir"
- The "Russian atrocities in Chechnya"
- Starving children in Iraq
- U.S. attacks in Afghanistan and Somalia (and no doubt, now, Iraq)
- Not respecting "the resolutions and policies of International Law"
- Propping up governments that prevent religious governments
- The treatment of prisoners at Guantánamo Bay
- Ignoring human rights

But the eight-page letter doesn't stop there. It also faults the United States and U.S. taxpayers for:

- Permitting "usury, forbidden by all religions" (e.g., the double-digit interest rates on our credit cards)
- Permitting drugs (this from a man who backed Afghanistan's heroin industry)
- Being immoral (apparently he hadn't noticed that the Christian Right is busy tidying up the country)
- "President Clinton's immoral acts committed in the official Oval Office"
- Exploiting "women like consumer products or advertising tools" (this from a man who supports genital mutilation, full-body covering, and death by stoning to accused female adulterers)
- Unleashing "AIDS as a Satan American Invention" (certainly more of a concern for those who take four wives)

But for all his visibility now, the truth of the matter is that Osama bin Laden certainly didn't appear to be much of a problem back in the 1980s when the United States was helping fund his mujahideen warriors in Afghanistan. He certainly wasn't mouthing off about the United States when he returned to Saudi Arabia as a war hero. What in fact launched the group that would become al-Qaeda appears to be nothing more than Osama bin Laden's pathetically wounded male ego. When Saddam Hussein invaded Kuwait in August 1990, bin Laden wanted to fight the Iraqi with his loyal Muslim warriors who were looking for some more battle action. And the royal Saudi family told him no. Instead they invited in the United States and other foreign armies, non-Muslims whom Osama bin Laden believed defiled the Saudi lands, the home to Islam's most sacred sites, Mecca and Medina.

By 1992, bin Laden was bad-mouthing the royal family so loudly they pushed him out of the country—and he ended up in Sudan. He continued to so vitriolically slam the Saudis that they stripped him of his Saudi citizenship in 1994. He posed such a threat that reportedly the mayor of Riyadh hired someone two years later to poison him; some believe that bin Laden suffers severe kidney problems as a result.

The introduction of Osama bin Laden to Ayman al-Zawahiri, an exiled Egyptian living in Sudan, was when al-Qaeda really took form. Al-Zawahiri's initial beef was that the United States and Britain had westernized Egypt and other Arab/Muslim countries, and were preventing religious governments from forming. Bin Laden's big complaint was that the Saudis had sold out—and allowed the United States to dictate everything from their oil prices to who fought their wars. With bin Laden's millions and al-Zawahiri's brains, the two angry radicals laid the foundation for the group that would launch the most dramatic and terrifying terrorist attack in modern history.

> In 1998, Osama bin Laden issued a fatwa, an edict typically released by a religious leader. In it, he urged all loyal Muslims to attack Americans and Zionists.

While the United States was the initial target, bin Laden hasn't left the Saudi royal family out of his plans. Now al-Qaeda is unleashing its full force in bin Laden's motherland, where suicide bombings have killed hundreds of foreigners and Saudis over the past two years. Al-Qaeda's newest target appears to be Britain, where the group is believed to have set off bombs that killed fifty in July 2005. The reason, claimed al-Qaeda of Europe, was Britain's support for U.S.-led wars.

Behind the Scenes

For obvious reasons, terrorists want us to be afraid. But, perhaps, so do some politicians. After the United States was hit on September 11, the mediocre approval ratings for President Bush soared to all-time highs—with 90 percent of Americans standing behind him in October 2001. Scared lawmakers are easy to manipulate: Congressmen now blame the administration's creation of an environment of fear as the reason they passed the USA Patriot Act. A trembling public is quick to sign off on its freedoms to give the government new powers that would never be granted during more rational times. And a world united against terrorism (theoretically) gave the United States the right to unleash its military wherever terrorists may lurk.

Certainly the dramatic rise in terrorism signaled a need for governments worldwide to get on the ball. Certainly groups from al-Qaeda to Hamas show that there are some individuals who are willing to kill themselves and thousands of others willing to express their unhappiness with the status quo. But the great beneficiaries of the Age of Terrorism aren't the terrorists themselves, but the governments who use the tool of fear to intimidate and control their own people.

Iraqi Insurgents
Rebels Without a (Unified) Cause

Nobody knows exactly how many Iraqi insurgents there are, although some estimates go as high as 200,000—more than the number of U.S. troops in Iraq. Exactly what they want is even more of a mystery, but they don't necessarily want the same thing. One thing is for sure: With car bombs and rocket attacks numbering over sixty a day, the insurgents in Iraq are on a bloody rampage that appears to be getting more vicious with time. Since the U.S. invasion in spring 2003, these hellions have killed over 1,400 American troops and thousands more of Iraqis who worked with them. They've also massacred hundreds of civilians, mostly Kurds and Shi'a—in one attack killing over fifty worshippers praying at a shrine, and sometimes driving Iraqis out of their homes.

> *Insurgents are now targeting doctors. At least 10 percent of the physicians in Baghdad have closed their medicine bags and many have fled.*

Over five dozen factions are believed to make up the insurgents' disorganized ranks, and many of them are foreigners, some may be mercenaries. One of the movement's most vicious leaders is Abu Musab al-Zarqawi, a militant Jordanian, who may be part of al-Qaeda. A former mujahideen in Afghanistan, Zarqawi now has a $25 million bounty on his head, and is held responsible for recent bombings in Casablanca and Istanbul as well as for many of the publicized beheadings, including of Americans Nick Berg and Eugene Armstrong. Zarqawi may have gathered divergent forces under his wings after Fallujah—a stronghold for rebels and a center of the extreme Wahhabi sect—was retaken by U.S. forces in 2004, although the insurgents retook it several months later. Some of these fighters are former Afghan jihadists striking out against the infidel; some are Egyptians in Takwir al Hijra who want an Islamic government; some are Islamist Kurds from the group Ansar al-Islam; others may be organized by Syrian intelligence, or Saddam's former guards, or may be linked to Iran, and most of the suicide bombers are believed to be foreign zealots. But for all their differences, they share one commonality: They want the United States out of Iraq, and they apparently hope that the new government will fail.

Analysts believe that insurgents had hoped to prevent the Iraqi elections in January 2005—but nearly two-thirds of Iraqis showed up to vote even amid missiles and bombs. Those who didn't venture out were often in Sunni-held towns, and their absence heavily tipped the votes, with Shi'a Muslims taking the majority in government—a fact believed to inspire some Sunni insurgents.

> *The U.S. government and media keep raising the volume, insisting that the Iranian government is providing explosives to insurgents in Iraq—and the Iranian government continues to deny it vehemently. Whether Iran is indeed involved or whether the Vulcans are simply spewing more disinformation in a lead-up to a showdown in Iran remains to be seen.*

36. ORGANIZED CRIMINALS:

Modern Misfits

Groups: Russian "mafiya," Japanese Yakuza, Chinese Triads, Italian mafia,
       Italian American mob
Headquarters: Worldwide
Founded: Some go back for centuries, but all found new life in the 1990s

Notable Number

- $1 trillion: Total estimated income of crime groups globally

Snapshot

Nobody adores twenty-first-century life more than the millions now working in organized crime syndicates, who look at the rapid changes taking place and see a vast sea of suckers. As the world becomes one tangled global village where oceans are crossed in mere hours, distant computers communicate in seconds, money can be instantly zapped to far corners of the planet, and borders are easily penetrated, the effect is to welcome crime outfits from all parts of the map—from Hong Kong, Moscow, Tokyo, Albania, and everywhere in between—to set up operation across South America, Europe, Australia, Asia, and, increasingly, Canada and the United States.

Traditionally, criminals who moved abroad kept their business in the family, so to speak: The Russian mob tormented ethnic Russians who'd moved to Brooklyn's Brighton Beach, Chinese gangsters demanded "protection" payments in foreign Chinatowns. The victims were easy targets since they understood the criminals' threats in the native tongue, and the thugs could threaten to rough up family still in the homeland. Now, however, incoming villains, particularly those from Eastern

Europe and Russia, are hitting up the locals as well: Some say the mobs from the Balkans and Russia extort money from over half of Amsterdam's bars and cafés, and in German cities such as Hamburg, the Russians simply moved their business into the legal red light district; after a few murders, it was easy to get the rest of the established businesses to hightail it out. The slavic and Eastern European mafia have set up serious roots in the United States as well, much to the surprise of the established criminals. Recently Albanians simply walked in and shoved the openmouthed Italian mobs out of much of their gambling business, and Russians have moved into Italian American territory with a whole new bag of fraud.

The ne'er-do-wells are running quite a polished racket these days, modernizing operations, upgrading their tools, and expanding their capabilities. Brandishing high-tech equipment and staffed with economists, strategists, and legal experts, they make more money than most countries and rattle everybody from international banks to heads of governments. Groups that once contented themselves with shaking down ma-and-pa corner stores now extort corporations; modern underworld sorts don't merely run brothels, they run a slave trade. These gangsters supply more than handguns, they sell missile launchers and the makings for dirty bombs; they don't just steal cars, they hijack cargo ships and make them part of their "phantom" fleets. The folks that smuggle in contraband cigarettes, cocaine, and China White heroin also deal in human organs; the mobsters who once monopolized trash pickup, charging outrageous fees, now haul toxic waste, which they dump wherever they please. And the outlaws that once robbed banks' safes can now steal far more by hacking directly into banks' computer systems.

THE NATASHA BUSINESS

Every year more than 250,000 girls are plucked from villages across the Ukraine, Russia, Moldova, Latvia, and other Eastern European lands. Lured by newspaper ads or local agencies, the girls believe they are being hired as waitresses, nannies, and housekeepers to work in Florida or Israel, Brussels or Budapest. Their passports taken by the recruiters who transport them out of their towns, these girls, called "Natashas"—many in their teens—soon discover that they are in fact slaves. Their new owners are the Russian mob, who will work them as prostitutes. Sold from owner to owner, they are herded like cattle across the world, some shuttled to Istanbul, Tel Aviv, Cyprus, or Dubai, some to Vienna, Amsterdam, or London, some shipped off to Canada, Florida, or New York. Kept under guard, they are forced to have sex with dozens of men each day, usually without protection (which is why one in three are believed to have AIDS). Natashas often end up drug addicts as well, though not by choice: Their pimps shoot them with heroin or methamphetamine to cultivate habits that make them more docile. Once part of the slave system, few Natashas get out, unless freed during a raid, which only leads to their deportation back to their town, where many are shunned by their families. There is another way to avoid turning tricks: Some Nastashas become recruiters. Some 70 percent of the bogus employment agents in countries such as the Ukraine are themselves female slaves, who've come to lure more future Natashas into the mafiya's system.[1]

Young men too are tricked from their villages, but they usually suffer another ghastly fate: Taken to a foreign land, they're trapped by thugs and forced to part with a kidney. Granted, they too have a choice: They can either go through with the operation—which, with commonly botched surgeries, often leave them ill for life—and receive their bus ticket home or they can be killed and have it yanked from their warm corpse. The tragedy doesn't end with a gaping wound, however: The men, when they return home, are often scorned by society as weaklings.

The Russian mafiya, a major player in the worldwide slave trade, is not alone. Japanese Yakuza and syndicates in Italy and Albania are also among the global mafia that traffic between 1 million and 2 million women and children in the slave trade each year—many also coming from Africa and Southeast Asia.

> Between 27 million and 200 million people in the world are believed to be living as slaves,[2] with upwards of 50,000 entering the United States annually.

Now nearly everything we do may be linked to organized crime, whether we know it or not. Some activities are obviously dicey—it is no surprise that counterfeit purses and CDs sold on the street put money into organized crime's piggy banks, as do most illegal drugs and prostitution. But we can be snagged in the crime web in the most innocuous ways. The clothes that we buy may pay for Italian mob "protection" in Manhattan's Garment District, and the gas we pump may have come from the Russian mob's oil companies. That Chinese buffet could be "employing" indentured servants snuck into the country by smuggling networks to whom they will be indebted for years. Organized crime is everywhere: The chips at the casino might clean up dirty money, that cigarette smoked after dinner could be contraband, that seafood in the sushi may have been illegally caught, and even that stock we bought yesterday may be controlled by gangsters in suits. Most people are absolutely unaware of the scope of organized crime's creeping activities, since these shadowy sorts try to keep knowledge of their involvement very hush-hush. After all, they have a hell of a lot of money on the line.

Of the $1 trillion or so that organized crime groups collectively earn, half is made in the United States. Illegal drugs provide a good chunk of their "paychecks," being a $500 billion a year industry. The entire GDP of the United States, by way of comparison, is $11 trillion.

Even though organized crime groups typically don't have a political goal, radical groups work with syndicates to get their contraband, they may use their networks, and they rely on mafia-style moneymakers—such as extortion—to fund their political cause. Al-Qaeda made a bundle selling Afghan heroin to international crime groups, Chechen terrorists earn their jack running arms and oil in Chechnya's black market, Albanian cigarette smugglers funnel money into nationalist causes, and the IRA and Irish Loyalists both squeeze Northern Ireland's businesses for "donations" to their causes. And when terrorist groups are looking for arms and other weaponry, they look up mafia sorts to provide them. Russian organized crime groups, in particular, have greatly enriched terrorists' arsenals: They are believed to have gotten their mitts on suitcase nukes, radiological compounds, nerve gas, and other odds and ends left over from the Cold War, and nobody knows exactly where those are now.

NUCLEAR TWITCHINGS

When the Soviet Union collapsed in 1991, a whole new landscape blossomed for crime syndicates. Spies, military men, and police officers, suddenly out of jobs, signed on with the Russian mob. The sudden downturn in fortune for government-paid nuclear scientists, energy plant workers, and soldiers at military bases in Russia, Ukraine, and Kazakhstan, where top secret weapons were stored, was a lucky break for criminal gangs as well. It wasn't too hard to convince workers who hadn't seen their paychecks for months to lift radioactive materials or to raid the Cold War experimental weapons cabinet; the Lithuanian mafia was offering missiles and suitcase nukes fresh from a base in Kiev. But the mobsters picked up more than nasty ingredients to make weapons; they also hired the brains that knew how to unleash them, a valuable commodity for terrorist organizations and to young and poor countries struggling to build up their arsenals. How many scientists were hired away and the extent of nuclear theft are unknown: There were at least twenty seizures of small amounts of plutonium and high-grade uranium between 1993 and 2001 according to the International Atomic Energy Agency—and nobody knows how much successfully made it where it was going. There are also questionable reports that the Chechen mafia sold twenty nuclear warheads to Osama bin Laden sometime around 1998.[3]

The Nunn-Lugar program (named after Sam Nunn and Dick Lugar, who sponsored the bill passed by Congress in 1991) gives U.S. funding to guard, secure, and destroy "loose nukes" in the former Soviet Union.

Of all the world's organized crime groups, the one that scares crime experts the most are the ones under the Russian umbrella. "Russian" better describes their common language during the Soviet era than their ethnicity, since those in the Russian mob may be Georgian, Ukrainian, Lithuanian, Chechen, or Tajikistani, to name but a few. Since the fall of the Communist regime, the Russian mafiya grabbed control of so much of the Russian state—from its mineral companies to its judicial system—that some believe they could simply take it over, and to some extent, they already have.

Close-up

If you are wondering why so many criminal syndicates have popped up on our radar recently, the answer is easy: Most of them have always been around, albeit lurking about mostly in their own countries. During the 1990s, they began moving abroad for three reasons: 1) because travel became easier, 2) because they wanted to expand business operations, and 3) because the heat was on and/or opportunities had dried up in their own countries. Over the past fifteen years, the Soviet Union fell apart and Russia went broke, prompting some Russian organized crime groups to set up international branches. When the Brits gave up Hong Kong and Portugal returned Macau to Communist China, the handovers prompted many Chinese Triads to bolt, fearing that Chinese rule would be more severe. The Bosnian War and attacks on Kosovo kicked Albanian criminals into action, first smuggling out Albanians and Kosovars—objects of Serbian genocide—and later hauling drugs and slaves. The crash of the organized-crime-riddled real estate market in Japan and crackdowns on gangsters prompted Japanese thugs to shoot new roots as well.

PICK YOUR POISON

Back in the good old days, most drugs, from heroin to cocaine, could be linked to the Italian mob. Now, however, some drugs are a specialty of certain groups of organized crime. Here's where the drug money often ends up:

- Ecstasy: Distribution dominated by Russian mafiya, some working with Israelis
- China White heroin, opium: Chinese Triads
- Methamphetamine (Ice): Japanese Yakuza (particularly in Hawaii and California)

- Black tar heroin: Mexican mob
- Crack cocaine: Jamaican posses
- Contraband cigarettes: Albanian and Italian organized crime

Even though the Italian mob in the United States at the moment is more or less crushed thanks to decades of busts, high-placed moles, and squealers, the Italian American mobster hasn't entirely gone away. He's merely slipped on a tie and headed over to the financial district.

In addition to slick Armani-clad golden boys, secretaries rushing down to the metro in their sneakers, and shouting street vendors trading doughnuts for dough, Wall Street's bestiary has recently welcomed a discreet newcomer: the Italian American mob. After being tossed from Fulton Fish Market, and thrown out of the waste-hauling industry in the early 1990s, Manhattan gangsters sniffed out new ventures. They soon realized that they were just a quick jaunt away from the biggest concentration of money movers in the world—Wall Street and its 100,000-plus brokers. For over a decade, they have forcefully managed so-called boiler rooms by forcing brokerage firms to work with them to manipulate stock—even pushing stock of companies that didn't exist on the unwary investor. Now the Italian mafia (and increasingly the Russian mob) have made global finance an essential engine of global crime. Working with the best accountants, lawyers, and financiers that money can buy, they are organizing complex financial schemes to launder their money, including cleaning it up on Wall Street.

In one well-documented case, members of the Bonanno and Genovese families controlled much of the stock for Health Tech, traded on the Nasdaq small-cap market. They muscled into several firms, bribing and extorting brokers to push the stock and create artificial demand—and the price of Health Tech soared during 1996. The following year the mafia grifters and their conspirators ditched their stock, making millions from the transactions; investors were left with nearly worthless pieces of paper and a busy signal every time they tried to get their broker on the phone.

—MELIK BOUDEMAGH

With the Italian American mobsters trying to keep their fingernails clean, an assortment of other criminal groups are taking over their dirtier, street-level games, from extortion and prostitution to gambling and drugs, while adding a few tricks of their own. As much as they like their anonymity, the effects of the stealthful swindlers are rather hard to ignore: They have become so huge a force, "employing" millions worldwide (up to 3 million in Russia alone), commanding so many billions of dollars (mobsters in Italy generate over $120 billion a year), and having such a dramatic effect (creating a slave trade, arming militias, and depleting tax revenues among them) that they are now society's biggest menace. So expansive is their reach and so rapidly have they diversified their tricks that in the 1990s governments, international organizations, and think tanks all sat up with a jolt and announced that organized crime was the most alarming problem on the planet and that it needed to be halted before it unraveled the interwoven threads of global society any further.

ORGANIZED CRIME: A VARIETY PACK

An overview of some of the major players in the underground:

- **Russian mob:** The slickest, the smartest, and the scariest, these organized gangs of ex-KGB, military officers, bankers, and thugs are arms dealers, drug smugglers, slave drivers, insurance fraudsters, car thieves, bank hackers, and hit men. They are very well-integrated in Russia, where they run between 60 and 80 percent of all banks, control much of the government and courts, and are very involved in sports: They are believed to have been behind the vote-swinging ice-skating scandal at the 2000 summer Olympics.
- **Albanian syndicates:** Every bit as brutal as the Russian mob, they are often the middlemen—transporting drugs or slaves from point to point mid-journey. They also work with the mafia in southeasternmost Italy, transporting illegal cigarettes.
- **Chinese Triads:** Descendents of ancient monks who rebelled against the Ching dynasty, Triads specialize in making counterfeit everything—from CDs and DVDs to software and Viagra. Known for extortion—young Triads shake down their classmates at school—they are also involved in smuggling Chinese migrants from the mainland to the United States, Canada, and Australia, where the migrants, who already paid tens of thousands of dollars to be illegally transported to wherever they are, find themselves hit with unexpected debts of tens of thousands more.
- **Japanese Yakuza:** Preferring to think of themselves as gentlemen outlaws, Yakuza (whose name means "the Losers") often have total body tattoos and may chop off a pinkie to show respect to their gang's leader, to whom they present the bloody digit. They run an Asian slave trade, buying women for their brothels, between peddling "ice" and building hospitals and golf courses to launder their ill-gotten dough. Their claim to fame, however, is corporate extortion.

- **Italian mob:** The Sicilian gangsters have declared a truce with the government and have quieted down recently; the 'Ndrangheta in Calabria (the toe of the boot) have stopped kidnapping so much; and the Sacra Corona Unita in Puglia (the heel of the boot) are mostly involved in the cigarette, slave, and heroin trade. The real hell-raisers in Italy are the Camorra around Naples: Now that women are running the mafia show—their men so often dead or in prison—they've launched old-style gang wars, and they have taken their waste-hauling business to a new dangerous extreme.

Organized crime, however, takes so many forms and is running amok in so many countries that it often defies the most dedicated efforts to halt its creeping into society. Whether you call them the mafia, organizatsiya, posses, gangs, cartels, babas, or syndicates, the money-hungry wolves now have long-reaching networks, a surprising level of sophistication, and a novel attitude of sharing operations as they sniff out all the vulnerabilities in modern life. Guided by the same goal as contemporary corporations—to turn a handsome profit—today's organized crime has evolved. Today's underworld criminals are high tech savvy. Working with video cameras, computers, Palm Pilots, and the Internet, they pull off sophisticated scams including recording PIN numbers and coding magnetic strips used at cash machines.

CYBERCRIMINALS

The Internet has provided organized crime groups with a myriad of ways to snatch mountains of money from unsuspecting consumers—to the tune of $50 billion or more a year. No group has been more adept than the Russians, whose years studying at technological institutes certainly did not go to waste, and who are happy to demonstrate their skills for the mafiya. The Web may serve as a marketplace to peddle drugs or child porn videos, but cybercriminals have also devised means that defraud users of their identities and credit card numbers. While some have hacked into online "banks" such as PayPal and emerge with millions of credit card numbers, another popular means is to set up a fake site offering goods—perhaps software, electronics, or pharmaceuticals— at way below market prices. When consumers punch in their credit card numbers, the order is never really placed: The goods aren't delivered and the consumer isn't charged, but the credit card may begin shopping on its own. Organized crime groups have hacked into telephone companies and have obtained millions of calling card numbers; they've hacked into banks and wired millions to their accounts; they've used the Internet to launder money. And it's believed that worms such as Mydoom were dreamed up by Russians, not only as a means to screw up computers but to access passwords and identity information. Another trick: cracking a corporation's computer system to gain sensitive information, and then "cyberextorting" for millions, threatening to reveal the info or crash the company's system if not paid. Hackers working out of Russia have also penetrated the Pentagon's system, although that's nothing new. It's believed that a quarter of a million computer nerds break into that high-security computer system every year.

Modern mobsters set their sights higher: The money handed over by a corporation whose arm they are twisting is likely to have a few more zeroes attached than the money from the cash box at the corner store. No group has better infiltrated the corporate system than Japan's Yakuza: Members even have their own offices and business cards. And they have devised a means to manipulate their country's strict social codes and extreme reliance on honor to great effects, using shame and humiliation to coax millions out of Japanese firms every year.

THE SHAME GAME

The Japanese simultaneously juggle a strict social protocol, high personal expectations, and a huge need to preserve honor and save face above all else. Some Yakuza gangsters recently began exploiting the country's corporate world with *sokaiya*—shaming for profit. In the past two decades, a new breed of outlaw rose up by buying stocks in major corporations and then digging up dirt on the companies' VIPs. Extramarital affairs, tax evasion, shady dealings, poor work conditions, or partaking in sex trips (of which Yakuza members often had firsthand knowledge since they organized them) are all liabilities that Yakuza extortionists threaten to publicize at shareholder meetings unless the corporations' VIPs pay up, by subscribing to "professional" journals at outlandish prices, or buying $50,000 worth of tickets to golf tournaments and charity balls (for a "foundation" that doesn't exist).

The shame game was first noted in 1976, when Yakuza godfather Yoshio Kodama was paid $2 million by Lockheed Martin to pressure the head of All Nippon Airways to reconsider Lockheed Martin's bid to manufacture a new fleet of commercial aircraft.[4] When the airline's president nevertheless rejected Lockheed Martin's bid, Yakuza smeared his name and caused a ruckus at a shareholders' meeting, planting rumors that he had taken illegal loans totaling in the millions. The president was quickly shamed into resigning.

The mafia in Italy has also been skilled at using business covers to pull off their dirty deeds. Whereas one of their former specialties was running trash-hauling businesses, they now haul industrial poisons, with disastrous results.

THE ECO-MAFIA

Few in Italy recognized exactly how problematic industrial wastes can be until the 1980s, when the government passed recycling laws—and put the squeeze on industries to responsibly deal with their leftover poisons. The Italian mafia saw just how profitable the field could be, with these new laws requiring that industries properly dispose of lead, arsenic, carcinogenic chemical compounds, and radioactive materials. Costs for safely getting rid of the hazardous materials were high—until the mafia snaked in with the proper permits and papers (provided by corrupt officials), offering to alleviate the headache for a tenth of the price that other haulers were bidding. Winning contract after contract from paper mills, tanneries, and chemical companies, the mafia loaded up their trucks with their carcinogenic cargo with no intention of taking it to a safe treatment facility. Sometimes they off-loaded the poisons in mafia-run municipal landfills, which aren't meant to hold hazardous waste. Sometimes they dumped them into the ocean or caves and sometimes they illegally dug deep pits and filled them with the chemical and heavy metal waste, not concerned that it would contaminate the water supply; to cover up their tracks, they sometimes built concrete factories over the subterranean waste dumps. Recently, however, the mafia sunk to a new low: They mixed the toxic sludge with fertilizer and, posing as salesmen, gave it to farmers free of charge to try out.[5] Now hundreds of thousands of acres of farmland are poisoned, cows and buffalo produce toxin-laced milk, and the costs of cleanup are in the billions of dollars.[6] It's so alarming that locally made mozzarella was banned in some southern towns due to contamination of cattle;[7] worse, cancer rates have soared—in some parts quadrupling within a few years.[8]

One of the most sensitive areas in global commerce is shipping, particularly in Southeast Asia, where geographic peculiarities put ships at greater risk for attack. And nobody knows that better than Chinese Triads, who've devised a method to make millions from a twisted modern-day take on piracy.

Piracy and hijackings of ships costs world shipping and industry around $25 billion a year.[9]

"PHANTOM" SHIPS

In case you imagined that there is an old salt sitting at a radar screen in Norway monitoring the whereabouts of the tens of thousands of ships plying the sea, guess again: Unlike commercial air traffic, nobody has a clue about the big picture of what ships are out there, where they are going, or how far on their way they are, which is exactly the sort of vulnerability and confusion that pirates prey on. No place better illustrates the soft underbelly of the maritime world than the Strait of Malacca, a narrow finger of water that runs between mangrove-fringed Indonesia and the cliffs of Malaysia. It is the shortest route from Southeast Asia to Europe, and a quarter of the world's commercial vessels cross it during their voyages. At any given time some five hundred vessels push through its six hundred miles of narrow shipping lanes, encountering the world's greatest risks of piracy (a daily occurrence) and hijackings (at least one a week is reported— although that is a fraction of what occurs).[10] As inky darkness descends and weary crews head to berth, small boats dart out from Indonesia's villages and mangrove swamps, sneaking up on that night's targets. Barefoot pirates hoist themselves over the sides of yachts, demanding TV, stereo, and clothes; they climb the chains of oil tankers, holding guards at knifepoint and demanding they open the safe, which might contain $40,000 or more. But lately Triads (and other organized crime groups) are directing many more involved operations. Pirates with automatic weapons begin by overtaking a crew, usually killing them as they hijack the ship; then they quickly repaint and rename the vessel. They sell and unload the haul—which might be worth millions of dollars in oil, sugar, or rice— and then con unsuspecting shippers at the new ports into giving them new cargoes, which never make it to where they're supposed to go. By the time the shipper grows concerned, the "phantom" ship has been renamed, repainted, and is sporting new papers again. Sometimes the hijacked ships are sold to unsuspecting buyers, but often they become part of fleets run by organized crime or terrorist groups. Hundreds of ships disappear this way every year. And some of them make their way into the fleets of terrorists: Al-Qaeda, for one, is believed to own at least twenty "phantom" ships.

"The number of attacks [on ships is] staggering. At the beginning of the 1990s there were about a hundred attacks a year. By the end of the 1990s it was about five hundred attacks a year. And that's just the tip of the iceberg. Conventional wisdom holds that the real number of attacks are at least four times more than what's reported."

—ANDREW LININGTON OF UK MARITIME UNION NUMAST[11]

Organized crime groups thrive because they meet society's desires—be they for drugs, sex, or even difficult-to-acquire food. One place you might not expect to see contraband goods is the sushi counter, but the demand for raw fish is so high in Japan that most everyone ignores the question of how it got from sea to chopstick. The suppliers are surprisingly often Russian organized crime groups, who are sending out crews to "overfish" in Russian waters and the Bering Sea and supply over $1 billion of illegal crab and other seafood every year to Japan.[12] It's serious business: In 2002, when a general in the Russian border guard tried to stop the practice by installing black boxes on Russian boats, his house was firebombed and he was killed in the blaze.

Behind the Scenes

One of the more unusual aspects of today's global crime scene is that the different organizations are beginning to work together. Historically prone to blow each other away in storms of gunfire, organizations in different countries are linking arms in international businesses during this era of "pax mafiosa." Turkish babas and Armenians work with Albanians to bring heroin into Europe, Colombians work with Nigerians to deliver cocaine, Russians were reportedly helping Colombians build a submarine to stealthily deliver their goods, and the Italian mob is sometimes called out to give strategic advice. While governments pour billions into fighting them, and loudly declare their "war on organized crime," the reality is that this war can't be won simply by boldly announced "crackdowns" or propaganda.

> The FBI now has an office in Budapest, Hungary, to help trail organized crime in this city, which is a hotbed for it. Intelligence groups sometimes work with organized criminals as well: Not only do they know what's going on on the street, they also can off-load the heroin and cocaine that previously the CIA, for one, was reportedly looking to sell.[13]

Many criminals enter this slimy underworld not for kicks, but because it's the best-paying job option for these guys, many of whom come from lower-class backgrounds in societies that are often economically strapped. Given the opportunity to find decent jobs, some of them would probably quit. And that's exactly what is happening in Japan right now, where businesses are opening doors to the former gangsters. Some Yakuza are having their tattoos removed, and their pinkies grafted back on, and marching into the gleaming towers of the corporate world.

PART IX

WHAT'S NEXT

"May you live in interesting times."

—CHINESE CURSE

Well, it's not going to be boring. Life in the twenty-first century has started out with a rip-roaring, earth-shattering bang, and the future is littered with mind-bending possibilities. One thing most everybody agrees on, whether you're talking with reporters or scientists, privacy experts or political pundits, sociologists or evangelicals: We are right at the brink of something very big. Humanity is poised to make a great leap or take a huge fall—or perhaps both.

> "You would never have thought it possible to pick up an atom and actually move it a few atomic diameters away. It is equivalent to reaching out to the planets and being able to touch a planet and move it from one orbit to another."
>
> —JOSEPH STROSCIO, PHYSICIST, NATIONAL INSTITUTE OF STANDARDS AND TECHNOLOGY, TALKING ABOUT THE UPCOMING NANOTECHNOLOGY REVOLUTION[1]

The most thrilling addition to our world—the thing that makes even the doomsayers lighten up—is the Internet. No force possesses a greater possibility for positive change—whether through increasing knowledge, slaying lies, or communicating with people in far-flung parts of the world. The mainstream media already offer special in-depth features online—from interactive graphics to downloadable reports—and as the traditional outlets continue to plummet in readership, viewership, and believability, the Internet is picking up the slack, offering news junkies alternative sources and alternative information. As developing countries tune in, they may be able to leapfrog in both education and economic development, connecting with new markets for their wares, including textiles and art. Access to the Internet will be easier (via wireless) and faster, and new channels of cybertravel beyond the World Wide Web will open up. Some envision that

the Internet will connect with our bodies (via a physical chip or a sensory sur-
round box), and the need for actual physical social interaction may decrease as
our social life comes via our electronic box. The anonymity of today's Internet
may soon vanish, however—already some public libraries require that users be
identified by their fingerprints. Given the problems of child pornography, financial
scams, and hacking, the Internet of tomorrow may broadcast who we are from
the minute we go online.

> *Wikipedia, an "open source" encyclopedia created by software designer Jimmy*
> *Wales, illustrates the possibilities of future Internet use. Readers can "contest"*
> *entries or even edit them, and numerous sources are linked at the bottom of*
> *each. One problem: Not only can PR firms post their marketing spin about*
> *companies and their products, pranksters can alter copy and photos as well.*
> *Recently, the smiling photo of President George W. Bush in the same-named*
> *entry was briefly replaced with a photo of an anus.*

Scientists and inventors, those pied pipers of the future, will be drawing us
down any number of mind-boggling paths that will revolutionize our lives. Stem
cell research is already helping the paralyzed to walk, and parents may soon
freeze their newborn's fluids and umbilical cords—which hold the keys for curing
many diseases and body malfunctions they may encounter in their lifetimes. The
unraveling of genetic codes, and the pioneering efforts of scientists such as
Craig Ventor, are playing out in numerous ways—from treating diseases to creating superwarriors and überathletes: Olympic committees are worried that they
will have to devise ways to test for genetic modification by the 2012 Olympics.

> *Nanotechnology involves rearranging atoms and molecules, which exist at a*
> *level invisible to the naked eye. Atoms are about 1/80,000 of the width of a*
> *human hair and nanotechnology develops "machines" and systems that work*
> *in this tiny arena.*

Corporations and governments are already sinking billions of dollars into
nanotechnology—rearrangement of matter on the molecular level. Car doors
that reassemble themselves after being smashed, facial creams that fill in wrin-
kles, and artificial flavors on the nanolevel are already in the marketplace. The
very near future will bring all sorts of marvels—some say microorganisms will
"eat" the greenhouse gases and that nanotech operations will "grow" the TVs

and cars that are today manufactured in factories. One problem, however, is that we don't know what we're really dealing with on this level, and the process is so novel and complicated that legislators have no idea what laws to make to govern it. Some worry that the more we tinker around on the atomic level, the more likely we are to make a mess of it all, including a possibility of turning our world into material-less "gray goo."

With petroleum prices skyrocketing and old fields drying up, we will be transitioning to other energy forces in the near future, starting with natural gas. Even though, thanks to the fiascos at Three Mile Island and Chernobyl, no new nuclear plants have been built in the United States for thirty years, the Bush administration is celebrating the idea of returning to nuclear energy—and making it more attractive with financial incentives. Regardless of what ExxonMobil tells us (it says half the country would have to be covered with cornfields to produce enough methane for American car use), others are looking to biofuels; Cargill, for example, is shipping them in from Brazil. Futurists such as Jeremy Rifkin, however, say we need to transition to hydrogen as a fuel and that a battle is already on between those who want to monopolize that fuel source (including oil companies Shell and BP) and those who want to keep it decentralized.

> "There are rare moments in history when a generation of human beings are given a new gift with which to rearrange their relationship to one another and the world around them. This is such a moment. . . . Hydrogen is a promissory note for humanity's future on Earth. Whether that promise is squandered . . . or used wisely on behalf of our species and our fellow creatures is up to us."
>
> —JEREMY RIFKIN, THE HYDROGEN ECONOMY

Geopolitically, the situation will be tricky. Led by Venezuela's President Hugo Chavéz and Brazil's President Lula da Silva, South America is beginning to wriggle out of the United States' economic and political lassos and assert its independence. Chávez is talking of cutting off oil sales to the United States and da Silva is telling the Americans that it doesn't want their money for Bush-style abstinence-only AIDS education. At a recent meeting of the U.S.-dominated Organization of American States, Latin American countries infuriated Secretary of State Condoleezza Rice by rejecting her insistent proposal to establish a democracy board to monitor their treatment of human rights.

Agricultural output from Brazil is soaring and some believe that the South American country will be the world's next breadbasket. Predictably, Monsanto is busily selling its seeds to Brazilian farmers.

The United States is sniping at Iran and Syria, both of whom support anti-Israeli terrorists, and the Bush administration is making unproven claims about their weapons of mass destruction in blustery words that some fear may lead to war. While Kim Jong II is leading North Korea, that country continues to be worrisome, and the rhetoric out of DC is amping, as if screaming about Kim's "irresponsibility" pardons the Bush administration for not diplomatically dealing with the situation back when it should have in 2002. But whether we're talking about resources, space issues, or the ability to ravage the economy, the biggest threat to the United States is Asia, specifically China.

 ZOOM ▶ ## The Making of China's Threat

President: Hu Jintao
Capital: Beijing
GDP: $7.3 trillion
GDP per capita: $5,600
Literacy: women 86 percent, men 95 percent

China is no longer an "emerging power." The dragon has fully emerged, with its 1.3 billion residents and its galloping $7.3 trillion economy (growing at over 9 percent a year) and its garments supplying over half of the American and European clothing markets. And now that the giant is awake, the United States wishes it would go straight back to bed. Now when one hears about "China" it is usually followed by the word "threat." China needs to fix its exchange rates, announces the Federal Reserve's Alan Greenspan. China should address its human rights issues, snipes the State Department, prompting China to reply that the United States appears to have a few human rights problems of its own. China is snuggling up to countries the United States has cut off, from Iran to Sudan, the Bush administration announces.

> According to the U.S. State Department, 250 protesters are still imprisoned from the 1989 Tiananmen Square protest.

China, it appears, is moving into U.S. territory: Drivers are wishing that China would just keep its paws off "our" oil, since its demands are sending our prices into new orbits. The air force's Space Command frets that China's recently launched "nanosatellite" could damage our satellites in space. What nobody really wants to even admit is how very deeply involved in our economy China has become. The United States is now importing almost $200 billion worth of goods from China a year, creating a $160 billion trade deficit, and China holds so many U.S. treasury bonds—some $120 billion worth[2]—that it could seriously wound the American economy and the value of the dollar if it wished.

STOMPING ON EGGSHELLS

Every country has its bugbears, and with China they can easily be summed up in one word: islands. Japan, the island chain to the southeast, invaded China in the 1930s, killing millions and brutally occupying the mainland, killing nearly 300,000 during the so-called Rape of Nanking—an event and an era that still plays large in Chinese history books. Although Japan has forked over tens of billions of dollars' worth of development grants and every so often whispers an apology, Japanese revisionists have hit the delete button with their own history books. When a new Japanese textbook came out in spring 2005, downplaying Japan's ruthless treatment of the Chinese, the news triggered riots on the mainland, complete with kicking out windows of the Japanese embassy. The foreign minister said relations were the worst since the two normalized relations in 1972.

But that wasn't the first time Japan ticked off China recently. In 2004, Japan and the United States stomped on China's sorest point: Taiwan. The two countries sent a joint message "encouraging the peaceful resolution of issues concerning the Taiwan Strait," a message that prompted China to ask that they both stop meddling in Chinese affairs. Taiwan has pretty much functioned independently since 1949, when Mao Tse-tung and his Communists overtook the mainland and Chiang Kai-shek and his Kuomintang nationalists hightailed it to the southeastern island. Back then, the United States recognized Taiwan's capital Taipei as the capital of China and boosted Taiwan's profile, selling it lots of arms and setting up U.S. bases. In 1972, however, Nixon switched the focus. To thaw relations with Beijing, the United States stopped recognizing Taiwan, began recognizing Beijing, and heeded the mainland's main line: "One China." Beijing tolerates Taiwan having its own government headed by its own president; China doesn't hamper business; and in many ways Taiwan is (don't tell Beijing) independent. But China refuses to make it official, and recently even passed an "antisecession law," saying that if Taiwan tried to politically saw itself off, China would invade. And according to the Bush administration's 2002 Nuclear Posture Review, if China invades Taiwan the United States might respond with nuclear weapons.

In summer 2005, China unsuccessfully tried to buy U.S. companies Unocal and Maytag.

China sees as a threat several U.S. behaviors, including:

▶ Selling arms to Taiwan
▶ Saying that it supports Taiwanese independence
▶ Saying that it will defend Taiwan
▶ Trying to dominate space (and refusing to heed China's, Russia's, and the rest of the world's request not to weaponize the commons)
▶ Building a National Missile Defense program, claiming that it relates to North Korea (while experts are whispering that it is ready to prepare for a future war with China)

There are indeed "issues" between the United States and China, including espionage, and nobody can paint China (or the United States) as a shimmering angel. Even though the country poses new challenges in its changing relationship with the Americans, it doesn't mean that China is our foe. The Bush administration, neocons, and the paranoid ultraright, however, are winding up a new propaganda campaign that paints China as a serious military woe. Defense Secretary Rumsfeld launched it at a June 2005 meeting of Asian government officials gathered in Singapore, where he noted that China missiles could now "reach targets in many areas of the world," even though this hasn't been news for about four decades.

"Since no nation threatens China," sniped Defense Secretary Rumsfeld, apparently forgetting that the Pentagon listed China on its "Might Nuke" list, "one wonders: Why this investment? Why these continuing large weapons purchases [by China]?"

The Chinese responded to Rumsfeld's hostility with diplomatic aplomb. "Chinese defence spending has indeed increased a little," admitted foreign ministry spokesman Liu Jianchao. "But the bulk of the increase is for the improvement of the living conditions of the officers and soldiers. China has not the intention nor the capability to drastically increase its military buildup. We hope that the US side will respect such facts and do more to serve a healthy development of China-US relations."[3]

> According to arms calculations from SIPRI, China spent about $34 billion on arms in 2003, $374 billion less than the United States.[4,5]

Suddenly, neocon think tanks, including the Hudson Institute, are holding emergency seminars on the heightened China threat. Just in time for the latest Bush misinformation campaign kickoff, an alarming new book, *The Gathering Threat* by the late Constantine Menges, a neocon who advised the CIA and the

Reagan White House, is causing stomachs to twist and fingers to point to the East. The machine is kicking into action and articles in conservative papers are shrieking that China:

▶ "[C]an launch nuclear weapons that in 30 minutes could kill one-hundred million Americans"[6]
▶ "[H]as defined the United States as its 'main enemy'"
▶ "Has threatened to destroy entire American cities if the U.S. were to help democratic Taiwan defend itself from a Chinese military assault"
▶ "[B]uys weapons from Russia designed to sink U.S. aircraft carriers"

It's all sounding frighteningly familiar. Except the last time we heard this kind of talk, the demon country was Iraq.

Another issue of grave concern is the world's poor. AIDS and starvation kill tens of thousands a day, but there are billions more who are getting furious that they can't get ahead in this world, be it due to geography, weather, their own country's corruption, or the acts of the international lending community geared to keep them down. The imbalance of riches, food, water, and resources may play out in violence: Hungry people are desperate people and the desperate who have nothing to lose are those most likely to resort to violence, and even terrorism.

Other big players on the world scene:

● **The European Union:** With 455 million inhabitants, the umbrella organization of twenty-five European countries represents the biggest economic bloc on the planet.
● **The United Nations:** One hundred ninety countries are represented in this world organization, but power resides in the Security Council. The five countries that hold permanent seats and have veto power are the United States, Britain, Russia, China, and France.
● **WTO:** The World Trade Organization is the referee board for world trade matters.
● **The Federal Reserve:** An independent entity within the U.S. government, the Federal Reserve oversees the creation of money and greatly affects the prime rate for bank loans to consumers. Headed by Alan Greenspan.
● **Group of Eight (G8):** The industrialized world's most powerful and richest countries—Canada, France, Germany, Italy, Japan, Russia, the United Kingdom, and the United States—send their leaders to annual economic/political summits where they adopt common policies and try to tackle problems. Notably, China not invited into the club.

The future, full of promises, full of problems, is at the moment being constructed and directed mostly by profit-driven corporations as well as a handful of
governments who are happy to deceive us to promote their own agendas while
yanking power out of our hands. That isn't the way it has to be. The rest of the
world is waiting for the residents of the United States—the most powerful citizens on the planet—to sit up, pay attention, demand accountability from their
leaders, and begin figuring out how to take back their country and change its current crash course. Who is really ruling the world? We are. With our actions and
our inaction, our votes, our grassroots efforts, and our information campaigns,
we have more say in scripting the future than anyone else. We are the future
agents of change—that is, if we decide to organize and take back our power.

Notes

I. THE RIGHT

Chapter 1. Briefing: The Mighty Right

1. Robert Dreyfuss, "Grover Norquist: Field Marshal of the Bush Plan," *Nation*, 14 May 2001.
2. For more information, see "Q and A," C-SPAN, 27 Mar. 2005, http://qanda.org/Transcript/?ProgramID=1016.
3. Paul Weyrich, "Letter to Conservatives," Free Congress Foundation, 18 Feb. 1999.
4. Paul Weyrich, "Separate and Free," *Washington Post*, 7 Mar. 1999.
5. Mission statement of Howard Phillips's Constitution Party. See http://www.constitutionparty.com/.
6. Sarah Posner, "Just Who Is the Council for National Policy, and Why Isn't It Paying Taxes?" AlterNet, 1 Mar. 2005. See http://www.theocracywatch.org/coucil_for_national_policy_march1_05.htm.
7. Ibid.
8. Jeremy Leaming and Rob Boston, "Behind Closed Doors," *Church and State*, Oct. 2004.

Chapter 2. The Christian Right

1. According to a 2002 CNN/Time poll.
2. "A Faith-Based Partisan Divide," *Pew Forum on Religion and Public Life*, Jan. 2005.
3. Estimate of Chip Berlet and Nikhil Aziz of progressive Boston think tank Public Eye; *Business Week* uses the figures of 36–26 percent white evangelicals and 10 percent black evangelicals in its May 18, 2005, cover story. *Business Week* source: John C. Green, University of Akron.
4. 2005 AP/Ipsos Poll, "Religious Fervor in the US Surpasses Faith in Many Other Industrialized Countries," 6 June 2005, http://www.ap-ipsosresults.com/.
5. Paul Weyrich, "Separate and Free," *Washington Post*, 7 Mar. 1999.

6. "Left Behind, but Not Forgotten," *Economist*, 15 Apr. 2004.
7. Carolyn Weaver, "Unholy Alliance," *Mother Jones*, Jan. 1986. See Maureen Farrell, "On a Mission from God," BuzzFlash, 9 Mar. 2004, http://www.buzzflash.com/farrell/04/03/far04007.html.
8. Robert Dreyfuss, "Reverend Doomsday," *Rolling Stone*, 19 Feb. 2004.
9. Chip Berlet, "Religion and Politics in the United States: Nuances You Should Know," *Public Eye*, Summer 2003, www.publiceye.org/magazine/v17n2/evangelical-demographics.html. Also see www.wheaton.edu/isae/Gallup-Bar-graph.html.
10. "A Faith-Based Partisan Divide," *Pew Forum on Religion and Public Life*, Jan. 2005.
11. Bob Moser, "The Crusaders," *Rolling Stone*, 7 Apr. 2005.
12. Dr. Bruce Prescott, "Christian Reconstructionism," Interfaith Alliance forum on Religious Extremism, Westminster Presbyterian Church, 11 Apr. 2002. www.mainstreambaptists.org/dominionism.htm.
13. "The Rise of the Religious Rise in the Republican Party," theocracywatch.org, http://www.theocracywatch.org/biblical_law2.htm#Biblical.
14. Kevin Phillips, *American Dynasty* (New York: Penguin, 2004).
15. Bible source pointed out by Katherine Yurica, "What Did Mr. Bush's 2nd Inaugural Address Really Mean?" 21 Feb. 2005.
16. Don Monkerud, "Bush Administration's 'Faith-based' Initiatives—Transforming America 'One Soul at a Time,'" IRC Right Web, International Relations Center, 18 Feb. 2005.
17. David Van Biema, Cathy Booth Thomas, Massimo Calabresi, John F. Dickerson, et al., "The 25 Most Influential Evangelicals in America," *Time*, 7 Feb. 2005.
18. So reports Katherine Yurica of the *Yurica Report*.
19. Deborah Zabarenko, "US Draws Jeers for Abortion Comments at UN," Reuters, 5 Mar. 2005.
20. "Religious Right to Boycott Microsoft," *Telegraph*, 15 May 2005.
21. Culture Wars hit Corporate America, *Business Week,* 19 May 2005.
22. Ibid.
23. Interview with author. See www.publicchristian.com.
24. Bruce Prescott, "How Does God Speak in a Pluralistic Society," speech given at the Interfaith Alliance of Oklahoma, 23 Mar. 2000. www.mainstreambaptists.org/interfaith_conscience.htm.

Chapter 3. The Bushes

1. "The Buying of the President 2004: President George W. Bush," Center for Public Integrity, publicintegrity.org.
2. Lucy Morgan, "While Cabinet Profits, Jeb's Fortune Declines," *St. Petersburg Times*, 20 Feb. 2005.
3. Timothy J. Christmann, "Vice President Bush Calls World War II Experience Sobering," *Naval Aviation News*, Mar.–Apr. 1985.

4. The latter is one of the implications of Kevin Phillips's book *American Dynasty* (New York: Penguin, 2004).

5. Marjorie Perloff, "Mommy Dearest," *New Republic*, 5 Oct. 1992.

6. Christopher Hitchens, "Minority Report: Corruption in George Bush's Family," *Nation*, 12 Nov. 1990. This real estate deal is also brought up by the Recall Jeb Bush/Rescue Florida Movement headed by Margaret Richards.

7. Stephen Pizzo, "Bush Family Values," *Mother Jones*, 1 Sept. 1992.

8. Ibid.

9. So reports Bush family biographer Kitty Kelly in *The Family: The Real Story of the Bush Dynasty* (New York: Doubleday, 2004).

10. David D. Kirkpatrick, "In Secretly Taped Conversations, Glimpses of the Future President," *New York Times*, 20 Feb. 2005.

11. "Bush Brother's Divorce Reveals Sex Romps," CNN, 25 Nov. 2003.

12. Duncan Campbell, "The Bush Dynasty and the Cuban Criminals," *Guardian*, 2 Dec. 2002. Also see: Ann Louise Bardach, *Cuba Confidential* (New York: Vintage, 2003).

13. So says Bush biographer Kitty Kelly, and so asserted the late J. H. Hatfield.

14. Duncan Campbell, "The Bush Dynasty and the Cuban Criminals," *Guardian*, 2 Dec. 2002.

15. George Bush and Brent Scowcroft, *A World Transformed* (New York: Vintage, 1998).

16. Simon English, "Bush on the Board Not Worth Much, says Carlyle Founder," *Telegraph*, 7 Sept. 2003.

Chapter 4. Bush Insiders

1. Well, so says *Ebony* magazine. But indeed is there another woman more powerful?

2. U.S. Treasury Dept., "Annual Report 2004: Outlays by Function." The FY 2004 budget marks an increase of $50.6 billion over 2003. See http://www.fms. treas.gov/annualreport/cs2004/outlay.pdf.

3. Center for Arms Control and Nonproliferation, "Highlights of the FY '05 Budget."

4. U.S. Treasury Dept., "Annual Report 2004: Financial Highlights." See http://www.fms.treas.gov/annualreport/cs2004/finhigh.pdf.

5. Some figures put the ultimate price tag for National Missile Defense at over $1 trillion. (See "Congress Considers National Defense Costs," CNN.com, 5 May 2005.) According to *Defense Week*, as of 2001, DoD estimated that costs would reach over $100 billion (John M. Donnelly, "US Missile-Defense Costs to Exceed $100 Billion," *Defense Week*, 2 April 2001) and over $100 billion had already been sunk into NMD. According to the Center for Defense Information (2003), the budget for 2002–09 alone exceeds $62 billion.

6. John Isaacs, "The Ones to Watch," *Bulletin of the Atomic Scientists*, Mar./Apr. 2001.

7. Patrick W. Lang, "Drinking the Kool-Aid," *Middle East Policy*, 22 June 2004. Also see James Mann's *Rise of the Vulcans* (New York: Penguin, 2004).

8. Anthony Lappé and Stephen Marshall, *True Lies* (New York: Plume, 2004).

9. Dick Cheney's speech to the Conservative Party of New York, Mar. 12, 2002, in Stephen Marshall and Anthony Lappé's *True Lies*.

10. Russ Kick, who runs the memoryhole.org, broke the story. Associated Press ran with it. "Agency Planned Drill for Plane Crash Last Sept. 11," Associated Press, 22 Aug. 2002.

11. According to New York Mayor Rudy Giuliani's testimony before the 9/11 Commission.

12. White House press release, 29 May 2003, http://www.whitehouse.gov/g8/ interview5.html.

13. Among those who have reported that the cabal was called the "nuts" is CIA employee Ray McGovern as noted by T. D. Allman, "The Curse of Dick Cheney," *Rolling Stone*, 25 Aug. 2004.

14. Michael Isikoff and Evan Thomas, "Storm Warnings," *Newsweek*, 29 Mar. 2004.

15. "Dear Condoleezza," a letter to Condoleezza Rice from U.S. Representative Henry Waxman, 29 Apr. 2005, http://www.democrats.reform.house.gov/ Documents/20050429123407-78970.pdf.

16. As pointed out by Cooperativeresearch.org.

17. Interview with WBNG, 21 Feb. 2005, http://www.wbng.com/data/ web_7431.shtml; Hinchey also made such assertions on CNN.

18. "Cheney's Rise," *Time*, 22 Dec. 2002.

19. The *St. Petersburg Times* bought two Russian satellite photos, which, according to the NASA experts who examined them, didn't show troops building up at all.

20. "Lynne Cheney," www.wikipedia.org.

21. Aspartame was approved after being resubmitted by Rumsfeld when he was head of G. D. Searle. Previously rejected by the FDA, aspartame is now considered safe by the FDA. However, it is the subject of at least three lawsuits which assert that it is a neurotoxin and capable of producing brain tumors.

22. The cost of the Iraq War is about $4.5 billion a month.

23. See "Rumsfeld's War," *Frontline*, PBS, 26 Oct. 2004, http://www.pbs.org/wgbh/ pages/frontline/shows/pentagon/.

24. Barton Gellman, "Secret Unit Expands Rumsfeld Domain," *Washington Post*, 23 Jan. 2004.

25. Seymour Hersh, "The Gray Zone," *New Yorker*, 24 May 2004.

26. Report of the Commission to Assess United States National Security Space Management and Organization, 11 Jan. 2001.

27. See Hart Seely, "The Poetry of D. H. Rumsfeld," *Slate*, 2 Apr. 2003. Seely later published a book of Rumsfeld's sayings: *Pieces of Intelligence: The Existential Poetry of Donald Rumsfeld*. Composer Donald Kong set them to music, sung by soprano Elender Wall: "The Poetry of Donald Rumsfeld Set to Music," *Morning Edition*, NPR, 12 Mar. 2004. (Go to National Public Radio site for more info and to hear: http://www.npr.org/templates/story/story.php?storyId=1761585.)

28. Alan Gilbert, "Condi as You Never Knew Her," *New African*, June 2004.

29. "Europe Influence Seen as Positive," BBC News, 6 Apr. 2005, http://news.bbc.co .uk/1/low/world/europe/4413913.stm.

30. Ken Guggenheim, "Probe: U.S. Knew of Jet Terror Plots," Associated Press, 18 Sept. 2002.

31. Stephen Marshall and Anthony Lappé, *True Lies* (New York: Plume, 2004).

32. In 1996, the *San Jose Mercury News* ran a three-part article exploring the relationship between the CIA, California drug rings, and the Nicaraguan contras that was so damning that CIA director John Deutch launched an investigation. The CIA was not implicated in the investigation, but a few more holes were pierced into the Iran-Contra cover-up, which continues to this day.

33. "[John] Hull is very well known in Colombia and Central America for his activities and his reputation [for] dealing with CIA. . . . [Drug dealer Jorge Morales] also claims . . . that Hull's airstrip was used in loading and unloading of drugs . . . [and that] it was very well known John Hull's ranch was a facility for refueling and storing drugs. John Hull was in Morales' office in July 1983 . . . to arrange delivery of 40 grenade launchers from Opaloca, Florida, to El Salvador. Morales' cargo airliner flew the launchers for Hull." (CIA agent Fiers, briefing the Senate Select Committee on Intelligence [SSCI] about Hull's alleged relationship with Jorge Morales, July 31, 1987.) Source: cia.gov.

34. http://www.thesmokinggun.com/archive/hasenfus1.html.

Chapter 5. The Neocons

1. Adam Curtis, *The Power of Nightmares:* Part 1 "Baby, it's cold outside." This documentary, produced by the BBC originally aired in late 2004. It can be downloaded at http://www.archive.org/details/thepowerofnightmares.

2. Ibid.

3. Jim Lobe, "Ultra-Right State Dept. Official Clashes with Pyongyang," Inter Press Service, 8 Mar. 2005.

4. Ibid.

5. Rodica Buzescu, "The New Review: US Nuclear Policy," *Harvard International Review: Intelligence*, Fall 2002, http://hir.harvard.edu/articles/1069/.

6. Some of this information is drawn from Adam Curtis's BBC documentary "The Power of Nightmares," first shown in 2004.

7. Anne Hessing Cahn, "Team B: The Trillion-Dollar Experiment," *Bulletin of Atomic Scientists*, Apr. 1993.

8. Estimates Anne Hessing Cahn, ibid.

9. "Rebuilding America's Defenses," A Report of the Project for the New American Century, Sept. 2000. See: http://www.globalpolicy.org/empire/2000/09newcentury.pdf.

10. Richard J. Newman, "Corporate Kleptocracy," *U.S. News and World Report*, 13 Sept. 2004.

11. Jim Lobe, "Spy Probe Scans Neocon-Israel Tie," Inter Press Service, 1 Sept. 2004, http://www.commondreams.org/headlines04/0901-20.htm. Stephen Green, "Serving Two Flags," *Counterpunch*, 28 Feb. 2004.

12. Seymour Hersh, "Lunch with the Chairman," *New Yorker*, 17 Mar. 2003.

13. Joshua Chaffin and Thomas Catán, "Perle Pays the Price for Business Controversies," *Financial Times*, 28 Mar. 2003.
14. For more on Perle's recent scandals and threats of libel against *The New Yorker*, see Jack Shafer, "Richard Perle: Libel Watch, Week 4," *Slate*, 2 Apr. 2003, http://slate.msn.com/id/2081053/. Also see the many links there. Also see: Stephen Labaton, "Advisor to U.S. Aided Maker of Satellites," *New York Times*, 29 Mar. 2003.
15. Statement of Richard Perle, Fellow, American Enterprise Institute, Before the Committee on Armed Services, United States House of Representatives, 6 Apr. 2005. See http://www.house.gov/hasc/schedules/PerleIraq%20Lessons4-5-2005.pdf.
16. Jim Lobe, "Spy Probe Scans Neocon-Israel Tie," *Inter-Press Services*, 1 Sept. 2004.

II. FOOD AND DRUG

Chapter 6. Briefing: How Big Pharma Works

1. IMS Health World Review, 2005. See: M. Asif Ismail, "Drug Lobby Second to None," Center for Public Integrity, 7 June 2005.
2. Marcia Angell, *The Truth About Drug Companies* (New York: Random House, 2004).
3. Ibid.
4. The IMS Report, *Medical Marketing and Media*, May 2005.
5. M. Asif Ismail, "Prescription for Power," Center for Public Integrity, 28 Apr. 2005, http://www.publicintegrity.org/lobby/report.aspx?aid=685&sid=200.
6. Opensecrets.org.
7. "Hank McKinnell," *NewsHour with Jim Lehrer*, PBS, 9 Mar. 2004.
8. Rep. Ron Paul, MD, "The Therapeutic Nanny State," LewRockwell.com, 21 Sept. 2004; Ron Strom, "Rep. Ron Paul Seeks to Yank Program, Decries Use of Drugs on Children," WorldNetDaily, 9 Sept. 2004.

Chapter 7. FDA

1. Jason Lazarou, Bruce H. Pomeranz, and Paul N. Corey, "Incidence of Adverse Drug Reactions in Hospital Patients," *Journal of the American Medical Association*, Apr. 1998.
2. "Dangerous Prescription," *Frontline*, PBS, 13 Nov. 2003, transcript: http://www.pbs.org/wgbh/pages/frontline/shows/prescription/hazard/.
3. David Willman, "How a New Policy Led to Seven Deadly Drugs," *Los Angeles Times*, 20 Dec. 2000.
4. U.S. General Accountability Office, "Food and Drug Administration: Effect of User Fees on Drug Approval Times, Withdrawals and Other Agency Activities," GAO, 2002.
5. "Dangerous Prescription," *Frontline*, PBS, 13 Nov. 2003, transcript:

http://www.pbs.org/wgbh/pages/frontline/shows/prescription/interviews/woosley.html.

6. Jason Lazarou, Bruce H. Pomeranz, Paul N. Corey, "Incidence of Adverse Drug Reactions in Hospital Patients," *Journal of the American Medical Association*, Apr. 1998.
7. Testimony of David J. Graham, M.D., before Senate Finance Committee, 18 Nov. 2004, http://finance.senate.gov/hearings/testimony/2004test/111804dgtest.pdf.
8. Philip B. Fontanarosa et al., "Postmarketing Surveillance—Lack of Vigilance, Lack of Trust," *JAMA*, 1 Dec. 2004; D. Cauchon, "FDA Advisers Tied to Industry," *USA Today*, 26 Sept. 2000.
9. http://www.cdc.gov/epo/mmwr/preview/mmwrhtml/mm4910a1.htm.
10. The USDA improved its testing of cattle for mad dow disease during 2005.
11. Among the sources: "Aspartame History," National Institute on Science, Law and Public Policy. See http://www.swankin-turner.com/hist.html.
12. One interesting account of the aspartame controversy: "Aspartame: History of Fraud and Deception," by Dr. Joseph Mercola, can be found at http://www.mercola.com/article/aspartame/fraud.htm.
13. Thomas Maeder, "The FDA Meets the 21st Century," www.understandinggovt.org.
14. See Consumer Reports, "The Truth about Irradiated Meat," for an overview of the issue: http://www.consumerreports.org/main/detailv2.jsp?CONTENT%3C%3 Ecnt_id=322725&FOLDER%3C%3Efolder_id=162689.

Chapter 8. Pfizer

1. From IMS Health.
2. IMS National Sales Report, Feb. 2005.
3. Center for Public Integrity, LobbyWatch.
4. Center for Response Politics, www.opensecrets.org.
5. Mark Thomas, "Drug Donations: Corporate Charity or Taxpayer Subsidy?" *War on Want*, 2001.
6. Ibid.
7. Corporate Watch UK.

Chapter 9. Monsanto

1. In 1999, Monsanto merged with drug giant Pharmacia. The pharmaceutical kept Monsanto's drug department—Searle—and tossed Monsanto back in 2000. Monsanto is now an entirely independent company.
2. As of 2004. Monsanto.com.
3. William Hallman et al., "Public Perception of Genetically Modified Food," Rutgers Food Policy Institute, Oct. 2003., http://www.foodpolicyinstitute.org/docs/reports/NationalStudy2003.pdf.
4. The biotech manufacturer must provide studies if the gene is derived from a

known allergen, such as a Brazil nut, or a known toxin. No outside testing is required, and the FDA does not conduct its own tests.

5. Jim Nicholson, "Biotech Food for the Hungry," *International Herald Tribune*, Oct. 2–3, 2004.

6. Susan E. Harkison et al., "Circulating Concentrations of Insulin-like Growth Factor 1 and Risk of Breast Cancer," *Lancet* 351:9113, 9 May 1998; June M. Chan et al., "Plasma Insulin-like Growth Factor 1 and Prostate Cancer Risk: A Prospective Study," *Science* 279:5350, 23 Jan. 1998.

7. Michael Taylor also denies that he was involved in the Posilac decisions.

8. "Corn Growers Submit Recommendations to USDA Advisory Committee on Agricultural Biotechnology," CorpWatch, 8 May 2000, www.corpwatch.com.

9. Dan Baum, "Feeding Our Deepest Fears," *Playboy*, June 2004.

10. Dr. Charles Benbrook, "Evidence of the Magnitude and Consequences of the Roundup Ready Soybean Yield Drag from University-Based Varietal Trials in 1998," Benbrook Consulting Services, 13 Jul. 1999.

11. "Harvest of Fear," *Frontline*, PBS, 23 Apr. 1999, www.pbs.org/wgbh/harvest/interviews/grant.html.

12. To view an online video about Percy Schmeiser, "Heartbreak in the Homeland," see http://www.mindfully.org/GE/GE4/Heartbreak-In-The-Heartland21jul02.htm.

13. *Farm Journal*, 1996.

14. "Cargill," Datamonitor, 2004.

15. "Cargill to Process Monsanto's VISTIVE Low Linolenic Soybeans," 4 Oct. 2004, Monsanto.com.

III. SHADOWY STUFF

Chapter 10. Briefing: Spooks, Sneaks, and Snitches

1. Ryan Singel, "Data Scant for Watch List Usage," *Wired*, 17 May 2004, http://www.wired.com/news/privacy/0,1848,63478,00.html.

2. Kim Zetter, "No Real Debate for Real ID," *Wired*, 10 May 2005, http://wired.com/news/privacy/0,1848,67471,00.html.

3. Simon Cooper, "Who's Spying on You?" *Popular Mechanics*, Jan. 2005.

4. See "More Cities Deploy Camera Survelllance with Federal Grant Money," Electronic Privacy Information Center, May 2005, http://www.epic.org/privacy/surveillance/spotlight/0505.html.

5. Robert Jacques, "Spam Emails Hide Key Logger Virus," vnunet.com, 3 July 2003.

6. See Congressional Testimony, Donald H. Kerr, Asst. Director, Laboratory Division, FBI, 6 Sept. 2000, http://www.fbi.gov/congress/congress00/kerr090600.htm.

7. Clay Wilson, "Computer Attacks and Cyberterrorism: Vulnerabilities and Policy Issues for Congress," Congress Research Service, 17 Oct. 2003, http://www.fas.org/irp/crs/RL32114.pdf.

8. Paul Roberts, "Your PC May Be Less Secure Than You Think," IDG, 25 Oct. 2004, http://www.pcworld.com/news/article/0,aid,118311,00.asp.

9. Michael Shnayerson, "The Net's Master Data-Miner," *Vanity Fair*, 31 Jan. 2005, http://www.vanityfair.com/commentary/content/printables/050131roco01?print=true.

10. Ibid.

11. June 2005 interview with author.

12. See Bob Sullivan, "ChoicePoint Files Found Riddled with Errors," MSNBC, 8 Mar. 2005, http://www.msnbc.msn.com/id/7118767/. Also see the links there.

13. Testimony of Don McGuffey before the House Committee on Financial Services, 4 May 2005, http://www.choicepoint.com/privacyatchoicepoint/statement_dmc050405.html.

14. Greg Palast, *The Best Democracy Money Can Buy* (New York: Plume, 2003). Also see www.gregpalast.com and "Jim Crow in Cyberspace" (excerpts from Palast book), http://www.thirdworldtraveler.com/Palast_Greg/JimCrow_Cyberspace_TBDMCB.html.

15. Data-mining company ChoicePoint acquired DBT, the company hired by the state of Florida for the voter purge. A 2004 ChoicePoint press release asserts that a) DBT told the state of Florida that due to wide parameters the lists would include voters that were in fact eligible, and the state of Florida told DBT not to worry about it and b) that the figure of 50,000 used by Palast is high; however, ChoicePoint does not know the correct number, saying that the state of Florida has that figure. See http://www.choicepoint.net/news/2000election.html.

16. After a lawsuit was filed against Florida by the NAACP, ChoicePoint donated $75,000 to the organization.

17. Michael Shnayerson, "The Net's Master Data-Miner," *Vanity Fair*, 31 Jan. 2005.

18. Bob Sullivan, "Data Theft Affects 145,000," MSNBC 18 Feb. 2005, http://www.msnbc.msn.com/id/6979897/.

19. ChoicePoint press release, "Response to 5/3 Article in *Wall Street Journal*," 5 Apr. 2004, http://www.choicepoint.net/news/statement_050405_1.html.

Chapter 11. Post-9/11 World

1. Dan Eggen and Julie Tate, "U.S. Campaign Produces Few Convictions," *Washington Post*, 12 June 2005.

2. According to documents from FBI retrieved by ACLU under Freedom of Information Act. See http://aclu.org/torturefoia/released/FBI.121504.4940_4941.pdf.

3. Scott Shane, "The Costs of Outsourcing Interrogation," 29 May 2005.

4. Stephen Brill, *After: How America Confronted the September 12 Era* (New York: Simon and Schuster, 2003). See "Now with Bill Moyers," 18 Apr. 2003 http://www.pbs.org/now/transcript/transcript_brill.html.

5. Ibid.

6. John Ashcroft, "Welcoming Big Brother," *Washington Times*, Aug. 12, 1997, as pointed out by Jon B. Gould, "Playing with Fire: The Civil Liberties Implications of September 11th," *Public Administration Review*, Sept. 2002.

7. Stephen Brill, *After: How America Confronted the September 12 Era*.

8. Dick Meyer, "Minister of Fear," CBS News, *Against the Grain*, 12 June 2002.

9. Michael Duffy, "Could It Happen Again?" *Time*, 4 Aug. 2003. Patrick Thibudeau, "FBI Expects Two-Year Wait to Replace Old Computers," *Computerworld*, July 2002.

10. Fairness and Accuracy in Reporting, www.fair.org.

11. The U.S. government disavowed knowledge of torture or giving authority to do so. See Mike Allen and Susan Schmidt, "Memo on Interrogation Tactics Is Disavowed," *Washington Post*, 23 June 2004, http://www.washingtonpost.com/wp-dyn/articles/A60719-2004Jun22.html.

12. FBI memo released to ACLU under Freedom of Information Act. It should be noted that it appears that those who committed the torture were typically not FBI agents. http://www.aclu.org/torturefoia/released/FBI.121504.5053.pdf.

13. According to documents from FBI retrieved by ACLU under Freedom of Information Act; see http://aclu.org/torturefoia/released/FBI.121504.4940_4941.pdf.

14. "Memorandum for Alberto R. Gonzales, Counsel to the President, Re: Standards of Conduct for Interrogation under 18 U.S.C. 2340-2340A," memo from the U.S. Department of Justice, Office of Legal Counsel, Office of the Assistant Attorney General, 1 Aug. 2002.

15. Dana Priest and R. Jeffrey Smith, "Memo Offered Justification for Use of Torture," *Washington Post*, 8 June 2004. Also see http://www.derechos.org/nizkor/us/doc/doj.pdf.

16. Rummy's inability to find the time to look at the reports on numerous occasions has been documented by writer Nick Turse. See "Rummy Dropped from the Loop," 22 Feb. 2005, TomDispatch and Commondreams, http://www.commondreams.org/views05/0222-23.htm; and "Rummy Rules: Rummy Watch II," 3 June 2005, TomDispatch and Commondreams, http://www.commondreams.org/views05/0222-23.htm.

17. Kate Zernike, "Newly Released Reports Show Early Concern on Prison Abuse," *New York Times*, 6 Jan. 2005.

18. Michael Hirsh and John Barry, "The Abu Ghraib Scandal Cover-up," *Newsweek*, 7 June 2005.

19. "CIA Flying Suspects to Torture?" *60 Minutes*, CBS, 6 Mar. 2005, www.cbsnews.com/stories/2005/03/04/60minutes/main678155.shtml.

20. One of the documents released to ACLU. This is an e-mail from an FBI employee. http://aclu.org/torturefoia/released/FBI.121504.4940_4941.pdf.

21. See ACLU for all the documents: http://action.aclu.org/site/PageServer?pagename=torturefoia.

22. Terence Hunt, "Bush Calls Human Rights Report Absurd," Associated Press, 31 May 2005.

23. "American Gulag," editorial, *Washington Post*, 22 May 2005.

Chapter 12. Foreign Intelligence

1. Dana Priest, "Jet Is Open Secret in Terror War," *Washington Post*, 27 Dec. 2004. See http://www.washingtonpost.com/ac2/wp-dyn/A27826-2004Dec26?language=printer.
2. Michael E. Sulla, "An Investigation into the CIA's 'Black Budget,'" Center for Global Peace/School of International Services at American University, 30 Jan. 2004, http://www.scoop.co.nz/stories/HL0401/S00151.htm.
3. Mark Zepezauer, *The CIA's Greatest Hits* (Tucson: Odonian Press, 2003).
4. Reuel Marc Gerecht, "The Counterterrorist Myth," *Atlantic*, July/Aug. 2001.
5. So says former Bush counterterrorism advisor Richard Clarke.
6. See Report at http://www.wmd.gov/report/wmd_report.pdf.
7. "'We Don't Do Torture,' says CIA Director," *AP*, 17 Mar. 2005, as reported on Msnbc.com.
8. John Diamond, "Intelligence Changes Thwarted by Confusion," *USA Today*, 7 June 2005.
9. John Suggs, "The Spies Who Came in from the Art Sale," *Creative Loafing*, 20 Mar. 2002, http://atlanta.creativeloafing.com/2002-03-20/fishwrapper.html.
10. "Allies and Espionage," *Jane's Intelligence Digest*, 13 Mar. 2002.
11. John Suggs, "The Spies Who Came in from the Art Sale," *Creative Loafing*, 20 Mar. 2002, http:atlanta.creativeloafing.com/2002-03-20/fishwrapper.html.
12. Yossi Melman, "New Evidence of Mossad Involvement in Belgian Murder Case," *Ha'aretz*, 1 May 2003.
13. Tim McGirk, "India v. Pakistan," *Time Asia*, 29 Apr. 2002.
14. Stephen Marshall and Anthony Lappé, *True Lies* (New York: Plume, 2004), p. 72.
15. Sarah Chayes, "With a Little Help from Our Friends," *New York Times*, 26 May 2005.
16. James Bamford, *Body of Secrets* (London: Arrow Books, 2002), pp. 427–28.
17. James Woolsey, "Why We Spy on Our Allies," *Wall Street Journal*, 17 Mar. 2000.

IV. CONSUMERISM

Chapter 13. Wal-Mart

1. According to Anthony Bianco, "Is Wal-Mart Too Powerful?" *Business Week*, 28 Sept. 2003.
2. According to Wal-Mart lawyer Thomas Mars, Wal-Mart was hit with 6,000 legal cases in 2002. This figure is for average business day. Thomas Mars, "Wal-Mart Legal Department Diversity," American Bar Association, Goal IX News, Fall 2004, http://www.abanet.org/minorities/publications/g9/v10n4/mars.html.
3. According to Burt Flickinger of Strategic Resource Group, as quoted by Abigail Goldman and Nancy Cleeland, "An Empire Built on Bargains Remakes the Working World," *Los Angeles Times*, 23 Nov. 2003.
4. "Wal Around the World," *Economist*, 6 Dec. 2001.
5. David Faber, "With a Small-Town Culture, Wal-Mart Dominates," MSN Money/CNBC TV, 10 Nov. 2004.

6. This and the following figures are from Jerry Useem, "One Nation Under Wal-Mart," *Fortune*, 18 Feb. 2003.

7. See National Trust press release: http://www.nationaltrust.org/news/docs/20040524_11most_vermont.html.

8. Rep. George Miller, "Everyday Low Wages: The Hidden Price We All Pay for Wal-Mart," 16 Feb. 2004; see http://edworkforce.house.gov/democrats/WALMARTREPORT.pdf. Rep. Miller's information is drawn from Steven Greenhouse, "Workers Assail Lock-Ins by Wal-Mart," *New York Times* 1 (18 Jan. 2004).

9. Based on Wal-Mart's stated wage of $9.68 and its definition of full-time employment as thirty-two hours.

10. "Toys of Misery," National Labor Committee, Jan. 2002.

11. Sam Walton, *Made in America: My Story* (New York: Bantam, 2003).

12. "Unionizing Behind the Wal," KOMU TV, http://www.komu.com/html/htmlfall2004/Behindthewal7.htm.

13. Rep. George Miller, "Everyday Low Wages: The Hidden Price We All Pay for Wal-Mart," 16 Feb. 2004; see http://edworkforce.house.gov/democrats/WALMARTREPORT.pdf.

14. "Is Wal-Mart Good for America?" *Frontline*, PBS, 16 Nov. 2004. See show and transcripts, www.pbs.org/wgbh/pages/frontline/shows/walmart.

15. Center for Responsive Politics, Opensecrets.org.

16. John F. Harris and William Branigan, "Bush Signs Class-Action Changes into Law," *Washington Post*, 18 Feb. 2005.

17. Andy Server, "The Waltons: Inside America's Richest Family," *Fortune*, 15 Nov. 2004.

Chapter 14. Credit Card Companies

1. According to U.S. Public Interest Research Group.

2. Tamara Draut and Javier Silva, "Borrowing to Make Ends Meet," Dēmos, 8 Sept. 2003. See http://www.demos-usa.org/pub1.cfm.

3. According to American Bankruptcy Institute. See Lewis Schiff, "Staying Out of Bankruptcy Court," *CNN/Money*, 2 Feb. 2005. http://www.cnn.com/2005/02/02/pf/armchair/bankruptcy.

4. "Secret History of the Credit Card," *Frontline*, PBS, www.pbs.org/wgbh/pages/frontline/shows/credit.

5. See http://www.occ.treas.gov/ftp/release/2000-49d.txt.

6. Tamara Draut and Javier Silva, "Borrowing to Make Ends Meet," Dēmos, 8 Sept. 2003. See http://www.demos-usa.org/pub1.cfm.

7. Teresa A. Sullivan, Deborah Thorne, and Elizabeth Warren, "Young, Old, and In Between: Who Files for Bankruptcy?" *Norton Bankruptcy Law Advisor*, Issue No. 9A, Sept. 2001.

8. March 2004 addendum to "The Buying of the President." See http://www.publicintegrity.org/bop2004/report.aspx?aid=220&sid=200.

9. According to Harvard professor Elizabeth Warren in a 2004 interview in "Secret History of the Credit Card," *Frontline*, PBS, www.pbs.org/wgbh/pages/frontline/shows/credit/interviews/warren.htm.

10. "Secret History of the Credit Card," *Frontline*, PBS, 23 Nov. 2004, www.pbs.org/wgbh/frontline/shows/credit/interviews/dodd.htm.

11. Ibid.

V. PERSUADERS

Chapter 15. Public Relations Companies

1. So says a report by the House Government Reform Committee looking at the Bush administration's first four years.

2. For more information on video news releases see www.sourcewatch.org/index.php?title=video_news_releases.

3. "Department of Health and Human Services, centers for Medicare & Medicaid Service—Video News Releases, B-302710," GAO, 19 May 2004. See www.gao.gov/decisions/appro/302710.htm.

4. Robert Pear, "Dems Attack Videos Promoting Medicare Law," *New York Times*, 15 Mar. 2004.

5. Office of National Drug Control Policy—Video News Release, B-303495, Government Accountability Office, 4 Jan. 2005, http:www.gao.gov/decisions/appro/303495.pdf.

6. John R. MacArthur, *Second Front: Censorship and Propaganda in the Gulf War* (Berkeley: University of California Press, 1992). As noted on PR Watch's Web site, www.prwatch.org.

7. The information in this piece is drawn from various sources, including John R. MacArthur, "Remember Nayirah, Witness for Kuwait," *Seattle Post-Intelligencer*, 12 Jan. 1992; and John Stauber and Sheldon Rampton, *Toxic Sludge Is Good for You* (London: Robinson, 2004). See http://www.prwatch.org/books/tsigfy10.html.

8. Jeff Stein, "When Things Turn Weird, the Weird Turn Pro," TomPaine.com, 26 Feb. 2002. www.tompaine.com/feature.cfm/ID/5188.

9. James Dao and Eric Schmitt, "Pentagon Readies Efforts to Sway Sentiments Abroad," *New York Times*, 19 Feb. 2002. See www.commondreams.org/headlines02/0219-01.htm.

10. Amy Goodman, *The Exception to the Rulers* (New York: Hyperion, 2004).

11. "Misperceptions, the Media and the Iraq War," Program of International Policy Attitudes/Knowledge Network, 2 Oct. 2003.

12. Gary Younge, "Don't Mention the Dead," *Guardian*, 7 Nov. 2003.

13. As reported by *Los Angeles Times*, 9 Apr. 2003.

14. See photos at www.informationclearinghouse.info/article2842.htm.

15. Sheldon Rampton and John Stauber, "How to Sell a War," *In These Times*, 4 Aug. 2003. www.inthesetimes.com/comments.php?=299_0_1_0_C.

16. "ACLU Sharply Criticizes White House Propaganda Scheme," ACLU Press Release, 14 Jan. 2000, www.aclu.org.
17. See www.sourcewatch.org/index.php?title=Front_groups.
18. Sen. John Kerry and Sen. Hank Brown, "The BCCI Affair: A Report to the Committee on Foreign Relations," U.S. Senate, Dec. 1992. Information in this section also provided by Corporation Watch.
19. John Carlisle, "Public Relationships: Hill & Knowlton, Robert Gray and the CIA," *Covert Action Quarterly*, Spring 1993.

Chapter 16. Rupert Murdoch

1. "Forbes 400," *Forbes,* 2004.
2. Jeff Chester, "A Present for Murdoch," *Nation,* 22 Dec. 2003.
3. News Corp's list of subsidiaries filed with SEC can be seen at www.sec.gov/Archives/edgar/data/788509/000095013002008792/dex998.htm.
4. Steven Kull, Clay Ramsey and Evan Lewis, "Misperceptions, the Media and the Iraq War," the PIPA/Knowledge Networks Poll, 2 Oct. 2003. www.pipa.org.
5. Edward A. Gargar, "Get Ready for Mao's Heirs," *New York Times Hong Kong*, 19 Mar. 2003.
6. "Who's Afraid of Rupert Murdoch?" *Frontline*, PBS, 7 Nov. 1995.
7. Diana B. Henriques, "How the Emperor Got His Clothes," *Columbia Journalism Review*, Nov./Dec. 2002.
8. Russ Baker, "Murdoch's Mean Machine," *Columbia Journalism Review*, May/June 1998.

Chapter 17. Think Tanks

1. People for the American Way, www.pfaw.org.
2. Ibid.
3. 2004 Annual Report, Cato Institute.
4. See "The Heritage Foundation" file at Media Transparency's Web site for more information. http://www.mediatransparency.org/recipientprofile.php?recipientID=153.
5. See Group Watch, "The Heritage Foundation," for a startling overview of this group's effects: http://rightweb.irc-online.org/groupwatch/hf.php.
6. Robert G. Kaiser and Ira Chinoy, "Scaife: Funding Father of the Right," *Washington Post*, 2 May 1999.
7. Gregory Conko and Henry I. Miller, "Misnamed Activists Are Thorns in Rose of Agbiotech Foods," *Investors Business Daily*, 3 Mar. 2004.
8. SourceWatch, "Competitive Enterprise Institute," www.sourcewatch.org.
9. People for the American Way, "Buying a Movement," pfaw.org/pfaw/dfiles/file_33pdf.

Chapter 18. Council on Foreign Relations

1. Peter Grosse, "Council on Foreign Relations: History/Mission—'War and Peace'" CFR Web site, cfr.org/about/grosse04/php.

2. Peter Grosse, "'X' Leads the Way," CFR Mission/History, www.cfr.org/about/grosse06.php.

3. "George Kennan," *NewsHour with Jim Lehrer*, PBS, 18 Apr. 1996, http://www.pbs.org/newshour/gergen/kennan.html. Reprinted with permission from MacNeil-Lehrer Productions.

Chapter 19. George Soros

1. Listen to the interview with George Soros at http://www.npr.org/templates/story/story.php?storyId=4635465.

2. Judith Miller, "With Big Money and Brash Ideas, A Billionaire Redefines Charity," *New York Times*, 17 Dec. 1996.

3. Laura Blumenthal, "Soros' Deep Pockets v. Bush," *Washington Post*, 11 Nov. 2003.

4. "Soros Calls for Regime Change in US," BBC News, 30 Sept. 2003.

5. As reported by Steve Inskeep, *Morning Edition*, NPR, 9 May 2005, http://www.npr.org/templates/story/story.php?storyId=4635465.

Chapter 20. Rev. Sun Myung Moon

1. Jason Howell, "Public Faith in NGOs Remains Strong Despite Scandals," *Korea Times*, 12 Apr. 2005.

2. This list draws on Don Lattin, "Moonies Knee-Deep in Faith-Based Funds," *San Francisco Chronicle*, 3 Oct. 2004.

3. Kevin Phillips, *American Dynasty*, p. 234 (New York: Viking, 2004).

4. John Gorenfeld, "Hail to the Moon King," *Salon*, 21 June 2004.

5. "US Presidents Endorse Sun Myung Moon from 'Spirit World,'" *Church and State*, 1 Oct. 2003.

6. Felicity Barringer, "Decisions Differ on Religious Ad," *New York Times*, 22 July 2002.

7. Ibid.

8. "US Presidents Endorse Sun Myung Moon from 'Spirit World,'" *Church and State*, 1 Oct. 2003.

9. Maureen Farrell gives an interesting overview of the weaving together of several religious elements in "On a Mission from God," BuzzFlash, 9 Mar. 2004, http://www.buzzflash.com/farrell/04/03/far04007.html.

10. Former Moonie Steven Hassen, now a counselor specializing in mind control, has insights as well. See "Moonies Use *Washington Times* as Front Group to Gain Power and Legitimacy," http://www.freedomofmind.com/resourcecenter/groups/m/moonies/wash_times_20.htm.

11. Carolyn Weaver, "Unholy Alliance," *Mother Jones*, Jan. 1986.

12. As quoted in the *St. Petersburg Times* (of Russia) 16 Feb. 2001, http://www.times.spb.ru/archive/times/645/opinion/o_2201.htm.

13. "The Resurrection of Reverend Moon," *Frontline*, PBS, 21 Jan. 1992.

14. Bruce Cumings, "Korean Scandal or American Scandal?" JPRI Working Paper 20, Japan Policy Research Institute, May 1996.

15. Investigation of Korean-American Relations, report of the Subcommittee in International Relations, U.S. House of Representatives, 31 Oct. 1978.
16. Eric Alterman, "In Moon's Orbit: The Messiah with Money," *New Republic*, 27 Oct. 1986.
17. Philip Taubman, "A Departure Leaves Few Regrets at the CIA," *New York Times*, 19 July 1981.
18. Robert Parry, "Rev. Moon, the Bushes and Donald Rumsfeld," *Consortium News*, 3 Jan. 2003. Also see David E. Kaplan and Alec Dubro, *Yakuza* (Berkeley: University of California Press, 2003).
19. Nansook Hung, Moon's former daughter-in-law, wrote of Moon's escapades in *In the Shadows of the Moons*.
20. Robert Parry, "Rev. Moon, the Bushes and Donald Rumsfeld," *Consortium News*, 3 Jan. 2003.

Chapter 21. Media Matters

1. This and the following figures are from "Public More Critical of Press, but Goodwill Persists," Pew Research Center for the People and the Press, 26 June 2005. Figures add up to over 100 percent because respondents could mention two sources.
2. Interview with author, May 2005.
3. Helen Thomas, "No Wonder Bush Doesn't Connect with the Rest of the Country," Hearst Newspapers, 15 Oct. 2003, http://seattlepi.nwsource.com/opinion/143851_thomas15.html.
4. Interview with author, May 2005.
5. "You Can't Say the President Is Lying," *Extra*, Jan./Feb. 2005, Fair.org, http://www.fair.org/index.php?page=2481.
6. Amy Goodman, *The Exception to the Rulers* (New York: Hyperion, 2004).
7. Rory O'Conner, "The Military Channel," Mediachannel.org, 3 Dec. 2004.
8. Daniel Okrent, "Weapons of Mass Destruction? Or Mass Distraction?" *New York Times*, 30 May 2004.
9. Howard Kurtz, "The Post on WMDs: An Inside Story," *Washington Post*, 12 Aug. 2004.
10. Ibid.
11. Interview with author, June 2005.
12. Thomas Curley, "Letter to USA Today," 29 July 1998, Public Citizen, www.citizen.org.
13. Peter Hart and Julie Hollar, "Extra! Fear & Favor 2003: The Fourth Annual Report," Fair.org.
14. According to media analyst Paul Waldham at Mediamatters.org.
15. Jack Shafer, "Glass Houses," *Slate*, 15 May 1998.
16. "Phil Donahue: We Have an Emergency in the Media and We Have to Fix It," *Democracy Now with Amy Goodman*, 24 Mar. 2004.
17. "Misperceptions, the Media and the Iraq War," PIPA/Knowledge Networks Poll, Oct. 2003.

18. Ibid.

19. Ibid.

20. "Study of Bias or Biased Studies?" FAIR press release, 14 May 1992. Also see "*Wash. Post*, Fox Cite Flawed CMPA Study," *Media Matters Action Network*, 19 May 2005.

21. Charles Lewis, "The Culture of Secrecy," Center for Public Integrity, 3 Feb. 2005.

22. "For Third Year in a Row Oprah Retains Her Position as America's Favorite TV Personality," Harris Poll, 29 Dec. 2004.

23. Sheldon Rampton and John Stauber, "One Hundred Percent All Beef Baloney . . . ," Prwatch.org.

24. So calculates Brigham Young University economist Richard Butler.

VI. WAR MACHINE

Chapter 22. Briefing: Defense Maneuverings

1. William D. Hartung, *How Much Are You Making on the War, Daddy?* (New York: Nation Books, 2003).

2. For more about the classified nuclear posture review, see "Excerpts from Nuclear Posture Review Report," 8 Jan 2002, posted at Global Security, http://www.globalsecurity.org/wmd/library/policy/dod/npr.htm. Also see Carnegie Endowment for International Peace, Nuclear Posture Review resource page: http://www.ceip.org/files/projects/npp/resources/nuclearposturereview.htm.

3. The Committee on the Present Danger and Project for a New American Century, both of which have members who own stock and/or work for and/or do business with the defense industry, are among the scaremongers who benefit financially when the Defense buying department agrees with their reports and suggestions.

4. André Verlöy, Daniel Politi, and Aron Pilhofer, "Advisors of Influence: Nine Members of Defense Policy Board Have Ties to Defense Contractors," Center for Public Integrity, 28 Mar. 2003, http://www.publicintegrity.org/report. aspx?aid=91&sid=200.

5. White House, DoD budget summary, www.whitehouse.gov/omb/budget/fy2006/ pdf/budget/defense/pdf.

6. Proposed Defense Dept. budget for FY 2006 can be viewed at http://www. whitehouse.gov/omb/budget/fy2006/pdf/budget/defense.pdf. The entire proposed budget can be seen at http://www.whitehouse.gov/omb/budget/fy2006/ budget.html.

7. As pointed out by Robert Higgs of the Independent Institute, http://www. independent.org/newsroom/article.asp?id=1253. Robert Higgs, "The Defense Budget Is Bigger than You Think," *San Francisco Chronicle*, 18 Jan. 2004.

8. Noah Shachtman, "More Robot Grunts Ready for Duty," *Wired*, 1 Dec. 2004.

9. Ibid.

10. Air Force Space Command Fact Sheet, http://www.af.mil/factsheets/ factsheet.asp?fsID=155.

11. Richard F. Grimmet, "Conventional Arms Transfers to Developing Nations 1996–2003," Congressional Research Service, Library of Congress, 26 Aug. 2004.

12. Wade Boese, "Pentagon Split on Missile Defense," *Arms Control Today*, Apr. 2005.

13. Ibid.

14. "LG-118 A Peacekeeper," Wikipedia, en.wikipedia.org.

15. Armscontrolcenter.org, http://www.armscontrolcenter.org/archives/000286.php.

16. For timeline, see Union of Concerned Scientists missile defense timeline, http://www.ucsusa.org/global_security/missile_defense/page.cfm?pageID=565.

17. Some information drawn from Sherry Jones, "Missile Wars," *Frontline*, PBS, 10 Oct. 2002, http://www.pbs.org/wgbh/pages/frontline/shows/missile/.

18. Richard Behar, "Rummy's North Korea Connection," *Fortune*, 30 Apr. 2003; Randeep Ramesh, "The Two Faces of Rumsfeld," *Guardian*, 9 May 2003.

19. Sherry Jones, writer and producer, "Missile Wars," *Frontline*, PBS, 10 Oct. 2002, http://www.pbs.org/wgbh/pages/frontline/shows/missile/.

20. Some information is drawn from Michael Cabbage, "Billions Spent on Untested Shield," *Orlando Sentinel*, 17 Oct. 2004.

21. Michael Cabbage, "Star Power Helps Tout Missile Defense," *Orlando Sentinel*, 19 Oct. 2004.

22. Rupert Cornwall, "The Real Star Wars," *Independent*, 30 May 2005.

Chapter 23. DARPA

1. Department of Defense Fiscal Year 2005 Budget Estimates, Vol. 1—Defense Advanced Research Projects Agency, Feb. 2004.

2. Dan Morgan, "Critics Decry Secret Pentagon Spending," *Washington Post*, 31 Aug. 2003.

Chapter 24. Lockheed Martin

1 "Federal Contractor Misconduct: Failures and the Suspension and Debarment System," Project on Government Oversight, 10 May 2002, http:www.pogo.org/p/contracts/co-020505-contractors.html#top43GovCon.

2. Richard Girard, "Lockheed Martin: The Weapons Manufacturer That Does It All," Polaris Institute, Oct. 2004.

3. "Outsourcing the Pentagon: Top Contractors by Dollars," Center for Public Integrity, 18 Nov. 2004, www.publicintegrity.org/pns/default.aspx (see Company Directory).

4. Tim Weiner, "Lockheed and the Future of Warfare," *New York Times*, 28 Nov. 2004.

5. Richard Girach, "Lockheed Martin: The Weapons Manufacturer That Does It All," Polaris Institute, Oct. 2004.

6. Lockheed Martin profile, CorpWatch, Corpwatch.org.

Chapter 25. Halliburton

1. Fortune 500, 2004.

2. Note: Halliburton tops military contractors; Lockheed Martin tops *all* government contractors.

3. To simplify matters, Halliburton's subsidiary Kellogg, Brown & Root is sometimes referred to by the parent company's name—Halliburton.

4. According to Representative Henry Waxman's Fact Sheet, "Halliburton's Iraq Contracts Now Worth Over $10 billion," 9 Dec. 2004.

5. "Military Operations: DoD's Extensive Use of Logistics Support Contract Requires Strengthened Oversight," GAO-04-854, Government Accountability Office, July 2004.

6. "Federal Deployment Center Forward Operations at the Kuwait Hilton," Coalition Provisional Authority Inspector General, 25 June 2004.

7. Charlie Cray, "The Halliburton Fix," *Multinational Monitor*, May/June 2004.

8. "Administration Withheld Halliburton Overcharges from International Auditors," U.S. House of Representatives Committee on Government Reform Minority Office, 3 Mar. 2003, www.democrats.reform.house.gov/story.asp?ID=812#. (Here you can see redacted document too.)

9. Peter Stone, "Halliburton Probes Take Their Toll," *National Journal*, 2 Oct. 2004.

10. Dan Briody, *The Halliburton Agenda* (New York: John Wiley & Sons, 2004).

11. Ibid.

12. Peter W. Singer, "Warriors for Hire in Iraq," *Salon*, 15 Apr. 2004.

13. Julian Borger and Martin Hodgson, "A Plane Is Shot Down and the US Proxy War on Drugs Unravels," *Guardian*, 2 June 2001.

14. Tucker Carlson, "Hired Guns," *Esquire*, Mar. 2004.

15. According to CACI, PMC employees are typically briefed by military about the Geneva Conventions. However, the U.S. Department of Justice says the Geneva Conventions don't apply in Guantánamo Bay or in case of al-Qaeda prisoners or other "enemy combatants."

16. Employees of Aviation Development Corporation apparently signaled the Peruvian air force that the missionaries' plane was suspicious, leading to the fatal shootdown. Source: Julian Borger and Martin Hodgson, "A Plane Is Shot Down and the US Proxy War on Drugs Unravels," *Guardian*, 2 June 2001.

17. Peter W. Singer, "Warriors for Hire in Iraq," *Salon*, 15 Apr. 2004. (Singer is a National Security Fellow at Brookings Institution.)

18. Dan Briody, *The Halliburton Agenda*.

19. Duncan Campbell, "Making a Killing," Center for Public Integrity, 30 Oct. 2002.

Chapter 26. The Carlyle Group

1. M. Asif Ismail, "Investing in War," Center for Public Integrity, 18 Nov. 2003

2. Dan Briody, *The Iron Triangle* (New York: John Wiley & Sons, 2003).

3. Melanie Warner, "The Big Guys Work for the Carlyle Group," *Fortune*, 11 Mar. 2002.

4. "Carlyle Group Establishes Mainland China Presence," Carlyle Group press release, 20 Apr. 2004.

5. Tim Shorrock, "US–Taiwan: The Guiding Hand of Frank Carlucci," *Asian Times*, 13 Mar. 2002.

6. Dan Briody, *Iron Triangle*.

7. Stephen Marshall and Anthony Lappé, *True Lies* (New York: Plume, 2004).
8. "Baker's Unearned Reputation," testimony of Rep. Barney Frank in House of Representatives, 24 July 1992.
9. Ibid.

Chapter 27. Bechtel

1. David R. Baker, "Bechtel Sees Record Revenue in 2004," *San Francisco Chronicle*, 29 Mar. 2004.
2. Steve Kretzmann and Daphne Wysham, "Crude Vision," Sustainable Energy and Economy Network/Institute of Policy Studies, 13 Aug. 2002.
3. According to the 2003 report "Bechtel: Profiting from Destruction," written by watchdogs Public Citizen, CorpWatch, and Global Exchange; www.citizen.org/cmep/.
4. All of the following claims are from Bechtel's site: "Bechtel Response to the Nation," www.bechtel.com/iraqthenationresponse.htm.
5. Clayton Hirst, "The World's at Bechtel's Beck and Call," *Independent Sunday*, 20 Apr. 2003.
6. Environmental Protection Agency.

VII. PRECIOUS LIQUIDS

Chapter 28. Briefing: Oil and Water

1. According to Gibson Consulting, http://www.gravmag.com/oil.html.
2. According to chemical engineering professor Michael J. Economides at the University of Houston.
3. Jeff Sanford, "Ship of Fuels," *Canadian Business*, 21 June 2004; Chris Hellman, "The Earl of Oil," *Forbes*, 5 July 2004.
4. According to International Maritime Bureau; reported acts are believed to be a small fraction of the actual piracy attacks.
5. John S. Burnett, "The Next 9/11 Could Be Here," *New York Times*, 22 Feb. 2005.
6. Environmental Protection Agency.

Chapter 29. The Oil Beast

1. From the International Energy Agency; estimates for 2005 shoot to 84 million barrels per day.
2. Approximations based on EIA Monthly Energy Review 2002.
3. Sources: U.S. Dept. of Energy, U.S. Energy Information Administration.
4. Source: U.S. Energy Information Administration.
5. "Environmental Change and Human Health," World Resources Institute, 1998–99.
6. Marianne Lavelle, "Hostage to Oil," *U.S. News and World Report*, 10 Jan. 2005.

Chapter 30. The al-Saud

1. *CIA World Factbook*, 2005.
2. "Country Analysis: Saudi Arabia," Energy Information Administration, U.S. Dept. of Energy, Jan. 2005.
3. Ibid.
4. This and the remaining figures in the list are from the *CIA World Factbook*, 2005.
5. In December 2004, the Saudi government announced it might have 200 million barrels more in proven reserves than previously estimated; if true, Saudi Arabia would hold nearly half of the world's proven reserves.
6. Some of the following information is drawn from "Saudi Arabia Backgrounder: Who Are the Islamists?" ICG Middle East Report, 21 Sept. 2004.
7. In 2002, Prince Nayef bin Sultan bin Fawwaz al-Shaalan was charged with using diplomatic immunity to smuggle two tons of coke into France on a Saudi royal plane.
8. Craig Unger, *House of Bush, House of Saud* (New York: Scribner, 2004).
9. Prince Turki is also known as Turki al-Faisal.
10. *Financial Times*, 7 Sept. 1988.
11. Tanya C. Hsu, "The United States Must Not Forget Saudi Arabian Invesments," *Saudi-American Forum*, 23 Sept. 2003.
12. Ibid.
13. "The Al-Qaeda Threat to Saudi Arabia's Oil Sector," Jerusalem Center for Public Affairs, 6 Jan. 2005.
14. Jean Sasson, *Princess: A True Story of Life Behind the Veil in Saudi Arabia* (Van Nuys: Windsor-Brooke, 2001).

Chapter 31. OPEC

1. U.S. Dept. of Energy estimates, 2005. See "OPEC," http://www.eia.doe.gov/emeu/cabs/opec.html.
2. "Oil & Gas: Production and Marketing," Standard & Poor's, 21 Oct. 2004.
3. Greg Palast, "Secret U.S. Plans for Iraq's Oil," 17 Mar. 2005, Commondreams.org.
4. Robert Parry, "Bush Sr.'s Iraq-Iran Secrets," Consortiumnews.com, 25 May 2004.
5. Siddharth Varadaraian, "Chávez Is India's Passport to L.A.," 4 Mar. 2005.

Chapter 32. Non-OPEC Oil Producers

1. Ipsos-Reid poll, May 3–5, 2002; see www.pollingreport.com/canada.htm.
2. "While 60% of Canadians Consider U.S.A. Canada's Closest Friend and Ally, Only 18% of Americans Name Canada as Same," Ipsos-Reed press release, 7 May 2002, www.ipsos-reid.com/media/dsp_pre_more_cdn.cfm.
3. Just ask a Canadian or a Brit (Britain fought on the Canadian side).
4. "Non-OPEC Fact Sheet: Top World Oil Producers and Top World Net Exporters 2004," Energy Information Administration, www.eia.doe.gov/emeu/cabs/topworldtables1_2.html.

5. "To Change Mexico, Fox Must First Change Pemex," *Alexander's Gas and Oil Connection*, 20 Feb. 2003, http://www.gasandoil.com/goc/company/cnl30873.htm.
6. Kevin Sullivan, "Past Catches Up with Mexico's Oil Monopoly," *Washington Post*, 18 Jan. 2005, http://www.washingtonpost.com/wp-dyn/articles/A16500-2005Jan17.html.
7. So predicts the U.S. Dept of Energy. "Mexico Country Profile," EIA. gov.

Chapter 33. Veolia and Suez

1. Suez is also an energy company. Total 2004 revenues for all of Suez totaled 40.7 billion (approximately $54 billion).
2. "Cholera and the Age of the Water Barons," Center for Public Integrity, 3 Feb. 2003.
3. Ibid.
4. Frank Koller, "No Silver Bullet," CBC News, 5 Feb. 2002, www.cbc.ca.
5. World Bank Web site.
6. Ibid.
7. IMF Web site.
8. Figures as of 2000. Source: Statement from NGO Debt Caucus, 15 Oct 2001, http://www.un.org/esa/ffd/1001ngo-debt_caucus.htm.
9. John Perkins, *Confessions of an Economic Hit Man* (San Francisco: Berrett-Koehler, 2004).
10. Ibid.
11. "The Water Barons: Promoting Privatization," Center for Public Integrity, Mar. 2003.
12. Catherine Caufield, "The World Bank," *Foreign Policy in Focus*, Sept. 2001, http://www.fpif.org/pdf/vol3/32ifwb.pdf.
13. According to John Perkins, *Confessions of an Economic Hit Man*.

VIII. ROGUES

Chapter 34. North Korea

1. According to the CIA World Factbook, 2005.
2. Ibid; dollars are calculated as purchasing power parity.
3. Randeep Armes, "The Two Faces of Rumsfeld," *Guardian,* 9 May 2003. Richard Behar, "Rummy's North Korea Connection," *Fortune*, 30 Apr. 2003, http://www.fortune.com/fortune/articles/0,15114,447429,00.html.

Chapter 35. Terrorists

1. The source of this listing is the U.S. Department of State, Office of Counterterrorism, Center for Defense Information, Terrorism Project.
2. This U.S. State Department estimate may be low.
3. See "Terrorist Attacks on Americans, 1979–1988," *Frontline*, PBS, http://www.pbs.org/wgbh/pages/frontline/shows/target/etc/cron.html.

4. "Full Text: bin Laden's 'Letter to America,'" *Observer*, 24 Nov. 2002.
5. Ibid.

Chapter 36. Organized Criminals

1. Donna Hughes, "The Natasha Trade: The Transnational Shadow Market in Women," *Journal of International Affairs*, spring 2000, http://www.uri.edu/artsci/wms/hughes/natasha_nij.pdf.
2. "Arresting Transational Crime," the U.S. State Department, Aug. 2001, http://www.iwar.org.uk/ecoespionage/resources/transnational-crime/ijge0801.htm.
3. According to an article by Lee Rensselaer in *Parameters* ("Nuclear Smuggling: Patterns and Responses," 22 Mar. 2003), the Parisian paper *al-Watan al-Arabi* reported in November 1998 that bin Laden had bought twenty nuclear warheads through Chechens; Rensselaer questions whether Chechens would even have been able to lay their hands on so many warheads.
4. Anthony Bruno, "Yakuza: Origins and Traditions," crimelibrary.com.
5. Gail Edmondson and Kate Carlisle, "Italy and the Eco-Mafia," *Business Week*, 27 Jan. 2003.
6. Francesca Colombo, "Mafia Dominates Garbage Industries," *Terramérica*, 21 Jun. 2003; Sophie Arie, "Italy's Mafia Banks on Trash," *Christian Science Monitor*, 5 Aug. 2004.
7. Sophie Arie, "Italy's Mafia Banks on Trash," *Christian Science Monitor*, 5 Aug. 2004.
8. Gail Edmondson and Kate Carlisle, "Italy and the Eco-Mafia," *Business Week*, 27 Jan. 2003. Also see report: "The Illegal Trafficking in Hazardous Waste in Italy and Spain," by Gruppo Abele-Nomos, Legambiente, GEPECC, Oct. 2003.
9. Author interview with John S. Burnett, author of *Dangerous Waters* (New York: Plume, 2003).
10. Based on interviews with Capt. Potengal Mukundan, International Maritime Bureau, and John S. Burnett, author of *Dangerous Waters*.
11. 2002 interview with author.
12. Velisarios Kattoulas, "The Death of Sushi?" *Far East Economic Review*, 15 Aug. 2002.
13. One of the original sources looking at the CIA's involvement in heroin in Vietnam: Alfred McCoy, *The Politics of Heroin in Southeast Asia* (New York: Harper and Row, 1972).

IX. WHAT'S NEXT

1. Marcia Walton, "Will Nanotechnology Save the World or Is It Mostly Hype?" 16 Apr. 2004, http://www.cnn.com/2004/TECH/science/04/15/nanotech.ideas/. Also see "The Little Big Down: A Small Introduction to Nano-Scale Technologies," ETC Group, June 2004, www.etcgroup.org/article.asp?newsid=471.

2. Matt Forney, "Tug of War Over Trade," *Time*, 22 Dec. 2003.
3. "China Rejects Rumsfeld Claims of Military Buildup as 'Totally Groundless,'" Agence France-Presse, 7 June 2005.
4. SIPRI, "The Major Spenders in 2003." These figures use the market exchange rate for 2003.
5. According to China it spent only $24 billion in 2004.
6. This and the following comments are collected in Constantine Mendes, *The Gathering Storm*, as quoted by Dave Eberhart, "Menges' Last Book Gives Dire China Warning," Newsmax, 24 May 2005, http://www.newsmax.com/archives/articles/2005/5/23/204304.shtml.

Bibliography

ONLINE MAGAZINES, NEWSPAPERS, AND INTERNET SITES

Air America Radio (www.airamericaradio.com)
AlterNet (alternet.org)
Americans United for Separation of Church and State (www.au.org)
BBC (news.bbc.co.uk)
Bulletin of the Atomic Scientists (www.thebulletin.org)
Business Week (www.businessweek.com)
BuzzFlash (buzzflash.com)
CNN (www.cnn.com)
Center for Defense Information (www.cdi.org)
Center for Public Integrity (www.publicintegrity.org)
Common Dreams (www.commondreams.org)
CorpWatch (www.corpwatch.org)
Corporate Watch (www.corporatewatch.org)
The Economist (www.economist.com)
Financial Times (news.ft.com)
Forbes (www.forbes.com)
Fortune (www.fortune.com)
The *Guardian* (www.guardian.co.uk)
Inter Press Service (www.ips.org)
The *Los Angeles Times* (www.latimes.com)
MSNBC (www.msnbc.msn.com)
The Nation (www.thenation.com)
National Public Radio (www.npr.org)
The New Republic (www.tnr.com)
Newsweek (newsweek.com)
The New Yorker (www.newyorker.com)
The New York Times (www.nytimes.com)
Open Society Institute (www.soros.org)

PBS (www.pbs.org)
PR Watch (www.prwatch.org)
Public Citizen (www.citizen.org)
Salon (salon.com)
Slate (slate.com)
SpinWatch (www.spinwatch.org)
TheocracyWatch (www.theocracywatch.org)
Time (www.time.com)
U.S. News and World Report (www.usnews.com)
The *Washington Post* (www.washpost.com)
SourceWatch (www.sourcewatch.org)
Union of Concerned Scientists (www.ucsusa.org)
Wikipedia (en.wikipedia.org)
World Resources Institute (www.wri.org)
Worldwatch Institute (www.worldwatch.org)

Alterman, Eric, and Mark Green. *The Book on Bush* (New York: Penguin, 2004)
Ambrose, Stephen, E., and Douglas G. Brinkley. *Rise to Globalism* (New York: Penguin, 1997)
Angell, Marcia. *The Truth About the Drug Companies* (New York: Random House, 2004)
Bacevich, Andrew J. *American Empire: The Realities and Consequences of U.S. Diplomacy* (Cambridge, MA: Harvard University Press, 2003)
Baer, Robert. *Sleeping with the Devil: How Washington Sold Our Soul for Saudi Crude* (New York: Three Rivers Press, 2003)
Bamford, James. *Body of Secrets* (New York: Arrow Books, 2002)
Barnett, Thomas P. M. *The Pentagon's New Map* (New York: G. P. Putnam, 2004)
Barsamian, David, and Noam Chomsky. *Propaganda and the Public Mind, 2001.* (London: Pluto Press, 2001)
Blum, William. *Rogue State* (Monroe, ME: Common Courage Press, 2000)
———. *Killing Hope* (New York: Black Rose Books, 1998)
Bodansky, Yossef. *Bin Laden, the Man Who Declared War on America* (New York: Prima, 1999)
Briody, Dan. *The Halliburton Agenda* (New York: John Wiley & Sons, 2004)
———. *The Iron Triangle* (New York: John Wiley & Sons, 2003)
Chenoweth, Neil. *Rupert Murdoch: The Untold Story of the World's Greatest Media Wizard* (New York: Crown Business, 2001)
Cohen, Jay S., M.D. *Overdose: The Case Against Drug Companies* (New York: Penguin, 2004)
Domhoff, G. William. *Who Rules America?* (Mountain View, CA: Mayfield, 1998)
Godson, Roy. *Dirty Tricks or Trump Cards: U.S. Covert Action and Counterintelligence* (New Brunswick, NJ: Transaction Publishers, 2001)
Goodman, Amy. *The Exception to the Rulers* (New York: Arrow, 2001)

Goozner, Merrill. *The $800 Million Pill: The Truth Behind the Cost of New Drugs* (Berkeley: University of California Press, 2004)

Hartung, William. *How Much Are You Spending on the War, Daddy?* (New York: Nation Books, 2003)

Helms, Harry. *Inside the Shadow Government: National Emergencies and the Cult of Secrecy* (Los Angeles: Feral House, 2003)

Herman, Edward S., and Noam Chomsky. *Manufacturing Consent: The Political Economy of the Mass Media* (New York: Vintage, 1994)

Hertz, Noreena. *The Silent Takeover* (London: Arrow, 2001)

Hightower, Jim. *Thieves in High Places* (New York: Penguin, 2003)

Jackson, Devon. *Conspiranoia!* (New York: Plume, 2000)

Jensen, Derrick, and George Draffan. *Welcome to the Machine* (White River Junction, VT: Chelsea Green Publishing, 2004)

Kean, Thomas H., and Lee H. Hamilton. *The 9/11 Report: The National Commission on Terrorist Attacks upon the United States* (New York: St. Martin's Press, 2004)

Klare, Michael. *Blood and Oil* (New York: Hamish Hamilton, 2004)

———. *Resource Wars* (New York: Henry Holt, 2002)

Klein, Naomi. *No Logo* (London: HarperCollins, 2000)

Landau, Saul. *The Pre-Emptive Empire: A Guide to Bush's Kingdom* (London: Pluto Press, 2003)

Lapham, Lewis. *Gag Rule* (New York: Penguin, 2004)

Laqueur, Walter. *The New Terrorism: Fanaticism and the Arms of Mass Destruction* (London: Phoenix Press, 2002)

Lessig, Lawrence. *Free Culture* (New York: Penguin, 2004)

Levy, Joel. *Secret History: Hidden Forces That Shaped the Past* (London: Vision Paperbacks, 2004)

Lewis, Tom. *Divided Highways* (New York: Penguin, 1999)

Mann, Michael. *Incoherent Empire* (London: Verso, 2003)

Marrs, Jim. *Rule by Secrecy* (New York: HarperCollins, 2000)

McDonald, Bernadette, and Douglas Jehl (editors). *Whose Water Is It?* (Washington, DC: National Geographic Society, 2003)

Micklethwait, John, and Adrian Wooldridge. *The Right Nation: Conservative Power in America* (London: Allen Lane, 2004)

Napoleoni, Loretta. *Terror Inc.* (London: Penguin, 2004)

Nestle, Marion. *Safe Food: Bacteria, Biotechnology and Bioterrorism* (Berkeley: University of California Press, 2003)

Palast, Greg. *The Best Democracy Money Can Buy* (New York: Plume, 2003)

Perkins, John. *Confessions of an Economic Hit Man* (San Francisco: Berrett-Koehler, 2004)

Phillips, Kevin. *American Dynasty* (New York: Viking, 2004)

Pilger, John. *The New Rulers of the World* (London: Verso, 2002)

———. *Hidden Agendas* (London: Vintage, 1999)

Rifkin, Jeremy. *The Hydrogen Economy* (New York: Jeremy P. Tarcher, 2003)

Robbins, Alessandra. *Secrets of the Tomb: Skull and Bones, the Ivy League, and the Hidden Paths of Power* (New York: Little, Brown, 2002)

Roy, Arundhati. *War Talk* (Cambridge, MA: South End Press, 2003)

———. *Power Politics* (Cambridge, MA: South End Press, 2001)

Schlosser, Eric. *Fast Food Nation* (New York: Penguin, 2002)

Shiva, Vandan. *Water Wars* (London: Pluto Press, 2002)

Snow, Nancy. *Information War, American Propaganda, Free Speech and Information Control Since 9-11* (New York: Seven Stories Press, 2003)

———. *Propaganda, Inc.* (New York: Seven Stories Press: 2003)

Soros, George. *The Bubble of American Supremacy* (New York: Public Affairs/Perseus Group, 2004)

Stauber, John, and Sheldon Rampton. *Toxic Sludge Is Good for You* (London: Constable and Robinson, 2000)

Suskind, Ron. *The Price of Loyalty* (New York: Simon & Schuster, 2004)

Tudge, Colin. *So Shall We Reap: What's Gone Wrong with the World's Food—and How to Fix It* (London: Allen Lane, 2003)

Unger, Craig. *House of Bush, House of Saud* (New York: Scribner, 2004)

Vidal, Gore. *Perpetual War for Perpetual Peace: How We Got to Be So Hated* (New York: Nation Books, 2002)

Zepezauer, Mark. *The CIA's Greatest Hits* (Tucson: Odonian Press, 2003)

Resources

While researching this book, I culled information from interviews as well as thousands of reports, articles, and books. I offer my utmost thanks to all the organizations, experts, reporters, and authors whose insights and hard work are reflected in this book. You can read many of these reports and articles at this book's affiliated site, www.runningtheworld.com.

INVALUABLE RESOURCES

Several sources influenced and provided needed info for nearly every section of this book. These invaluable resources include:

- *Frontline.* The weekly PBS documentary program hits the most compelling topics of the day—from Wal-Mart to the making of missile defense—and many programs can be viewed online. Even better, the *Frontline* site is packed with fabulous information, including transcripts of the full-length interviews with experts. (www.pbs.org/wgbh/pages/frontline/)

- *The NewsHour with Jim Lehrer.* Another PBS gem, the hour-long nightly news show looks at issues in depth, and also posts transcripts online. (www.pbs.org/newshour/)

- *The Economist.* Filled with flashy photos and witty captions, this British magazine is the international businessman's bible because it makes complex issues understandable. Editorials lean to the Right, but the information is vital. Some articles can be read free online. (www.economist.com)

- *The Guardian.* It may not be the most widely read daily in London, but the range of coverage, the reports from afar, and the clever writing style make this left-leaning paper Britain's best. (www.guardian.co.uk)

- Common Dreams. This online roundup service pulls together must-read articles from around the English-writing world that originally appeared in everything from the *Financial Times* to the *New York Times*, with lots of articles from the alternative media as well. (www.commondreams.org)

- Congressional Research Services Reports. Most citizens are unaware of the straightforward, nonpartisan reports published through the Library of Congress. Here's where congresspeople get the straight dope, and you can download many of the reports from the government sites for free. You may want to download quick—some congressmen want to keep reports closed from public access. (fpc.state.gov)

- The Center for Public Integrity. Investigative reporters share their findings at this site, with reports on topics from "outsourcing the war" to "water barons." Also features LobbyWatch, which tallies the amount individual companies spend on their lobbyists. (www.publicintegrity.org)

- Wikipedia. An "open source" Internet encyclopedia that anybody can edit, Wikipedia is not the definitive source—and some of the information is contested—but it's always a lively starting place. The links alone can entertain sufferers of attention deficit disorder for days. (en.wikipedia.org)

In addition to the sources above, here a few helpful resources by chapter—all of which were used in the writing of this book.

I. THE RIGHT

Chapter 1. Briefing: The Mighty Right

Media Stars: John Micklethwait and Adrian Wooldridge. Never mind that they're Brits, these *Economist* writers offer the most astute look at what the Right is doing, in their book *The Right Nation: Why America Is Different* (London: Allen Lane, 2004).

Web Sites:
- People for the American Way, a progressive group, offers extensive profiles of right-wing organizations (pfaw.org)
- Find information on groups and individuals at the Interhemispheric Resource Center (rightweb.irc-online.org/groupwatch)
- Discover the issues important to the Right and see how they organize, at the Focus on the Family site (www.family.org)

Chapter 2. The Christian Right

Media Star: Katherine Yurica. The investigative reporter offers up-to-date articles from numerous sources (www.yuricareport.com).
Web Sites:
- Dr. Bruce Prescott discusses religious issues and the blur between religion and state on his blog (mainstreambaptist.blogspot.com)
- Liberal Christians give their take in articles at www.publicchristian.com
- This looks like a conspiracy site, but it is actually affiliated with Cornell University and the links are fantastic (www.theocracywatch.org)
- An academic take on the rise of the Christian Right is offered at Political Research Associates (publiceye.org)
- Americans United for Separation of Church and State publishes *Church and State* magazine (www.au.org)

Chapter 3. The Bushes

Media Star: Kevin Phillips. The former Republican strategist takes a hard look at the Bush family in his fascinating book *American Dynasty* (New York: Viking, 2004).
Book: Alterman, Eric, and Mark Green, *The Book on Bush* (New York: Penguin, 2004)
Web Sites:
- See chapter 5 listing, below
- *Frontline*, "The Jesus Factor" (www.pbs.org/wgbh/pages/frontline/shows/jesus/president) for insight into George W. Bush Christian conversion
- Also see PBS, Religion and Ethics (www.pbs.org/wnet/religionandethics/)

Chapter 4. Bush Insiders

Media Stars: Anthony Lappé and Stephen Marshall of the Guerrilla News Network. They investigate some of the overlooked issues of the Bush era in their book *True Lies* (New York: Plume, 2004).
Book: Suskind, Ron. *The Price of Loyalty* (New York: Simon & Schuster, 2004) Former Treasury Secretary Paul O'Neill gives his take on the goofy bunch in this book.
Web Sites: See chapter 5 listing, below

Chapter 5. The Neocons

Media Star: Reporter Jim Lobe has been following the neocons since they were cutting their teeth in the Reagan administration. A collection of his articles can be found at antiwar.com/lobe/.

- Guerilla News Network (www.guerrillanews.com)
- A critical assessment of the Bush administration from *The Nation*, one of the foremost progressive magazines (www.thenation.com)
- Numerous articles from the alternative press at AlterNet (alternet.org)
- Access articles and information from the progressive radio network Air America Radio (www.airamericaradio.com)
- Also see: *Frontline*, "Rumsfeld's War" (www.pbs.org/wgbh/pages/frontline/shows/pentagon/)

II. FOOD AND DRUG

Chapter 6. Briefing: How Big Pharma Works

Media Star: Marcia Angell. The former editor in chief of the *New England Journal of Medicine*, Angell wrote *The Truth about the Drug Companies* (New York: Random House, 2004)—a book so upsetting to the corporate drug pushers that their lobby, PhRMA, devotes pages unconvincingly disputing it. A must-read if you want to understand the modern drug industry.

Chapter 7. FDA

Info Star: The FDA's History Office has put together a lovely and informative Web site (www.fda.gov/oc/history/default.htm) that documents the rise of the FDA in the twentieth century. This is the FDA we love and that we'd like to see return.

Chapter 8. Pfizer

Media Star: David Willman at the *Los Angeles Times* provides first-rate coverage of all pharmaceutical issues.
Web Sites:
- Public Citizen: Lots of reports condemning the drug industry (www.citizen.org); also see drug database at www.worstpills.org
- See *Frontline*, "Dangerous Prescriptions" (www.pbs.org/wgbh/pages/frontline/shows/prescription/)
- PhRMA: Get all the whitewash from Big Pharma's lobby at www.phrma.org
Books:
- Goozner, Merrill. *The $800 Million Pill* (Berkeley: University of California Press, 2004)
- Cohen, Jay S., M.D. *Overdose: The Case Against Drug Companies* (New York: Penguin, 2004)

Chapter 9. Monsanto

Media Star: Author Marion Nestle spills the beans on all issues of food in her book *Safe Food: Bacteria, Biotechnology and Bioterrorism* (Berkeley: University of California Press, 2003)

Web Sites:
- The Union of Concerned Scientists has put together numerous reports on this issue (www.usaucs.org)
- The Food Policy Institute: See how uninformed Americans are, in this 2004 report (www.foodpolicyinstitute.org/docs/reports/NationalStudy2004. pdf)
- For the European Union's take on the matter, see europa.eu.int/comm/ food/food/biotechnology/gmfood/index_en.htm
- The ETC Group: Great reports on issues from GM food to nanotechnology (etcgroup.org)
- *Frontline*, "Harvest of Fear" (www.pbs.org/wgbh/harvest/)

III. SHADOWY STUFF

Chapter 10. Briefing: Spooks, Sneaks, and Snitches
and Chapter 11. Post-9/11 World

Media Star: Wired. This magazine, about our high-tech world, consistently keeps an eye on privacy issues (www.wired.com)

Web Sites:
- Electronic Privacy Information Center: Keeps us attuned to the issues (www.epic.org)
- American Civil Liberties Union. Fighting for privacy rights (www.aclu.org)
- Don't Spy on Us: The most entertaining take on our diminishing privacy (www.dontspyonus.com)

Book: Jensen, Derrick, and George Draffan. *Welcome to the Machine* (White River Junction, VT: Chelsea Green Publishing, 2004)

Chapter 12. Foreign Intelligence

Media Star: Former intelligence agent William Blum uncovers CIA misdeeds in his books *Rogue State* (Monroe, ME: Common Courage Press, 2000) and *Killing Hope* (New York: Black Rose Books, 1998).

Books:
- Bamford, James. *Body of Secrets* (New York: Arrow Books, 2002)
- Godson, Roy. *Dirty Tricks or Trump Cards: U.S. Covert Action and Counterintelligence* (New Brunswick, NJ: Transaction Publishers, 2001)
- Zepezauer, Mark. *The CIA's Greatest Hits* (Tucson: Odonian Press, 2003)

IV. CONSUMERISM

Chapter 13. Wal-Mart

Media Stars: Los Angeles Times reporters Abigail Goldman and Nancy Cleeman garnered a Pulitzer for their multipart look at the retail giant. (See www.pulitzer.org/year/2004/national-reporting/works/).
Web Site: Frontline, "Is Wal-Mart Good for America?" (www.pbs.org/wgbh/pages/frontline/shows/walmart)

Chapter 14. Credit Card Companies

Media Star: Harvard Law Professor Elizabeth Warren. In books (*The Two-Income Trap: Why Middle-Class Mothers and Fathers Are Going Broke*), testimony, and meetings, she keeps hammering the system for hammering the consumer. (See www.pbs.org/wgbh/pages/frontline/shows/credit/interviews/warren.)
Web Sites:
- Demos.org has numerous reports on credit cards and bankruptcy. (See www.demos-usa.org/page38.cfm)
- Also see *Frontline*, "The Secret History of the Credit Card" (www.pbs.org/wgbh/pages/frontline/shows/credit)

V. PERSUADERS

Chapter 15. Public Relations Companies

Media Star: Center for Media and Democracy. It points out faux "front groups"—organizations that appear to represent the interests they are actually fighting against—and detail the misdeeds of assorted PR groups (www.sourcewatch.org). What's more, two writers from the center, John Stauber and Sheldon Rampton, expose numerous PR scams in articles and in their book *Toxic Sludge Is Good for You* (London: Constable and Robinson, 2000).
Book: Snow, Nancy. *Information War, American Propaganda, Free Speech and Information Control since 9-11* (New York: Seven Stories Press, 2003)

Chapter 16. Rupert Murdoch

Book: Neil Chenoweth. *Rupert Murdoch: The Untold Story of the World's Greatest Media Wizard* (New York: Crown Business, 2001)

Chapter 17. Think Tanks

Web Sites: What better way to understand what they are about than to visit the sites themselves? Don't miss the Heritage Foundation (www.heritage.org).

Chapter 18. Council on Foreign Relations

Info Star: The CFR itself. (www.cfr.org)

Chapter 19. George Soros

Web Site: Open Society Institute (www.soros.org)
Book: Soros, George. *The Bubble of American Supremacy* (New York: Public Affairs/Perseus Group, 2004)

Chapter 20. Rev. Sun Myung Moon

Media Star: John Gorenfeld covers the continuing rise of Moon for *Salon* (See www.salon.com/news/feature/2004/06/21/moon/index_np.html).
Web Site: The official Unification Church Web site (www.unification.net)

Chapter 21. Media Matters

Info Star: Fairness and Accuracy in Reporting (FAIR). This group points out all that's wrong with the media (www.fair.org).
Web Sites:
- The Project for Excellence in Journalism, affiliated with the Columbia Graduate School of Journalism, comprehensively reports on the state of the news media (www.stateofthenewsmedia.org/2005/index.asp)
- Media Matters: A progressive view on the news (www.mediamatters.org)
- Society of Professional Journalists (www.spj.org)
- AlterNet: Covers the media (alternet.org)

VI. WAR MACHINE

Chapter 22. Briefing: Defense Maneuverings

Media Star: William Hartung takes aim at the burgeoning war machine at the World Policy Institute's Arms Trade Resource Center (www.worldpolicy.org/projects/arms/reports.html) and in books, including *How Much Are You Spending on the War, Daddy?* (New York: Nation Books, 2003)
Web Sites:
- Center for Defense Information (www.cdi.org)
- Federation of Atomic Scientists (www.fas.org)
- Arms Control Association (www.armscontrol.org)
- World Policy Institute—Arms Trade Resource Center (www.worldpolicy.org/projects/arms/reports.html)
- Also see *Frontline*, "Missile Wars"(www.pbs.org/wgbh/pages/frontline/shows/missile/)

Chapter 23. DARPA

Web Sites:
- Wired News (www.wired.com)
- *Jane's Defence Weekly* (jdw.janes.com)

Chapter 25. Halliburton

Media Star: The Center for Public Integrity takes a close look at military outsourcing in general and Halliburton in specific (See www.publicintegrity.org/icij/).
Book: Briody, Dan. *The Halliburton Agenda* (New York: John Wiley & Sons, 2004)

Chapter 26. The Carlyle Group

Media Star: Dan Briody was one of the first to invest time uncovering what's going on at this investment firm. See his book *The Iron Triangle* (John Wiley & Sons, 2003).
Web Site: PR Watch (www.prwatch.org)

Chapter 27. Bechtel

Info Star: CorpWatch was part of a collaborative effort to report on Bechtel activities in "Bechtel: Profiting from Destruction" (See www.corpwatch.org/article.php?id=6975).

VII. PRECIOUS LIQUIDS

Chapter 28. Briefing: Oil and Water
and Chapter 29. The Oil Beast

Media Star: Michael Klare has been predicting what's ahead and documenting what's happening, in his lucid articles and books, including *Resource Wars* (New York: Henry Holt, 2002) and *Blood and Oil* (New York: Hamish Hamilton, 2004).

Chapter 30. The al-Saud

Media Star: Craig Unger. He digs up the dirt in his book *House of Bush, House of Saud* (New York: Scribner, 2004).

Chapter 31. OPEC
and Chapter 32. Non-OPEC Oil Producers

Info Star: The Department of Energy gives the necessary info at www.eia.doe.gov/emeu/cabs/opec.html.

Chapter 33. Veolia and Suez

Info Star: The Polaris Institute reports on nearly every aspect of water, from bottled water to water barons (www.polarisinstitute.org)
Books:
- McDonald, Bernadette, and Douglas Jehl (editors). *Whose Water Is It?* (Washington, DC: National Geographic Society, 2003)
- Shiva, Vandan. *Water Wars* (London: Pluto Press, 2002)

VIII. ROGUES

Chapter 34. North Korea

Media Star: Fred Kaplan covers the Hermit Kingdom, and Bush's goofs with it, at *Slate.* (See slate.msn.com/id/2117761/)

Chapter 35. Terrorists

Media Star: The *New York Times* pulled down a Pulitzer for its reporting on Osama bin Laden and terrorism (See www.pulitzer.org/year/2002/explanatory-reporting/works/).
Books:
- Bodansky, Yossef. *Bin Laden, the Man Who Declared War on America* (New York: Prima, 1999)
- Napoleoni, Loretta. *Terror Inc.* (London: Penguin, 2004)

Chapter 36. Organized Criminals

Info Star: Louise Shelley at American University tracks the scoundrels at www.american.edu/traccc/.

IX. WHAT'S NEXT

Media Star: Futurist Jeremy Rifkin has followed everything from the rise of genetically modified food to the reorganization of Europe. Now he's saying hydrogen could be the energy source of the future. In *The Hydrogen Economy* (New York: Jeremy P. Tarcher, 2003) he also gives a great overview of oil.

Index